# THE MARY DALY READER

# The Mary Daly Reader

Mary Daly

*Edited by*

Jennifer Rycenga *and* Linda Barufaldi

*Preface by Robin Morgan*

*Biographical Sketch by Mary E. Hunt*

NEW YORK UNIVERSITY PRESS

New York

NEW YORK UNIVERSITY PRESS
New York
www.nyupress.org



Library of Congress Cataloging-in-Publication Data
Names: Daly, Mary, 1928–2010, author. | Rycenga, Jennifer, editor.
Title: The Mary Daly reader / Mary Daly ; edited by Jennifer Rycenga and Linda Barufaldi ; preface by Robin Morgan ; biographical sketch by Mary E. Hunt.
Description: New York : NYU Press, 2016. | Includes bibliographical references and index.
Identifiers: LCCN 2016024252| ISBN 9781479892037 (hbk : alk. paper) | ISBN 9781479877768 (pbk : alk. paper)
Subjects: LCSH: Daly, Mary, 1928–2010. | Feminists—United States. | Women theologians—United States. | Feminist theology—Unied States.
Classification: LCC HQ1413.D23 A25 2016 | DDC 305.420973—dc23
LC record available at https://lccn.loc.gov/2016024252

New York University Press books are printed on acid-free paper, and their binding materials are chosen for strength and durability. We strive to use environmentally responsible suppliers and materials to the greatest extent possible in publishing our books.

Manufactured in the United States of America

10 9 8 7 6 5 4 3 2 1

Also available as an ebook

*To Mary Daly herSelf,*
*whose brilliance transformed Philosophy*
*and whose passion Sparked the*
*minds of her time and beyond.*

Overcoming the silencing of women is an extreme act,
a sequence of extreme acts.
—Mary Daly, *Gyn/Ecology*

CONTENTS

# PREFACE

ROBIN MORGAN

I can almost feel her sitting across from me as I write this, snarling lovingly that it's unfair of me to outlive her so she can't defend herself. Ah Mary, I come to praise you, never fear. As she might say, if you can't be there in the flesh, being there in spirit is the next best thing—and actually, who dares to say they're different?

We had a forty-year friendship, filled with collegiality, work, arguments, work, gleefully making trouble for the patriarchy, arguments, work, plotting, giggles and guffaws, work—and arguments. There were numerous bonds, doubtless saving the world chief among them. But one great bond was a shared love of good puns, and another was, well, intellect: we clung together especially during periods when the women's movement went through anti-intellectual fads.

Whenever we fell out with one another—"difficult twins" was Mary's nickname for our friendship—we somehow always fell back in again. To the very last. And if we hadn't seen one another or spoken by phone for months, somehow we always picked right up where we'd left off, as if no time had intervened.

Of all the memories, two stand out, one public and one private.

The public recollection is of the time when (yet again) Boston College was (yet again) persecuting her for some perceived (yet again) offense—perhaps this time it was, as she waggishly called it, "moral turpentine." In any event, there was a rally in some BC gymnasium packed with people, and I recall starting my support speech with the war cry, "Sisters, we meet on bloody Jesuit ground!"[1]

The roar in reply from the audience met with Mary's approval—that memorable Irish grin. Afterwards, she said she decidedly liked my part of the rally best, and since then would sign letters and books to me, "with love, respect, admiration—and indigestion." The lack of a qualifier in her praise was unsettlingly delightful.

The private, prized memory is of a time, probably in the 1970s, when I came to give a speech at Harvard and do a benefit for . . . well, for some group doing excellent work, I'm sure. Battery refuges. Rape crisis centers. Underground railway stations for then illegal abortions. Women's centers. Whatever.

I stayed overnight at Mary's. *Stayed*—not slept.

Because I had brought her a largeish bottle of Irish Mist as a house gift, and we sat up all night long—polishing off the *entire* bottle—while (what else?) arguing.

This time is was Aquinas versus Dante.

Mary's position, or rather imperious edict, was that all the philosophy and theology of the *Divina Commedia* was already evident in Aquinas, so there was really no need for the poem, which was just one big plagiarism. She got that twinkle in her eyes, knowing this would drive me crazy.

As a poet, I was indeed apoplectic: "It's a *POEM*, Mary, *forgodsake*, a great work of *art*, the origin of certain language and imagery that has transformed the global collective unconscious. *And* it was the first great work written in the vulgate, so that ordinary folks (at least those who were literate) could read it—a radical act!" Finally, I wound up with "Art goes where theology can't. And outlasts it."

Aha. Touché! Now *I* could twinkle.

Mary was apoplectic.

Another round of Irish Mist.

Finally, we dissolved in rib-aching, roll-on-the-floor-scare-the-cat laughter, agreeing that there was a nonplace for both Dante and Aquinas in the nonheaven we nonbelieved in and which we would jointly assault if we did.

The hilarity came when, at around 7 a.m., we realized that (a) we were drunk as loons yet famished for breakfast, and (b) if anyone had overheard such infamous "manhaters" quarreling over whose guy was best, our reputations would have been totally destroyed—not to speak of our dignity, which was already in shreds.

Mary was, of course, brilliant, funny, brave, a word-lover, angry, loving, bitter, both vulnerable and invulnerable—with an ego the size of

Montana, which, by the way, she'd earned. Passionately loved by many women—those who knew the woman and those who knew her solely through her books—she still was underestimated in her time. But her work will survive to transform future generations. She was a feminist philosopher, a radical theologian, a formidable professor, an activist agitator—and at times, a de facto stand-up comic.

The essays in this important book are samples of her range, the ferocity of her wit, and the depth of her daring. Read and savor them. Then go read her books. If rereading, you will find new revelations and insights in returning to old friends. If encountering them for the first time, welcome to the brain orgasms of Dalyworld.

For me, well, I miss her—her irascibility, humor, unique vision, her long telephone messages that blithely used up all my answering machine tape, the tenderness that lay beneath that tigress exterior. She was my friend, colleague, sister. She was my difficult twin, and I loved her.

I'm grateful to the women who assembled this volume, "Team Mary," for the jewel chest that this book is. Now it's in your hands. Cherish it.

May 4, 2012, New York City

# BIOGRAPHICAL SKETCH

MARY E. HUNT

Mary Daly was born of working-class Irish American parents in Schenectady, New York, where she grew up. Her father, Francis X. Daly, was a salesman; her mother, Anna Catherine Daly, would prove a lifelong support and friend to Mary, her only child.

Daly was educated in Catholic schools and graduated with a degree in English from St. Rose College in Albany, New York, in 1950, and an MA in English at The Catholic University of America in 1952. She earned her first doctorate in religion at St. Mary's College, Notre Dame, Indiana, in 1954, at a time when women were unwelcome in most U.S. doctoral programs in theology. After a few years of teaching, she supplemented her first PhD with two more doctorates in 1963, one in philosophy and the other in sacred theology from the University of Fribourg in Switzerland. In Fribourg, a lot of her studies were in Latin, a language skill that stood her in good stead in later creative endeavors. Her inveterate ability to articulate new ideas, coin new words, and redefine others always featured careful, critical attention to etymology.

Daly spent the 1960s in Europe studying and teaching. In a series of postcards to her mother (who spent some time with her in Switzerland), she wrote of her excitement at being in Rome for the Second Vatican Council. She was a young graduate student hanging around the edges of the Council, chatting up the press, learning about church politics, and collecting tidbits of ecclesial gossip. She was in her intellectual glory. Daly told her mother not to worry if she did not return to Fribourg on the appointed day, since she was having such a great time in the Eternal City.

She saw up close and personal in Rome the workings of a patriarchal organization. Gradually the reality of institutional sexism became painfully obvious and eventually too much to bear. As a woman, indeed as a Catholic woman with far more theological education than many of the assembled bishops and cardinals who had voting rights when she did not even have voice, Mary Daly simply had no place in the Roman Catholic Church.

She did attempt to remain in the church prior to leaving it. Accepting a teaching position at Boston College in 1966, she produced her first major book, *The Church and the Second Sex*, in 1968. This reformist effort, which pointed out the problems with the sexist legacy of the church, brought her some positive academic attention, but open hostility from her academic colleagues at Boston College. Their attempt to terminate her contract brought forth protests from academics, from her own students, and from defenders of academic freedom, leading to her vindication and retention at the college.

However, she took from this that being a reformer was, for her, ineffective. From that experience, and her travels around the globe, she launched her lifelong efforts to expose and change the inferior place of most women in the world. Gradually her scope enlarged to include special concern for animals and Earth, for the eradication of war and the end of poverty. But it was her insistence on the well-being of women that led her and other pioneering colleagues to create the feminist theologies that are taken for granted today.

Mary Daly was a writer and a teacher. Her writings speak for themselves, beginning with her dissertations and ending with her clarion call to "Sin Big." Her audience was the world, not the academy. She lectured widely and spoke often at conferences, bookstores, seminars, and even a restaurant. It is safe to say she is one of the few professors of philosophy/theology with a published interview in the *New Yorker* and an appearance on Roseanne Barr's television show.

This popular approach did not help her to become a full professor at Boston College; her application was rejected in 1975. The dean of the College of Arts and Sciences spelled out the problem in Daly's regard: "Nevertheless in arriving at a determination of an appropriate level of excellence in your publications, the Committee recognized the contrast between your works and the more typical demonstrations of scholarly methodology in publications by which candidates for promotion to Professor are judged" (*Outercourse*, p. 389). Indeed the contrast was and remains vivid, but not in the way the dean intended. The academy does not necessarily reward its best and brightest. More's the pity.

Daly considered her books to be her legacy. *Beyond God the Father* (1973) remains on the syllabi of many courses in feminist studies in religion, indeed of many general introductions to religion and women's studies. Sad to say, it is still fresh and provocative despite decades of efforts by many feminists to eradicate the problems Mary Daly pointed to in patriarchal religions. Exclusive use of male language and metaphors for the divine were but the tip of the patriarchal iceberg.

She received hundreds of letters (pre–e-mail) from women who thanked her for helping them make sense of their lives. The theologian Rita Nakashima Brock described Mary Daly as "perhaps the most transformative theologian of the 20th century," and asserted that "*Beyond God the Father* remains the landmark book in feminist theology."

The controversies opened in *Gyn/Ecology* (1978) remain part of contemporary conversation. Complexities of race, class, and nationality remain to be unpacked by Mary's successors. Debates about her positions on race and her opinions on transsexuals rage in blogs and at conferences long after her death. Few colleagues in religion exercised such a broad and diverse reach across disciplines and throughout activist groups. It may not have gained her an academic promotion, but her work certainly made an enormous difference in the world.

Mary Daly's autobiographical *Outercourse* is a compelling read about one woman's efforts to unmake the world. Her life was rather solitary, with her closest companion for many years a beloved cat. However, she was wonderfully well accompanied by people she never met who remain in her intellectual debt, as well as by close collaborators and friends. Happily, a small team of friends and colleagues, myself included, was privileged to accompany her in her waning years. We ensured that she lived and died with dignity and peace. She had taught us that sisterhood was important and we deepened in that knowledge as she aged.

Daly was at heart a teacher. Over her decades (1967–1999) on the faculty at Boston College, she loved the classroom and her students. While much has been made of her decision to teach men separately from women, few people realize that in the early years at Boston College her students were nearly all males. Some of them recall her very fondly, including a young man of color who was viciously harassed by some white racist classmates. He confided his situation not to his Jesuit professors, but to Mary Daly, who noticed his distress, listened to and understood his oppression because of her own, and supported him as he regained his academic and emotional footing. So much for claims that Daly disliked men.

She enjoyed the Socratic approach, always questioning her students, with keen interest in their answers. In later years, after she finished university teaching, I invited her to join my interns at WATER (Women's Alliance for Theology, Ethics and Ritual) for a seminar by telephone. She reveled in it, asking the young women what they *felt* about a topic as well as what they thought. She was wildly intuitive, a nice personal bookend to her raving rationality. She loved trees and plants; she enjoyed nothing more than a swim in the pond behind her apartment. She was part mystic.

Her last students were part of a "hedge school" she started. These were informal discussions and seminars with feminist graduate students in Boston who wanted to learn with her. Appropriately, the eighteenth- and nineteenth-century hedge schools were created by Catholics who resisted converting to the Anglican tradition. Daly, true to her roots, revived the idea to feminist ends.

Mary Daly attended many professional meetings. She said she went to the American Academy of Religion gatherings to see her friends. She was part of the group that initiated that organization's Women's Caucus. She was active early in the Women and Religion Section of the AAR. She always liked to have a panel on her latest publication even though she criticized "academentia" as a locus for intellectual work.

Mary Daly was controversial in her life and remains controversial after her death. She challenged basic assumptions about how the world ought to be. She asked no one's pardon for trying to make it different, especially when it came to women. Her methods were not universally appreciated, even by many who agreed with her goals. But she changed the world by opening up the hard philosophical questions of Being and Sinning, by positing the importance of all women, including Crones, Lesbians, and Hags, by unmasking patriarchy in its myriad disguises, by insisting on sharing "life energy" with all beings without exception.

Religious studies after Mary Daly is a new thing for which future generations are in her debt. Hers is a legacy to celebrate by delving deeply into tough questions that reshape the world and enjoying the process as much as she did.

She died in Gardner, Massachusetts, on January 3, 2010, at the age of eighty-one, after several years of declining health. She is buried in Mount Auburn Cemetery in Cambridge, Massachusetts.

## ACKNOWLEDGMENTS

This book has traveled on its own Wayward Voyage, from conception to spiraling out into the world. The editors would like to thank Mary Hunt, Emily Culpepper, the late Nancy Kelly, Nan O'Mealey, Xochitl Alvizo, Kathryn House, Marla Marcum, Tiffany Steinwert, and the late Judith Lennett. Julie Enszer kept us going when discouragement loomed with practical and Crone-logical advice. Janet Woods provided invaluable assistance with permissions. Lisa DeBoer ably crafted the Index.

Mary Daly's papers are permanently housed at the Sophia Smith Collection archives at Smith College. Users of this book are encouraged to contribute to the cataloging and maintenance of the collection.

Jennifer Rycenga would like to thank San José State University and my colleagues there, the birds of northeastern Massachusetts, Mary Daly's cat Cottie for desisting from her plans to kill me, and my late mother-in-law, Millie Wagner, for putting up with my long hours of proofreading. Thanks to my sisters Mary and Clara, and their families, as well as B.J. and Michaeleen for providing writing retreats and lots of treats. My nieces Miranda, Lydia, Liz, and Lauren inspire me to keep fighting for women's minds, which they display with brilliance. My mother, Dolores, and her dog Fagan befriended Mary Daly, and encouraged this project in many ways. My loving spouse, Peggy Macres, has aided all dimensions of the book from inception to manifestation.

Linda Barufaldi would like to thank Emily Culpepper, Jean MacRae, and Jan Raymond (a.k.a. the Tigers) for their lifelong friendship, Harvard Divinity School for providing financial support and atmosphere conducive to—or at least tolerant of—free thought, and Jennifer Rycenga for generously welcoming me into this project. Most of all I wish to thank Joyce Marieb, whose extraordinary life it has been my privilege to share for more than four decades.

# EDITORS' NOTE

Ellipses in square brackets indicate material that the editors have excised for the sake of brevity or clarity. Any ellipses not enclosed in square brackets are from the original publications.

In her works subsequent to *The Church and the Second Sex*, Mary Daly made it a practice to not capitalize the terms "christian," "catholic," "catholic church," and the names of other religions. This was a conscious decision to shrink the institutional inflation of the organizations she was analyzing. The editors have followed this practice in their introductory statements.

# Introduction

## *A Kick in the Imagination*

JENNIFER RYCENGA AND LINDA BARUFALDI

It requires a kick in the imagination, a wrenching of tired words, to realize that feminism is the final and therefore the first cause, and that *this* movement *is* movement. Realization of this is already the beginning of a qualitative leap in be-ing. . . . but the final cause that is *movement* is in our imaginative-cerebral-emotional-active-creative be-ing.
—Mary Daly, *Beyond God the Father*, p. 190

Mary Daly's writings—and her living presence when she was on the planet—proved to be a continuous "kick in the imagination" for her associates and perceptive readers. Sensing that the women's revolution required a philosophic arc to persist, she worked tirelessly to provide one. From the core of language to political creativity, from analyzing the horrors of patriarchy to celebrating women's communities, Daly synthesized the women's movement in thought, even as she lived it. That is a legacy worth celebrating and cerebrating, questioning and questing.

*The Mary Daly Reader* was first conceived by Mary Daly herself, with goading from Jennifer Rycenga, in the early years of the twenty-first century. The need for an anthology of her work emerged as it seemed that the impact and richness of her thought were disappearing as time receded. A further impetus was provided by the many professors who would ask how best to include Daly's work in their classes.

Conversations began in 2003, just as Daly was finishing *Amazon Grace*. As a systematic philosopher, Daly had initial misgivings about an excerpted reader, but overcame that resistance as the positive aspects of such a book became clear. Daly chose many excerpts herself, highlighting her most significant breakthroughs and ideas. She was particularly eager to include the "Final Cause" section from *Beyond God the Father,* the Harvard Memorial Exodus, and her writings on female friendship from *Gyn/Ecology* and *Pure Lust.* Other preliminary choices made by Rycenga—such as the opening chapters of *Beyond God the Father* and *Gyn/Ecology*—were enthusiastically endorsed by Daly. A few choices were made after her passing, particularly from *Outercourse.*

After Daly's death in 2010, Linda Barufaldi, who had been Daly's graduate student, friend, and reader during the writing of *Beyond God the Father* and *Gyn/Ecology,* joined the project. Over the next four years we met regularly to cull the best and most representative excerpts from Daly's eight books, writing introductions to each excerpt to contextualize them in the histories of philosophy, feminist thought, and women's activism.

Daly's work has inspired both of the editors to lifelong feminist thought and activism. We contend that Daly's work is foundational to feminist philosophy, but fear that academics and students are losing touch with it, or know it only in caricature. *The Mary Daly Reader* is meant to revive Daly's legacy as the groundbreaking thinker and scholar that she was.

This book runs in chronological order across Daly's work, starting with *The Church and the Second Sex.* The earliest excerpts find Daly still a member of, even an apologist for, the catholic church. From 1971 forward, Daly broke decisively with christianity and all patriarchal religions. This is reflected in later excerpts, starting with the Harvard Memorial Church walkout and her philosophic breakthrough in *Beyond God the Father.* From 1974 to 1984 Daly chronicled the atrocities patriarchy committed against women, and constructed a biophilic world surpassing those limitations, in *Gyn/Ecology* and *Pure Lust.* These two books also marked the full emergence of Daly's characteristically scintillating neologisms and wordplay as part of her creation/discovery of realms beyond patriarchy. Unfortunately, strong articulation of her ideas led to equally strong reactions and disagreements, most crucially within the feminist community. Third world women, women of color, and transgender people all had well-publicized disagreements with Daly, some of them resulting in permanent severing of connections and conversations. One of the goals of this reader is to revisit those conversations and arguments, forty years after the fact, to re-examine these fault lines.

Daly's idiosyncratic yet highly resonant development of language culminated in the publication of the *Websters' First New Intergalactic Wickedary of the English Language* (in cahoots with Jane Caputi) in 1987. This book includes an essay on words and language, but largely consists of definitions and etymologies of the words Daly developed for her philosophy. Therefore, we have woven Daly's playful and meaningful neologisms from the *Wickedary* as epigraphs to our editorial introductions.

Daly's final three books—*Outercourse*, *Quintessence*, and *Amazon Grace*—presumed the readers' familiarity with Daly's philosophic language. The autobiographical *Outercourse* yields many contextual clues about Daly's life. She was a product of her generation and of her upbringing in a segregated immigrant Catholic neighborhood. While that does not excuse her from any failings in her work, it helps us to comprehend the source of her limitations. We needn't deprive ourselves of her many brilliant insights to punish her for her lacunae, though. Her final two books, concerned with environmental collapse, are more topically focused, while also increasingly invested in a post-patriarchal world. The excerpts from these later books illustrate continuity in Daly's thought, and bring to light some hidden gems of insight.

In the years since Daly's passing the continued significance of her work, for reasons both substantial and controversial, has remained patent. The notion that "patriarchy is the prevailing religion of the entire planet"[1] is still all too real, whether one looks at terrorist violence, reduced access to reproductive health care, or attempts to restrict women's education. This anthology provides new readers with a guide to Daly's work and an invitation to explore it further. The bibliography of Daly's own writings opens one set of pathways; the extensive secondary sources listed here reveal the intellectual ferment that her works have created. The editors have also provided a thorough index that references philosophic terms, proper names, and Daly's own neologisms. Together these resources are intended to make this book a useful starting point for scholarship.

Daly's originality arises from her combination of feminist ethics, transcendent spiritual experience, philosophic dynamism, and linguistic enchantment, all simmering in an imagination shaped by catholic theology but decisively liberated from its institutional and scriptural limitations. Her love of perpetual transformation could be seen in her life, where she "communicate[d] a kind of contagious freedom."[2] This took on distinctly ontological dimensions in her thought. When she rejected divine revelation, she made it clear that "realizing reason is both dis-covering and participating in the unfolding, the Self-creation, of reason."[3] She championed an open cosmology, eschewing stability in favor of ever-expanding creativity:

> The women's revolution, insofar as it is true to its own essential dynamics, is an ontological, spiritual revolution, pointing beyond the idolatries of sexist society and sparking creative action in and toward transcendence. . . . [T]he vision of human becoming as a process of integration and transformation . . . potentially includes both the individualistic ontological dimension of depth and revolutionary participation in history.[4]

Daly was never a disinterested thinker. She maintained a "righteous fear of compromise,"[5] castigating academic objectivity as intrinsic to necrophilic thought. Instead, she adopted the mantle of constant fury/Fury at the erasure of countless generations of women, a resolute refusal to forget the context of women's lives. Daly even claimed that "Freed Fury makes hate, aversion, and sorrow biophilic. No longer twisted inward, devouring women's Selves, these passions purge our souls of horizontal violence."[6]

Daly's facility with wordplay makes an impression on most readers, but the depth of her commitment to the integrity and deep roots of language is not grasped as easily as her linguistic agility. She often declared that women have had the power of naming stolen from us, whether that meant naming our own experiences or naming the perpetrators of violence against us. Words and their etymologies became for Daly a lively link to pre-patriarchal times. Words "radiate knowledge of an ancient age, and . . . let us know that they, the words themselves, are treasures trying to be freed."[7] Her use of word-lore created a vocabulary that was off-putting to some readers but served others as a gateway to thinking beyond the given, creating neologisms to match not only the experience of feminism, but its yet-to-be-realized aspirations. She saw each of her books fulfilling a similar dialectic role, as "crystal balls, Glowing Globes" that "help us to foretell the future and to dis-cover the past" by making what was inarticulate into something that "we explicitly know, and therefore can reflect upon, criticize."[8]

In this compilation we have attempted to contextualize Daly's controversial positions on race and transgender identity to make them comprehensible, especially to those who find them unacceptable or repugnant. Daly was a participant in bruising debates over hierarchies of oppression. These debates, many of which still rage today, may affect readers' perception of Daly's feminist ethics. But the moral clarity that appears obvious today was often opaque to sincerely ethical feminists in the late 1970s. Contrary to the easy assumption that Daly was an "essentialist feminist," it is important to see that she had been influenced by Buber, wanting to see every person in their subjectivity, because no matter how damaged that subjectivity was, it was never destroyed. Her anger, though, at those who attempted to destroy others' subjectivities and lives was in constant tension with a more embracing ideal.

Daly's influences form a heterogeneous mix of women and men, medieval and contemporary, feminists and leftists. Her appreciation for foresisters like Simone de Beauvoir, Elizabeth Gould Davis, Virginia Woolf, Sojourner Truth, and preeminently Matilda Joslyn Gage will be evident. Her contemporaries and allies included Nelle Morton, Emily Culpepper, Sally Roesch Wagner, Louky Bersianik, and Robin Morgan. Theological students will be interested by her references to Jacques Maritain, Johannes Metz, Martin Buber, Harvey Cox, Paul Tillich, and her ultimate touchstone, Thomas Aquinas. One charming instance of this connection is how medieval angelology fascinated her, offering a legacy of philosophic speculation on a qualitatively different way of be-ing, free from the limitations that plagued the patriarchal foreground.[9]

The second wave of feminism emerged in midcentury after a few decades of quiescence following the success of the suffrage movement in the 1920s. While women's freedom expanded with factory work in World War II, the aftermath of the war eagerly reinscribed strict gender-role stereotypes. Reflections on living through that time, by such major thinkers as Sylvia Plath, Audre Lorde, and Adrienne Rich, speak to the sense of entrapment that women felt. Mary Daly's situation, as a young white working-class woman aligned with the explicitly patriarchal catholic church, meant that she was subject to the full brunt of this conformism. Her intellect, though, provided her a sanctuary in the realms of philosophy, theology, and academia.

The second wave of feminism came fully to life from within leftist activism in the 1960s, including the anti-war, free speech, farmworker, and civil rights movements. Women were participants in these movements but found themselves frequently relegated to second-class status, making coffee, typing leaflets, running mimeograph machines, and cleaning the hall after a meeting, but overlooked as authors, speakers, or leaders. The same logic that led to calls for equal rights across lines of race and class was extrapolated to gender by thinking women. However, because of the legacy of the Left, issues of religion were often ignored or treated as examples of "false consciousness" by early feminist activists.

From 1960 to 1966, Mary Daly was studying philosophy and theology in Europe. Upon her return to accept a teaching position at Boston College, the women's liberation movement was already in its nascent stages. Her topic for her first major publication—*The Church and the Second Sex*—demonstrates her connection to the new movement. She also engaged with the major existing philosophic source of feminist thought, wrestling with Simone de Beauvoir's *The Second Sex*, at that time little known to American women.

To understand Daly's relation to second wave feminism, the reader must keep in mind the particularities of her situation: her emphasis on intellectual work, her concern for the religious imagination (both destructive and constructive uses), and a deep commitment to the women's liberation movement, but always with a sense that she had arrived to that movement with an agenda distinct from its founders'. Her catholic heritage means that Daly might be one of the few major thinkers who came to feminism from a conservative bastion rather than from within the Left (though Daly would certainly be characterized as a progressive catholic in the Vatican II mold of the 1960s).

It is over forty years since the publication of *Beyond God the Father.* The impact of this work in feminist thought, theology, and philosophy still reverberates, due to Daly's adroit combination of ethical outrage, ontological insight, and reimagining of the divine from static being to dynamic verb. The bulk of her life's writings developed from that insight, growing alongside the feminist movement of the late twentieth century. She was an active participant in such controversies as the environmental crisis, the anti-nuclear movement, the persistence of racism in the United States, the emergence of transgender politics, and the lesbian and gay rights movement. Her positions on some of these issues may come across as dated, even offensive, to contemporary readers, but they emerged from specific circumstances, both historical and personal.

Roseanne Barr, the famed comedian, has said that reading *Gyn/Ecology* with her sister and other feminists helped her to find her voice as a comic and gave her the strength to pursue that goal. Regardless of history's eventual judgment of Mary Daly, the importance her thought had on women at that moment is integral to a clear understanding of that period. Those were heady times, and Daly's writing sparked many feminists' heads. Some of what made the movement so powerful for women was how the emotions generated by freedom and liberation were grounded in serious intellectual rigor that took women's history and situation into account. Daly was key in fleshing out the philosophical and ethical bases upon which the movement moved. Recall that when Daly was writing *Beyond God the Father*, women could rarely support themselves, obtain credit in their own names, or even imagine themselves above the glass ceiling.

Not only did Mary Daly insist that women think outside the box, she made it imperative to ask who set up the box in the first place, and why. A systematic thinker, Daly practiced a hermeneutics of suspicion that drove her ethical outrage at the treatment of women, yet always took care to balance that outrage with a vision of hope. The letters that Daly received from readers after the publication of *Beyond God the Father* indicate that she had indeed kicked the imagination into action for many. Women wrote that they were going to pursue their ambitions because of the boost in confidence that the book gave them, including one woman who wrote that, at age eighty, to find someone saying aloud what she had been thinking to herself all of her life meant she could now die happy!

Mary Daly's personality paralleled her work: enthusiastic, supremely self-confident, generous yet quickly defensive, brilliant, often personable, even charming, yet equally quick with derisive responses. She was revered, loved, and challenged by her students. Daly was capable of incredible kindness, taking her students to dinner and creating academic opportunities for them. In fact, she treated her students as equals in the struggle, a new stance for a professor, even stating, in the introduction to *Beyond God the Father*, that her graduate students' "friendship, ideas, and process of becoming are woven into the fabric of this book."[10]

She was also capable of withering contempt. Strongly intuitive, but also used to the solitary work of a philosopher, she could be impatient. As Mary Hunt has observed, none of those who loved her ever accused her of being easy to get along with. We can't say she didn't exacerbate some of the famous disputes she was engaged in. However, Daly was not the only strong and self-confident personality in the women's liberation movement; none of the fierce debates of the time can be separated from the personalities that drove them.

The transformative power of Daly's thought has had a lasting impact on many readers. Even those who later came to disagree with her recognize how their initial encounter with her work revealed, as Barufaldi recalls, how "everything before was a great lie."[11] She had turned her own world around, from being deeply ensconced within the catholic church to bursting through the inadequacies of that system. Having liberated herself, she threw the doors open to legions of readers.

Daly's work, in its daring scope, needs to be seen in the context of the disparities in life opportunities that existed between women and men in America at that time. Daly outlines some of these restrictions on her own education and prospects in the excerpts included here from *Outercourse.* Her response, though, to these limitations consistently involved a radical break from the given. As she wrote in *Beyond God the Father,* "Women are not merely 're-thinking' philosophy and theology but are participating in new creation. The process implies beautiful, self-actualizing anger, love, and hope."[12]

As a living person, Mary Daly had a delightful and flirtatious smile to complement her great cackling laugh. She reveled in being a crone, swimming in the lake behind her dwelling into her mid-seventies, conversing with the ducks and geese that flew overhead. She lived with numerous feline familiars (who make cameo appearances in her writings). Her connection to animals and her love of nature were charmingly small in scale, intimate yet cosmic.

Women's lives, women's minds, women's spiritual freedom—these were the touchstones in Daly's work. She glimpsed—and tried to live—a vision of women as biophilic creatures, opposing the death-dealers of the twentieth century in essence and in deed. Philosophic debates over whether or not Daly was an "essentialist" can fruitfully draw from this volume, but her hope that women's liberation would show the way out of the destructive history of the world was what guided her ethical thought. She always sounded a note of courage to balance her anger and outrage:

> This writing has been done in hope. Hopefully it represents not merely a continuation but a new beginning. Certainly it is not The Last Word. But insofar as it brings forth the right word it will be heard, for the right word will have the power of reality in it.[13]

PART I

# Winds of Change (to 1971)

Mary Daly's life as a thinker and writer began with deep roots in the catholic church—as a belief system, as an institution, and as a tradition. While she later renounced her affiliation to catholicism, and to all institutional forms of religion, she made that definitive move from a distinct place: the centuries-long accumulation of catholic metaphysical thought.

Daly's higher education started at the College of St. Rose, including stops at Notre Dame and The Catholic University of America, before reaching its apogee in Fribourg for two PhDs: one in philosophy and the other in sacred theology. While her extended stay in Europe during the early to mid-1960s meant that she was absent from the growing social movements in the United States, her education there included shocking examples of the depth of sexism embedded in "civilized" European culture in general and in theological academia in particular.

Her experience in Fribourg was isolating and hurtful. The all-male catholic students ostracized her, both in class and socially, and the hierarchy made it perfectly clear that she was unwelcome and that her presence was inappropriate. Still, Daly forged on, gaining the degrees she had sacrificed much to obtain. While in Fribourg, in the fall of 1965, she traveled to Rome to observe the proceedings of the Second Vatican Council; here, once again, "no one had invited" her and she "had no official role." While she found the cardinals' discourse to be "silly," she did have the opportunity to converse with social activists and thinkers who shared her "exhilarating" hope for change.[1]

When she returned to America in 1966, she began her career as a professor at Boston College, and as an author. Her first book (aside from her doctoral theses), published in 1968, *The Church and the Second Sex,* forms the content of this first part. Later in her career, Daly would sneer somewhat at the timid, reformist character of this work, but its perspective marks a necessary stage in her development. A canny reader can detect kernels of her later ideas even in her faintest protests.

From her superb philosophical training she gained a lifelong affection for Thomas Aquinas. She also nurtured a connection to the aesthetic and mystic neo-Thomism of Jacques and Raïssa Maritain. Most significantly, she focused on the humanity and the intellect of women through her engagement with Simone de Beauvoir. It may be difficult for the contemporary reader to understand, but women's thought—even in the case of a public intellectual like Simone de Beauvoir—was so consistently belittled, erased, or simply ignored, that Daly's choice to take de Beauvoir seriously (even if critically) was a feminist act.

1

# The Case against the Church

From chapter 1 of *The Church and the Second Sex*, pp. 27–31. All page numbers from *The Church and the Second Sex* are from the original first edition. Reissued editions in 1975 and 1985 included extensive additional materials, resulting in repagination.

*Courage to See:* the Courage to become dis-illusioned, to See through male mysteries, to become a Seer.
—*Wickedary*, p. 69

*The Church and the Second Sex* was the first full-length book that Daly wrote following her return to the United States and the launch of her teaching career at Boston College. As Daly took her place in what Emily Culpepper termed *philosophia*—a female train of thought—the title itself evidenced the stimulus provided through another female philosopher, Simone de Beauvoir (1908–1986), particularly her work *The Second Sex* (1949). The excerpt here shows a Catholic and thus still partially cautious Daly explaining how and why she has chosen to highlight de Beauvoir, particularly the latter's critique of the church and its role in the oppression of women. Significantly, Daly acknowledged and agreed with de Beauvoir's view that "femininity" is a social construct rather than an eternal, unchanging essence. Given later critiques of Daly as an "essentialist," knowing that she understood what was at stake in essentialist/constructionist debates from the beginning of her own philosophic career is significant. Some of Daly's later characteristic impatience with the Catholic Church can be heard in her disgust at philosophically simplistic solutions and the church's defensiveness in the face of atheistic critiques. But the retention of the male generic to include both men and women marks this as an early stage in Daly's development. Finally, in a nugget of self-understanding, Daly outlined her own role as an activist philosopher when she wrote, "The thinker need not be a helpless spectator of the course of history. There is both place and need for creative thought and action."
—Editors

## Facing the Problems

It has been claimed that since Simone de Beauvoir's writings presuppose a certain philosophical attitude, that of the atheistic existentialism of Jean-Paul Sartre, her interpretation of the facts should be rejected *a priori* by a Christian. On this basis, a naïve and pietistic rebuttal of her thesis runs something like this: "An atheist cannot really understand the doctrine and practice of the Church." Unfortunately this sort of defensive stance, understandable though it may be, rests upon a highly questionable hypothesis. It simplistically assumes that non-Christians can have no valid insights concerning the expressions of belief and the behavior of Christians. Implicit in this attitude is the idea that the Church is a congregation of disembodied spirits, living on a wholly "supernatural" plane, whose "official" utterances and behavior are totally beyond the scope of merely psychological or sociological analysis. In fact, however, Christians are human beings, subject to the same kinds of failings as other people, and often owe a debt of gratitude to non-believers for their criticisms. Non-believers are an aid in the continual struggle to purify Christian doctrine of its inevitable admixture of nonsense and Christian practice of the tendency to hypocrisy and injustice. A certain callousness to the harmful effects of some ideas and situations, cloaked by the supranaturalist justification that "it will all come out right at the last judgment," has led to—one might almost say "necessitated"—violent reactions.

Simone de Beauvoir's atheistic existentialism does of course embody several salient ideas that are particularly relevant to her treatment of the problem of women. First, according to this philosophy, which is one of despair, there is only this life and what one makes of oneself in this life. Given such a perspective, the failure to develop what human talents one has—to lead the life of the escapist, and thus the life of the typical woman as de Beauvoir sees her—has the dimensions of high tragedy. Since the compensations of an after-life are denied, present injustice is seen and felt in all its poignancy. It is futile to speak about what a person might have done or might have been. He or she is the sum total of his works and nothing more. A second, closely related point is that since there is no God who might have a "plan" for this world, there are no fixed essences. There is no fixed "human nature." Thirdly, it follows that one is not born man or woman; one becomes thus. This is not to deny biological differences. What it means is that the characteristic attitudes of men and women are acquired; they are cultural, the results of conditioning. Thus, "masculinity" and "femininity" are the effects of historical processes. What is called "femininity" is really only a situation of fact in a given culture. It is not definitely grounded either in biology or in a mysterious feminine essence. Fourthly, the masculine-feminine opposition is alienating. Woman, as "the Other," is exploited, duped. . . . In order to be liberated, she must first become conscious of her situation. She will then cease to be imprisoned in the false values of "femininity," in a pseudo-nature. Once conscious of her real situation, she can be free to become whatever she makes of herself.

There is no cheap and easy answer to these basic elements in de Beauvoir's philosophical position. In regard to the first point: to answer this life-view simply by superimposing belief in an afterlife upon the tragedy of the human situation on earth (with reference to the tragedy of woman's situation in particular) is to miss the point of the modern atheist's protest. De Beauvoir claims that such a belief is itself alienating: it distracts from the need to face the harmfulness of the given situation. Thus the "cure" perpetuates the illness. Religious thinkers increasingly recognize that there is meaning and value in this atheistic criticism of Christian belief. Faith in an afterlife can indeed be used as a psychological gimmick which helps to distract attention from present injustice.

In regard to the point about fixed essences: in the face of modern evolutionary theory, it is extremely difficult to uphold the idea of a fixed human nature, which is supposedly grasped by a process of abstraction, nor does there seem to be any justification for clinging to a medieval theory of knowledge. However, many contemporary Christian thinkers would deny Sartre's thesis (adopted by de Beauvoir) that belief in the existence of God is inseparably linked with the assertion that there is an immutable human nature. Believing Christians also see man as an evolving being. Moreover, even if it is legitimate to speak of a human "nature," this does not imply possession of an exhaustive or even exact knowledge of this "nature" through some mysterious process of abstraction of essences. Man's knowledge of man is also continually evolving.

As to whether one is born or becomes man or woman, dogmatic assertions about an unchanging feminine essence do not find anything like general acceptance among those who follow developments in modern philosophy and in the social sciences and psychology. In fact, our awareness of the profound and subtle effects of conditioning upon the human personality is continually increasing. There is an impressive stock of evidence in support of de Beauvoir on this point, and despite the tenacious hold of the "eternal feminine" upon the popular mind, the concept of woman is changing, whether one is existentialist or not.

Finally, the fact that woman has been exploited and that the fixed images of masculine and feminine have been used to further her exploitation is indeed demonstrable, as de Beauvoir among others has shown. There is nothing in all this to justify a refusal of the wealth of insight which her work brings to the problem.

What, then, can the Christian who is truly sensitive to the problem of women and the Church offer as an adequate response in the dialogue initiated by de Beauvoir?

As we have suggested, it will not be fruitful to begin with an opposition of philosophical or theological "principles" to her position. This offers too easy a way of avoiding the real issues. Indeed, many who are not adherents of Sartre's atheistic existentialism agree in large measure with de Beauvoir's analysis of woman's situation. Since human knowledge does not begin with "principles" but with experience, the most fruitful approach will begin with an effort honestly to answer the question: "To what extent is this interpretation of Christianity's role in the oppression of women in accord with the data of experience, that is, with historical fact?" This approach will entail an examination of sources—scripture, the writings of the Fathers and of theologians, and papal statements.

It is often the case that disagreement with a critic bears less upon what he has actually said than upon what he has failed to say. Therefore, one should ask a further question: has de Beauvoir omitted any significant data? There is a suggestion (probably an unwitting one) that she has, in the passages on St. Teresa, for whom, de Beauvoir says, the Church provided the needed condition for rising above the handicap of her sex. What are the implications of this? Why does de Beauvoir not develop this theme? It must be asked whether her analysis has brought into its perspective all of the important dimensions.

Before closing this chapter there is one other matter deserving consideration. It seems essential to this writer that we recognize that religious doctrine and practice are not in fact static, but rather are continually evolving. This is in large measure the effect of developments in the physical and social sciences, and in psychology, mixed with the influences of changing social conditions. While there have been harmful distortions of doctrine and practice, it is not necessary that these remain with us. A constant purification of doctrine and reform of practice are not only possible but necessary. The insight necessary to effect this evolution comes from human experience, and especially from the challenge of encounter with opposed viewpoints. There are, clearly, promising elements already present in Christian thought which can be sources of further development toward a more personalist conception of the man-woman relationship on all levels. These seminal elements must be distinguished from the oppressive, life-destroying ideas with which they have been confused, and by which they are in danger of being choked off. The distinction having been made, there remains the necessity of seeking to bring about, insofar as our own historically conditioned insights enable us, conditions in which a genuinely life-fostering evolution can take place. For the thinker need not be a helpless spectator of the course of history. There is both place and need for creative thought and action.

2

# Christian History

## *A Record of Contradictions*

From chapter 2 of *The Church and the Second Sex*, pp. 46–53.

*"Faith of Our Fathers"*: hideous hymn extolling a long dead faith of fatherland; perverted paean to dead faith, which is the patriarchal parody and reversal of Wholly Heathen Faith.
—*Wickedary*, p. 197

In *The Church and the Second Sex*, Mary Daly tackled the history of misogyny in the Catholic Church. Daly's work on women's place in the theology of the church was genuinely pioneering, both because she compiled original material and because her philosophic and Christian theological training enabled her to use forms of argument and analysis more sophisticated than those available to critics external to Christianity. For instance, she tried to understand the reasoning behind even the most odious of theological arguments against women's full personhood. At the same time, the reason that Daly, after writing *Beyond God the Father*, referred to *The Church and the Second Sex* as written by a foresister of hers, can be detected here, in the attempt to defend the ultimate coherence of Catholic thought, the hope that a few sensible reforms might correct the surface errors caused by mistaken social notions of previous eras.

Despite not yet being able to unfurl the full implications of what she was seeing, Daly here grasped the structural nature of women's ontological place in the schemas of the church fathers (she still capitalizes "Fathers"). In this excerpt, she isolated the theory of exceptionalism, noting that "the existence of exceptions, no matter how numerous, did not change the generalizations about feminine 'nature.'" Her dry wit and caustic disgust at what she named the "fierce misogyny" of the fathers come through in a taste of the sarcasm she would later utilize when the mere act of reading a text aloud exposes its sexism: "When woman achieves this transcendence which is, of course, not due to her own efforts but is a 'supernatural' gift, she is given the compliment of being called 'man.'"

The most significant aspect of this excerpt for understanding Daly's thought concerns her presentation of Thomas Aquinas (1225–1274). Those who have difficulty comprehending her lifelong attachment to Aquinas will see how, for her, his philosophic framework and principles outstripped the flaws of his particularities: Aquinas's sexism reveals itself as a cultural artifact, while the "deep roots of Thomas's thought . . . clearly support the genuine equality of men and women with all of its theoretical and practical consequences." Thus, Daly explained that "if woman has an intellectual nature, then her end cannot be man, for intellectuality is the radical source of autonomous personhood." Throughout her career, Daly would return to Aquinas, for his embrace of intellectual rationality, his universalization of intellect to humans, angels, and beyond, and his rigor in applying rational categories to understanding the world. Reading her gloss on Aquinas at this point in her career holds this advantage: Daly did not have to rationalize her use of a Catholic source! Aside from her earlier scholarly article, "The Problem of Speculative Theology," this gives the best explanation of why she found Aquinas useful to her radical feminism.[1]
—Editors

## The Patristic Period

For the [Church] Fathers, woman is a temptress of whom men should beware. That the problem might be reciprocal is not even considered.

There were attempts to balance the alleged guilt-laden condition of the female sex, but these, unfortunately, did not take the form of an admission of guilt shared by the sexes. Instead, Eve was balanced off by Mary. Thus, for example, Origen remarks that as sin came from the woman so does the beginning of salvation.[2] Augustine wrote that woman is honored in Mary.[3] He claimed that since man (*homo*) fell through the female sex, he was restored through the female sex. "Through the woman, death; through the woman, life."[4] This type of compensation produced an ambivalent image of woman. Mary was glorified, but she was unique. Women in the concrete did not shake off their bad reputation and continued to bear most of the burden of blame. The sort of polemic, therefore, which attempts to cover the antifeminism of the Fathers by pointing to their glorification of Mary ignores the important point that this did not improve their doctrine about concrete, living women. In fact there is every reason to suspect that this compensation unconsciously served as a means to relieve any possible guilt feelings about injustice to the other sex.

In the mentality of the Fathers, woman and sexuality were identified. Their horror of sex was also a horror of woman. There is no evidence that they realized the projection mechanisms involved in this misogynistic attitude. In fact, male guilt feelings over sex and hyper-susceptibility to sexual stimulation and suggestion were transferred to "the other," the "guilty" sex. The idea of a special guilt attached to the female sex gave support to the double moral standard which prevailed. For example, in cases of adultery, the wife had to take back her unfaithful husband, but if the wife was unfaithful, she could be rejected.

Even in the face of such oppressive conditions a few women managed to attain stature. Jerome admitted that many women were better than their husbands.[5] But more significant is the fact that the existence of exceptions, no matter how numerous, did not change the generalizations about feminine "nature." Hence the strange ambivalence which we have noted.

On the whole, then, the Fathers display a strongly disparaging attitude toward women, at times even a fierce misogynism. There is the recurrent theme that by faith a woman transcends the limitations imposed by her sex. It would never occur to the Fathers to say the same of a man. When woman achieves this transcendence which is, of course, not due to her own efforts but is a "supernatural" gift, she is given the compliment of being called "man" (*vir*). Thus there is an assumption that all that is of dignity and value in human nature is proper to the male sex. There is an identification of "male" and "human." Even the woman who was elevated by grace retained her abominable nature. No matter what praise the Fathers may have accorded to individuals, it is not possible to conclude that in their doctrine women are recognized as fully human. [ . . . ]

## The Middle Ages

Theological opinion of women was hardly better in the Middle Ages, although some of the fierceness of tone was mitigated. The twelfth century theologian, Peter the Lombard, whose *Sentences* became a standard textbook to be commented upon by teachers of theology, went so far as to write that woman is sensuality itself [ . . . ].[6]

What was new in the picture in the Middle Ages was the assimilation into theology of Aristotelianism, which provided the conceptual tools for fixing woman's place in the universe and which, ironically, could have been used to free her. In the writings of Thomas Aquinas, which later came to have a place of unique pre-eminence in the Church, Aristotelian thought was wedded to the standard biblical interpretations, so that the seeming weight of "science" was added to that of authority. Thus, following Aristotle, Aquinas held that the female is defective as regards her individual nature. He wrote that she is, in fact, a misbegotten male, for the active force in the male seed tends to the production of a perfect likeness in the masculine sex. Her existence is due to some defect in the active force (that of the father), or to some material indisposition, or even to some external influence, such as that of the south wind, which is moist. He adds that, as regards human nature in general, woman is not misbegotten, but is included in nature's intention as directed to the work of generation.[7] She has, then, a reason for being—that is, she is needed in the work of generation. It seems that this really is all she is good for, "since a man can be more efficiently helped by another man in other works."[8]

It would be a mistake, however, to conclude that Thomas thought woman has a major or even an equal role, even in her one specialty, i.e. reproduction. He wrote:

> Father and mother are loved as principles of our natural origin. Now the father is principle in a more excellent way than the mother, because he is the active principle, while the mother is a passive and material principle. Consequently, strictly speaking, the father is to be loved more.[9]

He continues:

> In the begetting of man, the mother supplies the formless matter of the body; and the latter receives its form through the formative power that is in the semen of the father. And though this power cannot create the rational soul, yet it disposes the matter of the body to receive that form.[10]

Thus, the role of the woman in generation is purely passive; she merely provides the matter, whereas the father disposes this for the form. This view of woman as a purely passive principle which merely provides the "matter" of the offspring is, of course, linked to an entirely outdated and false biology: that the mother is, in fact, equally "active" in the production of the child was unknown in the thirteenth century.

This idea of women as "naturally" defective, together with the commonly accepted exegesis of the texts concerning woman in Genesis and the Pauline epistles, and the given social situation of women in a condition of subjection are three factors whose influence can be detected in Thomas's arguments supporting the traditional androcentric views. Thus, in regard to marriage, he judged that, although there is proportional equality between man and wife, there is not strict equality; neither in regard to the conjugal act, in which that which is nobler is due to the man, nor in regard to the order of the home, in which the woman is ruled and the man rules.[11] Moreover, the exclusion of women from Holy Orders is upheld on the basis that a sacrament is a sign, and that in the female sex no eminence of degree can be signified, since the woman has the state of subjection.[12] There is no probability at all that Thomas was able to see this "state of subjection" as merely the result of social conditioning, of a situation which could change. He believed that social inferiority was required by woman's "natural" intellectual inferiority: "So by such a kind of subjection woman is naturally subject to man, because in man the discretion of reason predominates."[13] This, he thought, would have been the case even if sin had not occurred, i.e. even before the Fall. Thus, in Thomas's view, the question of woman's autonomy is hopelessly closed. The best she could hope for, even in the best of worlds, would be a kind of eternal childhood, in which she would be subject to man "for her own benefit."

The puzzlement which characterized patristic thought on women is again starkly evident in Thomas's writings. This is all the more striking because his thought is worked out in an ordered synthesis; it is not a collection of disconnected snatches of rhetoric, as is sometimes the case with the Fathers. The very existence of women seems to have been an awkward snag in the orderly universe which he envisaged. For the modern reader, it is startling to read the question posed in the *Summa Theologiae*: "Whether woman should have been made in the first production of things?"[14] The very existence of the question is significant. Although Thomas argues that human bi-sexuality[15] should have been "from the beginning," his whole mode of argument reveals a naïvely androcentric mentality which assigns what is properly human to the male and views sexual union as merely "carnal." Woman is seen as a sort of anomaly.

The anomaly of woman had nevertheless to be assimilated into the system. A striking ambiguity, which looks very much like a contradiction, resulted. It was necessary to admit, for example, that the image of God is found both in man and in woman, for this Thomas recognized to be the teaching of Genesis. Yet Paul had said that "woman is the glory of man," and indicated that she was not the image of God. Thomas concludes that

> in a secondary sense the image of God is found in man, and not in woman: for man is the beginning and end of woman; as God is the beginning and end of every creature.[16]

The degrading idea that "man is the beginning and end of woman" is reinforced by the parallel: man:woman::God:creature. Besides the intrinsic unacceptableness of this idea, there is an extreme difficulty in reconciling it with the assertion in the same paragraph that the image of God in its principal meaning (i.e. the intellectual nature) is found in both man and woman. If woman has an intellectual nature, then her end cannot be man, for intellectuality is the radical source of autonomous personhood [ . . . ].

It is abundantly clear, therefore, that even according to Thomas's own principles, the alleged defectiveness of women, both as to their role in generation and considered as products of the generative process, becomes extremely difficult to uphold. Indeed, in the light of these principles it becomes impossible to uphold. According to Thomas, it is the intellectual soul which makes the human person to be the image of God.[17] This is neither caused by the male, nor is it essentially different in man and woman.

We said earlier that there is a striking difference between Thomas and the Fathers. The latter often manifest an unresolved tension between their idea of woman in her "nature" and woman with grace, to such an extent that when she has grace, she no longer is called "woman," but "man." Thus, there is an identification of "male" and "human," which is overcome to some extent by grace. Thomas, of course, shares the feeling that women as such are not quite human. However, leaving all questions of grace aside, there is indecision in his thought on the level of nature itself. For Thomas, possession of an intellectual soul is natural and essential to men and women. In the light of this radical natural equality, it makes little sense to say that man is the principle and end of woman. Why, then, does he say it?

The discord between the philosophical anthropology of Thomas and his androcentric statements is due to the then commonly accepted biblical exegesis, Aristotelian biology, and the prevailing image and social status of women. The deep roots of Thomas's thought—his philosophical conceptions of the body-soul relationship, of intellect, of will, of the person, and his theological ideas of the image of God in the human being and of man's last end—clearly support the genuine equality of men and women with all of its theoretical and practical consequences. In opposition to the outdated exegesis and biology which he accepted, these Thomistic principles are radically on the side of feminism. Thomas himself could not see—or would not permit himself to see—the implications of these principles in regard to women. And we have seen why: the logical conclusions he might have drawn would at that time have appeared contrary to faith and contemporary experience.

Today, fidelity to truth and justice requires that thinkers who are aware of these implications make them explicit, rather than parroting as "Thomistic doctrine" harmful and untenable ideas which Thomas surely would not propose, were he alive today.[18]

# 3

# The Pedestal Peddlars

From chapter 4 of *The Church and the Second Sex*, pp. 114–22.

*Godfather, Son & Company 1:* the christian trinity *2:* the church, the state, the family, and all other firms dedicated to the propagation of the male line.
—*Wickedary*, p. 203

No matter how conciliatory *The Church and the Second Sex* attempted to be, Mary Daly's righteous anger at the systematic mistreatment of women often became apparent, as in this excerpt from the fourth chapter. Many elements of Daly's later themes and style can be detected here, such as concern with the effects of language and the interlocking totality of patriarchy in systems as disparate as psychology, advertising, education, and theology. She even painted a picture of the Eternal Woman who, while not yet ready to cackle loudly, at least can "laugh behind her veil" at the pretensions of the patriarchs.

There are three themes worth noting in this excerpt: (1) the misuse of authoritarian language to shut down creative philosophic thought via the church's appeal to "the divine plan"; (2) the male elaboration of Mary (the mother of Jesus) as a symbolic representation of women; and (3) the resulting generalizations created by a misplaced symbolic mode of thought.

Each of these themes was present when Daly took apart a work by a French Jesuit, Fr. Galot, that purported to be a systematic approach to the church's position on woman. Daly's disgust with his abstract pedestal grew increasingly manifest. She wrote that to

> consider a person—a subject—as a symbol is to treat him or her as an object, which is fundamentally an egoistic and hostile act. . . . It is characteristic of this species of symbol-oriented writing that it nearly always refers to "woman," rather than to "women." The static, symbolic point of view does not take into account plurality, which implies variety. It is hierarchical, but not pluralistic. It sees polarity, but not individuality; specific complementarity, but not the likeness and autonomous self-realization which are the basis of all genuine friendship.

Her insistence on plurality as a positive good and her opposition to the symbolic castigation of women remained consistent themes in her feminist thought; reading them in the context of *The Church and the Second Sex* allows the clarity of these principles to be seen prior to the development of Daly's alternative words and worlds.

Daly's quoting of patently misogynistic church writers may seem to the modern reader to be a setting up of a "straw man." It is important to realize that, as recently as the 1970s, this drivel bespoke the common attitude and discourse to which women and girls were subjected. Her use of words such as "egoistic" and "hostile" to describe a respected Jesuit was, at the time, dangerous to her career, yet she wrote them.
—Editors

## Theological Distortions

Another aspect of the "eternal feminine" phenomenon must be considered in this context, and this is the use of Catholic doctrine to perpetuate the symbol syndrome. Before we do so, we need to agree that there are many other contributing sources which have nothing directly to do with the Church, although they undoubtedly influence Catholic authors. These non-church sources include the myths of advertisers who reduce the image of woman to that of sex object; the theories of educators who promote a rigid, role-determining program of studies for girls; theories of doctrinaire Freudian psychologists who classify women's efforts at being human as "penis-envy"; and the operative philosophy of the editors of women's magazines that glorify only the "happy housewife heroine." These have been studied in other books. What we are concerned with here is a species of delusion peculiar to Catholic thinking which is especially potent because it surrounds itself with an aura of alleged divine approval. This delusion is rather complex. It can best be described in connection with two phrases familiar to Catholic ears which, though they may be innocuous in themselves, tend to accumulate assumptions and associations which are highly questionable. These two phrases are "the divine plan" (with its variations, such as "God's plan," "God's ordinance," "divinely ordained," "Christ's plan," "inspired by God"), and "Mary as the model of all women."

"The divine plan," to start with, is often used by religious authors and speakers to buttress claims for which there is no conclusive argument. Generally, the phrase or one of its variations is accompanied by some claims about "nature" and her "laws." Since the various sciences keep turning up with more and more disconcerting facts and theories which defy the old simplifications about mother nature and her "laws," the need is seen to appeal to a higher court. What could be higher or more unassailable than "the divine plan"? Thus, Father Arnold alludes to "the divinely ordained hierarchy between man and woman in marriage, in the family and in public life."[1] Monsignor Alberione, Italian author of a work on women which was translated into English and published in the United States, illustrates the technique so obviously that the unconscious parody would make even the Eternal Woman see the point and laugh behind her veil:

> Lest we forget, let it be repeated here once more: Woman's true sphere is within the family circle. He who would substitute anything else, frustrates her true nature, disrupts the providential plan of God and creates serious problems for society at large, which becomes filled with neurotic, unhappy, useless and very often, and worst of all, disruptive women![2] [ . . . ]

[ . . . ] When an audience which has been conditioned by Catholic training hears or sees the words "divine plan," "divinely ordained," etc., there tends to be a response of awe and reverence, and an inclination to assent to whatever is being proposed as God's plan. This effect is greatly increased if the people are made to feel that the speaker or writer has a position of authority in the Church and a claim to some esoteric body of knowledge which they themselves lack. Therefore the popularity of such devices as the "God's plan" rhetoric among clerical authors and speakers is not surprising. Nor is it surprising that the phrase occurs with great frequency when the doctrine proposed is open to attack as contrary to reason, or to custom, or to social justice. "God," after all, could propose nothing unreasonable, unfitting, or unjust. The Eternal Woman proponents are now especially in need of such a device, since they are working against an aspect of social evolution which is constantly gaining momentum.

In the second place, the "God's plan" theme is very frequently used to close discussion on positions which are not only open to challenge from the various "profane" sciences, but from theology as well. These authors take advantage of their readers' ignorance of the fact that theology, too, is evolving, and of the fact that there is a variety of opinion among scholars and theologians on the interpretation of nearly every significant document and on the approach to nearly every important problem. The fact is that theological opinion concerning the man-woman relationship is evolving, and shows every sign of continuing to do so, largely because of pressure from social processes and because of new insights from non-theological disciplines. Theological opinion about the place of women in the Church is also changing. There are all shades of opinion on the many issues surrounding these two central themes. The writers who are prone to invoke the "divine plan" hide this variety behind the monolithic mask of a supposedly changeless ideology.

We may say, in the third place, that the use of such terminology not only suggests the user's rhetorical purpose but also reflects a naïve simplicism. It requires a lack of appreciation of the complexity of reality, and a lack of insight concerning the limitations, projection mechanisms and other "tricks" of one's own mind, to be able to set down with a clear conscience the specifics of the "divine plan." To whom has God confided his blueprints? Upon reflection, therefore, it appears that such verbal devices, which are meant to arouse reverence, should instead be recognized as warning signals.

The second seemingly innocent but loaded phrase deserving review—a phrase which is often both the effect and the cause of delusions—is "Mary as the model of all women." The dimensions of the problem with which we are confronted here are suggested by the following remark:

> Devotion to Mary is, without fail, the best experience capable of opening to the priest "the metaphysical world of woman."[3]

It does not require a specialized knowledge of psychology to be aware of some of the difficulties involved in supporting this hypothesis. First, there are the projection mechanisms by which one may be deluded in his well-meaning "devotion to Mary." Not to be forgotten is the fact that the promotion of Marian devotion has largely been the work of a celibate clergy, whose manner of life has cut them off not only from marriage and sexual experience, but also from most of the normal day to day personal relationships which alone can provide a realistic understanding of persons of the opposite sex. The confessional is hardly a situation for normal dialogue, and it is probable that the types of women who turn consistently to the clergy for advice are often over-dependent and obsessive. Even in apparently normal social contacts between a woman and a priest, there are psychological barriers on both sides. The isolated seminary education of the priest has ill-prepared him for such social encounters, so that what takes place is often play-acting rather than honest dialogue. Not infrequently, therefore, one finds among the Catholic clergy a warped and pessimistic view of women which is based upon narrow, selective, or even vicarious experience.

Some of the excesses of Marianism may well be accounted for by this situation of the celibate clergy. There is evidence enough to give rise to suspicions that compensation mechanisms have a great deal to do with some forms of devotion to Mary. A seminarian in Rome remarked that his "spiritual director" told him that when he was troubled by "bad thoughts" he should immediately try to think about Mary. Such advice appears to be rather common, if not always as crude and obvious as this. In any case, the "beloved in heaven" idea leaves something to be desired. What it can spawn is that dream world which is precisely "the metaphysical world of woman," the ideal, static woman, who is so much less troublesome than the real article. Since she belongs to "another world," she cannot compete with man. Safely relegated to her pedestal, she serves his purpose, his psychological need, without having any purpose of her own. For the celibate who prefers not to be tied down to a wife, or whose canonical situation forbids marriage, the "Mary" of his imagination could appear to be the ideal spouse [ . . . ].

The idea, then, that "devotion to Mary is, without fail, the best experience capable of opening to the priest 'the metaphysical world of woman'" is highly questionable. How does the priest know that his devotion is not, at least in part, a confused product of his own psychology? The realism that comes from dialogue, from the realm of concrete human experience, is a more trustworthy source of understanding of the opposite sex. Moreover, when this understanding is developed, it will be discovered that there is no "metaphysical world" peculiar to women, except in the foggy realm of the mind's own symbols. But women in fact are not symbols; they are people, and each person is a unique subject. To consider a person—a subject—as a symbol is to treat him or her as an object, which is fundamentally an egoistic and hostile act.

[. . . A]ssumptions are operative in much writing on woman's place in the Church, notably in that of the Jesuit theologian J. Galot, who attempts to outline in detail the "divine plan" for women on the basis of a universalization of certain ideas about Mary contained in Vatican II's Dogmatic Constitution on the Church (*Lumen Gentium*). Admitting that the Council did not have the purpose of envisaging the mission which God assigns in general to women in the Church, but rather confines itself to some statements about Mary, Father Galot seizes upon these statements and adds to them considerably:

> In Mary are revealed the intentions of the divine plan concerning the whole of femininity.[4]

This assumption invokes the whole fallacious process of spinning a "theology of woman" out of Marian doctrine, in which process fantasy fills the void left by unknown historical fact and universalizes with naïve abandon.

The most catastrophic aspect of this method is its simplistic analogizing from the Christ-Mary relationship to the man-woman relationship in general. The inevitable fruit of this method, despite the elaborate precautions of its proponents, is the relegating of the woman to a hopelessly inferior situation. Thus, Father Galot argues that as Christ *operated* and Mary, being totally dependent, merely *cooperated*, so it is, analogously, with the respective roles of men and women in the Church. The clue to the meaning of women's "cooperation" is "receptivity." Thus it follows, we are told, that man has the mission to preach and woman has the mission to listen. However, we are assured this does not reduce the feminine role to something small, for "in willing to listen and assimilate, woman is rendering service to the man who speaks."[5] There is no evidence that the author intends the obvious irony. With incredible naïveté the argument concludes with the affirmation that this silence is what permits woman to play a veritable role, that of receiving the word of God and thus of making it penetrate more deeply into humanity.[6] If logic were at all operative here, it would follow that, given this total identification of the individual with a fixed sex "role," it should be impossible for the male to receive the word of God, and then, of course, it would follow that he could not transmit it. However, in this happy dream world of reified symbols, no embarrassing logic or facts are admitted.

Inevitably, given this framework, woman is seen as a "relative being." Submission and self-effacement are her lot. Since it is impossible to stay on the wave length of the Christ-Mary analogy without becoming at least subliminally aware of interference from reality, the analogy is generally supported with affirmations about woman's "nature" which make it all appear to turn out just right. She is said to be "disposed by nature" to subordinate her nature to another, to be "docile," to be "less apt at reasoning." Thus, Father Galot supports his flimsy analogical argument for the exclusion of women from preaching with a pronouncement about "her" (never "their") capacities. "God's choice," he writes, "is based upon masculine aptitudes." Having spent two hundred pages exaggerating woman's "receptivity," he now comes to the real issue:

> She is less capable of receiving the doctrinal deposit objectively, of mastering its essential lines by a vigorous synthesis, of submitting it to a rational work of elaboration and of explicitation, and of transmitting it objectively after having re-thought it.[7]

The generalizing "she" suggests that all women are inferior in this respect, or should be, according to their "nature." Regressing to the stage of theological development represented by the most antifeminist of the Fathers, Father Galot sees woman as a weak daughter of Eve:

> She has not lost the dispositions of impressionability and mobility which Eve had manifested in the initial drama of humanity. She remains fragile, more subject to an unreflected impulse, and more accessible to seduction.[8]

It is characteristic of this species of symbol-oriented writing that it nearly always refers to "woman," rather than to "women." The static, symbolic point of view does not take into account plurality, which implies variety. It is hierarchical, but not pluralistic. It sees polarity, but not individuality; specific complementarity, but not the likeness and autonomous self-realization which are the basis of all genuine friendship.

4

# The Second Sex and the Seeds of Transcendence

From conclusion to *The Church and the Second Sex*, pp. 178–81.

*Be-Longing:* transcending the patriarchally-embedded need to belong; ontological yearning for participation in Metabeing; Realizing one's Lust for the intensely focused ontological activity which is Happiness.
—*Wickedary*, p. 64

This short encomium to hope closes *The Church and the Second Sex*. In distinguishing between her perspective and de Beauvoir's, Daly clarified that she (at that point) remained a Catholic because of the trajectory toward social change that she thought (hoped?) exists in Christian theology. While Daly accepted the negation inherent in de Beauvoir's condemnation of the church's role in patriarchy, she insisted on a second negation, a turn to the positive. Certain phrases ring ironically here, such as Daly's call to "shake off" the "archaic." She would later proudly reclaim the Archaic for women (this neologistic use develops in the early 1980s, specifically in *Pure Lust*; see chapter 22 in this collection for this later use of "Archaic," starting with Daly's epigraphs). Her reference to the civil rights movement indicated Daly's awareness of the issues of race that so marked the critical milieu in which she was evaluated from the late 1970s forward.
—Editors

I do best by obeying and serving my sovereign Lord—that is, God.
—Joan of Arc

We are now witnessing and participating in a period of growth [ . . . ]. The slaves have been freed, the Negroes are no longer willing to play the subservient role assigned to them, the women are beginning to become conscious of their latent potentialities. The archaic heritage is being shaken off. Humanity appears to be in a transitional stage and is therefore haunted by unnamed anxieties, for it is not possible to predict with certainty what the next stage will be or where we are going, ultimately. In this situation, we are experiencing a dramatic cleavage between those who, looking to the horizon, affirm that the world is moving, and those who stubbornly insist that nothing changes. This fundamental division between liberal and conservative cuts across all others. Thus, for example, a liberal Christian feels more at home talking to an open and honest agnostic than to his conservative fellow believers, who cling to their vision of a static Church.

In this situation, it is not astonishing that many of those whose psychic structures are robust enough to welcome change have lost all patience with organizations and ideologies which appear to hold back the evolutionary process. To these, total rejection of the old appears to be a normal and necessary part of maturation. This could in some cases be a neurotic reaction, just as clinging to the past can be a sign of immaturity. However, there is no reason to think that it is always so. Thus, an *ad hominem* attack upon Simone de Beauvoir's rejection of Christianity is not an answer; it is an escape.

We have said that we are in fundamental agreement with de Beauvoir concerning the facts of history. Is there no disagreement, then? We have already suggested the answer to this. Disagreement may bear more upon the attitude concerning the facts and interpretation than upon the facts themselves. It also may bear more upon what a critic has omitted than upon what is actually said.

The fundamental difference between Simone de Beauvoir's vision of the Church and women and that which motivated this book is the difference between despair and hope. For this reason our approach is fundamentally far more radical than that of the French existentialist. De Beauvoir was willing to accept the conservative vision of the Church as the reality, and therefore has had to reject it as unworthy of mature humanity. However, there is an alternative to rejection, an alternative which need not involve self-mutilation. This is commitment to radical transformation of the negative, life-destroying elements of the Church as it exists today. The possibility of such commitment rests upon clear understanding that the seeds of the eschatological community, of the liberating, humanizing Church of the future, are already present, however submerged and neutralized they may be. Such commitment requires hope and courage.

De Beauvoir herself has acknowledged that religion has been able to work a transformation, enabling women to perform works comparable to men, although the only examples she cites are Catherine of Siena and Teresa of Avila. We have seen that she becomes quite lyrical concerning the case of Teresa who, it is claimed, lived out the situation of humanity, taking her stand beyond the earthly hierarchies, and setting her pride beyond the sexual differentiation. We could well argue that there have been others in all ages who have transcended "the earthly hierarchies," and, although they have been comparatively few, they have served as beacons, signaling to others the fact of undreamed of possibilities in themselves. We can truly say that the Church has, indeed, worked to bring about this transformation, that it has inspired men and women to reach beyond the limitations imposed by their environments, even beyond the limitations imposed by itself as institution.

It is essential, however, that we do not dupe ourselves, supporting our optimism with a facile apologetic. It is easy to say that Christianity has "always taught" the dignity of the human person, and indeed it is true that the prophetic voice has always called out from the depths, however muffled that voice may have been by alienating notions spawned in an alienated society. However, it is not necessary to belabor this point defensively. Our optimism is not dependent upon the past; rather, it arises from a call, a summons into the future. Harvey Cox expressed the Christian condition accurately when he said that Jesus Christ comes to his people not primarily through ecclesiastical traditions, but through social change, that he "goes before" first as a pillar of fire. There is no need, then, to be obsessed with justification of the past. In fact, while it is necessary to watch the rear-view mirror, this does not tell us where we are going, but only where we have been.

Simone de Beauvoir rejects Christianity as burdensome baggage inherited from the past. The life-affirming alternative to this is response to that liberating Power which calls us to transcend the archaic heritage and move toward a future whose seeds are already within us. Our response to the French existentialist is one of friendly respect and gratitude, for without her light we may not have recognized so acutely our own darkness and therefore may not have discovered the dimensions of our own light. Rather than a philosophy of despair, we choose a theology of hope, not because the former is "false," but because we think it represents an incomplete and partial vision.

It is part and parcel of Christian hope and courage that these qualities do not allow us ultimately to rest in the illusion that we are in possession of fixed blueprints for our future. God is present, yet always hidden, and the summons from that Presence gives a dimension of transcendence to our activity, by which we are propelled forward.

In the exercise of self-transcending creative activity, inspired and driven forward by faith and hope, sustained by courage, men and women can learn to "set their pride beyond the sexual differentiation." Working together on all levels they may come at last to see each other's faces, and in so doing, come to know themselves. It is only by this creative personal encounter, sparked by that power of transcendence which the theologians have called grace, that the old wounds can be healed. Men and women, using their best talents, forgetful of self and intent upon the work, will with God's help mount together toward a higher order of consciousness and being, in which the alienating projections will have been defeated and wholeness, psychic integrity, achieved.

PART II

# From God to Be-ing (1972–1974)

To a contemporary reader, *The Church and the Second Sex* may seem mild in its critique of the church, but when the book was published in 1968, it created a firestorm around Daly. In fact, the Boston College Theology Department intended to fire her for having the temerity to critique "Mother Church." She was given a one-year terminal contract, in effect denying her tenure. As Daly wrote, her

> "case" became a cause célèbre. It was 1969, a year of demonstrations, and the students wanted a symbol in their crusade for "academic freedom." I was it.[1]

Daly's students (all male) and many academics around the country rallied to her support, citing both academic freedom and the intellectual integrity of her important work. Though Boston College reversed itself and awarded her tenure, Daly learned a principle of political struggle that she would never forget: there is no reward in reformism. The radical Mary Daly would never be suppressed or timid of voice again.

The controversy over *The Church and the Second Sex* provided Daly with visibility, and in the intellectual environment of Boston, that meant that graduate students sought her out. Similarly, Boston's centrality to the political movements in the United States in the late 1960s and early 1970s meant that the stimulation and palpable progress of the women's liberation movement immersed Daly in the cross-currents of radicalism.

The signal convergence of these forces was the Harvard Memorial Church Exodus on November 14, 1971. This event, planned by Daly and her graduate students, combined collective community consciousness, a strong metaphysical break with both the ideas and institutions of christianity, and connections to the American protest traditions (dating back to similar church walkouts in the founding of Black churches and the Abolitionist crusade against church support for slavery).[2] The text of

Daly's sermon forms the first chapter in this part. This moment became a touchstone, the definitive break from institutional religion for Daly (and many others).

The rest of this section consists of excerpts from *Beyond God the Father,* which some maintain is Daly's best work. It is assuredly her most consequential book theologically (though not necessarily her most significant philosophically or politically). Her unique combination of anger, ridicule, sarcasm, hope, creativity, immanence, and transcendence emerges. Furious at the illusions and lies of christianity (and all religions), she used theological tools to expose the inanity of mythology, doctrine, and above all hierarchic oppression. Far more important, though, is her understanding of a deity who cannot be reified, but is instead God the Verb. She coined the term "Be-ing" to describe this concept of a participatory divine energy.

Once again, Boston College was unimpressed and outraged, leading to Daly's being denied promotion to full professor in 1975. A member of the committee dared to compare the groundbreaking *Beyond God the Father* to the hackneyed popular novel of the day, *Love Story* (see chapter 39 in this collection for the full story).

# 5

# The Women's Movement

## *An Exodus Community*

From "The Women's Movement: An Exodus Community," in *Women and Religion: A Feminist Sourcebook of Christian Thought*, ed. Elizabeth Clark and Herbert Richardson (New York: Harper and Row, 1977), pp. 265–71. Originally published in *Religious Education* 67 (September–October 1972): 327–33.

*Courage to Leave:* Virtue enabling women to depart from all patriarchal religions and other hopeless institutions; resolutions springing from deep knowledge of the nucleus of nothingness which is at the core of these institutions.
—*Wickedary*, p. 69

This historically significant document, reproduced in full, summarizes Daly's radical feminist insights on the verge of *Beyond God the Father.* This speech, given at Harvard Memorial Church on November 14, 1971, was, amazingly, the first "sermon" ever preached by a woman there (Harvard opened in 1636). Daly took the podium only to renounce it, and led a walkout of women (and some sympathetic men) from the chapel. More on the background and context of the walkout can be read in chapter 36 of this collection.

The content of the speech provides a fine *précis* of Daly's fast-developing thought; it will be appreciated by students of feminist thought and feminist history alike. Many of the themes Daly would develop over her next few books are here, albeit without her creative neologisms bedazzling the text. Her analysis of patriarchy included themes of its universal nature, the existence of a sexual caste system, the fact that religious sexism is both ancient and modern, and the continuities (structural and substantive) between religious institutions and psychology. She also commenced her use of "synchronicity" to explain symbolic actions taken by male-supremacist institutions to crush nascent female self-definition: here she connected the rise of psychiatry to the need to suppress the energies of the first wave of women's liberation.

One of the large-scale organizing elements in each of Daly's books, and in her thought as a whole, is a dialectic movement between the harshest, most thorough critique possible of injustice, and then the recovery of hope and creativity as a realistic (and verifiable) response to the wreckage caused by the critique. In this speech, she called on women to abandon "prudence" and choose instead an "existential courage . . . to *see* and to *be*." Daly calls on women to reject subservient and auxiliary roles, to pry out the internalized "male chauvinist pig," and to leave the church behind rather than settle for tokenistic inclusion. Daly declared women's liberation "an event which is new under the sun." This was a proclamation of both its historical uniqueness and its potential going forward. In the hands of her critics, it was also an example of the undifferentiated way she used the category of "women."

Finally, this speech was the first location in which one of Daly's most important contributions to feminist philosophy and theology was made: "as long as God is imaged exclusively as male, then the male can feel justified in playing God." Her enunciation of this idea would be fine-tuned later, but its startlingly descriptive nature (for the Western monotheisms) made an impact in 1971. The dual nature of the problem—males' projection of themselves onto God, and the idea of a God who upheld sexism in *his* own being—lifts this idea to a central principle for feminist theologies.
—Editors

Sisters and other esteemed members of the congregation:

There are many ways of refusing to see a problem—such as the problem of the oppression of women by society in general and religion in particular. One way is to make it appear trivial. For example, one hears: "Are you on that subject of women again when there are so many important problems—like war, racism, pollution of the environment." One would think, to hear this, that there is no connection between sexism and the rape of the Third World, the rape of the Blacks, or the rape of land and water. Another way of refusing to see the problem of the oppression of women is to particularize it. For instance, one hears: "Oh, that's a Catholic problem. The Catholic church is so medieval." One would imagine, to listen to this, that there is no patriarchy around here. Another method of refusing to see is to spiritualize, that is, to refuse to look at concrete oppressive facts. There is a significant precedent for this in Christian history: Paul wrote that "in Christ there is neither male nor female," but was not exactly concerned about social equality for women. The repetition of that famous line from Paul by would-be pacifiers of women invites the response that even if "in Christ there is neither male nor female," everywhere else there damn well is. Finally, some people, especially academics, attempt to make the problem disappear by universalizing it. One frequently hears: "But isn't the real problem *human* liberation?" The difficulty with this is that the words spoken may be "true," but when used to avoid the issue of sexism they are radically untruthful.

There *is* a problem. It is this: There exists a world-wide phenomenon of sexual caste, which is to be found not only in Saudi Arabia but also in Sweden. This planetary sexual caste system involves birth-ascribed, hierarchically ordered groups whose members have unequal access to goods, services, prestige, and physical and mental well-being. This exploitative system is masked by sex role segregation. Thus it is possible for a woman with a Ph.D. to fail to recognize any inequity in church regulations which forbid her to serve Mass while permitting a seven year old retarded boy to do so. Sexual caste is masked also by women's duality of status, for women have a derivative status stemming from relationships with men, which serves to hide our infrahuman condition *as women*. Finally, it is masked by ideologies and institutions that alienate women from our true selves, deluding us with false identifications, sapping our energies, deflecting our anger and our hope.

It is easy, then, to fail to see the problem of sexual caste. Moreover, patriarchal religion has made it more difficult to see through the injustices of the system by legitimating and reinforcing it. The long history of legitimation of sexism by religion is too well known to require detailed repetition here. I need not recite those infamous Pauline passages on women. I need not allude to the misogynism of the church Fathers—for example, Tertullian, who informed women in general: "You are the devil's gateway," or Augustine, who opined that women are not made to the image of God. I can omit reference to Thomas Aquinas and his numerous commentators and disciples who defined women as misbegotten males. I can overlook Martin Luther's remark that God created

Adam lord over all living creatures but Eve spoiled it all. I can pass over the fact that John Knox composed a "First Blast of the Trumpet against the Monstrous Regiment of Women." All of this, after all, is past history.

Perhaps, however, we should take just a cursory glance at more recent history. Pope Pius XII more or less summarized official ecclesiastical views on women when he wrote that "the mother who complains because a new child presses against her bosom seeking nourishment at her breast is foolish, ignorant of herself, and unhappy." In another address he remarked that "she loves it the more, the more pain it has cost her." It may be objected, however, that in the year 1970 the official Catholic position leaped into the twentieth century, for in that year chaste lay women (c-h-a-s-t-e) willing to take vows of chastity were offered special consecration in what was called the answer to the modern world's obsession with sex. . . . The question unasked was: Just *whose* obsession is this?

Meanwhile on the Protestant front things have not really been that different. Theologian Karl Barth proclaimed that woman is ontologically subordinate to man as her "head." Dietrich Bonhoeffer in his famous *Letters and Papers from Prison*, in which he had proclaimed the attack of Christianity upon the adulthood of the world to be pointless, ignoble, and unchristian—in this very same volume—insists that women should be subject to their husbands.

Theology which is overtly and explicitly oppressive to women is by no means a thing of the past. Exclusively masculine symbolism for God, for the notion of divine "incarnation" in human nature, and for the human relationship to God reinforces sexual hierarchy. Tremendous damage is done, particularly in ethics, when theologians construct one-dimensional arguments that fail to take women's experience into account. This is evident in biased ethical arguments concerning abortion—for example, those of some well-known professors at this university. To summarize briefly the situation: The entire conceptual apparatus of theology, developed under the conditions of patriarchy, has been the product of males and serves the interests of sexist society.

To a large extent in recent times the role of the church in supporting the sexual caste system has been assumed by psychoanalysis. Feminists have pointed out that it is by no accident that Freudian theory emerged as the first wave of feminism was cresting. This was part of the counter-revolution, the male backlash. Psychoanalysis has its own creeds, priesthood, spiritual counseling, its rules, anathemas, and jargon. Its power of psychological intimidation is enormous. Millions who might smile at being labeled "heretic" or "sinful" for refusing to conform to the norms of sexist society can be cowed and kept in line by the labels "sick," "neurotic," or "unfeminine." This Mother Church of contemporary secular patriarchal religions has sent its missionaries everywhere, not excluding the traditional churches themselves.

It isn't "prudent" for women to see all of this. Seeing means that everything changes: the old identifications and the old securities are gone. Therefore the ethic that is emerging in the women's movement is not an ethic of prudence but one whose dominant theme is existential courage. This is the courage to *see* and to *be* in the face of the nameless anxieties that surface when a woman begins to see through the masks of sexist society and to confront the horrifying fact of her own alienation from her authentic self.

The courage to be and to see that is emerging in the women's revolution expresses itself in sisterhood—an event which is new under the sun. The so-called "sisterhoods" of patriarchy were and are in fact mini-brotherhoods, serving male interests and ideals. The ladies' auxiliaries of political parties, college sororities, religious orders of nuns—all have served the purposes of sexist society. In contrast to these, the new sisterhood is the bonding of women for liberation from sex role socialization. The very word itself says liberation and revolution.

There is no reason to think that sisterhood is easy. Women suffer from a duality of consciousness, as do the members of all oppressed groups. That is, we have internalized the image that males have created of "the woman," and this is in constant conflict with our authentically striving selves. One of the side effects of this duality is a kind of paralysis of the will. This is sometimes experienced as fear of ridicule, or of being considered abnormal, or—more basically—simply of being rejected, unwanted, unloved. Other effects of this dual consciousness are self-depreciation and emotional dependence. All of this is expressed in feminine antifeminism—the direction by women of our self-hatred toward each other. Each of us has internalized the "male chauvinist pig." It exists inside our heads and it is a devil that must be exorcised and exterminated.

How can we do this? For women, the first salvific moment comes when we realize the fact of our exploitation and oppression. But—and this is an important "but"—unless the insight gives birth to externalized action it will die. This externalized action, or *praxis*, authenticates insight and creates situations out of which new knowledge can grow. It must relate to the building of a new community, to the bonding of women in sisterhood.

Sisterhood is both revolutionary and revelatory. By refusing—together—to be objects, we can break down the credibility of sex stereotyping and bring about a genuine psychic revolution. By the same token, sisterhood is revelation. The plausibility of patriarchal religion is weakening. Nietzsche, the prophet, asked: "What are these churches now if they are not the tombs and sepulchres of God?" Nietzsche's misogynism did not permit him to see that the God who had to die was the patriarchal tyrant. Women who are "getting it together" are beginning to see that as long as God is imaged exclusively as male, then the male can feel justified in playing God. The breakdown of the idols of patriarchal religion, then, is consequent upon women's new consciousness. Out of our courage to be in the face of the absence of these idols—in the face of the experience of non-being—can emerge a new sense of transcendence, that is, a new and more genuine religious consciousness. This means that a transvaluation of values can take place. Faith, instead of being blind acceptance of doctrines handed down by authority, can be a state of ultimate concern that goes beyond bigotry. Hope, instead of being reduced to passive expectation of a reward for following rules allegedly set down by the Father and his surrogates, can be a communal creation of the future. Love, instead of being abject acceptance of exploitation, can become clean and free, secure in the knowledge that the most loving thing we can do in an oppressive situation is to work against the structures that destroy both the exploited and the exploiter. The transvaluation of values that is implied in the revolution of sisterhood touches the very meaning of human life itself. It may be the key to turning our species away from its course of destroying life on this planet.

Sisterhood, then, is in a very real sense an anti-church. In creating a counter-world to the society endorsed by patriarchal religion women are at war with sexist religion *as sexist*. This is true whether we concern ourselves directly with religion or not. Women whose consciousness has been raised are spiritual exiles whose sense of transcendence is seeking alternative expressions to those available in institutional religion.

Sisterhood is also functioning as church, proclaiming dimensions of truth which organized religion fails to proclaim. It is a space set apart, in which we can be ourselves, free of the mendacious contortions of mind, will, and feeling demanded of us "out there." It is a charismatic community, in which we experience prophecy and healing. It is a community with a mission to challenge the distortions in sexually unbalanced society, to be a counter-force to the prevailing sense of reality by building up a new sense of reality. Finally, sisterhood is an *exodus community* that goes away from the land of our fathers—leaving that behind because of the promise in women that is still unfulfilled. It is an exodus community that, perhaps for the first time in history, is putting our own cause—the liberation of women—*first*. It is a positive refusal to be co-opted any more—a positive refusal based on the prophetic insight that the sisterhood of women opens out to universal horizons, pointing outward to the sisterhood of man.

Sisters:

The sisterhood of man cannot happen without a real exodus. We have to go out from the land of our fathers into an unknown place. We can this morning demonstrate our exodus from sexist religion—a break which for many of us has already taken place spiritually. We can give physical expression to our exodus community, to the fact that we must go away.

We cannot really belong to institutional religion as it exists. It isn't good enough to be token preachers. It isn't good enough to have our energies drained and co-opted. Singing sexist hymns, praying to a male god breaks our spirit, makes us less than human. The crushing weight of this tradition, of this power structure, tells us that *we do not even exist.*

The women's movement is an exodus community. Its basis is not merely in the promise given to our fathers thousands of years ago. Rather its source is in the unfulfilled promise of our mothers' lives, whose history was never recorded. Its source is in the promise of our sisters whose voices have been robbed from them, and in our own promise, our latent creativity. We can affirm *now* our promise and our exodus as we walk into a future that will be our *own* future.

Sisters—and brothers, if there are any here: Our time has come. We will take our own place in the sun. We will leave behind the centuries of silence and darkness. Let us affirm our faith in ourselves and our will to transcendence by rising and walking out together.

6

# The Problem, the Purpose, the Method

From *Beyond God the Father*, pp. 1–12.

*Exorcism:* series of A-mazing Acts of Dis-possession, expelling both internal and external manifestations of the godfather; Naming the demons who block each passage of the Otherworld Journey and thereby ousting these obstacles to the Ecstatic Process.
—*Wickedary*, p. 75

*Beyond God the Father* established the principles from which Daly would spiral out for the remainder of her life. This introduction is so rich that any attempt to summarize it would necessarily revert to quoting it. Thematically, she blended hope and fury, praxis and abstraction, history and transcendence, creating "beautiful, self-actualizing anger, love, and hope." She revealed herself to be in conversation with the women's liberation movement, with her critics, with those thinkers who influenced her, and with her own sense of Self. While she had not yet created the full range of neologisms that would mark her later writings poetically, she had built her theory of language: there are words that have to be discarded as unusable, while others have dimensions that have been hidden under conditions of oppression; these meanings emerge as women reclaim the power to name reality.

Much of the first section of the introduction to *Beyond God the Father* literally repeats the Harvard Memorial walkout speech; these have been edited out here, with the exception of the analyses of particularization and spiritualization, which she articulated here with a sharper edge than before. Especially instructive is her dismissal of the argument that the most damaging New Testament passages about women (e.g., 1 Timothy 2) are deutero-Pauline rather than by Paul. She retorted that it didn't matter who wrote them; what matters is how they were used as evidence of divine sanction for patriarchal oppression of women. The simple elegance and fury of her argument skewered the scholars who are "more concerned with justifying an author long dead . . . than with the deep injustice itself that is being perpetrated by religion."

Daly seems to have prepared the outlines for her own journey in describing the path for feminists in this introduction. She expounded the concept of "boundary" living, while warning against succumbing to "cooptable reformism that nourishes the oppressive system." A warning against tokenism provided the antidote: a preference for "dramatic action" that is "multidimensional" and provides "signals and clues of transcendence" to give "impetus for future actions."

The writing itself carried a self-certainty beyond Daly's previous writings, reflected in sentence structures that can be read as imperative, imperious, aphoristic, encouraging, or just plain out there, depending on the reader and her mood.

For those who lived it, the reality of the time (1972–1973) is difficult to convey in words. It was heady: a time of exuberance, confrontation, and intellectual breakthroughs, a time of political action, a time in which every thought was subject to revisiting, rethinking, embracing or rejecting. It brought an intoxicating intellectual and personal self-trust that most of the participants had never experienced before. More than thinking outside the box, the questions became how the box got there, who had set it up, and who benefited from it. Returning naïvely to the box was not an option.

Finally, the depth of alienation from the patriarchal world that Daly expressed may seem to the modern reader to be hyperbole. Bear in mind as you read this that in 1970–1971, as Daly wrote, there were almost no women in academia or in professional or governmental leadership. For example, when one of the editors entered Harvard Divinity School in 1970, there were twelve women in a student body of five hundred, and there had never been a female faculty member (since 1636).

Female college graduates at the time found jobs as teachers, secretaries, and assistants. Married women could not hold property or get credit in their own names. Sexism and sexist structures, such as the "glass ceiling," are still present and operative today (albeit several floors above where it was in the 1970s), but generally less obvious, writ less large. Sporadic eruptions, such as recent obsessions of the far right with compulsory transvaginal ultrasounds and preventing insurance coverage for contraceptives for women (while supporting Viagra coverage for men), reveal the extent to which virulent institutional patriarchy and degrading patriarchal attitudes still shape our lives and our institutions. Recent events that we find

shocking would not have surprised any woman prior to the second wave of feminism.
—Editors

I want a women's revolution like a lover.
I lust for it, I want so much this freedom,
this end to struggle and fear and lies
we all exhale, that I could die just
with the passionate uttering of that desire.
—Robin Morgan

When you are criticizing the philosophy of an epoch, do not chiefly direct your attention to those intellectual positions which its exponents feel it necessary explicitly to defend. There will be some fundamental assumptions which adherents of all the various systems within the epoch unconsciously presuppose. Such assumptions appear so obvious that people do not know what they are assuming because no other way of putting things has ever occurred to them.
—Alfred North Whitehead

Recent years have witnessed a series of crescendos in the women's movement. Women of all "types," having made the psychic breakthrough to recognition of the basic sameness of our situation as women, have been initiated into the struggle for liberation of our sex from its ancient bondage. The bonding together of women into a sisterhood for liberation is becoming a widespread feature of American culture, and the movement is rapidly taking on worldwide dimensions.

The bonding is born out of shared recognition that there exists a worldwide phenomenon of sexual caste, basically the same whether one lives in Saudi Arabia or in Sweden. This planetary sexual caste system involves birth-ascribed hierarchically ordered groups whose members have unequal access to goods, services, and prestige and to physical and mental well-being. Clearly I am not using the term "caste" in its most rigid sense, which would apply only to Brahmanic Indian society. I am using it in accordance with Berreman's broad description, since our language at present lacks other terms to describe systems of rigid social stratification analogous to the Indian system.[1]

It may be that the psychological root of selective nit-picking about the use of the term "caste" to describe women's situation is a desire not to be open to the insights made available by the comparison.[2] Such rigidity overlooks the fact that language develops and changes in the course of history. The term is the most accurate available. Precisely because it is strong and revealing, many feminists have chosen to employ it. As Jo Freeman points out, caste systems are extremely difficult although not impossible to change. Moreover, since they are composed of interdependent units, to alter one unit is to alter all.[3]

The exploitative sexual caste system could not be perpetuated without the consent of the victims as well as of the dominant sex, and such consent is obtained through sex role socialization—a conditioning process which begins to operate from the moment we are born, and which is enforced by most institutions. [ . . . ]

There are many devices available both to women and to men for refusing to see the problem of sexual caste. [ . . . ] Particularization is not uncommon among scholars, who frequently miss the point of the movement's critique of patriarchy itself as a system of social arrangements, and become fixated upon one element or pseudo-element of feminist theory as a target for rebuttal. That is, they spend energy answering questions that women are not really asking. An example of this is the labored defense of Paul by Scripture scholars who would have us know that "the real Paul" was not the author of the objectionable passages against women and was *not* the all time male chauvinist.[4] From the point of view of scriptural scholarship the distinction between the deutero-Pauline authors and "the real Paul" is important, no doubt. However, the discussion is hardly central to women's concern with the oppressiveness of patriarchal religion. The point is that for nearly two thousand years the passages have been used to enforce sexual hierarchy. They represent an established point of view. It is rather obscene to be more concerned with justifying an author long dead and with berating women for an alleged lack of scholarship than with the deep injustice itself that is being perpetrated by religion. The women's critique is not of a few passages but of a universe of sexist suppositions.

Another related method of refusing to see is *spiritualization*, that is, refusal to look at concrete oppressive facts. For example, would-be pacifiers of women seem to be fond of quoting the Pauline text which proclaims that "in Christ there is neither male nor female." This invites the response that *even if* this were true, the fact is that everywhere else there certainly is. Moreover, given the concrete facts of social reality and given the fact that the Christ-image is male, one has to ask what meaning-content the passage possibly can have.

## The Purpose of This Book

It is easy, then, simply not to see. So overwhelming and insidious are the dynamics that function to support the sexist world view that women are constantly tempted to wear blinders—even in the very process of confronting sexism. Then the result is cooptable reformism that nourishes the oppressive system. In the process of writing this book, I have tried to be constantly aware of this dynamic. Asked if this work is intended to be a "new theology," I must point out that the expression is misleading. To describe one's work as "theology" or even as "new theology" usually means that the basic assumptions of patriarchal religion will be unchallenged and that they constitute a hidden agenda of the work. I am concerned precisely with questioning this hidden agenda that is operative even in so-called radical theology. I do not intend to apply "doctrine" to women's liberation. Rather, my task is to study the potential of the women's revolution to transform human consciousness and its externalizations, that is, to generate human becoming. If one must use traditional labels, my work can at least as accurately be called philosophy. Paul Tillich described himself as working "on the boundary" between philosophy and theology. The work of this book is not merely on the boundary *between* these (male-created) disciplines, but on the boundary *of* both, because it speaks out of the experience of that half of the human species which has been represented in neither discipline.

But if the word "theology" can be torn free from its usual limited and limiting context, if it can be torn free from its function of legitimating patriarchy, then my book can be called an effort to create theology as well as philosophy. For my purpose is to show that the women's revolution, insofar as it is true to its own essential dynamics, is an ontological, spiritual revolution, pointing beyond the idolatries of sexist society and sparking creative action in and toward transcendence. The becoming of women implies universal human becoming. It has everything to do with the search for ultimate meaning and reality, which some would call God.

Women have been extra-environmentals in human society. We have been foreigners not only to the fortresses of political power but also to those citadels in which thought processes have been spun out, creating a net of meaning to capture reality. In a sexist world, symbol systems and conceptual apparatuses have been male creations. These do not reflect the experience of women, but rather function to falsify our own self-image and experiences. Women have often resolved the problems this situation raises by simply not seeing the situation. That is, we have screened out experience and responded only to the questions considered meaningful and licit within the boundaries of prevailing thought structures, which reflect sexist social structures.

As Simone de Beauvoir sadly notes, women who have perceived the reality of sexual oppression usually have exhausted themselves in breaking through to discovery of their own humanity, with little energy left for constructing their own interpretation of the universe. Therefore, the various ideological constructs cannot be imagined to reflect a balanced or adequate vision. Instead, they distort reality and destroy human potential, female and male. What is required of women at this point in history is a firm and deep refusal to limit our perspectives, questioning, and creativity to any of the preconceived patterns of male-dominated culture. When the positive products of our emerging awareness and creativity express dimensions of the search for ultimate meaning, they can indeed be called both philosophical and theological, but in the sense of pointing beyond the God of patriarchal philosophy and religion.

## The Problem of "Method"

The question arises, therefore, of the method I propose to use in this book in dealing with questions of religious symbols and concepts, and with ethical problems. I will begin my description with some indications of what my method is *not*. First of all it obviously is not that of a "kerygmatic theology," which supposes some unique and changeless revelation peculiar to Christianity or to *any* religion.[5] Neither is my approach that of a disinterested observer who claims to have an "objective knowledge about" reality.[6] Nor is it an attempt to correlate with the existing cultural situation certain "eternal truths" which are presumed to have been captured as adequately as possible in a fixed and limited set of symbols.[7] None of these approaches can express the revolutionary potential of women's liberation for challenging the forms in which consciousness incarnates itself and for changing consciousness.

The method that is required is not one of correlation but of *liberation*. Even the term "method" must be reinterpreted and in fact wrenched out of its usual semantic field, for the emerging creativity in women is by no means a merely cerebral process. In order to understand the implications of this process it is necessary to grasp the fundamental fact that women have had the power of *naming* stolen from us. We have not been free to use our own power to name ourselves, the world, or God. The old naming was not the product of dialogue—a fact inadvertently admitted in the Genesis story of Adam's naming the animals and the woman. Women are now realizing that the universal imposing of names by men has been false because partial. That is, inadequate words have been taken as adequate. In this respect—though with a different slant—the new woman-consciousness is in accord with the view of Josiah Royce that it is impossible to consider any term apart from its relations to the whole.[8]

To exist humanly is to name the self, the world, and God.[9] The "method" of the evolving spiritual consciousness of women is nothing less than this beginning to speak humanly—a reclaiming of the right to name. The liberation of language is rooted in the liberation of ourselves.

It would be a mistake to imagine that the new speech of women can be equated simply with women speaking men's words. What is happening is that women are really *hearing* our*selves* and each other, and out of this supportive hearing emerge *new words*.[10] This is not to say necessarily that an entirely different set of words is coming into being full blown in a *material* sense—that is, different sounds or combinations of letters on paper. Rather, words which, materially speaking, are identical with the old become new in a semantic context that arises from qualitatively new experience. The word *exodus* as applied to the community of women that is now emerging exemplifies this phenomenon.[11] The word's meaning is stripped of its patriarchal, biblical context, while at the same time speaking *to* and *beyond* that context. So also the word *sisterhood* no longer means a subordinate mini-brotherhood, but an authentic bonding of women on a wide scale for our own liberation.

Moreover, this liberation of language from its old context implies a breakthrough to new semantic fields. The new context has its source and its verification in the rising consciousness women have of ourselves and of our situation. Since this consciousness contradicts the established sense of reality which is reflected in the prevailing social and linguistic structures, its verbal expressions sometimes involve apparent contradictions. The words of women's becoming function in such a way that they raise questions and problems and at the same time give clues to the resolution of those problems. A number of examples of this naming process can be found in this book.

Occasionally such expressions may be deliberately transitional. When, for example, I have spoken of "the sisterhood of man" the result has been a sense of contradiction and a jarring of images. "Intellectually" everyone "knows" that "man" is a generic term. However, in view of the fact that we live in a world in which full humanity is attributed only to males, and in view of the significant fact that "man" also means male, the term does not come through as truly generic. For this reason many feminists would like to erase the specious generic term "man" from the language, and rightly so. What "sisterhood of man" does is to give a generic weight to "sisterhood" which the term has never before been called upon to bear. At the same time it emasculates the pseudo-generic "man." The expression, then, raises the problem of a sexually oppressive world and it signals other possibilities. I would not use the pseudo-generic "man" in any other kind of context than in this contradictory and problematic setting. The point is not to legitimate the use of "man" for the human species, but to point to the necessity of the death of this false word, its elimination from our language.

The method of liberation, then, involves a *castrating* of language and images that reflect and perpetuate the structures of a sexist world. It castrates precisely in the sense of cutting away the phallocentric value system imposed by patriarchy, in its subtle as well as in its more manifest expressions. As aliens in a man's world who are now rising up to name—

that is, to create—our own world, women are beginning to recognize that the value system that has been thrust upon us by the various cultural institutions of patriarchy has amounted to a kind of gang rape of minds as well as of bodies.

Feminists are accustomed to enduring such labels as "castrating females." Some have rightly retorted that if "to castrate" essentially means to deprive of power, potency, creativity, ability to communicate, then indeed it is women who have been castrated by a sexist society. However, I would push the analysis a bit further. It is also true that men are castrated by such a social system in which destructive competitiveness treats men who are low on the totem pole (e.g., black males, poor males, noncompetitive males, Third World males, etc.) *like women*. Yet all of these can still look down upon the primordially castrated beings—women. Now these primordial eunuchs are rising up to castrate not people but *the system* that castrates—that great "God-Father" of us all which indulges senselessly and universally in the politics of rape.

The cutting away of this phallocentric value system in its various incarnations amounts also to a kind of *exorcism* that essentially must be done by women, who are in a position to experience the demonic destructiveness of the super-phallic society in our own being. The *machismo* ethos that has the human psyche in its grip creates a web of projections, introjections, and self-fulfilling prophecies. It fosters a basic alienation within the psyche—a failure to lay claim to that part of the psyche that is then projected onto "the Other." It is essentially demonic in that it cuts off the power of human becoming.

The method of *liberation-castration-exorcism*, then, is a becoming process of "the Other"—women—in which we hear and speak our own words. The development of this hearing faculty and power of speech involves the dislodging of images that reflect and reinforce the prevailing social arrangements. This happens in one way when women assume active, creative roles. I am not referring to women as "role models" in the commonly accepted sense of patriarchy's "models." Rather, I mean to call attention to the emergence of free persons whose lives communicate a kind of contagious freedom.

This dislodging process requires a refusal of the false identity of tokenism. This refusal sometimes is expressed by dramatic action, which is multidimensional in meaning. There is no single prescription for such symbolic acts. They grow organically out of particular situations. They are revelatory, since they not only unmask the fact of sexism but also give signals and clues of transcendence. Generally they involve rejection of tokenism, breaking with the past, dramatic action, the living out of something really new—which gives the impetus for further action.[12]

Women may judge that in some cases the names imposed upon reality by male-dominated society and sanctified by religion are basically oppressive and must be rejected. In other instances, it may be that partial truth has been taken for the whole in the past, and that the symbols and conceptualizations that are biased have to be liberated from their partiality. Women will free traditions, thought, and customs only by hearing each other and thus making it possible to speak our word. This involves interaction between insight and praxis, not in the sense of "reflection" upon "social action" (a false dualism), but rather in the sense of a continual growth, flexibility, and emergence of new perceptions of reality—perceptions that come from being where one is.[13]

The becoming of women in sisterhood is the countercultural phenomenon *par excellence* which can indicate the future course of human spiritual evolution. As I have pointed out, none of the methods acceptable to male philosophers and theologians can begin to speak to this task. Women are not merely "re-thinking" philosophy and theology but are participating in new creation. The process implies beautiful, self-actualizing anger, love, and hope.

## Overcoming Methodolatry

One of the false gods of theologians, philosophers, and other academics is called Method. It commonly happens that the choice of a problem is determined by method, instead of method being determined by the problem. This means that thought is subjected to an invisible tyranny. Susanne Langer wrote:

> The limits of thought are not so much set from outside, by the fullness or poverty of experiences that meet the mind, as from within, by the power of conception, the wealth of formulative notions with which the mind meets experiences. Most new discoveries are suddenly-seen things that were always there.[14]

The tyranny of methodolatry hinders new discoveries. It prevents us from raising questions never asked before and from being illumined by ideas that do not fit into pre-established boxes and forms. The worshippers of Method have an effective way of handling data that does not fit into the Respectable Categories of Questions and Answers. They simply classify it as nondata, thereby rendering it invisible.

It should be noted that the god Method is in fact a subordinate deity, serving Higher Powers. These are social and cultural institutions whose survival depends upon the classification of disruptive and disturbing information as nondata. Under patriarchy, Method has wiped out women's questions so totally that even women have not been able to hear and formulate our own questions to meet our own experiences. Women have been unable even to experience our own experience.

This book is an effort to begin asking nonquestions and to start discovering, reporting, and analyzing nondata. It is therefore an exercise in Methodicide, a form of deicide. The servants of Method must therefore unacknowledge its nonexistence (a technique in which they are highly skilled). By the grace of this double negative may they bless its existence in the best way they know. High treason merits a double cross.

This writing has been done in hope. Hopefully it represents not merely a continuation but a new beginning. Certainly it is not The Last Word. But insofar as it brings forth the right word it will be heard, for the right word will have the power of reality in it.

7

# After the Death of God the Father

## Chapter 1 of *Beyond God the Father*, pp. 13–43.

*Be-ing 1:* Ultimate/Intimate Reality, the constantly Unfolding Verb of Verbs which is intransitive, having no object that limits its dynamism *2:* the Final Cause, the Good who is Self-communicating, who is the Verb from whom, in whom, and with whom all true movements move.
—*Wickedary*, p. 64

Arguably the most important pages of Daly's career, the opening chapter of *Beyond God the Father* makes clear that Daly had abandoned the staleness of received theological traditions in favor of a constantly creative, dynamic sense of God the Verb. Supremely confident, buoyant with hope, yet certain of the difficulties ahead, Daly articulated a philosophy that reconciles individual and community, mysticism and social justice.

What she named so effectively here is that when transcendence becomes objectified, it becomes static. The move to God the Verb breaks the cycle of "fixing names *upon* God, which deafened us to our own potential for self-naming." In place of "a super-reified Something" Daly proposed "a power of being which both is, and is not yet," a divine that "is form-destroying, form-creating, transforming power that makes all things new." Her notion of God finds "the creative potential itself in human beings that is the image of God." Her use of the plural here is not a mistake: she meant this collectively. She suggested that the "self-awareness of women is a *creative political ontophany*, . . . creating a counterworld to the counterfeit 'this world'" in which we find ourselves. This creativity, which Daly has already divinized, she now proclaimed "is participation in eternal life."

Daly insisted, in a way that may make a contemporary reader uneasy, on the primacy of women's liberation as a transformative movement. Her logic had to do with the universal nature of patriarchy: "women have been the most radically alienated of all segments of society." She had referred before to the idea that males in oppressed groups are treated like women, and therefore deduced that male/female inequality is the primary paradigm for oppression. If all women in all religious and cultural systems came to consciousness about the depth of sexism that has limited women's abilities to participate as full human beings, it would upset the entire operation of patriarchy. So Daly anticipated "the present awakening of the hitherto powerless sex," which would demand "an explosion of creative imagination that can withstand the disapproval of orthodoxy and overreach the boundaries cherished by conventional minds." She remained uneasy with strict secularism, because for her the dimension of transcendence defined human longing and, she predicted, would also allow for the full depth of critique and creativity that the women's liberation movement needed: "The new wave of feminism desperately needs to be not only many-faceted but cosmic and ultimately religious in its vision."

Throughout this chapter, the imprint of Daly's theological education and extensive reading and study is clear; she also began to critique almost all of her male sources for their failure even to notice the glaring ontological deficiencies in their understanding of women. Buried, however, in the footnotes is an ode to the mystical "intuition of being" that she imbibed from Jacques Maritain. Despite acknowledging that Maritain "was hardly a feminist or social revolutionary," Daly credited him with "an exceedingly fine sensitivity to the power of this intuition [of being], which, if it were carried through to social consciousness, would challenge the world." The significance of this resonance between intuition and transformation would remain with Daly from the beginning to the end of her career as a writer and thinker. She never categorically dismissed Maritain (or his wife, Raïssa).
—Editors

> The first step in the elevation of women under all systems of religion is to convince them that the great Spirit of the Universe is in no way responsible for any of these absurdities.
> —Elizabeth Cady Stanton

The biblical and popular image of God as a great patriarch in heaven, rewarding and punishing according to his mysterious and seemingly arbitrary will, has dominated the imagination of millions over thousands of years. The symbol of the Father God, spawned in the human imagination and sustained as plausible by patriarchy, has in turn rendered service to this type of society by making its mechanisms for the oppression of women appear right and fitting. If God in "his" heaven is a father ruling "his" people, then it is in the "nature" of things and according to divine plan and the order of the universe that society be male-dominated.

Within this context a mystification of roles takes place: the husband dominating his wife represents God "himself." The images and values of a given society have been projected into the realm of dogmas and "Articles of Faith," and these in turn justify the social structures which have given rise to them and which sustain their plausibility. The belief system becomes hardened and objectified, seeming to have an unchangeable independent existence and validity of its own. It resists social change that would rob it of its plausibility. Despite the vicious circle, however, change can occur in society, and ideologies can die, though they die hard.

As the women's movement begins to have its effect upon the fabric of society, transforming it from patriarchy into something that never existed before—into a diarchal situation that is radically new—it can become the greatest single challenge to the major religions of the world, Western and Eastern. Beliefs and values that have held sway for thousands of years will be questioned as never before. This revolution may well be also the greatest single hope for survival of spiritual consciousness on this planet.

## The Challenge: Emergence of Whole Human Beings

There are some who persist in claiming that the liberation of women will only mean that new characters will assume the same old roles, and that nothing will change essentially in structures, ideologies, and values. This supposition is often based on the observation that the very few women in "masculine" occupations often behave much as men do. This kind of reasoning is not at all to the point, for it fails to take into account the fact that tokenism does not change stereotypes or social systems but works to preserve them, since it dulls the revolutionary impulse. The minute proportion of women in the United States who occupy such roles (such as senators, judges, business executives, doctors, etc.) have been trained by men in institutions defined and designed by men, and they have been pressured subtly to operate according to male rules.[1] There are no alternate models. As sociologist Alice Rossi has suggested, this is not what the women's movement in its most revolutionary potential is all about.[2]

What *is* to the point is an emergence of woman-consciousness such as has never before taken place. It is unimaginative and out of touch with what is happening in the women's movement to assume that the becoming of women will simply mean uncritical acceptance of structures, beliefs, symbols, norms, and patterns of behavior that have been given priority by society under male domination. Rather, this becoming will act as catalyst for radical change in our culture. It has been argued cogently by Piaget that structure is maintained by an interplay of transformation laws that never yield results beyond the system and never tend to employ elements external to the system.[3] This is indicative of what *can* effect basic alteration in the system, that is, a potent influence *from without*. Women who reject patriarchy have this power and indeed *are* this power of transformation that is ultimately threatening to things as they are.

The roles and structures of patriarchy have been developed and sustained in accordance with an artificial polarization of human qualities into the traditional sexual stereotypes. The image of the person in authority and the accepted understanding of "his" role has corresponded to the eternal masculine stereotype, which implies hyper-rationality (in reality, frequently reducible to pseudo-rationality), "objectivity," aggressivity, the possession of dominating and manipulative attitudes toward persons and the environment, and the tendency to construct boundaries between the self (and those identified with the self) and "the Other." The caricature of human being which is represented by this stereotype depends for its existence upon the opposite caricature—the eternal feminine. This implies hyper-emotionalism, passivity, self-abnegation, etc. By becoming whole persons women can generate a counterforce to the stereotype of the leader, challenging the artificial polarization of human characteristics into sex-role identification. There is no reason to assume that women who have the support of each other to criticize not only the feminine stereotype but the masculine stereotype as well will simply adopt the latter as a model for ourselves. On the contrary, what is happening is that women are developing a wider range of qualities and skills. This is beginning to encourage and in fact demand a comparably liberating process in men—a phenomenon which has begun in men's liberation groups and which is taking place every day within the context of personal relationships. The becoming of androgynous human persons implies a radical change in the fabric of human consciousness and in styles of human behavior.

This change is already threatening the credibility of the religious symbols of our culture. Since many of these have been used to justify oppression, such a challenge should be seen as redemptive. Religious symbols fade and die when the cultural situation that gave rise to them and supported them ceases to give them plausibility. Such an event generates anxiety, but it is part of the risk involved in a faith which accepts the relativity of all symbols and recognizes that clinging to these as fixed and ultimate is self-destructive and idolatrous.

The becoming of new symbols is not a matter that can be decided arbitrarily around a conference table. Rather, symbols grow out of a changing communal situation and experience. This does not mean that we are confined to the role of passive spectators. The experience of the becoming of women cannot be understood merely conceptually and abstractly but through active participation in the overcoming of servitude. Both activism and creative thought flow from and feed into the evolving woman-consciousness. The cumulative effect is a surge of awareness beyond the symbols and doctrines of patriarchal religion.

## The Inadequate God of Popular Preaching

The image of the divine Father in heaven has not always been conducive to humane behavior, as any perceptive reader of history knows. The often cruel behavior of Christians toward unbelievers and toward dissenters among themselves suggests a great deal not only about the values of the society dominated by that image, but also about how that image itself functions in relation to behavior. There has been a basic ambivalence in the image of the heavenly patriarch—a split between the God of love and the jealous God who represents the collective power of "his" chosen people. As historian Arnold Toynbee has indicated, this has reflected and perpetuated a double standard of behavior.[4] Without debating the details of his historical analysis, the insight is available on an experiential level. The character of Vito Corleone in *The Godfather* is a vivid illustration of the marriage of tenderness and violence so intricately blended in the patriarchal ideal. The worshippers of the loving Father may in a sense love their neighbors, but in fact the term applies only to those within a restricted and unstable circumference, and these worshippers can "justifiably" be intolerant and fanatic persecutors of those outside the sacred circle.

How this God operates is illustrated in contemporary American civil religion.[5] In one of the White House sermons given during the first term of Richard Nixon, Rabbi Louis Finkelstein expressed the hope that a future historian may say "that in the period of great trials and great tribulations, the finger of God pointed to Richard Milhous Nixon, giving the vision and the wisdom to save the world and civilization; and also to open the way for our country to realize the good that the twentieth century offers mankind."[6] Within this context, as Charles Henderson has shown, God is an American and Nixon is "his" anointed one.[7] The preachers carefully selected for the White House sermons stress that this nation is "under God." The logical conclusion is that its policies are right. Under God, the President becomes a Christ figure. In 1969, the day the astronauts would set foot on the moon, and when the President was preparing to cross the Pacific "in search of peace," one of these preachers proclaimed:

> And my hope for mankind is strengthened in the knowledge that our intrepid President himself will soon go into orbit, reaching boldly for the moon of peace. God grant that he, too, may return in glory and that countless millions of prayers that follow him shall not have been in vain.[8]

A fundamental dynamic of this "theology" was suggested by one of Nixon's speech writers, Ray Price, who wrote:

> Selection of a President has to be an act of faith. . . . This faith isn't achieved by reason: it's achieved by charisma, by a feeling of trust. . . .[9]

Price also argued that the campaign would be effective only "if we can get people to make the *emotional* leap, or what theologians call 'leap of faith.'"[10] This is, of course, precisely the inauthentic leap that Camus labeled as philosophical suicide. It is the suicide demanded by a civil religion in which "God," the Savior-President, and "our nation" more or less merge. When the "leap" is made, it is possible simply not to see what the great God-Father and his anointed one are actually doing. Among the chosen ones are scientists and professors who design perverse methods of torture and death such as flechette pellets that shred the internal organs of "the enemy" and other comparable inhumane "anti-personnel" weapons. Also among the elect are politicians and priests who justify and bestow their blessing upon the system that perpetrates such atrocities. "Under God" are included the powerful industrialists who are making the planet uninhabitable.

Sophisticated thinkers, of course, have never intellectually identified God with a Superfather in heaven. Nevertheless it is important to recognize that even when very abstract conceptualizations of God are formulated in the mind, images survive in the imagination in such a way that a person can function on two different and even apparently contradictory levels at the same time. Thus one can speak of God as spirit and at the same time imagine "him" as belonging to the male sex.[11] Such primitive images can profoundly affect conceptualizations which appear to be very refined and abstract. So too the Yahweh of the future, so cherished by the theology of hope, comes through on an imaginative level as exclusively a He-God, and it is consistent with this that theologians of hope have attempted to develop a political theology which takes no explicit cognizance of the devastation wrought by sexual politics.

The widespread conception of the "Supreme Being" as an entity distinct from this world but controlling it according to plan and keeping human beings in a state of infantile subjection has been a not too subtle mask of the divine patriarch. The Supreme Being's plausibility and that of the static worldview which accompanies this projection has of course declined, at least among the more sophisticated, as Nietzsche prophesied. This was a projection grounded in specifically patriarchal societal structures and sustained as subjectively real by the usual processes of producing plausibility such as preaching, religious indoctrination, and cult. The sustaining power of the social structure has been eroded by a number of developments in recent history, including the general trend toward democratization of society and the emergence of technology. However, it is the women's movement which appears destined to play the key role in the overthrow of such oppressive elements in traditional theism, precisely because it strikes at the source of the societal dualism that is reflected in traditional beliefs. It presents a growing threat to the plausibility of the inadequate popular "God" not so much by attacking "him" as by leaving "him" behind. Few major feminists display great interest in institutional religion. Yet this disinterest can hardly be equated with lack of spiritual consciousness. Rather, in our present experience the woman-consciousness is being wrenched free to find its own religious expression.

It can legitimately be pointed out that the Judeo-Christian tradition is not entirely bereft of elements that can foster intimations of transcendence. Yet the liberating potential of these elements is choked off in the surrounding atmosphere of the images, ideas, values, and structures of patriarchy. The social change coming from radical feminism has the potential to bring about a more acute and widespread perception of qualitative differences between the conceptualizations of "God" and of the human relationship to God which have been oppressive in their connotations, and the kind of language that is spoken from and to the rising woman-consciousness.

## Castrating "God"

I have already suggested that if God is male, then the male is God. The divine patriarch castrates women as long as he is allowed to live on in the human imagination. The process of cutting away the Supreme Phallus can hardly be a merely "rational" affair. The problem is one of transforming the collective imagination so that this distortion of the human aspiration to transcendence loses its credibility.

Some religious leaders, notably Mary Baker Eddy and Ann Lee, showed insight into the problem to some extent and tried to stress the "maternal" aspect of what they called "God."[12] A number of feminists have referred to "God" as "she." While all of this has a point, the analysis has to reach a deeper level. The most basic change has to take place in women—in our being and self-image. Otherwise there is danger of settling for mere reform, reflected in the phenomenon of "crossing," that is, of attempting to use the oppressor's weapons against him. Black theology's image of the Black God illustrates this. It can legitimately be argued that a transsexual operation upon "God," changing "him" to "her," would be a far more profound alteration than a mere pigmentation change. However, to stop at this level of discourse would be a trivialization of the deep problem of human becoming in women.

## Beyond the Inadequate God

The various theologies that hypostatize transcendence, that is, those which in one way or another objectify "God" as a *being*, thereby attempt in a self-contradictory way to envisage transcendent reality as finite. "God" then functions to legitimate the existing social, economic, and political status quo, in which women and other victimized groups are subordinate.

"God" can be used oppressively against women in a number of ways. First, it occurs in an overt manner when theologians proclaim women's subordination to be God's will. This of course has been done throughout the centuries, and residues remain in varying degrees of subtlety and explicitness in the writings of twentieth century thinkers such as Barth, Bonhoeffer, Reinhold Niebuhr, and Teilhard de Chardin.[13]

Second, even in the absence of such explicitly oppressive justification, the phenomenon is present when one-sex symbolism for God and for the human relationship to God is used. The following passage illustrates the point:

> To believe that God is Father is to become aware of oneself not as a stranger, not as an outsider or an alienated person, but as a son who belongs or a person appointed to a marvelous destiny, which he shares with the whole community. To believe that God is Father means to be able to say "we" in regard to all men.[14]

A woman whose consciousness has been aroused can say that such language makes her aware of herself as a stranger, as an outsider, as an alienated person, not as a daughter who belongs or who is appointed to a marvelous destiny. She cannot belong to *this* without assenting to her own lobotomy.

Third, even when the basic assumptions of God-language appear to be nonsexist, and when language is somewhat purified of fixation upon maleness, it is damaging and implicitly compatible with sexism if it encourages detachment from the reality of the human struggle against oppression in its concrete manifestations. That is, the lack of explicit relevance of intellection to the fact of oppression in its precise forms, such as sexual hierarchy, is itself oppressive. This is the case when theologians write long treatises on creative hope, political theology, or revolution without any specific acknowledgment of or application to the problem of sexism or other specific forms of injustice. Such irrelevance is conspicuous in the major works of "theologians of hope" such as Moltmann, Pannenberg, and Metz. This is not to say that the vision of creative eschatology is completely irrelevant, but that it lacks specific grounding in the concrete experiences of the oppressed. The theorizing then has a quality of unreality. Perhaps an obvious reason for this is that the theologians themselves have not shared in the experience of oppression and therefore write from the privileged distance of those who have at best a "knowledge about" the subject.

Tillich's ontological theology, too, even though it is potentially liberating in a very radical sense, fails to be adequate in this regard. It is true that Tillich *tries* to avoid hypostatization of "God" (though the effort is not completely successful) and that his manner of speaking about the ground and power of being would be difficult to use for the legitimation of any sort of oppression.[15] However, the specific relevance of "power of being" to the fact of sexual oppression is not indicated. Moreover, just as his discussion of God is "detached," so is the rest of his theology—a point that I will pursue later on. This detachment from the problem of relevance of God-language to the struggle against demonic power structures characterizes not only Tillich but also other male theoreticians who have developed a relatively nonsexist language for transcendence. Thinkers such as Whitehead, James, and Jaspers employ God-language that soars beyond sexual hierarchy as a specific problem to be confronted in the process of human becoming.

The new insight of women is bringing us to a point beyond such direct and indirect theological oppressiveness that traditionally has centered around discussions of "God." It is becoming clear that if God-language is even implicitly compatible with oppressiveness, failing to make clear the relation between intellection and liberation, then it will either have to be developed in such a way that it becomes explicitly relevant to the problem of sexism or else dismissed. In asserting this I am employing a pragmatic yardstick or verification process to God-language in a manner not totally dissimilar to that of William James. In my thinking, the specific criterion which implies a mandate to reject certain forms of God-talk is expressed in the question: Does this language hinder human becoming by reinforcing sex-role socialization? Expressed positively—a point to be developed later on—the question is: Does it *encourage* human becoming toward psychological and social fulfillment, toward an androgynous mode of living, toward transcendence?

It is probable that the movement will eventually generate a new language of transcendence. There is no reason to assume that the term "God" will always be necessary, as if the three-letter word, materially speaking, could capture and encapsulate transcendent being. At this point in history, however, it is probable that the new God-word's essential newness will be conveyed more genuinely by its being placed in a different semantic field than by a mere material alteration in sound or appearance of the word. Since the women's revolution implies the liberation of all human beings, it is impossible to believe that during the course of its realization the religious imagination and intelligence will simply lie dormant. Part of the challenge is to recognize the poverty of all words and symbols and the fact of our past idolatry regarding them, and then to turn to our own resources for bringing about the radically new in our own lives. It is this living that is generating the new meaning context for God, some elements of which can now be examined.

## Women's Liberation and Revelatory Courage

I have already indicated that it would be unrealistic to dismiss the fact that the symbolic and linguistic instruments for communication—which include essentially the whole theological tradition in world religions—have been formulated by males under the conditions of patriarchy. It is therefore inherent in these symbolic and linguistic structures that they serve the purposes of patriarchal social arrangements. Even the usual and accepted means of theological dissent have been restricted in such a way that only some questions have been allowed to arise. Many questions that are of burning importance to women now simply have not occurred in the past (and to a large extent in the present) to those with "credentials" to do theology. Others may have been voiced timidly but quickly squelched as stupid, irrelevant, or naïve. Therefore, attempts by women theologians now merely to "up-date" or to reform theology within acceptable patterns of question-asking are not likely to get very far.

Moreover, within the context of the prevailing social climate it has been possible for scholars to be aware of the most crudely dehumanizing texts concerning women in the writings of religious "authorities" and theologians—from Augustine to Aquinas, to Luther, to Knox, to Barth—and at the same time to treat their unverified opinions on far more imponderable matters with utmost reverence and respect. That is, the blatant misogynism of these men has not been the occasion of a serious credibility gap even for those who have disagreed on this "point." It has simply been ignored or dismissed as trivial. By contrast, in the emerging consciousness of women this context is beginning to be perceived in its full significance and as deeply relevant to the worldview in which such "authorities" have seen other seemingly unrelated subjects, such as the problem of God. Hence the present awakening of the hitherto powerless sex demands an explosion of creative imagination that can withstand the disapproval of orthodoxy and overreach the boundaries cherished by conventional minds.

The driving revelatory force that is making it possible for women to speak—and to *hear* each other speak—more authentically about God is courage in the face of the risks that attend the liberation process. Since the projections of patriarchal religion have been blocking the dynamics of existential courage by offering the false security of alienation, that is, of self-reduction in sex roles, there is reason to hope for the emergence of a new religious consciousness in the confrontation with sexism that is now in its initial stages. The becoming of women may be not only the doorway to deliverance which secular humanism has passionately fought for—but also a doorway *to* something, that is, a new phase in the human spirit's quest for God.

This becoming who we really are requires existential courage to confront the experience of nothingness. All human beings are threatened by nonbeing. In Tillich's analysis, the resultant anxiety surfaces in relation to the threat of fate and death, guilt and condemnation, and meaninglessness.[16] While Tillich analyzes courage in universalist, humanist categories, he does not betray any awareness of the relevance of this to women's confrontation with the structured evil of patriarchy. I am suggesting that at this point in history women are in a unique sense called to be the bearers of existential courage in society.

People attempt to overcome the threat of nonbeing by denying the self. The outcome of this is ironic: that which is dreaded triumphs, for we are caught in the self-contradictory bind of shrinking our being to avoid nonbeing. The only alternative is self-actualization in spite of the ever-present nothingness. Part of the problem is that people, women in particular, who are seemingly incapable of a high degree of self-actualization have been made such by societal structures that are products of human attempts to create security. Those who are alienated from their own deepest identity do receive a kind of security in return for accepting very limited and undifferentiated identities. The woman who single-mindedly accepts the role of "housewife," for example, may to some extent avoid the experience of nothingness but she also avoids a fuller participation in being, which would be her only real security and source of community. Submerged in such a role, she cannot achieve a breakthrough to creativity. Many strong women are worn out in the struggle to break out of these limits before reaching the higher levels of intellectual discovery or of creativity.

The beginning of a breakthrough means a realization that there is an existential conflict between the self and structures that have given such crippling security. This requires confronting the shock of nonbeing with the courage to be. It means facing the nameless anxieties of fate, which become concretized in loss of jobs, friends, social approval, health, and even life itself. Also involved is anxiety of guilt over refusing to do what society demands, a guilt which can hold one in its grip long after it has been recognized as false. Finally, there is the anxiety of meaninglessness, which can be overwhelming at times when the old simple meanings, role definitions, and life expectations have been rooted out and rejected openly and one emerges into a world without models.

This confrontation with the anxiety of nonbeing is revelatory, making possible the relativization of structures that are seen as human products, and therefore not absolute and ultimate. It drives consciousness beyond fixation upon "things as they are." Courage to be is the key to the revelatory power of the feminist revolution.[17]

## The Struggle toward Self-Transcendence

The drive toward transcendence can be envisaged mythically in different but interrelated ways. This point has been made in an original way by Herbert Richardson, whose typology I am relating to sex role socialization in the following analysis.[18] The myth of separation and return (going away and coming home again—like Ulysses) is obviously a cyclic vision and it is often bound up with parental images. Birth means separation from the mother, but the child immediately returns to its parents in its dependency for the necessities of life. Popular Christianity envisages human life in these terms, looking forward to a return to the Father in heaven. The theme of *exitus-reditus* (exit and return) was commonly used in medieval theology to describe the human relationship to God. Although this theme was developed in a subtle and intricate way and although the journey did involve transformation through grace, the imagery of "return" that was attached to it lent itself easily to an attitude of detachment from social injustice. Taken on the imaginative level the myth of separation and return reflects quite well the limited sort of transcendence that has been the only possibility for most women in the course of history—separation from the home of parents only to return to paternalistic domination in the home of a husband. The eternal circle of separation from and return to infantile dependence has been the story of the feminine mode of existence.

Another kind of transcendence myth has been dramatization of human life in terms of conflict and vindication. This focuses upon the situation of oppression and the struggle for liberation. It is a short-circuited transcendence when the struggle against oppression becomes an end in itself, the focal point of all meaning. There is an inherent contradiction in the idea that those devoted to a cause have found their whole meaning in the struggle, so that the desired victory becomes implicitly an undesirable meaninglessness. Such a truncated vision is one of the pitfalls of theologies of the oppressed. Sometimes black theology, for example that of James Cone, resounds with a cry for vengeance and is fiercely biblical and patriarchal. It transcends religion as a crutch (the separation and return of much old-fashioned Negro spirituality) but tends to settle for being religion as a gun. Tailored to fit only the situation of racial oppression, it inspires a will to vindication but leaves unexplored other dimensions of liberation. It does not get beyond the sexist models internalized by the self and controlling society—models that are at the root of racism and that perpetuate it. The Black God and Black Messiah apparently are merely the same patriarchs after a pigmentation operation—their behavior unaltered.[19]

Fortunately, the danger that the new spiritual consciousness of women will be truncated in a similar way is greatly reduced by the fact that the stereotypically male symbols of Christianity do not lend themselves to this kind of easy adaptation by feminism. There is less "opportunity" for us to fall into facile repetition of the same mistakes. With the rise of feminism, women have indeed come to see the necessity of conflict, of letting rage surface and of calling forth a will to liberation. Yet—partially because there is such an essential contrast between feminism and patriarchal religion's destructive symbols and values, and partially because women's lives are intricately bound up with those of men—biologically, emotionally, socially, and professionally—it is quite clear that women's liberation is essentially linked with full human liberation. Women generally can see very well that the movement will self-destruct if we settle for vengeance. The more imminent danger, then, is that some women will seek premature reconciliation, not allowing themselves to see the depth and implications of feminism's essential opposition to sexist society. It can be easy to leap on the bandwagon of "human liberation" without paying the price in terms of polarization, tensions, risk, and pain that the ultimate objective of real human liberation demands.

A third myth of transcendence (still using Richardson's typology) is integrity and transformation. Within this perspective, the individual seeks self-transformation and spiritual rebirth. This involves the becoming of psychic unity, which means that one does not have to depend upon another for "complementarity" but can love independently. Richardson's analysis in this essay hints at but does not quite convey explicit recognition that such independence means the becoming of psychologically androgynous[20] human beings, since the basic crippling "complementarity" has been the false masculine/feminine polarity. Androgynous integrity and transformation will require that women cease to play the role of "complement" and struggle to stand alone as free human beings.

## Nonbeing, Power of Being, and Hope

The striving toward psychic wholeness, or androgyny, incorporates the insights and clues in the less adequate modes of envisaging transcendence. The separation and return motif, at its best, pointed to the dimension of depth in human existence. Its basis lay in intimations of the holiness of what *is*. The vision that it entailed, however, often tended to be nonsocial and abstracted from history, or—to borrow (somewhat out of context) a phrase from Moltmann—the nonhistorical mysticism of the solitary soul. At its best, this ontological-sacramental faith gave a kind of interior freedom. A high point of cyclic theological expression was the Thomistic synthesis. The conflict and vindication motif rests more upon a kind of moral faith, an intimation of the holiness of what *ought to be*. It too has tended to be individualistic and, with the help of Kant, has bred a kind of split-level consciousness in which personal struggles for transcendence can exist side by side with social conformity. In the recently developed theology of hope, the conflict and vindication motif is brought to a level of social concern that transcends some of the limitations of the Protestant ethic. Yet the ontological dimension of the holiness of what *is* is generally rejected as Hellenic and unbiblical. I am suggesting that the vision of human becoming as a process of integration and transformation, *as this vision is emerging in the women's revolution*, potentially includes both the individualistic ontological dimension of depth and revolutionary participation in history. It does this precisely because it strikes at the externalized structures and internalized images of patriarchy that have cut us off from realizing psychic wholeness in ourselves and consequently have cut down our capacity for genuine participation in history.

The seeds of such a synthesis were present to some extent in Tillich's vision, especially as expressed in *The Courage to Be*, even though this was not developed as a political theology. As he explains, existential courage is dynamic and it has two sides: the courage to be as a self and the courage to be as a part. I suggest that such courage makes creative, communal, revolutionary hope possible to the extent that the courage is expressed in confrontation with earthly powers and principalities that embody nonbeing in our patriarchal culture. It is this dimension of confrontation that makes courage give rise to creative hope.

This synthesis of hope and courage, potentially in the dynamics of the feminist revolution, includes separation and return since by breaking from the past and consciously creating our own history we change the past, that is, change and expand our understanding of it. This separation and return happens, for example, when we establish the significance of events that historians have disregarded, such as the achievements of great women and major landmarks in the history of the oppression of women. The synthesis also includes conflict and vindication, not in the sense of attempting to reduce those in power to objects, but in the sense of breaking down the masculine/feminine models thrust upon us by the powers and principalities that shrink the human potential of women and men.

If one were to judge by theological writings of the past several years, from Gogarten to Harvey Cox to Leslie Dewart to Pannenberg, it would appear that the sense of being is disappearing from the contemporary consciousness. Before jumping to such conclusions, however, it would be well to consider at least two points. In the first place, existential questions have never been expressed explicitly in ontological terms most of the time by most people, who indeed seem to have spent most of their energy evading such questions. The question of being and nonbeing (to be or not to be) in all of its poignancy, arises in times of great distress, that is, in "marginal situations" (Berger) such as proximity to death, and occasionally in times of extremely positive "peak experiences."[21] In the second place, it is becoming increasingly evident that among disaffected members of the younger generation—younger in years and/or in spirit—there is a resurgence of ontological awareness which theologians recently have tended to overlook.[22] It appears that there has been a loss of the sense of being in our culture, and that this is essentially what the alienated are experiencing and communicating—an awareness of depth of reality that liberates from false consciousness. As I have indicated, the liberation of women involves susceptibility to the experience of nonbeing in a most dramatic way, for women have been the most radically alienated of all segments of society.

I am proposing that all authentic human hope is ontological, that is, that it requires facing nothingness. This experience gives a sense of distance and relativity in relation to the symbols prevailing in one's culture. Without it, the mind tends to perceive these as literally "true" or at least as permanently adequate for all cultural situations, which means the human mind becomes paralyzed by its own products. This is, I think, the essential inadequacy of non-ontological "theology of hope," which obstinately stays within the terrain of biblical language.[23] When women reach the point of recognizing that we are aliens in this terrain, the sense of transcendence and the surge of hope can be seen as rooted in the power of being, which, perhaps for lack of a better word, some would still call "God."

## Why Speak about "God"?

It might seem that the women's revolution should just go about its business of generating a new consciousness, without worrying about God. I suggest that the fallacy involved in this would be an overlooking of a basic question that is implied in human existence and that the pitfall in such an oversight is cutting off the radical potential of the movement itself.

It is reasonable to take the position that sustained effort toward self-transcendence requires keeping alive in one's consciousness the question of ultimate transcendence, that is, of God. It implies recognition of the fact that we have no power *over* the ultimately real, and that whatever authentic power we have is derived from *participation in* ultimate reality. This awareness, always hard to sustain, makes it possible to be free of idolatry even in regard to one's own cause, since it tells us that all presently envisaged goals, lifestyles, symbols, and societal structures may be transitory. This is the meaning that the question of God should have for liberation, sustaining a concern that is really open to the future, in other words, that is really ultimate. Such a concern will not become fixated upon limited objectives. Feminists in the past have in a way been idolatrous about such objectives as the right to vote. Indeed, this right is due to women in justice and it is entirely understandable that feminists' energies were drained by the efforts needed to achieve even such a modicum of justice. But from the experience of such struggles we are in a position now to distrust token victories within a societal and structural framework that renders them almost meaningless. The new wave of feminism desperately needs to be not only many-faceted but cosmic and ultimately religious in its vision. This means reaching outward and inward toward the God beyond and beneath the gods who have stolen our identity.

The idea that human beings are "to the image of God" is an intuition whose implications could hardly be worked through under patriarchal conditions. If it is true that human beings have projected "God" in their own image, it is also true that we can evolve beyond the projections of earlier stages of consciousness. It is the creative potential itself in human beings that is the image of God.[24] As the essential victims of the archaic God-projections, women can bring this process of creativity into a new phase. This involves iconoclasm—the breaking of idols. Even—and perhaps especially—through the activity of its most militantly atheistic and a-religious members, the movement is smashing images that obstruct the becoming of the image of God. The basic idol-breaking will be done on the level of internalized images of male superiority, on the plane of exorcising them from consciousness and from the cultural institutions that breed them.

One aspect of this expurgation is dethronement of false Gods—ideas and symbols of God that religion has foisted upon the human spirit (granted that the human spirit has created the religions that do this). I have already discussed this to some extent, but it might be well to focus specifically upon three false deities who still haunt the prayers, hymns, sermons, and religious education of Christianity. The three usurpers I have in mind have already been detected and made the targets of attack by liberal male theologians, but the point in mentioning them here is to indicate the specific relevance of feminism to their demise.

One of the false deities to be dethroned is the God of explanation, or "God as a stop-gap for the incompleteness of our knowledge," as Bonhoeffer called him.[25] This serves sometimes as the legitimation of anomic occurrences such as the suffering of a child, a legitimation process which Peter Berger lucidly analyzes in discussing the problem of theodicy.[26] Such phenomena are "explained" as being God's will. So also are socially prevailing inequalities of power and privilege, by a justifying process which easily encourages masochistic attitudes. Clearly, this deity does not encourage commitment to the task of analyzing and eradicating the social, economic, and psychological roots of suffering. As marginal beings who are coming into awareness, women are in a situation to see that "God's plan" is often a front for men's plans and a cover for inadequacy, ignorance, and evil. Our vantage point offers opportunities for dislodging this deity from its revered position on the scale of human delusions.

Another idol is the God of otherworldliness. The most obvious face of this deity in the past has been that of the Judge whose chief activity consists in rewarding and punishing after death. As de Beauvoir indicated, women have been the major consumers of this religious product. Since there has been so little self-realization possible by the female sex "in this life," it was natural to focus attention on the next. As mass consumers of this image, women have the power to remove it from the market, mainly by living full lives here and now. I do not mean to advocate a mere re-utterance of the "secularization" theology that was so popular in the sixties. This obvious shape of the God of otherworldliness has after all been the target of male theologians for some time, and the result has often been a kind of translation of religion into humanism to such an extent that there is a kind of "self-liquidation of theology."[27] What I see beginning to happen with women coming into their own goes beyond this secularization. The rejection of the simplistic God of otherworldliness does not mean necessarily reduction to banal secularism. If women can sustain the courage essential to liberation this can give rise to a deeper "otherworldliness"—an awareness that the process of creating a counterworld to the counterfeit "this world" presented to consciousness by the societal structures that oppress us is participation in eternal life.

It should be noted that the God lurking behind some forms of Protestant piety has functioned similarly to the otherworldly God of popular Roman Catholic piety. In his analysis of the effects of Luther's doctrine of salvation by faith alone, Max Weber uncovers serious problems of ethical motivation, involving a complicated series of phenomena: "Every rational and planned procedure for achieving salvation, every reliance on good works, and above all every effort to surpass normal ethical behavior by ascetic achievement is regarded by religion based on faith as a wicked preoccupation with purely human powers."[28] Trans-worldly asceticism and monasticism tend to be rejected when salvation by faith is stressed, and as a result there may be an increased emphasis upon vocational activity within the world. However, as Weber explains, emphasis upon personal religious relationship to God tends to be accompanied by an attitude of individualism in pursuit of such worldly vocational activity. One consequence is an attitude of patient resignation regarding institutional structures, both worldly and churchly.[29] It is precisely this schizophrenic attitude that combines personal vocational ambition within the prevailing set of social arrangements and passive acceptance of the system that radical feminism recognizes as destructive.

A third idol, intimately related to those described above, is the God who is the Judge of "sin," who confirms the rightness of the rules and roles of the reigning system, maintaining false consciences and self-destructive guilt feelings. Women have suffered both mentally and physically from this deity, in whose name they have been informed that birth control and abortion are unequivocally wrong, that they should be subordinate to their husbands, that they must be present at rituals and services in which men have all the leadership roles and in which they are degraded not only by enforced passivity but also verbally and symbolically. Although this is most blatant in the arch-conservative religions, the God who imposes false guilt is hardly absent from liberal Protestantism and Judaism, where his presence is more subtle. Women's growth in self-respect will deal the death blow to this as well as to the other demons dressed as Gods.

## Women's Liberation as Spiritual Revolution

I have indicated that because the becoming of women involves a radical encounter with nothingness, it bears with it a new surge of ontological hope. This hope is essentially active. The passive hope that has been so prevalent in the history of religious attitudes corresponds to the objectified God from whom one may anticipate favors. Within that frame of reference human beings have tried to relate to ultimate reality as an object to be known, cajoled, manipulated. The tables are turned, however, for the objectified "God" has a way of reducing his producers to objects who lack capacity for autonomous action. In contrast to this, the God who is power of being acts as a moral power summoning women and men to act out of our deepest hope and to become who we can be. I am therefore in agreement with Johannes Metz that authentic hope will be active and creative.[30] The difference is that I see the specific experiential basis for this as an ontological experience. This experience in its first phase is one of nonbeing. In its second phase it is an intuition of being which, as Jacques Maritain described it, is a *dynamic* intuition.[31] Clearly, from what has preceded in this chapter, I see this ontological basis of hope to be particularly available to women at this point in history because of the marginal situation of females in an androcentric world.

This hope is communal rather than merely individualistic, because it is grounded in the two-edged courage to be. That is, it is hope coming from the experience of individuation *and* participation. It drives beyond the objectified God that is imagined as limited in benevolence, bestowing blessings upon "his" favorites. The power of being is that in which all finite beings participate, but not on a "one-to-one" basis, since this power is in all while transcending all. Communal hope involves in some manner a profound interrelationship with other finite beings, human and nonhuman. Ontological communal hope, then, is cosmic. Its essential dynamic is directed to the universal community.

Finally, ontological hope is revolutionary. Since the insight in which it is grounded is the double-edged intuition of nonbeing and of being, it extends beyond the superstitious fixations of technical reason. The latter, as Tillich has shown, when it is cut off from the intuitive knowledge of ontological reason, cannot get beyond superstition.[32] The rising consciousness that women are experiencing of our dehumanized situation has the power to turn attention around from the projections of our culture to the radically threatened human condition. Insofar as women are true to this consciousness, we have to be the most radical of revolutionaries, since the superstition revealed to us is omnipresent and plagues even the other major revolutionary movements of our time. Knowing that a Black or White, Marxist or Capitalist, countercultural or bourgeois male chauvinist deity (human or divine) will not differ essentially from his opposite, women will be forced in a dramatic way to confront the most haunting of human questions, the question of God. This confrontation may not find its major locus within the theological academy or the institutional churches and it may not always express itself in recognizable theological or philosophical language. However, there is a dynamism in the ontological affirmation of self that reaches out toward the nameless God.[33] In hearing and naming ourselves out of the depths, women are naming *toward* God, which is what theology always should have been about. Unfortunately it tended to stop at fixing names *upon* God, which deafened us to our own potential for self-naming.

## The Unfolding of God

It has sometimes been argued that anthropomorphic symbols for "God" are important and even necessary because the fundamental powers of the cosmos otherwise are seen as impersonal. One of the insights characteristic of the rising woman consciousness is that this kind of dichotomizing between cosmic power and the personal need not be. That is, it is not necessary to anthropomorphize or to reify transcendence in order to relate to this personally. In fact, the process is demonic in some of its consequences.[34] The dichotomizing-reifying-projecting syndrome has been characteristic of patriarchal consciousness, making "the Other" the repository of the contents of the lost self. Since women are now beginning to recognize in ourselves the victims of such dichotomizing processes, the insight extends to other manifestations of the pathological splitting off of reality into falsely conceived opposites. Why indeed must "God" be a noun? Why not a verb—the most active and dynamic of all? Hasn't the naming of "God" as a noun been an act of murdering that dynamic Verb? And isn't the Verb infinitely more personal than a mere static noun? The anthropomorphic symbols for God may be intended to convey personality, but they fail to convey that God is Be-ing. Women now who are experiencing the shock of nonbeing and the surge of self-affirmation against this are inclined to perceive transcendence as the Verb in which we participate—live, move, and have our being.

This Verb—the Verb of Verbs—is intransitive.[35] It need not be conceived as having an object that limits its dynamism.[36] That which it is over against is nonbeing. Women in the process of liberation are enabled to perceive this because our liberation consists in refusing to be "the Other" and asserting instead "I am"—without making another "the Other." Unlike Sartre's "us versus a third" (the closest approximation to love possible in his world) the new sisterhood is saying "us versus nonbeing." When Sartre wrote that "man [*sic*] fundamentally *is* the desire to be God," he was saying that the most radical passion of human life is to be a God who does not and cannot exist. The ontological hope of which I am speaking is neither this self-deification nor the simplistic reified images often lurking behind such terms as "Creator," "Lord," "Judge," that Sartre rightly rejects.[37] It transcends these because its experiential basis is courageous *participation* in being. This ontological hope also has little in common with the self-enclosed "ontological arguments" of Anselm or Descartes. It enables us to break out of this prison of subjectivity because it implies commitment together.

The idea that breakthrough to awareness of transcendence comes through some sort of commitment is not new, of course. It has not been absent from existential philosophy. Karl Jaspers, for example, writing of the problem of getting beyond the subject-object split (which, of itself, without awareness of the Encompassing, yields nothing but dead husks of words), affirms that this happens when people live in commitment, but it is not too clear what sort of commitment he had in mind—a not uncommon unclarity among existentialist philosophers.[38] The commitment of which I am speaking has a locus. It is a "mysticism of sorority." I hasten to put this phrase in quotes even though it is my own, since it is a re-baptism of Metz's "mysticism of fraternity"—a correction I deem necessary since—as by now is obvious—a basic thesis of this book is that creative eschatology must come by way of the disenfranchised sex.[39]

What I am proposing is that the emergence of the communal vocational self-awareness of women is a *creative political ontophany*. It is a manifestation of the sacred (*hierophany*) precisely because it is an experience of participation in being, and therefore a manifestation of being (*ontophany*). A historian of religions such as Eliade insists that there was a sort of qualitative leap made by the biblical religions in the realm of hierophany.[40] Whether or not this is historically true is not my concern at this point. What I do suggest is that the potential for *ontological* hierophany that is already beginning to be realized in the participatory vocational self-consciousness of women does involve a leap, bridging the apparent gap between being and history. In other words, women conscious of the vocation to raise up this half of humanity to the stature of acting subjects in history constitute an ontological locus of history. In the very process of becoming actual persons, of confronting the non-being of our situation, women are bearers of history.

In his analysis of history-bearing groups, Tillich saw vocational consciousness as a decisive element.[41] He did not believe that humanity as a whole can become the bearer of history instead of particular groups. There is a particular *eros* or sense of belonging which provides the identity of a group to the exclusion of others.[42] This much is true of the women's movement as existing essentially in polarity with the predominantly androcentric society and its institutions. However, there is an essential way in which the women's movement does *not* meet Tillich's specifications for a history-bearing group. I am suggesting that this "non-qualification" arises precisely from the fact that our transformation is so deeply rooted in being. Tillich insists that a history-bearing group's ability to act in a centered way requires that the group have a "central, law-giving, administering, and enforcing authority."[43] In contrast to this, our movement is *not* centrally administered—although it includes organizations such as NOW and WEAL[44]—and many (perhaps most) radicalized women resist attempts to bring this about because their outlook is nonhierarchical and multidimensional.

I am suggesting that the women's movement is *more than* a group governed by central authority in conflict with other such hierarchical groups. If it were only this it would be only one more subgroup within the all-embracing patriarchal "family." What we are about is the human becoming of that half of the human race that has been excluded from humanity by sexual definition. This phenomenon, which is mushrooming "up from under" (to use Nelle Morton's phrase) in women from various "classes," races, and geographical areas, can hardly be described as a group. What is at stake is a real leap in human evolution, initiated by women. The ground of its creative hope is an intuition of being which, as Janice Raymond has suggested, *is* an intuition of human integrity or of androgynous being.[45]

When this kind of sororal community-consciousness is present—this "us versus nonbeing"—there are clues and intimations of the God who is without an over-against—who is Be-ing. The unfolding of the woman-consciousness is an intimation of the endless unfolding of God. The route to be followed by theoreticians of the women's revolution, then, need not be contiguous with that followed by Marxist theoreticians such as Roger Garoudy and Ernst Bloch, even though we share their concern to maintain an absolutely open future, and even though in some sense we must share also in their insistence upon atheism. We agree with their atheism insofar as this means rejection of hypostatized God-projections and the use of these to justify exploitation and oppression.[46] However, there is a difference which I believe arises from the fact that Marxism does not fully confront patriarchy itself. Roger Garoudy wrote:

> If we reject the very name of God, it is because the name implies a presence, a reality, whereas it is only an exigency which we live, a never-satisfied exigency of totality and absoluteness, of omnipotence as to nature and of perfect loving reciprocity of consciousness.[47]

In effect, Garoudy distinguishes his position from that of even the most progressive Christian theologians by asserting that the exigency of the Christian for the infinite is experienced and/or expressed as presence, whereas for him it is absence. What I am suggesting is that women who are confronting the nothingness which emerges when one turns one's back upon the pseudo-reality offered by patriarchy are by that very act saying "I am," that is, confronting our own depth of *being*. What we are experiencing, therefore, is not *only* the sense of absence of the old Gods—a sense which we fully share with Garoudy and Bloch. Our exclusion from identity within patriarchy has had a totality about it which, when faced, calls forth an ontological self-affirmation. Beyond the absence, therefore, women are in a situation to experience *presence*. This is not the presence of a super-reified Something, but of a power of being which both is, and is not yet.

One could hasten to point out that various theories of a developing God have been expounded in modern philosophy. Some women might find it helpful to relate their perception of the spiritual dynamics of feminism to ideas developed by such a thinker as William James, who offers the possibility of seeing the perfecting of God as achieved through our active belief, which can be understood as an enrichment of the divine being itself.[48] Others might find it helpful to correlate this experience with Alfred North Whitehead's functional approach to the problem of God, who is seen as a factor implicated in the world and philosophically relevant.[49] Other helpful insights on the problem of the developing God can be found in the work of such thinkers as Max Scheler, Samuel Alexander, E. S. Brightman, and Charles Hartshorne. In my opinion it would not be the most fruitful expenditure of energy at this point to attempt to fit our thoughts concerning the spiritual implications of radical feminism into theories that might appear tempting as prefabricated molds. Rather, it seems to me far more important to listen to women's experiences to discover the spiritual dynamics of this revolution and to speak these dynamics in our own lives and words.

I have already said that this does not mean that an entirely new language for God, materially speaking, will emerge, *ex nihilo*, but rather that a new meaning context is coming into being as we re-create our lives in a new experiential context. Because the feminist experience is radically a coming out of nothing into a vocational/communal participation in being, I have suggested that it can be perceived in terms of ontological hope. Paradoxical though it may seem, this being-consciousness may mean that our new self-understanding *toward God* may be in some ways more in affinity with medieval thought than with some modern theological and philosophical language about God. It is fascinating to observe that in beginning to come to grips with the problem of our own self-naming in a world in which women are nameless, feminism is implicitly working out a naming toward God that is comparable to, though different from, the famous three "ways" the medieval theologians employed in speaking of God.[50]

There was first of all the *negative way*, variously described, but meaning essentially that we can show "what God is not" by systematically denying of God the imperfections of creatures. A prominent scholar has suggested that current epistemology, influenced by recent developments in science, holds resources for a comparable "negative way," but with a different slant. That is, science itself, by constantly opening up more and more unpredicted aspects of reality, is making us aware that there *is* an unknown, aspects of which may be transcendent. This doesn't "prove" Transcendence, but makes room for it.[51] I am suggesting that a new *via negativa* is coming not just from science but from the experience of liberation. Women are living out this negative way by discovering more and more the androcentrism of God-language and being compelled to reject this, and, beyond this, by discovering the male-centeredness of the entire society which this legitimates. Since women are excluded from the in-group of the male intellectual community, and since in fact we begin actively to *choose* self-exclusion as we become more conscious of the limitations on thought and creativity that the in-breeding of the power-holding group involves (witness the deadness of meetings and journals of the "learned societies"), we may be less trapped in the old delusions—such as word games about God that pass for knowledge among those who play them. This discovery, followed by active choice of "not belonging" on the part of creative women, can lead to our finding previously untapped resources within ourselves, and the process yields clues to further possibilities of becoming. The realization of our exclusion from the world-building process is a *neo-negative way*, in that we are discovering our previously unknown being, which points our consciousness outward and inward toward as yet unknown Being, that some would call the hidden God.

Second, there was the traditional *affirmative way*, which presupposed that God prepossesses all the perfections of creatures and that therefore any perfection found in a creature which does not by definition include limitation can be predicated of God. Thus it was considered legitimate to say that God is good, wise, etc.[52] I am suggesting that feminism is giving rise also to the beginnings of a *neo-affirmative way*. This is a *living* "analogy of being" (*analogia entis*), and the particular aspect of our existence from which we are enabled to draw the analogy is the courage that is experienced in the liberation process. The *analogia entis* of Aquinas involved an extremely complex reasoning, based upon certain premises, including the notion that God is the first cause of all finite reality and the idea that there is some kind of resemblance between effects and their causes.[53] By contrast, what I am pointing to by the use of the expression "analogy of being" is an experience of the dynamic content of the intuition of being as experienced in existential courage. Women now have a special opportunity to create an *affirmative way* that is not simply in the arena of speculation, but especially in the realm of active self-affirmation. Since through the existential courage now demanded of us we can have consciousness of *being toward* the image of God, this process can give us intimations of the Be-ing in and toward which we are participating. That is, it can be in some sense a theophany, or manifestation of God.

A third way of naming God, the traditional *way of eminence*, was not totally distinct from the other two "ways" but rather included both. Medieval theologians, including the so-called Denis the Areopagite and Thomas Aquinas, believed that even names said affirmatively of God fall far short of saying *what* God is: "So when we say 'God is good,' the meaning is not, [merely] 'God is the cause of goodness,' or 'God is not evil,' but the meaning is, 'Whatever good we attribute to creatures preexists in God' and in a more excellent and higher way."[54]

I propose that the becoming of women is potentially a new and very different *way of eminence*. The positive and unique element in our speaking toward God has to do with what Buber called "the primary word I-Thou [which] establishes the world of relation."[55] By refusing to be objectified and by affirming being, the feminist revolution is creating new possibilities of I-Thou. Therefore, the new *way of eminence* can be understood as follows:

In modern society, technical controlling knowledge has reached the point of violating the privacy and rights of individuals and destroying the natural environment. In reaction against this, social critics sometimes call for the awakening of interpersonal consciousness, that is, of intersubjectivity. But this cannot happen without communal and creative refusal of victimization by sexual stereotypes. This creative refusal involves conscious and frequently painful efforts to develop new lifestyles in which I-Thou becomes the dominant motif, replacing insofar as possible the often blind and semi-conscious mechanisms of I-It, which use the Other as object. In the realm of knowledge, this means removing the impediments to that realm of knowing which is subjective, affective, intuitive, or what the Scholastics called "connatural." It means breaking down the barriers between technical knowledge and that deep realm of intuitive knowledge which some theologians call ontological reason.[56]

Objective or technical knowledge is necessary for human survival and progress. It is the capacity for "reasoning." Clarity of thinking and the construction of language require its use. So also does the ability to control nature and society. However, by itself, cut off from the intuitive knowledge of ontological reason, technical knowledge is directionless and ultimately meaningless. When it dominates, life is deprived of an experience of depth, and it tends toward despair.

Technical knowledge of itself is detached. It depends upon a subject-object split between the thinker and that which is perceived. It is calculative, stripping that which is perceived of subjectivity. Technical knowledge, cut off from ontological reason, degrades its object and dehumanizes the knowing subject. Because it reduces both to less than their true reality, at a certain point it even ceases to be knowledge in any authentic sense. When it is thus separated from ontological reason, the psychological and social sciences which it dominates become dogmatic, manipulative, and destructive. Under its dominion, philosophy, theology, and all of religion deteriorate.

Widening of experience so pathologically reduced can come through encounter with another subject, an I who refuses to be an It. If, however, the encounter is simply a struggle over who will be forced into the position of It, this will not be ultimately redemptive. It is only when the subject is brought to a recognition of the other's damaged but never totally destroyed subjectivity as equal to his/her own, having basically the same potential and aspiration to transcendence, that a qualitatively new way of being in the world and toward God can emerge. What is perceived in this new way of being is the Eternal Thou, the creative divine word that always has *more* to say to us. This is the meaning of the women's movement as the new *way of eminence*.

## New Space: New Time

The unfolding of God, then, is an event in which women participate as we participate in our own revolution. The process involves the creation of new space, in which women are free to become who we are, in which there are real and significant alternatives to the prefabricated identities provided within the enclosed spaces of patriarchal institutions. As opposed to the foreclosed identity allotted to us within those spaces, there is a diffused identity—an open road to discovery of the self and of each other. The new space is located always "on the boundary." Its center is on the boundary of patriarchal institutions, such as churches, universities, national and international politics, families. Its center is the lives of women, whose experience of becoming changes the very meaning of center for us by putting it on the boundary of all that has been considered central. In universities and seminaries, for example, the phenomenon of women's studies is becoming widespread, and for many women involved this is the very heart of thought and action. It is perceived as the core of intellectual and personal vitality, often as the only part of the "curriculum" which is not dead.[57] By contrast, many male administrators and faculty view "women's studies" as peripheral, even trivial, perhaps hardly more serious than the "ladies' page" of the daily newspaper. Most "good" administrators do sense that there is something of vitality there, of course, and therefore tolerate or even encourage women's studies—but it remains "on the boundary." So too, the coming together of women on the boundary of "the church" is the center of spiritual community, unrecognized by institutional religion.

The new space, then, has a kind of invisibility to those who have not entered it. It is therefore inviolable. At the same time it communicates power which, paradoxically, is experienced both as power of presence and power of absence. It is not political power in the usual sense but rather a flow of healing energy which is participation in the power of being. For women who are becoming conscious, that participation is made possible initially by casting off the role of "the Other" which is the nothingness imposed by a sexist world. The burst of anger and creativity made possible in the presence of one's sisters is an experience of becoming whole, of overcoming the division within the self that makes nothingness block the dynamism of being. Instead of settling for being a warped half of a person, which is equivalent to a self-destructive nonperson, the emerging woman is casting off role definitions and moving toward androgynous being. This is not a mere "becoming equal to men in a man's world"—which would mean settling for footing within the patriarchal space. It is, rather, something like God speaking forth Godself in the new identity of women.[58] While life in the new space may be "dangerous" in that it means living without the securities offered by the patriarchal system for docility to its rules, it offers a deeper security that can absorb the risks that such living demands. This safety is participation in *being*, as opposed to inauthenticity, alienation, nonidentity—in a word, nonbeing.

The power of presence that is experienced by those who have begun to live in the new space radiates outward, attracting others. For those who are fixated upon patriarchal space it apparently is threatening. Indeed this sense of threat is frequently expressed. For those who are thus threatened, the presence of women to each other is experienced as an absence. Such women are no longer empty receptacles to be used as "the Other," and are no longer internalizing the projections that cut off the flow of being. Men who need such projection screens experience the power of absence of such "objects" and are thrown into the situation of perceiving nothingness. Sometimes the absence of women that elicits this anxiety is in fact physical. For example, when women deliberately stay away from meetings, social gatherings, etc., in order to be free to do what is important to ourselves, there is sometimes an inordinate response of protest. Sometimes the absence is simply non-cooperation, refusal to "play the game" of sex roles, refusal to flatter and agree, etc. This too hints at presence of another space that women have gone off to, and the would-be users are left with no one to use. Sometimes, of course, the absence of women takes the form of active resistance. Again, it throws those who would assume the role of exploiters back into their sense of nothingness.

In this way then, women's confrontation with the experience of nothingness invites men to confront it also. Many of course respond with hostility. The hostility may be open or, in some cases, partially disguised both from the men who are exercising it and from the women to whom it is directed. When disguised, it often takes seductive forms, such as invitations to "dialogue" under conditions psychologically loaded against the woman, or invitations to a quick and easy "reconciliation" without taking seriously the problems raised. Other men react with disguised hostility in the form of being "the feminist's friend," not in the sense of really hearing women but as paternalistic supervisors, analysts, or "spokesmen" for the movement. Despite the many avenues of nonauthentic response to the threat of women's power of absence, some men do accept the invitation to confront the experience of nothingness that offers itself when "the Other" ceases to be "the Other" and stands back to say "I am." In so doing men begin to liberate themselves toward wholeness, toward androgynous being. This new participation in the power of being becomes possible for men when women move into the new space.

Entry into the new space whose center is on the boundary of the institutions of patriarchy also involves entry into new time. To be caught up in these institutions is to be living in time past. This is strikingly evident in the liturgies and rituals that legitimate them. By contrast, when women live on the boundary, we are vividly aware of living in time present/future. Participation in the unfolding of God means also this time breakthrough, which is a continuing (but not ritually "repeated") process. The center of the new time is on the boundary of patriarchal time. What it is, in fact, is women's *own* time. It is our *life-time*. It *is* whenever we are living out of our own sense of reality, refusing to be possessed, conquered, and alienated by the linear, measured-out, quantitative time of the patriarchal system. Women, in becoming who we are, are living in a qualitative, organic time that escapes the measurements of the system. For example, women who sit in institutional committee meetings without surrendering to the purposes and goals set forth by the male-dominated structure, are literally working on our own time while perhaps appearing to be working "on company time." The center of our activities is organic, in such a way that events are more significant than clocks. This boundary living is a way of being in and out of "the system." It entails a refusal of false clarity. Essentially it is being alive now, which in its deepest dimension is participation in the unfolding of God.

It should be apparent, then, that for women entrance into our own space and time is another way of expressing integrity and transformation. To stay in patriarchal space is to remain in time past. The appearance of change is basically only separation and return—cyclic movement. Breaking out of the circle requires anger, the "wrath of God" speaking God-self in an organic surge toward life.[59] Since women are dealing with demonic power relationships, that is, with structured evil, rage is required as a positive creative force, making possible a breakthrough, encountering the blockages of inauthentic structures.[60] It rises as a reaction to the shock of recognizing what has been lost—before it had even been discovered—one's own identity. Out of this shock can come intimations of what human being (as opposed to half being) can be. Anger, then, can trigger and sustain movement from the experience of nothingness to recognition of participation in being. When this happens, the past is changed, that is, its significance for us is changed. Then the past is no longer static: it too is on the boundary. When women take positive steps to move out of patriarchal space and time, there is a surge of new life. I would analyze this as participation in God the Verb who cannot be broken down simply into past, present, and future time, since God is form-destroying, form-creating, transforming power that makes all things new.

8

# Beyond Good and Evil

From chapter 2 of *Beyond God the Father*, pp. 65–68.

*Fall:* women's Movement beyond patriarchy's "good" and "evil"; the Dreadful Biophilic Bounding of women from imposed ignorance and false guilt into Wicked Wisdom.
*fall, the:* one of patriarchy's Biggest Lies; the biblical story of the "original sin" of Adam and Eve, which projects all guilt upon the woman, enshrining the myth of feminine evil as revealed by god.
—*Wickedary*, p. 75

This brief excerpt illustrates Daly's technique of reversals, as she considered the Fall and the mythological Eve and "transvaluated" their meaning to positive terms. She reclaimed the term "witch," and called for a rejection of the scapegoat role by women. In reclaiming the Fall, she wrote,

> Rather than a Fall *from* the sacred, the Fall now initiated by women becomes a Fall *into* the sacred and therefore into freedom. . . . [I]f the symbols and myths of patriarchal religion are dying, this is hardly a total tragedy, since they have perpetuated oppression. To the extent that they have done this, they have represented a pseudo-sense of the sacred. The Fall beyond the false dichotomy between good and evil has the potential to bring us away not only from the false paradise of the pseudo-sacred symbols of patriarchy but also from [a] banal nonreligious consciousness. . . . It can bring *us* into a new meeting with the sacred.

Perhaps the most intriguing passage, though, is one that Daly hinted at in this and all her remaining books, but never worked out fully. This was the claim that the evils of patriarchy were themselves screens preventing a genuine encounter with evil. Once people exorcised the massive present evil of patriarchy, it might provoke "the dawn of real confrontation with the mystery of evil."
—Editors

The beginning of liberation comes when women refuse to be "good" and/or "healthy" by prevailing standards. To be female is to be deviant by definition in the prevailing culture. To be female and defiant is to be intolerably deviant. This means going beyond the imposed definitions of "bad woman" and "good woman," beyond the categories of prostitute and wife. This is equivalent to assuming the role of witch and madwoman. Though this might be suicidal if attempted in isolation (not less self-destructive, however, than attempting to live within the accepted categories), when done in sisterhood it amounts to a collective repudiation of the scapegoat syndrome. It is then tantamount to a declaration of identity beyond the good and evil of patriarchy's world, and beyond sanity and insanity.

It cannot be claimed that such a declaration of identity will cause the mystery of evil to disappear automatically from human existence. What it amounts to, however, is a massive exorcism. Repudiation of the scapegoat role and of the myth of the Fall by the primordial scapegoats may be the dawn of real confrontation with the mystery of evil.

Margaret Murray pointed out that the word "witch" is allied with "wit," basically meaning *to know*. The witch's knowledge has always been that of one who foretells. In addition, Murray indicated that when this is done in the name of one of the established religions it is called prophecy, but when divination is done in the name of a pagan god it is called "mere" witchcraft. This kind of prophetic knowing is characteristic of the women's movement. The knowledge that women are now acquiring is an experiential knowledge that drives beyond the inane "goodness" of the victimized "honest matron" (or respectable suburban housewife or docile nun). It also drives beyond the projected "wickedness" of the equally victimized whore whose options have been so few that the "evil" is less a choice than a forced limitation. This knowledge that drives beyond the unreal goodness and wickedness imposed upon women is both experiential and reflective. It is not reducible to "knowing" only in the sense of sexual experience. It is, rather, a knowing that comes with discovery of the self's potential in all areas of endeavor, in a way that has been denied to women not only by external deterrents, such as restrictive laws and rules, but also by internal deterrents, which are the result of upbringing. It brings with it an ability to assess and evaluate experiences independently of and in the face of the culture's imposed valuation. It is therefore prophetic knowledge, pointing beyond "things as they are."

In going beyond the imposed innocence which both the good woman and the bad woman have in common (i.e., lack of valuation and choice of identity by the self) women are gaining the psychological freedom required to challenge the destructive false innocence that is characteristic of our age. Albert Camus wrote of the contrast between the unabashed and honest crimes of earlier times and the hypocrisy of our age:

> But slave camps under the flag of freedom, massacres justified by philanthropy or by the taste for the superhuman, in one sense cripple judgment. On the day when crime dons the apparel of innocence—through a curious transposition characteristic of our times—it is innocence that is called upon to justify itself.[1]

This "innocence" is characteristic of the phallic morality that identifies good with "us" and bad with "them," particularly when such an attitude is carried to its logical conclusion. It can be seen through when those most victimized by it begin to come of age, that is, to find our integrity beyond such "good" and "evil."

This movement beyond patriarchy's good and evil can be seen mythically as "the Fall"—the dreaded Fall which is now finally beginning to occur, in which women are bringing ourselves and then the other half of the species to eat of the forbidden fruit—the knowledge refused by patriarchal society. This will be a Fall from false innocence into a new kind of adulthood. Unlike the old adulthood that required the arresting of growth, this demands a growing that is ever continuing, never completed.

In writing this way, I am tearing the image of "the Fall" from its context in patriarchal religion. I have suggested that the original myth revealed the essential defect or "sin" of patriarchal religion[2]—its justifying of sexual caste. I am now suggesting that there were intimations in the original myth—not consciously intended—of a dreaded future. That is, one could see the myth as prophetic of the real Fall that was yet on its way, dimly glimpsed. In that dreaded event, women reach for knowledge and, finding it, share it with men, so that together we can leave the delusory paradise of false consciousness and alienation. In ripping the image of the Fall from its old context we are also transvaluating it. That is, its meaning is divested of its negativity and becomes positive and healing.

Rather than a Fall *from* the sacred, the Fall now initiated by women becomes a Fall *into* the sacred and therefore into freedom. Mircea Eliade, at the close of his book *The Sacred and the Profane*, suggests that in the modern mind religion and mythology have been "eclipsed" in the darkness of the unconscious: "Or, from the Christian point of view it could also be said that nonreligion is equivalent to a new 'fall' of man."[3] I am proposing a different interpretation of the contemporary situation, arising from the new women's experience of liberation. That is, if the symbols and myths of patriarchal religion are dying, this is hardly a total tragedy, since they have perpetuated oppression. To the extent that they have done this, they have represented a pseudo-sense of the sacred. The Fall beyond the false dichotomy between good and evil has the potential to bring us away not only from the false paradise of the pseudo-sacred symbols of patriarchy but also from the banal nonreligious consciousness that Eliade deplores. It can bring *us* into a new meeting with the sacred.

In his insightful foreword to Montague Summers' *The History of Witchcraft*, Felix Morrow points out that Summers' justifications of the church's persecution of the witches spring from a concept of the supernatural in which God is inconceivable without the devil.[4] The Fall from this schizoid image of the supernatural can come when women refuse the schizoid identity foisted upon us. As we overthrow the unreal "good" and "evil" projected upon us, we will be overthrowing the unreally good "God" whose existence requires an incarnate devil to be persecuted (and to do the persecuting).

In a real sense the symbols of patriarchal religion deserved to "die." What women's becoming can mean is something beyond their death and beyond their rebirth. It is not a mere cyclic return or resurrection of the sacred into profane consciousness that is at stake. Rather, women's becoming is something more like a new creation. [ . . . ] it can mean the arrival of New Being.

9

# The Second Coming of Women and the Antichrist

From chapter 3 of *Beyond God the Father*, pp. 95–97.

*Second Coming of Women:* New arrival of Archaic Female Presence; spiritual awakening beyond christolatry and all patriarchal religions.
—*Wickedary*, p. 95

This brief passage annuls patriarchal reversals at the core of the Christian symbol system: the person of Christ. True to her project in *Beyond God the Father,* Daly replaced the singular male scapegoat of Christ with the positive, collective power of women's liberation: "In its depth, because it contains a dynamic that drives beyond Christolatry, the women's movement *does* point to, seek, and constitute the primordial, always present, and future Antichrist."

Notable here is Daly's use of the word "androgyny" (a term she would renounce a few years later in *Gyn/Ecology*). Her use here of "androgyny" illuminates the depth of the transformation she desired; it also shows that Daly was not a feminist essentialist, when, for instance, she writes,

> To the degree that it is true to its ontological dynamics, feminism means refusal to be captured again in a stereotypic symbol. It means the freeing of women and men from the sexist ethos of dichotomizing and hierarchizing that is destroying us all. Far from being a "return" to the past, it implies a qualitative leap toward psychic androgyny. The new arrival of female presence is the necessary catalyst for this leap.

—Editors

The absurd story of Eve's birth is an excellent example of a process that is prevalent in men's treatment of women and their accomplishments throughout the history of patriarchy. I shall simply call this phenomenon *reversal.* In some cases it is blatantly silly, as in this case of insistence that a male was the original mother, and that "God" (a male) revealed this. In other instances it has been pseudo-biological, as in the centuries-long insistence that women are "misbegotten males"—a notion refuted by modern genetic research, which demonstrates that it would be far more accurate to designate the male (produced by a Y chromosome, which is an incomplete X chromosome) as a misbegotten female. Very commonly, it consists simply in stealing women's ideas and assuming credit for them, that is, denial by men that the ideas ever came from their female originators. Many women are aware of this happening in their own lives, and many have consciously allowed it to happen, in the belief that this was the only way of getting acceptance for an idea or a plan, and that the latter was more important than credit for its authorship. I suggest that it is time not only to become conscious of this phenomenon but also to end complicity in its continuance. The *idea and actualization of feminism* is far more important than any idea that could succeed through such self-abnegating and humiliating tactics.

We should also consider the possibility that the reversal phenomenon has taken place in assertions that Christianity "has raised the status of women" and affirmed our "dignity." Women who have attempted to be feminists and at the same time Christians have generally gone along with this, believing that Christianity did advance the cause of women in the past but that it now (oddly) lags behind. However, the record of barbarous cruelty to women in Christendom hardly gives unequivocal support to this kind of apologetic. Christian theology widely asserted that women were inferior, weak, depraved, and vicious. The logical consequences of this opinion were worked out in a brutal set of social arrangements that shortened and crushed the lives of women.[1]

I propose that another form of reversal has been the idea of redemptive incarnation uniquely in the form of a male savior, for [ . . . ] this is precisely what is impossible. A patriarchal divinity or his son is exactly *not* in a position to save us from the horrors of a patriarchal world. Does this mean, then, that the women's movement points to, seeks, or in some way constitutes a *rival* to "the Christ"? On another, but related, level Michelet wrote that the priest has seen in the witch "an enemy, a menacing *rival.*"[2] In its depth, because it contains a dynamic that drives beyond

Christolatry, the women's movement *does* point to, seek, and constitute the primordial, always present, and future Antichrist. It does this by breaking the Great Silence, raising up female pride, recovering female history, healing and bringing into the open female presence.

I suggest that the mechanism of reversal has been at the root of the idea that the "Antichrist" must be something "evil." What if this is not the case at all? What if the idea has arisen out of the male's unconscious dread that women will rise up and assert the power robbed from us? What if it in fact points to a mode of being and presence that is beyond patriarchy's definitions of good and evil? The Antichrist dreaded by the patriarchs may be the surge of consciousness, the spiritual awakening, that can bring us beyond Christolatry into a fuller stage of conscious participation in the *living* God.

Seen from this perspective the Antichrist and the *Second Coming of women* are synonymous. This Second Coming is not a return of Christ but a new arrival of female presence, once strong and powerful, but enchained since the dawn of patriarchy. Only *this* arrival can liberate the memory of Jesus from enchainment to the role of "mankind's most illustrious scapegoat." The arrival of women means the removal of the primordial victim, "the Other," because of whom "the Son of God had to die." When no longer condemned to the role of "savior," perhaps Jesus can be recognizable as a free man. It is only female pride and self-affirmation that can release the memory of Jesus from its destructive uses and can *free* freedom to be contagious.

The Second Coming, then, means that the prophetic dimension in the symbol of the Great Goddess—later reduced to the "Mother of God"—is the key to salvation from servitude to structures that obstruct human becoming. Symbolically speaking, it is the Virgin who must free and "save" the Son. Anthropologically speaking, it is women who must make the breakthrough that can alter the seemingly doomed course of human evolution. Unlike the so-called "First Coming" of Christian theology, which was an absolutizing of men, the women's revolution is not an absolutizing of women, precisely because it is the *overcoming* of dichotomous sex stereotyping, which is the source of the absolutizing process itself. To the degree that it is true to its ontological dynamics, feminism means refusal to be captured again in a stereotypic symbol. It means the freeing of women and men from the sexist ethos of dichotomizing and hierarchizing that is destroying us all. Far from being a "return" to the past, it implies a qualitative leap toward psychic androgyny. The new arrival of female presence is the necessary catalyst for this leap.

As marginal beings who have no stake in a sexist world, women—if we have the courage to keep our eyes open—have access to the knowledge that neither the Father, nor the Son, nor the Mother *is* God, the Verb who transcends anthropomorphic symbolization. Such knowledge will entail a transvaluation of values undreamed of by Nietzsche or any other prophet whose prophecy was dwarfed by secret dread of the Second Coming. This event, still on its way, will mean the end of phallic morality. Should it not occur, we may witness the end of the human species on this planet.

10

# The Bonds of Freedom

## *Sisterhood as Antichurch*

From chapter 5 of *Beyond God the Father*, pp. 138–46.

*Antichurch, Sisterhood as*: the Movement of Feminist Spirituality understood as bringing forth Archaic be-ing, annihilating the credibility of patriarchal religious myths that have been contrived to legitimate the man-made world.
—*Wickedary*, p. 62

The substance of this excerpt from *Beyond God the Father* concerns ritual and the role it plays in patriarchal memory. Daly prized spontaneity and creativity, not repetition. She used the Harvard Memorial Exodus as an example of an event that need not be repeated nor reenacted in order to maintain its place in memory or its efficacious impact on those who participated in and/or know of it.

Daly's positive use of Herbert Marcuse and Abraham Maslow shows her engagement with the new Left, the counterculture, and contemporary psychology. Though she noted the lack of feminist perspectives in these fields, her ability to perceive parallel interests with these thinkers should be acknowledged, especially in light of the too-common parody that she rejected everything ever said or done by men.
—Editors

### Antiworld: Antichurch

To live in this new world is to be creating an Antiworld, by renaming the cosmos. To some it might appear to be a sort of trivialization to call this Antichurch, reducing the phenomenon to contradiction of only one cultural institution. However, this is to forget the power that religion has over the human psyche, linking the unsteady reality of social constructs (objectivations) to ultimate reality through myth. It would be naïve to think that religion in this sense has lost all of its power. The use of religion by both presidential candidates in the 1972 United States election bordered on the grotesque, suggesting that American civil religion has been carried through to the ultimate caricature of the battle between principalities and powers.[1] To affirm that sisterhood is Antichurch is not to speak on the level of denominational quarrels but on the level of a profound struggle within the human psyche trying to free itself from destructive social forces. It is to say we are dealing with powerful symbols that invade our beings from all sides, from the most banal television commercial or textbook, to the doctor's office, to a billboard with a three-dimensional figure of a local political candidate, telling voters to "put your faith in him." All say one thing: that to be human is to be male is to be the Son of God.

What is involved, then, is a religious struggle, and this is so because the conflict is on the level of being versus nonbeing. The affirmation of being by women is a religious affirmation, confronting the archaic heritage of projections that deny our humanity. However, since the conflict is more on the level of creation than of struggle for equal ground in sexist space, the term Antichurch must be understood in a positive way. It is the bringing forth into the world of New Being, which by its very coming annihilates the credibility of myths contrived to support the structures of alienation.

## Antichurch and Antichrist

Analyzing medieval Catholicism, Troeltsch wrote:

> The Church means the eternal existence of the God-Man: it is the extension of the Incarnation, the objective organization of miraculous power, from which . . . subjective results will appear quite naturally.[2]

Moreover, "in spite of all individual inadequacy the institution remains holy and divine."[3] Just as the incompetencies of the ascendent group count for nothing as evidence that the system is wrong, so too the brilliant "exceptions" within the subordinate group offer no substantial challenge. The system has been closed to new information.

The image of the church as the "bride of Christ" is another way of conveying that it is "the extension of the Incarnation," since a bride or wife in patriarchy is merely an extension of her husband. The potency of this image derives from the notion of the divinity of Jesus, for authority figures can derive credibility from the belief that they are representing the God-Man. The pope, who has been called "the vicar of Christ on earth," and the ecclesiastical hierarchy of Catholicism as distinguished from the laity, participate in this identification.

It has been argued, of course, that unlike the harsh patriarchates of pre-Christian culture, this system was construed as a patriarchalism of love. In regard to the family, for example, Troeltsch claims that "in this respect all that Christianity did was to modify from within this idea of male domination by its teaching about love and good will." It stressed *voluntary* submission. Authority and subordination were to continue as before, he maintains, "although with important and increasing security for the individual personality of women, children, and servants."[4] Such claims are so common that we tend to accept them as "true" without question. However, they leave out of account certain disturbing facts such as the barbarities of "good" Christians toward women, children, and servants that have been sanctioned by the church.[5] Such claims also leave out of account the fact that under Christianity the will to autonomy in women and other "lesser beings" has been stifled in a double way: feelings of fear have been reinforced by feelings of guilt. The alleged "voluntariness" of the imposed submission in Christian patriarchy has turned women against ourselves more deeply than ever, disguising and reinforcing the internalization process. As the Virgin-Mother Mary was alleged to have said: "Let it be done unto me according to *Thy* word."

There is a bond, then, between the significance of the women's revolution as Antichrist and its import as Antichurch. Seen in the positive perspective in which I have presented it, as a spiritual uprising that can bring us beyond sexist myths, the Antichrist has a natural correlative in the coming of the Antichurch, which is a communal uprising against the social extensions of the male Incarnation myth, as this has been objectified in the structures of political power. In order to see the relationship between the Second Coming of female presence not only as Antichrist but also as Antichurch, it will be helpful to consider some aspects of the relationship between myth and ritual.

### *Reinforcement of Myth through Cult*

Sociologists have perceived well enough the connections between myths and ritual. Durkheim observed:

> If the myth were withdrawn from religion, it would be necessary to withdraw the rite also; for the rites are generally addressed to definite personalities . . . and they vary according to the manner in which these personalities are conceived.[6]

Durkheim points out that the cult rendered to a divinity depends upon the character attributed to him [*sic*], and the myth determines this character. He adds that "very frequently, the rite is nothing more than the myth put into action."[7] If this is the case, then clearly a rejection of Christolatrous symbols in the rising woman-consciousness has an organic consequence in the rejection of sexist rituals. Although one might be tempted to see this as a simple logical consequence, a reduction of the process to "logic" would be utterly naïve. Berger has pointed out that the sacred cosmos provides the "ultimate shield against the terror of anomy."[8] To be in the position of confronting the Christocentric cosmos that shields many from facing "the terror of anomy" is to be exposed to the wrath of those who fear their own latent madness and therefore will inflict madness upon those who threaten their fragile "sanity." To assert this is not to be hyperbolic but rather to make an understatement. Robin Morgan expressed this realization in her poem "Monster":

> Oh, mother I am tired and sick.
> One sister, new to this pain called feminist consciousness
> For want of a scream to name it, asked me last week
> "But how do you stop from going crazy?"
> No way, my sister.
> No way.
> This is a pore war, I thought once, on acid.[9]

Berger, quite unaware that he is describing precisely the spiritual dimension of feminist consciousness as it converges to form Antichurch, writes:

> To be in a "right" relationship with the sacred cosmos is to be protected against the nightmare threats of chaos. To fall out of such a "right" relationship is to be abandoned on the edge of the abyss of meaninglessness.[10]

Berger continues to describe powerfully the horrible danger that one may lose all connection with the sacred and be swallowed up by chaos. "All the nomic constructions are designed to keep this terror at bay." Mircea Eliade graphically records human efforts to ward off this terror.[11]

The women's revolution as Antichurch represents this terror of chaos and says it will no longer be kept at bay. It rejects not only the myths of patriarchy but their externalization in ritual. This makes it more threatening than an abstract "intellectual" discussion about "myth and all that." One reason why it is threatening is that religious ritual maintains a continuum between the present and the religious tradition. It is essentially *a memory*. Sexist ritual is a false memory, placing present experience in the context of a history that is in fact a deadly fiction, a pernicious lie. The Antichurch dimension of women's liberation *reveals* that this expression of social memory is a lie. To use Berger again:

> Men [*sic*] forget. They must, therefore, be reminded over and over again. . . . Religious ritual has been a crucial instrument of this process of "reminding."[12]

Nietzsche said more than he realized when he wrote of this process:

> Whenever man [*sic*] has thought it necessary to create a memory for himself [*sic*] his effort has been attended with torture, blood, sacrifice.[13]

Antichurch means saying "No" to these "reminders."

The import of this "No" to the rituals that externalize the *machismo* myth may be gleaned from facing the fact that males have always marched to war amid blessings and prayers. The presence of military chaplains saying Mass and holding other religious services for "the boys" engaged in the business of killing those on "the other side" speaks for itself.[14] Females and males have been put to death amid rites and incantations. Thus violence is made to appear "sane." It is legitimated and made part of the social reality that is considered part of the normal scheme of things. To persons in whom the effects of socialization so overwhelm critical judgment that their sense of reality is co-extensive with the world legitimated by religious myth and ritual, the "reasonableness" of even the most bizarre and violent events thus legitimated seems unquestionable. Such persons will fearfully resist the "No" of the women's movement as Antichurch to such legitimations. Others, who wield ideological and political power and understand how to manipulate such fears will also resist this "No" by *using* religion and other instruments of social control. Such instruments include the myth and institutions of "mental illness." In the past, this control was exercised by the execution of heretics. In the present, well, as Robin Morgan puts it in her poem "Monster":

> I gripped the arms of my seat more than once
> to stop my getting up and screaming to the entire planeload
> of human beings what was torturing us all—stopped
> because I knew they'd take me for a crazy, an incipient
> hijacker perhaps, and wrestle me down until Bellevue Hospital
> could receive me at our landing in New York.[15]

The worshippers of the Yahweh of patriarchy, as they come to realize the potential of this Antichurch to bring about the transference of consciousness into another world, can be expected to use all the tools of violence at their command. For the social reality that they attempt to link with "Ultimate Reality" is precarious, and the danger of anomy or of "conversion" is a threat that lurks always behind the irrational dogmatism of the High Priests of war. The need for ritual "*reminders*" itself betrays the precariousness of the shields against anomy which these High Priests, both ecclesiastical and civil, wish to keep erect.

### *Ritual and Repressive Satisfaction*

Marcuse wrote:

> All liberation depends on the consciousness of servitude, and the emergence of this consciousness is always hampered by the predominance of

> needs and satisfactions which, to a great extent, have become the individual's own.[16]

Marcuse is here writing of false needs, that is, those "which perpetuate toil, aggressiveness, misery, and injustice."[17] Although his intent and context clearly were not precisely the same as those reflected in this book, there is a coincidence of insights. The rituals of patriarchy *do* create false needs, such as the need to lean on father-figures instead of finding strength in the self, or the need for compulsive "self-sacrifice" because one is brainwashed into thinking that one is sinful and "unworthy." They then respond to these needs by granting a transitory euphoria of unhappiness. This is repressive satisfaction. To let Marcuse speak again:

> The most effective and enduring form of warfare against liberation is the implanting of material and intellectual needs that perpetuate obsolete forms of the struggle for existence.[18]

The women's revolution, just by being ourselves, declares that such needs are not our true needs and such satisfaction is not satisfying. Saying this comes from the depths of feminists' new awareness. Once it is seen and said, we do not need "reminders" because it is the word of our very being that is spoken. We may become confused, lonely, despairing, or mad, but we cannot really "forget." This is because our revolution means life against death. It is not "losing oneself" for a cause, but living for oneself and therefore also living a cause. Because such consciousness is not contrived, its dawning marks a change and the mark is indelible. One of the women who walked out of Harvard Memorial Church in the 1971 Exodus wrote:

> What made the Memorial Church Exodus different [from skulking out the side door and feeling guilty for leaving], what made it possible, was the realization that the Church that does belong to me and to my experience is the exodus community of women and men who are prepared to get on with the business of living—living up to our potential, living in relationship, living creatively.[19]

As the same woman remarked over one year later: "It was once and for all. We don't need to walk out of churches over and over again." That is the point. The satisfaction of actively participating in being is real and not repressive. As another woman wrote of the same experience:

> As I left, I looked at the different faces in the pews—and kept on smiling. I saw leaving women I knew, old women, middle-aged women, their children, husbands, young women, all kinds and sorts of people. I knew that we were leaving to do whatever we had to do to become persons.[20]

Because this nonrepressive satisfaction is rooted in being, it in itself is not fragile but enduring. Not needing the inane "reminding" by ritual that reinforces false consciousness, it is creative and spontaneous. Women have not walked out of Memorial Church again, but have found other expressions suitable to new situations that arise. Feminist consciousness of being, then, is anti-ritual, because it is so deep.

### *"Feminist Liturgy": A Square Circle?*

A woman who proposed as her project for a course on "The Women's Revolution and Theological Development" an attempt to create a "Women's Liturgy," wrote a twelve-page journal recording her thought process as she tried to work this out. The description of the thought process is in the form of a day by day diary and shows her increasing skepticism of the possibility of a "Women's Liturgy." The problems as they evolved in her consciousness included distrust of anything rigidly structured; unwillingness to do research on "liturgies," which would suggest a mold into which to cast women's experience; dislike of appealing to the old liturgies of patriarchy for legitimation, since these reek of hierarchy; fear of failure in trying to do something completely new, which would be a vehicle rather than a product, so that women would be carried forward.[21]

All of these problems strike deep chords in women who are struggling with the tensions between remembrance of the past and experience of the present which contradicts our old beliefs. Probably the most striking reflection in this woman's journal was that just as antiracist, anti-war services never really seemed to change the racist and warlike beliefs of the participating Christians, so a feminist liturgy would change nothing, for "the *form* was *theirs*." It was the "form" that counted, no matter what the "content." The form was a dead shell, and the growth of the consciousness of women is an attempt to live without such shells. The result of her efforts was the creation of an *event*, a combination of readings and songs expressing anger, change, self-assertion and sisterhood—an event not to be repeated, but the story of which could be told repeatedly. It was called "Something of, by, and for Women."

A "feminist liturgy" is a contradiction in terms, given the legitimating function of liturgy in patriarchy to support sexism and consequently its offshoots: war, racism and all the destructive hierarchies of economic oppression. It is an attempt to put new wine, women's awareness, into the old skins of forms that kill female self-affirmation and turn female consciousness against itself. This is not to say that the impulse behind the desire to have something like a "women's liturgy" is not healthy and alive. There is every reason for women to celebrate our becoming and the discovery of our history, but in ever new ways, not encrusted in stagnant, repetitious ritual. The urge to celebrate is part of a precious new beginning. It springs from an ovarian insight.[22] But the impulse can be twisted against itself if we look for support and legitimation in the forms of patriarchal ritual, whether Jewish, Protestant, Catholic, Moslem, Hindu, or whatever. To know this, one needs only to open one's eyes to the "sacred" symbols and one's ears to the "sacred" words of the "sacred" cosmos that excludes our humanity. To straighten out the thought of Nietzsche: "What are these churches now if they are not the sepulchres of *women*?" In his confusion, Nietzsche wrote "sepulchres of God," but the real problem is that the churches have been the murderers of women. The corpse of "God" they contain is unfulfilled human being.

To put the matter in psychological terms, one might ask the question: "What is a self-actualizing person?" To this question Abraham Maslow has excellent answers in his list of qualities such people exhibit. They tend to have or better exhibit "boldness, courage, freedom, spontaneity, perspicuity, integration, and self-acceptance."[23] These healthy human specimens tend also to have clearer, more efficient perception of reality, more openness to experience, autonomy, detachment, recovery of creativeness, ability to fuse concreteness and abstractness, democratic character structure.[24] Such persons seem to have resolved "the civil war . . . between the forces of the inner depths and the forces of defense and control."[25] We need only to think of such qualities and then to think of what religion in our society has done to wipe them out in women. A "feminist liturgy," despite the healthy impulse behind it, would contribute to the legitimation of this "wiping out" process, because it would be *contained* to some extent in a traditional form (the admission of this is implicit in the word "liturgy"). It would reinforce—though in an ambivalent manner—false memory.

11

# Antichurch and the Sounds of Silence

From chapter 5 of *Beyond God the Father*, pp. 150–53.

*bibliolater:* a hot air type who attempts to contain the universe within the confines of one bible/bubble.
—*Wickedary*, p. 185

As if anticipating her own turn to a new language (one that would be ridiculed by critics, as she here predicted), Daly described women's communication as "the new sounds of silence" whose "vibrations . . . are too high for the patriarchal hearing mechanism." This new language arose from the situation of oppression, in which "male religion entombs women in sepulchres of silence in order to chant its own eternal and dreary dirge to a past that never was." The dialectic tension in this excerpt concerns absence and presence, suppression counterposed to creativity. One theme, though, that resounds increasingly through *Beyond God the Father* concerns the need to abandon all patriarchal religions. Here Daly is at her most categorical, when she extrapolated from the Catholic refusal to allow women priests, to declare that none of the traditions allow women to speak "officially":

> For the "sacred" words were all written by men and can only be repeated and echoed. In religions that cling to the past, whether by Bibliolatry or by tradition or both, no woman can break out of imposed silence.

—Editors

Male religion entombs women in sepulchres of silence in order to chant its own eternal and dreary dirge to a past that never was. The silence *imposed* upon women echoes the structures of male hierarchies. It is important to listen to the structures of this imposed silence in order to hear the flow of the new sounds of free silence that are the voice of sisterhood as Antichurch.

Durkheim wrote of the Warramunga tribe in Australia which imposed absolute silence upon women for long mourning periods (as long as two years). As a result, he claimed, the women developed communication through gestures. Some preferred to remain silent even for years after the imposed period of silence.[1] One woman was said to have been silent for twenty-four years. One wonders if the continuation of silence is because the women discover a better means of communication, an underground language of silence that men cannot understand.[2]

The Pauline text screamed (it doesn't matter at all whether this was written by Paul or some pseudo-Paul): "I permit no woman to teach . . . she is to keep silent." The point, it seems, was that women cannot "officially" speak—a claim still shrilly proclaimed by Roman Catholicism and orthodox Judaism and affirmed only a bit more subtly by Reformed Judaism and Protestant Christianity. For the "sacred" words were all written by men and can only be repeated and echoed. In religions that cling to the past, whether by Bibliolatry or by tradition or both, no woman can break out of imposed silence.

In modern times academia and the printed secular word have partially moved in on the territory of the sacred church and its sacred word. Here too women have been entombed in imposed silence, in the gross and obvious way of simply being excluded and in the more subtle way of only being allowed to echo male words. One may not dare to think out loud women's words—at least, not too much. We know the penalties for that.

As a result the new sounds of free silence may be hard for many to understand. They are many-faceted. We speak forth shapes and colors, utter textures, flash forth to each other in a flow of understanding what is too awesome to be understood: our own self-birth in sisterhood. Robin Morgan paints the silence:

> And I will speak less and less to you
> And more and more in crazy gibberish you cannot understand:
> witches' incantations, poetry, old women's mutterings. . . .[3]

This multi-faced communication that is being born among women in the modern technological jungle of America is nonspeech in the terms of our culture, just as truly as the gestures of the "primitive" Warramunga women were nonspeech to their men. Multi-leveled communication is of course not unknown to all men, but the rules of patriarchy try to write it out as much as possible. What is new when it happens with women is that it is the interflow of our own being, our affirmation of process that is our own process over and against sepulchral forms that almost but never quite did quench our fire.

Women are starting to know now the defects of language because it is not ours. It reflects the structures blessed by male religion. In order to say that women's speech breaks out of these bounds I have called it silence. It is silence in the sense of going beyond inauthentic speech, but to those who know only inauthentic speech it is meaningless. "Logical positivists" have claimed that one can ask only whatever questions language clearly expresses. To go outside this pre-established box is, supposedly, to use "pseudo-propositions," to say the unthinkable, the meaningless. What the logical positivists did not point out was that the pre-established box is patriarchal, which would mean that our new anti-patriarchal questions are *a priori* pseudo-questions. Other academicians, and non-academicians, though they would not call themselves logical positivists, share this view. To such persons, who crush thought and language into patriarchal space and time past, the new sounds are unhearable. A sexist language-bound world is deaf to these.

Susanne Langer wrote of the restriction on discourse that sets bounds to the complexity of speakable ideas. She saw this as an inherent defect of language, which is a poor medium for expressing emotions, ever-moving patterns, the ambivalences and intricacies of inner experience, the interplay of feelings and thought, memories and echoes of memories. The fine arts compensate for this built-in defect of language, she maintained.[4] But I would point out that poetry and the fine arts have been *individual* expressions of ontological reason—granting that in the case of great art many people can resonate to such expressions. They have remained by and large within patriarchy, which has neatly labeled them "fine arts," and entombed them in its museums and universities. Contained, they have not made a planetary rebellion. Indeed most art and poetry in our culture expresses patriarchal feelings. (Look at the flabby, unathletic bodies of Renaissance Madonnas; read the diarrheic outpourings of misogynism in Milton, Kipling, Claudel.) By contrast, the new sounds of silence, sparking forth a network of boundary communication, are the dawning of communal New Being. This is neither "public" nor "private," neither "objective" nor "subjective." It is intersubjective silence, the vibrations of which are too high for the patriarchal hearing mechanism. It is, then, ultrasonic.

# 12

# The Final Cause, the Future, and the End of the Looking Glass War

From chapter 7 of *Beyond God the Father*, pp. 180–83, 195–98. This excerpt was one that Daly was most eager to see included in this compilation.

> *Looking Glass Society 1:* patriarchy: the house of mirrors, the world of reversals *2:* the society in which women serve as magnifying mirrors reflecting men at twice their natural size *3:* society manufactured by phallocrats, who project their own deficiencies upon all Others, attempting to convert these into reflections of their own inadequate selves.
> —*Wickedary*, p. 208

The two excerpts presented here, from the final chapter of *Beyond God the Father*, show the meticulous philosophic precision that formed the jumping-off point for Daly's intuition of Be-ing. She champions the omnipresence of an immanent sacred—having shown such to be incompatible with Christian thought—by embracing the "manifold and unique manifestations of Be-ing."

In all of her major books, Daly composed her ending pages to serve as both summation and summons. It is in these conclusions that one can best experience the combination of rigor and poetry in her thought. The conclusion of *Beyond God the Father*, as it spins out the logic of the Mirror World of patriarchy, anticipated the flights of fantastical metaphors that Daly would pursue in her later works. Her sarcastic portrayal of self-important male religious clerics placed her analysis into a realm accessible to all, and the picture of males not knowing how to experience life without their female mirrors presented an interesting counterpoint to the exhilarating discovery of women's power of naming ourselves and reality.

As always, Daly ended optimistically, but with clarity about the stakes involved:

> The freedom-becoming-survival of our species will require a continual, communal striving in be-ing. This means forming the great

chain of be-ing in sisterhood that can surround nonbeing, forcing it to shrink back into itself. The cost of failure is Nothing.

—Editors

In a moment of illumination, a radical feminist exclaimed: "We are the final cause."[1] I believe that she was right. Hence the following philosophical analysis.

## The Final Cause and the Future

When Aristotle wrote of the "final cause" he intended "cause" to mean that which brings about an effect. Scholastic philosophers followed the Aristotelean theory of the "four causes" to explain change. According to this theory the material cause is that out of which something is made (as the wood in a table). The formal cause is that which determines its nature (as the shape of the wood which makes it a table and not a chair or something else). The efficient cause is the agent that produces the effect by her/his/its action (as the carpenter who produces the table). The final cause is the purpose which starts the whole process in motion (as the goal of having an object upon which to place books, papers, and other items). The final cause is therefore the first cause, since it moves the agent to act upon the matter, bringing forth a new form. [ . . . ] (This) theory for centuries provided a framework for thinking about problems of transformation and becoming[2] [ . . . ].

As it was conceived by Aristotle, the final cause or goal inspires the agent to act because it is apprehended as good. It causes by attracting, by drawing unto itself. This idea of the good as attracting, which Aristotle inherited from his teacher, Plato, might seem to be indicative of a futurist vision of a world on the move. However, it did not work out this way. The Greeks identified the concept of "the good" with the Parmenidian conception of "true being" which is changeless and already present. The goal of every action, therefore, already is. The future is essentially closed.

In the medieval philosophical synthesis of Thomas Aquinas, the good and true being were identical—the distinction being only in the mind.[3] Hence his thinking too remained bound within the same nonevolutionary circle. Aquinas did have an important distinction between the way creatures cause and God's causality. He thought that any finite agent can only work upon pre-existing matter, transforming it in a way that its potentiality will allow, which meant that it would "become" essentially the same as something already existing. In contrast to this, God, the First Cause, was said to be cause of being, for God brings creatures into existence out of nothing and sustains them in existence.[4] But in reality there was not an open future envisaged here, since God was understood as *changeless* Being, from whom all creatures proceed and to whom they return.[5]

Contemporary Christian theology ostensibly has tried to bring the future into the picture. The results have been remarkably unsuccessful. The problem is illustrated in the work of Wolfhart Pannenberg, a prominent exponent of the theology of hope. Pannenberg casts us into a state of real hopelessness by his fixation on the figure of Jesus. He contrasts "the coming-to-appearance of God in Jesus" with the "epiphanies of gods [*sic*] in human or animal form" claiming that in the latter cases "any particular form of the appearance, being replaceable, remains external to the essence of the deity." He continues:

> In the ministry of Jesus, on the contrary, the God of Israel, the future of his Reign, comes definitively to appearance once. He [*sic*] manifested himself in this single event conclusively and for all time, and just for this reason only once.[6]

This is indeed a theology of hopelessness. Pannenberg reconfirms this interpretation at the end of the same essay, when he writes:

> The arrival of what is future may be thought through to its conclusion only with the idea of repetition (which does not exclude the new), in the sense that in it the future *has* arrived in *a permanent* present [emphasis his].[7]

One is compelled to wonder what sort of future this might be. At any rate the symbolic message tells us that the prospects are dismal, and that this perspective is far more paralyzing than that of the Greeks. It is particularly depressing, though consistent, that this theologian finds the epiphanies of the "gods" (small "g") in *human* as well as in animal form to be external to the essence of the deity, apparently because these are *replaceable*. That is, there is no vision here of the universal presence of the Verb that is Be-ing, who has *not* been revealed once for all time, who can be revealed at any moment in a constant unfolding (not merely repeated) revelation. Genuine *hierophanies* (manifestations of the sacred) are not "replaceable." Rather, they are manifold and unique manifestations of Be-ing. The fact that they are many and new, and not once and for all, is precisely because *they are not external to the essence of the deity*. The manifold and new quality of genuine hierophanies—genuine in so far as they are manifestations of Be-ing—that is, *ontophanies* is possible because of *participation* in Being which is Be-ing. Be-ing encompasses and engulfs with healing power the false dichotomy between "true being" and becoming, revealing its unreality. [ . . . ]

Our planet is inhabited by half-crazed creatures, but there is a consistency in the madness. Virginia Woolf, who died of being both brilliant and female, wrote that women are condemned by society to function as mirrors, reflecting men at twice their actual size. When this basic principle is understood, we can understand something about the dynamics of the Looking Glass society. Let us examine once again the creatures' speech.

That language for millennia has affirmed the fact that Eve was born from Adam, the first among history's unmarried pregnant males who courageously chose childbirth under sedation rather than abortion, consequently obtaining a child-bride. Careful study of the documents recording such achievements of Adam and his sons prepared the way for the arrival of the highest of the higher religions, whose priests took Adam as teacher and model. They devised a sacramental system which functioned magnificently within the sacred House of Mirrors. Graciously, they lifted from women the onerous power of childbirth, christening it "baptism." Thus they brought the lowly material function of birth, incompetently and even grudgingly performed by females, to a higher and more spiritual level. Recognizing the ineptitude of females in performing even the humble "feminine" tasks assigned to them by the Divine Plan, the Looking Glass priests raised these functions to the supernatural level in which they alone had competence. Feeding was elevated to become Holy Communion. Washing achieved dignity in Baptism and Penance. Strengthening became known as Confirmation, and the function of consolation, which the unstable nature of females caused them to perform so inadequately, was raised to a spiritual level and called Extreme Unction.[8] In order to stress the obvious fact that all females are innately disqualified from joining the Sacred Men's Club, the Looking Glass priests made it a rule that their members should wear skirts. To make the point clearer, they reserved special occasions when additional Men's Club attire should be worn. These necessary accoutrements included delicate white lace tops and millinery of prescribed shapes and colors. The leaders were required to wear silk hose, pointed hats, crimson dresses and ermine capes, thus stressing detachment from lowly material things and dedication to the exercise of spiritual talent. They thus became revered models of spiritual transsexualism.

These anointed Male Mothers, who naturally are called Fathers, felt maternal concern for the women entrusted to their pastoral care. Although females are obviously by nature incompetent and prone to mental and emotional confusion, they are required by the Divine Plan as vessels to contain the seeds of men so that men can be born and then supernaturally (correctly) reborn as citizens of the Heavenly Kingdom. Therefore in charity the priests encouraged women to throw themselves gratefully into their unique role as containers for the sons of the sons of the Son of God. Sincerely moved by the fervor of their own words, the priests educated women to accept this privilege with awestruck humility.

Since the Protestant Reformation, spiritual Looking Glass education has been modernized in some rooms of the House of Mirrors. Reformed Male Mothers gradually came to feel that Maleness was overstressed by wearing dresses all the time and even decided to include a suitable proportion of females (up to one half of one percent) among their membership, thereby stressing that the time for Male Snobbism was over and the time for Democracy had come. They also came to realize that they could be just as supernatural without being hemmed in by a stiff sacramental system. They could give birth spiritually, heal and console, and give maternal advice. They therefore continued the Looking Glass tradition of Mother Adam while at the same time making a smooth transition to The Modern Age.

Thus, Western culture was gracefully prepared by its Supernatural Mothers called Fathers to see all things supernaturally, that is, to perceive the world backward clearly. In fact, so excellent had been our education that this kind of thinking has become like second nature for almost everybody. No longer in need of spiritual guidance, our culture has come of age. This fact is evident to anyone who will listen to it when it talks. Its statesmen clear-headedly affirm the fact that this is "the Free World." Its newscasters accurately report that there has been fighting in the demilitarized zone, that several people were killed in a nonviolent demonstration, that "our nation" is fighting to bring peace to Southeast Asia. Its psychiatrists proclaim that the entire society is in fact a mental institution and applaud this fact as a promising omen of increasing health for their profession.

In the Looking Glass society females, that is, Magnifying Mirrors, play a crucial role. But males have realized that it would serve no good purpose if this were to become known by females, who then might stop looking into the toy mirrors they have been taught to use incessantly. They might then begin looking inside or outside or backward or forward. Instead of settling for the vanity of parakeets they might fall into the sin of pride and refuse to be Magnifying Mirrors any longer.

The females, in the terrifying, exhilarating experience of becoming rather than reflecting, would discover that they too have been infected by the dynamics of the Mirror World. Having learned only to mirror, they would find in themselves reflections of the sickness in their masters. They would find themselves doing the same things, fighting the same way. Looking inside for something there, they would be confused by what at first would appear to be an endless Hall of Mirrors. What to copy? What model to imitate? Where to look? What is a mere mirror to do? But wait—How could a mere mirror even frame such a question? The question itself is the beginning of an answer that keeps unfolding itself. The question-answer is a verb, and when one begins to move in the current of the verb, of the Verb, she knows that she is not a mirror. Once she knows this she knows it so deeply that she cannot completely forget. She knows it so deeply that she has to say it to her sisters. What if more and more of her sisters should begin to hear and to see and to speak?

This would be a disaster. It would throw the whole society backward into the future. Without Magnifying Mirrors all around, men would have to look inside and outside. They would start to look inside, wondering what was wrong with them. They would have to look outside because without the mirrors they would begin to receive impressions from real Things out there. They would even have to look at women, instead of reflections. This would be confusing and they would be forced to look inside again, only to have the harrowing experience of finding *there* the Eternal Woman, the Perfect Parakeet. Desperately looking outside again, they would find that the Parakeet is no longer *out there.* Dashing back inside, males would find other horrors: All of the other Others—the whole crowd—would be in there: the lazy niggers, the dirty Chicanos, the greedy Jews, faggots and dykes, plus the entire crowd of Communists and the backward population of the Third World. Looking outward again, mirrorless males would be forced to see—people. Where to go? Paroxysm toward the Omega Point? But without the Magnifying Mirror even that last refuge is gone. What to do for relief? Send more bombing missions? But no. It is pointless to be killing The Enemy after you find out The Enemy is yourself.

But the Looking Glass society is still there, bent on killing itself off. It is still ruled by God the Father who, gazing at his magnified reflections, believes in his superior size. I say "believes," because the reflection now occasionally seems to be diminished and so he has to make a renewed act of faith in Himself.

We have been locked in this Eden of his far too long. If we stay much longer, life *will* depart from this planet. The freedom to fall out of Eden will cost a mirror-shattering experience. The freedom-becoming-survival of our species will require a continual, communal striving in be-ing. This means forming the great chain of be-ing in sisterhood that can surround nonbeing, forcing it to shrink back into itself. The cost of failure is Nothing.

Is this the war to end all wars? The power of sisterhood is not war-power. There have been and will be conflicts, but the Final Cause causes not by conflict but by attraction. Not by the attraction of a Magnet that is All There, but by the creative drawing power of the Good Who is self-communicating Be-ing, Who is the Verb from whom, in whom, and with whom all true movements move.

## PART III

# The Double-Edged Labrys of Outrageous/Outraged Philosophy (1975–1984)

Daly's work in part 3 dates from 1975 to 1984, years in which her reputation reached its high point (among feminists), but also began its decline amidst both ideological controversies and personality clashes. In this period, she came out publicly as a lesbian during a time when lesbian-feminism was growing within the women's liberation movement. Lesbian separatism, representing a sizeable and vocal minority in the women's liberation movement, is often misunderstood as solely a hatred of men. In contrast, lesbian separatists understood their politics as taking time away from the patriarchy to be able to hear their own thoughts without the constant clamor of their socialization. For Daly, this perspective was a natural fit and informed the pages of *Gyn/Ecology* and her decision to provide an all-female learning experience for her students (now at a co-ed Boston College). A common myth about Mary Daly is that she refused to teach men. In reality, she offered male students independent study (a privilege that some of her women students coveted!). There can be no doubt, however, that the world of *Gyn/Ecology* is a female-centered world; this is more than a compensatory gesture: it is a reframing of reality.

Daly's perspective of this period, compared to the period of *Beyond God the Father*, now deepened and widened, seeing a meta-level where she analyzed patriarchy as universal, rather than focusing on defrocking particular institutions and legacies (e.g., the catholic church). The impatience that would increasingly come to characterize her thought manifested now as disgust with the artificial limits and mind-numbing pettiness of academentia (as she termed it), while she retained and extolled the virtues of constant intellection and rigor. Certainly her rhetorical tone suggested that she was taking no prisoners in her search-and-destroy mission against patriarchy; those targeted included Paul Tillich, whose thought had so influenced her previously.

A major thematic shift came with Daly's term "biophilia." The life-loving metaphysics that she wanted to write and live, as well as the growth of both environmentalism and ecofeminism throughout the 1970s, presented her with a rich source of connection to the world she loved and an endless store of metaphors and images. Daly had a lifelong affection for animals, particularly the cats she kept as familiars, and farm animals. Starting with *Gyn/Ecology*, Daly's work is a crucial resource for ecofeminism.

There was another change, culturally, since the time of *Beyond God the Father*. By 1978, when *Gyn/Ecology* was published, the feminist movement had expanded, creating a critical mass of serious feminist thinkers, sufficient to engender dialogues, diatribes, and differences of opinion. This meant that the controversies created by *Gyn/Ecology* were no longer only between the patriarchy and feminism, but also among feminists themselves. Boston College—a typical representative of patriarchal institutions—continued to make Daly's life difficult, but significantly its reaction to *Gyn/Ecology* is not important: what makes *Gyn/Ecology* a turning point in perceptions of Mary Daly is precisely how it divided feminist opinions. Unintentionally, inadvertently, but inevitably, *Gyn/Ecology* became contested and divisive territory among women. All of this occurred in a lively, indeed rambunctious, network of women's bookstores, feminist festivals, and womyn's music—in effect, a parallel feminist culture. Within that culture, Daly was a revered figure, but increasingly a polarizing one as well, a lightning rod for both attack and admiration.

The two most significant criticisms of *Gyn/Ecology* focused on Daly's scholarship in the "Second Passage," where she was reporting on atrocities committed against women, and how those atrocities fit her "Sado-Sublime" paradigm. Numerous feminists—most notably Elly Bulkin in *Signs*—took issue with Daly's use of imperialist sources and perceived cross-cultural insensitivity. Daly's stand was that stopping crimes of this magnitude against women was a moral imperative for any feminist, and superseded concerns for "tradition" and "culture." Far more famously, Black Lesbian-Feminist Audre Lorde wrote an "Open Letter to Mary Daly," challenging Daly's one-sided representation of African women in the chapter on genital mutilation (included as chapter 16). The history of Lorde's "Open Letter," its anthologization, and its profound effects on issues of race within the feminist community contributed to the decline of Daly's prominence and popularity. Any dream of feminist unity vanished forever, and with it went much of Daly's leadership within the movement. Instead of taking positions against patriarchy, taking a position for or against Mary Daly became a kind of litmus test among feminists. Decades later, the tangled history of Daly's response to Lorde took an unexpected turn, when Lorde's biographer, Alexis De Veaux, discovered evidence of Daly's response in Lorde's papers; see chapter 44 for the details.

The stark contrast between the critiques and adulation that *Gyn/Ecology* received happened against a rapidly changing political landscape. The Iranian Revolution, followed by the ascendancy of conservative political leaders such as Margaret Thatcher and Ronald Reagan, marked a changed and dangerous world for revolutionary thinkers like Mary Daly. Previously she had been operating in a progressive environment, as a leading voice on the edge. Now that progressive movement morphed into reactive mode—and that was a mode that Mary Daly had long outgrown, and would never adopt.

Some of this increasing discomfort surfaced in the third book of her mature thought, *Pure Lust*, published in that ominously Orwellian year of 1984. *Pure Lust* did not dwell on real-world historic specifics, but instead harkened back to some of the themes of *Beyond God the Father*, with Thomistic categories and philosophic concerns taking the lead. *Pure Lust* would be difficult to understand without familiarity with Daly's previous books, as it synthesizes their perspectives.

Daly had to address the controversies that *Gyn/Ecology* had provoked; however, she did this indirectly and ineffectively. Her attempts to address questions of race were either flippantly dismissive or hopelessly tone-deaf. They are, at best, defensive responses against an avalanche of often acerbic attacks that Daly found both hurtful and irrelevant to her thought.

*Pure Lust*, though, may be her most successful combination of philosophy and poetry—one of Daly's stated life goals. The juxtaposition of her dense and rigorous written style with elements of her spoken style realizes her dream of a new language, filled with living words.

13

# Preface to *Gyn/Ecology*

From preface to *Gyn/Ecology*, pp. xi–xvi.

*Spinning 1:* Gyn/Ecological creation; Dis-covering the lost thread of connectedness within the cosmos and repairing this thread in the process; whirling and twirling the threads of Life on the axis of Spinsters' own be-ing *2:* turning quickly on one's heel; moving Counterclockwise; whirling away in all directions from the death march of patriarchy.
—*Wickedary*, p. 96

From the first moments of *Gyn/Ecology*, an exultant world of words greets the reader. Even a sentence as simple as the opening—"This book voyages beyond *Beyond God the Father*"—contains humor and multiple meanings of "voyage." This voyaging includes internal and external dimensions, and moves at ontological levels, as marked by Daly's use of capitalization (a New England philosophical tradition, from Ralph Waldo Emerson to Mary Baker Eddy to Daly):

> Be-ing at home on the road means continuing to Journey. This book continues to Spin on, in other directions/dimensions. It focuses beyond christianity in Other ways.

While Daly invented new words, and infused others with poetic resonance, there are some old words she here explicitly rejected: God, homosexuality, and androgyny. It is here that she first introduced her identification of patriarchy with "necrophilia," an analysis that she would retain through her works, setting the strongest possible contrast with biophilia. It is interesting to compare Daly's use of the term "necrophilia"—a graphic term with active imagistic and emotional content—to what she called, in *Beyond God the Father*, the patriarchs' ability to "embody nonbeing" (see chapter 7 in this collection).

While language represents the most obvious change in Daly's tone from *Beyond God the Father*, what should not be overlooked is her passionate defense of intellection. She knew that academic gatekeepers—who had showered her with scathing critiques of *Beyond God the Father* and *The Church and the Second Sex*—would prove incapable of understanding *Gyn/Ecology*; she expected and even desired that response from the small-minded. But Daly never wanted feminists to embrace what she named as a "downward mobility of the mind." She made it clear that the ontological, cosmological, and philosophic levels of the feminist project cannot be sloughed off.

> Yes-saying by the Female Self and her Sisters involves intense work—playful cerebration. The Amazon Voyager can be anti-academic. Only at her greatest peril can she be anti-intellectual. Thus this book/Voyage can rightly be called anti-academic because it celebrates cerebral Spinning.

She insisted that feminists need to comprehend the workings of patriarchy in order not to be tricked by its alluring way stations and dead ends. Criticism of patriarchy "has nothing to do with 'jumping over' tough discipline of the mind."

Another change in tone came from her use of female and feminist sources: Julia Penelope, Virginia Woolf, Marilyn Frye, *Sinister Wisdom*, as well as Simone de Beauvoir. The building of a female train of thought—what Emily Culpepper dubs *philosophia*—became an explicit part of Daly's project here.

—Editors

This book voyages beyond *Beyond God the Father.*[1] It is not that I basically disagree with the ideas expressed there. I am still its author, and thus the situation is not comparable to that of *The Church and the Second Sex,* whose (1968) author I regard as a reformist foresister, and whose work I respectfully refute in the New Feminist Postchristian Introduction to the 1975 edition.[2]

Going beyond *Beyond God the Father* involves two things. First, there is the fact that be-ing continues. Be-ing at home on the road means continuing to Journey. This book continues to Spin on, in other directions/ dimensions. It focuses beyond christianity in Other ways. Second, there is some old semantic baggage to be discarded so that Journeyers will be unencumbered by malfunctioning (male-functioning) equipment. There are some words which appeared to be adequate in the early seventies, which feminists later discovered to be false words. Three such words in *Beyond God the Father* which I cannot use again are *God*, *androgyny*, and *homosexuality*. There is no way to remove male/masculine imagery from *God*. Thus, when writing/speaking "anthropomorphically" of ultimate reality, of the divine spark of be-ing, I now choose to write/speak gynomorphically. I do so because *God* represents the necrophilia of patriarchy, whereas *Goddess* affirms the life-loving be-ing of women and nature. The second semantic abomination, *androgyny*, is a confusing term which I sometimes used in attempting to describe integrity of be-ing. The word is misbegotten—conveying something like "John Travolta and Farrah Fawcett-Majors scotch-taped together"—as I have reiterated in public recantations. The third treacherous term, *homosexuality*, reductionistically "includes," that is, excludes, gynocentric be-ing/Lesbianism.

Simply rejecting these terms and replacing them with others is not what this book is about, however. The temptation/trap of mere labeling stops us from Spinning. Thus Goddess images are truthful and encouraging, but reified/objectified images of "The Goddess" can be mere substitutes for "God," failing to convey that Be-ing is a Verb, and that She is many verbs. Again, using a term such as *woman-identified* rather than *androgynous* is an immeasurable qualitative leap, but Spinning Voyagers cannot rest with one word, for it, too, can assume a kind of paralysis if it is not accompanied by sister words/verbs.

The words *gynocentric be-ing* and *Lesbian* imply separation. This *is* what this book is about, but not in a simple way. In *Beyond God the Father* I wrote:

> For those who are . . . threatened, the presence of women to each other is experienced as an absence. Such women are no longer empty receptacles to be used as "the Other," and are no longer internalizing the projections that cut off the flow of being. Men who need such projection screens experience the power of absence of such "objects" and are thrown into the situation of perceiving nothingness. . . .
>
> In this way, then, women's confrontation with the experience of nothingness invites men to confront it also.[3]

The primary intent of women who choose to be present to each other, however, is not an invitation to men. It is an invitation to our Selves. The Spinsters, Lesbians, Hags, Harpies, Crones, Furies who are the Voyagers of *Gyn/Ecology* know that we choose to accept this invitation for our Selves. This, our Self-acceptance, is in no way contingent upon male approval. Nor is it stopped by (realistic) fear of brutal acts of revenge. As Marilyn Frye has written:

> Male parasitism means that males *must* have access to women; it is the Patriarchal Imperative. But feminist no-saying is more than a substantial removal (re-direction, re-allocation) of goods and services because access is one of the faces of power. Female denial of male access to females substantially cuts off a flow of benefits, but it has also the form and full portent of assumption of power.[4]

The no-saying to which Frye refers is a consequence of female yes-saying to our Selves. Since women have a variety of strengths and since we have all been damaged in a variety of ways, our yes-saying assumes different forms and *is* in different degrees. In some cases it is clear and intense; in other instances it is sporadic, diffused, fragmented. Since Female-identified yes-saying is complex participation in be-ing, since it is a Journey, a process, there is no simple and adequate way to divide the Female World into two camps: those who say "yes" to women and those who do not.

The Journey of this book, therefore, is (to borrow an expression from the journal *Sinister Wisdom*) "for the Lesbian Imagination in All Women."[5] It is for the Hag/Crone/Spinster in every *living* woman.[6] It is for each individual Journeyer to decide/expand the scope of this imagination within her. It is she, and she alone, who can determine how far, and in what way, she will/can travel. She, and she alone, can dis-cover the mystery of her own history, and find how it is interwoven with the lives of other women.

Yes-saying by the Female Self and her Sisters involves intense work—playful cerebration. The Amazon Voyager can be anti-academic. Only at her greatest peril can she be anti-intellectual. Thus this book/Voyage can rightly be called anti-academic because it celebrates cerebral Spinning. If this book/Voyage could be placed neatly in a "field" it would not be this book. I have considered naming its "field" Un-theology or Un-philosophy. Certainly, in the house of mirrors which is the universe/university of reversals, it can be called Un-ethical.

Since Gyn/Ecology is the Un-field/Ourfield/Outfield of Journeyers, rather than a game in an "in" field, the pedantic can be expected to perceive it as "unscholarly." Since it *confronts* old molds/models of question-asking by being itself an Other way of thinking/speaking, it will be invisible to those who fetishize old questions—who drone that it does not "deal with" *their* questions.

Since Gyn/Ecology Spins around, past, and through the established fields, opening the coffers/coffins in which "knowledge" has been stored, re-stored, re-covered, its meaning will be hidden from the Grave Keepers of tradition. Since it seeks out the *threads of connectedness* within artificially separated/segmented reality, striving "to put the severed parts together,"[7] specious specialists will decry its "negativity" and "failure to present the whole picture." Since it Spins among fields, leaping over the walls that separate the halls in which academics have incarcerated the "bodies of knowledge," it will be accused of "lumping things together."

In fact, *Gyn/Ecology* does not belong to any of their de-partments. It departs from their de-partments. It is the Department/Departure of Spinning. Since the Custodians of academic cemeteries are unable to see or hear Spinning, they will attempt either to box it out or to box it in to some pre-existing field, such as basket weaving.[8] Cemetery librarians will file and catalogue it under *gynecology* or *female disorders*. None of this matters much, however, for it is of the nature of the Departure of Spinning that it gets around. Moreover, it is of the nature of Women's Movement that we are on the move. Eventually we find each other's messages that have been deposited in the way stations scattered in the wilderness.

The cerebral Spinner can criticize patriarchal myth and scholarship because she knows it well. Her criticism has nothing to do with "jumping over" tough discipline of the mind. The A-mazing Amazon has no patience with downward mobility of the mind and imagination. She demands great effort of herself and of her sisters.[9] For she must not only know the works of The Masters; she must go much further. She must see through them and make them transparent to other Voyagers as well.[10] To borrow an expression from Virginia Woolf, she must take a "vow of derision":

> By derision—a bad word, but once again the English language is much in need of new words—is meant that you must refuse all methods of advertising merit, and hold that ridicule, obscurity and censure are preferable, for psychological reasons, to fame and praise.[11]

Who and where are "the deriders"? The reader/Journeyer of this book will note that it is not addressed only to those who now call themselves members of "the women's community." Many women who so name themselves are Journeyers, but it is also possible that some are not. It seems to me that the change in nomenclature which gradually took place in the early seventies, by which *the women's movement* was transformed into *the women's community*, was a symptom of settling for too little, of settling *down*, of being too comfortable. I must ask, first, just *who* are "the women"? Second, what about *movement*? This entire book is asking the question of movement, of Spinning. It is an invitation to the Wild Witch in all women who long to spin. This book is a declaration that it is time to stop putting answers before the Questions. It is a declaration/Manifesto that in our chronology (Crone-ology) it is time to get moving again. It is a call of the wild to the wild, calling Hags/Spinsters to spin/be beyond the parochial bondings/bindings of any comfortable "community." It is a call to women who have never named themselves Wild before, and a challenge to those who have been in struggle for a long time and who have retreated for awhile.

As Survivors know, the media-created Lie that *the women's movement* "died" has hidden the fact from many of our sisters that Spinners/Spinsters have been spinning works of genesis and demise in our concealed workshops. Feminists have been creating a rich culture, creating new forms of writing, singing, celebrating, cerebrating, searching. We have been developing new strategies and tactics for organizing—for economic, physical, and psychological survival. To do this, we have had to go deep inside our Selves. We have noted with grief that meanwhile another phenomenon has appeared in the foreground of male-controlled society: pseudo-feminism has been actively promoted by the patriarchs. The real rebels/renegades have been driven away from positions of patriarchally defined power, replaced by reformist and roboticized tokens.

This book can be heard as a Requiem for *that* "women's movement," which is male-designed, male-orchestrated, male-legitimated, male-assimilated.[12] It is also a call to those who have been unwittingly tokenized, to tear off their mindbindings and join in the Journey. It is, hopefully, an alarm clock for those former Journeyers who have merged with "the human (men's) community," but who can still feel nostalgia for the present/future of their own be-ing.

14

# The Metapatriarchal Journey of Exorcism and Ecstasy

Chapter 1 of *Gyn/Ecology*, pp. 1–34.

> *Crone:* Great Hag of History, long-lasting one; Survivor of the perpetual witchcraze of patriarchy, whose status is determined not merely by chronological age, but by Crone-logical considerations; one who has Survived early stages of the Otherworld Journey and who therefore has Dis-covered depths of Courage, Strength, and Wisdom in her Self.
> —*Wickedary*, p. 114

*Gyn/Ecology* marks the most definitive break in Daly's career in content and style. By its 1978 publication, the women's movement had grown substantially, and there was a ready audience of radical feminists, lesbian-feminists, lesbian separatists, and politically active women eager for the ideas Daly articulated here. At the same time, the decisive absolutism of some of her characterizations of patriarchy, and its identity with men as a class, proved a stumbling block for some readers.

Daly's notion of history became more definitive: there was a time before patriarchy, which women can remember, as well as the current patriarchy in which we are living. She termed these "Background" and "foreground," terms she retained throughout the remainder of her life: "In writing of the deep *Background* which is the divine depth of the Self, I capitalize, while the term *foreground*, referring to surface consciousness, generally is not capitalized."

She exposed the eight deadly sins of patriarchy and named their reversals in a writing style that cannot help but make one smile: "Patriarchy has stolen our cosmos and returned it in the form of *Cosmopolitan* magazine and cosmetics." The ecstasy of the writing and the visions in it provide high humor and highly precise analysis: "This demystification process, a-mazing The Lies, *is* ecstasy." Her identification with nature steals the stage in her final lines about the end of the patriarchal paradise ("the image is one of stagnation [in a stag-nation]"): "Breaking through the foreground which is the Playboys' Playground means letting out the bunnies, the bitches, the beavers, the squirrels, the chicks, the pussycats, the cows, the nags, the foxy ladies, the old bats and biddies, so that they can at last begin naming themselves."

The poetic humor in her language led her to encourage others to read aloud, and drew an admission from her that, at times, the words seemed to want to go in their own direction, without her supervision. But what she did with language exemplifies "ludic cerebration," the kind of focused and evocative listening that she wanted for all women and sentient nature: "When I play with words I do this attentively, deeply, paying attention to etymology, to varied dimensions of meaning, to deep Background meanings and subliminal associations."

This freeing of language to live out its multivalence finds a parallel in the cackling of the Crones, which Daly relished:

> There is nothing like the sound of women really laughing. The roaring laughter of women is like the roaring of the eternal sea. Hags can cackle and roar at themselves, but more and more, one hears them roaring at the reversal that is patriarchy. . . . [T]his laughter is the one true hope, for as long as it is audible there is evidence that someone is seeing through the Dirty Joke.

Her explanation of the title and subtitle of the book established the sweeping nature of her project here; in particular, her choice of the term "metapatriarchal" demonstrated an unwillingness to entertain any kind of reformism. Perhaps the easiest comparison between the still assimilable language of *Beyond God the Father* and the uncompromising *Gyn/Ecology* can be heard between these two quotes:

> In its depth, because it contains a dynamic that drives beyond Christolatry, the women's movement *does* point to, seek, and constitute the primordial, always present, and future Antichrist. (*Beyond God the Father*; in this book chapter 9)

> We are be-ing in the Triple Goddess, who is, and is not yet. (*Gyn/Ecology*)

One final distinction worth noting: *Gyn/Ecology's* language did not shrink from being bawdy and earthy. While Daly had no patience with the

genitally obsessed fetishisms of patriarchal attitudes toward sex, she no longer played only in her head: her own embodiment feels livelier in this book than in its predecessors.
—Editors

All mother goddesses spin and weave. . . . Everything that is comes out of them: They weave the world tapestry out of genesis and demise, "threads appearing and disappearing rhythmically."
—Helen Diner, *Mothers and Amazons*

This book is about the journey of women becoming, that is, radical feminism. The voyage is described and roughly charted here. I say "roughly" by way of understatement and pun. We do not know exactly what is on the Other Side until we arrive there—and the journey *is rough.* The charting done here is based on some knowledge from the past, upon present experience, and upon hopes for the future. These three sources are inseparable, intertwined. Radical feminist consciousness spirals in all directions, dis-covering the past, creating/dis-closing the present/future.

The radical be-ing of women is very much an Otherworld Journey. It is both discovery and creation of a world other than patriarchy. Patriarchy appears to be "everywhere." Even outer space and the future have been colonized. As a rule, even the more imaginative science-fiction writers (allegedly the most foretelling futurists) cannot/will not create a space and time in which women get far beyond the role of space stewardess. Nor does this colonization exist simply "outside" women's minds, securely fastened into institutions we can physically leave behind. Rather, it is also internalized, festering inside women's heads, even feminist heads.

The Journey, then, involves exorcism of the internalized Godfather in his various manifestations (his name is legion). It involves dangerous encounters with these demons. Within the christian tradition, particularly in medieval times, evil spirits have sometimes been associated with the

"Seven Deadly Sins," both as personifications and as causes.[1] A standard listing of the Sins is the following: pride, avarice, anger, lust, gluttony, envy, and sloth.[2] The feminist voyage discloses that these have all been radically misnamed, that is, inadequately and perversely "understood." They are particularized expressions of the overall use of "evil" to victimize women. Our journey involves confrontations with the demonic manifestations of evil.

Why has it seemed "appropriate" in this culture that the plot of a popular book and film (*The Exorcist*) centers around a Jesuit who "exorcises" a girl who is "possessed"? Why is there no book or film about a woman who exorcises a Jesuit?[3] From a radical feminist perspective it is clear that "Father" is precisely the one who cannot exorcise, for he is allied with and identified with The Possessor. The fact that he is himself possessed should not be women's essential concern. It is a mistake to see men as pitiable victims or vessels to be "saved" through female self-sacrifice. However possessed males may be within patriarchy, it is *their* order; it is they who feed on women's stolen energy. It is a trap to imagine that women should "save" men from the dynamics of demonic possession; and to attempt this is to fall deeper into the pit of patriarchal possession. It is women ourselves who will have to expel the Father from ourselves, becoming our own exorcists.

Within a culture possessed by the myth of feminine evil, the naming, describing, and theorizing about good and evil has constituted a maze/haze of deception. The journey of women becoming is breaking through this maze—springing into free space, which is an a-mazing process.

Breaking through the Male Maze is both exorcism and ecstasy. It is spinning through and beyond the fathers' foreground which is the arena of games. This spinning involves encountering the demons who block the various thresholds as we move through gateway after gateway into the deepest chambers of our homeland, which is the Background of our Selves. As Denise Connors has pointed out, the Background is the realm of the wild reality of women's Selves. Objectification and alienation take place when we are locked into the male-centered, monodimensional foreground.[4] Thus the monitors of the foreground, the male myth-masters, fashion prominent and eminently forgettable images of women in their art, literature, and mass media—images intended to mold women for male purposes.

The Background into which feminist journeying spins is the wild realm of Hags and Crones. It is Hag-ocracy. The demons who attempt to block the gateways to the deep spaces of this realm often take ghostly/ghastly forms, comparable to noxious gases not noticeable by ordinary sense perception.[5] Each time we move into deeper space, these numbing ghostly gases work to paralyze us, to trap us, so that we will be unable to move further. Each time we succeed in overcoming their numbing effect, more dormant senses come alive. Our inner eyes open, our inner ears become unblocked. We are strengthened to move through the next gateway and the next. This movement inward/outward is being. It is spinning cosmic tapestries. It is spinning and whirling into the Background.

The spinning process requires seeking out the sources of the ghostly gases that have seeped into the deep chambers of our minds. "The way back to reality is to destroy our perceptions of it," said Bergson. Yes, but these deceptive perceptions were/are implanted through language—the all-pervasive language of myth, conveyed overtly and subliminally through religion, "great art," literature, the dogmas of professionalism, the media, grammar. Indeed, deception is embedded in the very texture of the words we use, and here is where our exorcism can begin. Thus, for example, the word *spinster* is commonly used as a deprecating term, but it can only function this way when apprehended exclusively on a superficial (foreground) level. Its deep meaning, which has receded into the Background so far that we have to spin deeply in order to retrieve it, is clear and strong: "a woman whose occupation is to spin." There is no reason to limit the meaning of this rich and cosmic verb. A woman whose occupation is to spin participates in the whirling movement of creation. She who has chosen her Self, who defines her Self, by choice, neither in relation to children nor to men, who is Self-identified, is a Spinster, a whirling dervish, spinning in a new time/space. Another example is the term *glamour*, whose first definition as given in Merriam-Webster is "a magic spell." Originally it was believed that witches possessed the power of glamour, and according to the authors of the *Malleus Maleficarum*, witches by their glamour could cause the male "member" to disappear. In modern usage, this meaning has almost disappeared into the Background, and the power of the term is masked and suffocated by such foreground images as those associated with *Glamour* magazine.

Journeying is multidimensional. The various meanings and images conjured up by the word are not sharply distinguishable. We can think of mystical journeys, quests, adventurous travel, advancement in skills, in physical and intellectual prowess. So also the barriers are multiple and intertwined. These barriers are not mere immobile blocks, but are more like deceptive tongues that prevent us from hearing our Selves, as they babble incessantly in the Tower of Babel which is the erection of phallocracy.[6] The voices and the silences of Babel pierce all of our senses. They are the invasive extensions of the enemy of women's hearing, dreaming, creating. *Babel* is said to be derived from an Assyrian-Babylonian word meaning "gate of god." When women break through this multiple barrier composed of deceptions ejaculated by "god" we can begin to glimpse the true gateways to our depths, which are the Gates of the Goddess.

Spinsters can find our way back to reality by destroying the false perceptions of it inflicted upon us by the language and myths of Babel. We must learn to dis-spell the language of phallocracy, which keeps us under the spell of brokenness. This spell splits our perceptions of our Selves and of the cosmos, overtly and subliminally. Journeying into our Background will mean recognizing that both the "spirit" and the "matter" presented to us in the Fathers' foreground are reifications, condensations. They are not really "opposites," for they have much in common: both are dead, inert. This is unmasked when we begin to see through patriarchal language. Thus, the Latin term *texere*, meaning to weave, is the origin and root for both *textile* and for *text*. It is important for women to note the irony in this split of meanings. For our process of cosmic weaving has been stunted and minimized to the level of the manufacture and maintenance of textiles. While there is nothing demeaning about this occupation in itself, the limitation of women to the realm of "distaff" has mutilated and condensed our Divine Right of creative weaving to the darning of socks. If we look at the term *text* in contrast to *textile*, we see that this represents the other side of the schizoid condensations of weaving/spinning. "Texts" are the kingdom of males; they are the realm of the reified word, of condensed spirit. In patriarchal tradition, sewing and spinning are for girls; books are for boys.

Small wonder that many women feel repugnance for the realm of the distaff, which has literally been the sweatshop and prison of female bodies and spirits. Small wonder that many women have seen the male kingdom of texts as an appealing escape from the tomb-town of textiles which has symbolized the confinement/reduction of female energy.[7] The kingdom of male-authored texts has appeared to be the ideal realm to be reached/entered, for we have been educated to forget that professional "knowledge" is our stolen process. As Andrée Collard remarked, in the society of cops and robbers, we learn to forget that the cops are the robbers, that they rob us of everything: our myths, our energy, our divinity, our Selves.[8]

Women's minds have been mutilated and muted to such a state that "Free Spirit" has been branded into them as a brand name for girdles and bras rather than as the name of our verb-ing, be-ing Selves. Such brand names brand women "Morons." Moronized, women believe that male-written texts (biblical, literary, medical, legal, scientific) are "true." Thus manipulated, women become eager for acceptance as docile tokens mouthing male texts, employing technology for male ends, accepting male fabrications as the true texture of reality. Patriarchy has stolen our cosmos and returned it in the form of *Cosmopolitan* magazine and cosmetics. They have made up our cosmos, our Selves. Spinning deeper into the Background is courageous sinning against the Sins of the Fathers. As our senses become more alive we can see/hear/feel how we have been tricked by their texts. We begin unweaving our winding sheets. The process of exorcism, of peeling off the layers of mindbindings and cosmetics, is movement past the patriarchally imposed sense of reality and identity. This demystification process, a-mazing The Lies, *is* ecstasy.

Journeying centerward is Self-centering movement in all directions. It erases implanted pseudodichotomies between the Self and "other" reality, while it unmasks the unreality of both "self" and "world" as these are portrayed, betrayed, in the language of the fathers' foreground. Adrienne Rich has written:

> In bringing the light of critical thinking to bear on her subject, in the very act of *becoming more conscious* of her situation in the world, a woman

> may feel herself coming deeper than ever into touch with her unconscious and with her body.[9]

Moving into the Background/Center is not navel-gazing. It is be-ing in the world. The foreground fathers offer dual decoys labeled "thought" and "action," which distract from the reality both of deep knowing and of external action. There is no authentic separation possible.

The Journey is itself participation in Paradise. This word, which is said to be from the Iranian *pairi* (meaning around) and *daēza* (meaning wall), is commonly used to conjure an image of a walled-in pleasure garden. Patriarchal Paradise, as projected in Western and Eastern religious mythology, is imaged as a place or a state in which the souls of the righteous after death enjoy eternal bliss, that is, heaven. Despite theological attempts to make this seem lively, the image is one of stagnation (in a stag-nation) as suggested in the expression, "the Afterlife." In contrast to this, the Paradise which is cosmic spinning is not containment within walls. Rather, it is movement that is not containable, weaving around and past walls, leaving them in the past. It moves into the Background which is the moving center of the Self, enabling the Self to act "outwardly" in the cosmos as she comes alive. This metapatriarchal movement is not Afterlife, but Living now, dis-covering Life.

A primary definition of *paradise* is "pleasure park." The walls of the Patriarchal Pleasure Park represent the condition of being perpetually parked, locked into the parking lot of the past. A basic meaning of *park* is a "game preserve." The fathers' foreground is precisely this: an arena where the wildness of nature and of women's Selves is domesticated, preserved. It is the place for the preservation of females who are the "fair game" of the fathers, that they may be served to these predatory Park Owners, and service them at their pleasure. Patriarchal Paradise is the arena of games, the place where the pleas of women are silenced, where the law is: Please the Patrons. Women who break through the imprisoning walls of the Playboys' Playground are entering the process which is our happening/happiness. This is Paradise beyond the boundaries of "paradise." Since our passage into this process requires making breaks in the walls, it means setting free the fair game, breaking the rules of the games, breaking the names of the games. Breaking through the foreground which is the Playboys' Playground means letting out the bunnies, the bitches, the beavers, the squirrels, the chicks, the pussycats, the cows, the nags, the foxy ladies, the old bats and biddies, so that they can at last begin naming themselves.

I have coined the term *metapatriarchal* to describe the journey, because the prefix *meta* has multiple meanings. It incorporates the idea of "postpatriarchal," for it means occurring later. It puts patriarchy in the past without denying that its walls/ruins and demons are still around. Since *meta* also means "situated behind," it suggests that the direction of the journey is into the Background. Another meaning of this prefix is "change in, transformation of." This, of course, suggests the transforming power of the journey. By this I do not mean that women's movement "reforms" patriarchy, but that it transforms our Selves. Since *meta* means "beyond, transcending," it contains a built-in corrective to reductive notions of mere reformism.

This metapatriarchal process of encountering the unknown involves also a continual conversion of the previously unknown into the familiar.[10] Since the "unknown" is stolen/hidden know-ing, frozen and stored by the Abominable Snowmen of Androcratic Academia, Spinsters must melt these masses of "knowledge" with the fire of Female Fury.

Amazon expeditions into the male-controlled "fields" are necessary in order to leave the fathers' caves and live in the sun. A crucial problem for us has been to learn how to re-possess righteously while avoiding being caught too long in the caves.[11] In universities, and in all of the professions, the omnipresent poisonous gases gradually stifle women's minds and spirits. Those who carry out the necessary expeditions run the risk of shrinking into the mold of the mystified Athena, the twice-born, who forgets and denies her Mother and Sisters, because she has forgotten her original Self. "Re-born" from Zeus, she becomes Daddy's Girl, the mutant who serves the master's purposes. The token woman, who in reality is enchained, possessed, "knows" that she is free. She is a useful tool of the patriarchs, particularly against her sister Artemis, who knows better, respects her Self, bonds with her Sisters, and refuses to sell her freedom, her original birthright, for a mess of respectability.

A-mazing Amazons must be aware of the male methods of mystification. Elsewhere I have discussed four methods which are essential to the games of the fathers.[12] First, there is *erasure* of women. (The massacre of millions of women as witches is erased in patriarchal scholarship.)

Second, there is *reversal.* (Adam gives birth to Eve, Zeus to Athena, in patriarchal myth.) Third, there is *false polarization.* (Male-defined "feminism" is set up against male-defined "sexism" in the patriarchal media.) Fourth, there is *divide and conquer.* (Token women are trained to kill off feminists in patriarchal professions.) As we move further on the metapatriarchal journey, we find deeper and deeper layers of these demonic patterns embedded in the culture, implanted in our souls. These constitute mindbindings comparable to the footbindings which mutilated millions of Chinese women for a thousand years. Stripping away layer after layer of these mindbinding societal/mental embeds is the a-mazing essential to the journey.

Spinsters are not only A-mazing Amazons cutting away layers of deceptions. Spinsters are also Survivors. We must survive, not merely in the sense of "living on," but in the sense of living beyond. Surviving (from the Latin *super* plus *vivere*) I take to mean living above, through, around the obstacles thrown in our paths. This is hardly the dead "living on" of possessed tokens. The process of Survivors is meta-living, be-ing.

## The Title of This Book

The title of this book, *Gyn/Ecology*, says exactly what I mean it to say. "Ecology" is about the complex web of interrelationships between organisms and their environment. In her book, *Le Féminisme ou la mort*, Françoise d'Eaubonne coins the expression "eco-féminisme."[13] She maintains that the fate of the human species and of the planet is at stake, and that no male-led "revolution" will counteract the horrors of overpopulation and destruction of natural resources. I share this basic premise, but my approach and emphasis are different. Although I am concerned with all forms of pollution in phallotechnic society, this book is primarily concerned with the mind/spirit/body pollution inflicted through patriarchal myth and languages on all levels. These levels range from styles of grammar to styles of glamour, from religious myth to dirty jokes, from theological hymns honoring the "Real Presence" of Christ to commercial cooing of Coca-Cola as "The Real Thing," from dogmatic doctrines about the "Divine Host" to doctored ingredient-labeling of Hostess Cupcakes, from subliminal ads to "sublime" art. Phallic myth and language generate, legitimate, and mask the material pollution that threatens to terminate all sentient life on this planet.

The title *Gyn/Ecology* is a way of wrenching back some wordpower. The fact that most gynecologists are males is in itself a colossal comment on "our" society. It is a symptom and example of male control over women and over language, and a clue to the extent of this control. Add to this the fact, noted by Adrienne Rich, of "a certain indifference and fatalism toward the diseases of women, which persists to this day in the male gynecological and surgical professions."[14] And add to this the fact that the self-appointed soul doctors, mind doctors, and body doctors who "specialize" in women are perpetrators of *iatrogenic disease.*[15] That is, soul doctors (priests and gurus), mind doctors (psychiatrists, ad-men, and academics), and body doctors (physicians and fashion designers) are by professional code causes of disease in women and hostile to female well-being.[16] Gynecologists fixate upon what they do not have, upon what they themselves cannot do. For this reason they epitomize and symbolize the practitioners of other patriarchal -ologies, and they provide important clues to the demonic patterns common to the labor of all of these. In their frantic fixation upon what they lack (biophilic energy)[17] and in their fanatic indifference to the destruction they wreak upon the Other—women and "Mother Nature"—the phallic -ologists coalesce. Their corporate merger is the Mystical Body of knowledge which is gynocidal gynecology.

Note that the *Oxford English Dictionary* defines *gynecology* as "that department of medical science which treats of the functions and diseases peculiar to women; also *loosely*, the science of womankind." I am using the term *Gyn/Ecology* very loosely, that is, freely, to describe the science, that is the process of know-ing, of "loose" women who choose to be subjects and not mere objects of enquiry. Gyn/Ecology is by and about women a-mazing all the male-authored "sciences of womankind," and weaving world tapestries *of our own kind*. That is, it is about discovering, de-veloping the complex web of living/loving relationships *of our own kind*. It is about women living, loving, creating our Selves, our cosmos. It *is* dis-possessing our Selves, enspiriting our Selves, hearing the call of the wild, naming our wisdom, spinning and weaving world tapestries out of genesis and demise. In contrast to gynecology, which depends upon fixation and dismemberment, Gyn/Ecology affirms that everything is connected.

Since "o-logies" are generally static "bodies of knowledge," it might at first glance seem that the name *Gyn/Ecology* clashes with the theme of the Journey. However, a close analysis unveils the fact that this is not so. For women can recognize the powerful and multidimensional gynocentric symbolism of the "O."[18] It represents the power of our moving, encircling presence, which can make nonbeing sink back into itself. Our "O" is totally other than "nothing" (a fact demonically distorted and reversed in the pornographic novel, *The Story of O*). As Denise Connors has pointed out, it can be taken to represent our aura, our O-Zone.[19] Within this anti-pollutant, purifying, moving O-Zone, the aura of gynocentric consciousness, life-loving feminists have the power to affirm the basic Gyn/Ecological principle that everything is connected with everything else. It is this holistic process of knowing that can make Gyn/Ecology the O-logy of all the -ologies, Gyn/Ecology can reduce their pretentious facades to Zero. It can free the flow of their "courses" and overcome their necrophilic circles, their self-enclosed processions, through spiraling creative process. It is women's own Gyn/Ecology that can break the brokenness of the "fields," deriding their borders and boundaries, changing the nouns of knowledge into verbs of know-ing.

## The Subtitle of This Book

By the subtitle, *The Metaethics of Radical Feminism*, I intend to convey that this book is concerned with the Background, most specifically of language and myth, which is disguised by the fathers' foreground fixations. Merriam-Webster gives as one of the definitions of the prefix, *meta*: "of a higher logical type—in nouns formed from names of disciplines and designating new but related disciplines such as can deal critically with the nature, structure, or behavior of the original ones (*meta*language, *meta*theory, *meta*system)." Despite the dullness of dictionary diction, there are clues here. I would say that radical feminist metaethics is of a *deeper intuitive* type than "ethics." The latter, generally written from one of several (but basically the same) patriarchal perspectives, works out of hidden agendas concealed in the texture of language, buried in mythic reversals which control "logic" most powerfully because unacknowledged. Thus for theologians and philosophers, Eastern and Western, and particularly for ethicists, woman-identified women do not exist. The metaethics of radical feminism seeks to uncover the background of such logic, as women ourselves move into the Background of this background. In this sense, it can be called "of a higher [read: deeper] logical type." It is, of course, a new discipline that "deals critically" with the nature, structure, and behavior of ethics and ethicists. It is able to do this because our primary concern is *not* male ethics and/or ethicists, but our own Journeying.

This book has to do with the mysteries of good and evil. To name it a "feminist ethics" might be a clue, but it would also be misleading, pointing only to foreground problems. It would be something like arguing for "equal rights" in a society whose very existence depends upon inequality, that is, upon the possession of female energy by men. The spring into free space, which is woman-identified consciousness, involves a veritable mental/behavioral mutation. The phallocratic categorizations of "good" and "evil" no longer apply when women *honor* women, when we become honorable to ourselves.[20] As Barbara Starrett wrote, we are developing something like a new organ of the mind.[21] This development both causes and affects qualitative leaping through galaxies of mindspace. It involves a new faculty and process of valuation. None of the dreary ethical texts, from those of Aristotle down to Paul Ramsey and Joseph Fletcher, can speak to the infinitely expanding universe of what Emily Culpepper has named "gynergy."[22] Indeed, the texts of phallocratic ethicists function in the same manner as pornography, legitimating the institutions which degrade women's be-ing. Gyn/Ecological metaethics, in contrast to all of this, functions to affirm the deep dynamics of female be-ing. It is gynography.

There are, of course, male-authored, male-identified works which purport to deal with "metaethics." In relation to these, gynography is meta-metaethical. For while male metaethics claims to be "the study of ethical theories, as distinguished from the study of moral and ethical conduct itself,"[23] it remains essentially male-authored and male-identified theory about theory. Moreover, it is only theory about "ethical theories"—an enterprise which promises boundless boringness. In contrast to this, Gyn/Ecology is hardly "metaethical" in the sense of masturbatory meditations by ethicists upon their own emissions. Rather, we recognize that the essential omission of these emissions is of our own life/freedom. In the name of our life/freedom, feminist metaethics O-mits seminal omissions.

In making this metapatriarchal leap into our own Background, feminists are hearing/naming the immortal Metis, Goddess of wisdom, who presided over all knowledge. In patriarchal myth she was swallowed by Zeus when she was pregnant with Athena. Zeus claimed that Metis counseled him from inside his belly. In any case, the Greeks began ascribing wisdom to this prototype of male cannibalism. We must remember that Metis was originally the parthenogenetic mother of Athena. After Athena was "reborn" from the head of Zeus, her single "parent," she became Zeus's obedient mouthpiece. She became totally male-identified, employing priests, not priestesses, urging men on in battle, siding against women consistently.[24] Radical feminist metaethics means moving past this puppet of Papa, dis-covering the immortal Metis. It also means dis-covering the parthenogenetic Daughter, the original Athena, whose loyalty is to her own kind, whose science/wisdom is of womankind. In this dis-covering there can be what Catherine Nicholson named "the third birth of Athena."[25] As this happens, Athena will shuck off her robothood, will re-turn to her real Source, to her Self, leaving the demented Male Mother to play impotently with his malfunctioning machine, his dutiful dim-witted "Daughter," his broken Baby Doll gone berserk, his failed fembot. The metaethics of radical feminism means simply that while Zeus, Yahweh, and all the other divine male "Mothers" are trying to retrieve their dolls from the ashcan of patriarchal creation, women on our own Journey are dis-covering Metis and the third-born Athena: our own new be-ing. That is, we are be-ing in the Triple Goddess, who is, and is not yet.[26]

## The Tradition of This Book: Hag-ography

*Hagiography* is a term employed by christians, and is defined as "the biography of saints; saints' lives; biography of an idealizing or idolizing character." Hagiology has a similar meaning; it is "a description of sacred writings or sacred persons." Both of these terms are from the Greek *hagios*, meaning holy.

Surviving, moving women can hardly look to the masochistic martyrs of sadospiritual religion as models. Since most patriarchal writing that purports to deal with women is pornography or hagiography (which amount to the same thing), women in a world from which woman-identified writing has been eliminated are trying to break away from these moldy "models," both of writing and of living. Our foresisters were the Great Hags whom the institutionally powerful but privately impotent patriarchs found too threatening for coexistence, and whom historians erase. *Hag* is from an Old English word meaning harpy, witch. Webster's gives as the first and "archaic" meaning of *hag*: "a female demon: FURY, HARPY." It also formerly meant: "an evil or frightening spirit." (Lest this sound too negative, we should ask the relevant questions: "Evil" by whose definition? "Frightening" to whom?) A third archaic definition of *hag* is "nightmare."[27] (The important question is: Whose nightmare?). *Hag* is also defined as "an ugly or evil-looking old woman." But this, considering the source, may be considered a compliment. For the beauty of strong, creative women is "ugly" by misogynist standards of "beauty." The look of female-identified women is "evil" to those who fear us. As for "old," ageism is a feature of phallic society. For women who have transvaluated this, a Crone is one who should be an example of strength, courage and wisdom.

For women who are on the journey of radical be-ing, the lives of the witches, of the Great Hags of our hidden history are deeply intertwined with our own process. As we write/live our own story, we are uncovering their history, creating Hag-ography and Hag-ology. Unlike the "saints" of christianity, who must, by definition, be dead, Hags live. Women traveling into feminist time/space are creating Hag-ocracy, the place we govern. To govern is to steer, to pilot. We are learning individually and together to pilot the time/spaceships of our voyage. The vehicles of our voyage may be any creative enterprises that further women's process. The point is that they should be governed by the Witch within—the Hag within.

In living/writing Hag-ography it is important to recognize that those who live in the tradition of the Great Hags will become haggard. But this term, like so many others, must be understood in its radical sense. Although *haggard* is commonly used to describe one who has a worn or emaciated appearance, this was not its original or primary meaning.

Applied to a hawk, it means "untamed." So-called obsolete meanings given in Merriam-Webster include "intractable," "willful," "wanton," and "unchaste." The second meaning is "wild in appearance: as a) *of the eyes:* wild and staring b) *of a person:* WILD-EYED." Only after these meanings do we find the idea of "a worn or emaciated appearance." As a noun, *haggard* has an "obsolete" meaning: "an intractable person, especially: a woman reluctant to yield to wooing."

Haggard writing is by and for haggard women, those who are intractable, willful, wanton, unchaste, and, especially, those who are reluctant to yield to wooing. It belongs to the tradition of those who refuse to assume the woes of wooed women, who cast off these woes as unworthy of Hags, of Harpies. Haggard women are not man-wooed. As Furies, women in the tradition of the Great Hags reject the curse of compromise.

The Great Hags of history, when their lives have not been prematurely terminated, have lived to be Crones. Crones are the long-lasting ones.[28] They are the Survivors of the perpetual witchcraze of patriarchy, the Survivors of The Burning Times.[29] In living/writing, feminists are recording and creating the history of Crones. Women who can identify with the Great Crones may wish to call our writing of women's history Crone-ography.[30]

It is also appropriate to think of our writing in this tradition as Crone-ology. *Chronology*, generally speaking, means an arrangement (as of data, events) in order of time of occurrence or appearance. In a specific sense, however, it refers to "the classification of archeological sites or prehistoric periods of culture." Since the history of Hags and Crones is truly Prehistoric in relation to patriarchal history—being prior both in time and in importance—haggard women should consider that our Crone-ology is indeed our chronology. In writing/recording/creating Crone-ography and in studying our own Prehistoric chronology, we are unmasking deceptive patriarchal history, rendering it obsolete. Women who refuse to be wooed by patriarchal scholarship can conjure the chronicles of the Great Crones, foresisters of our present and future Selves. In Greek mythology, the crow is an oracular bird. Whether or not an etymological connection can be demonstrated, the association between Crones and oracular utterances is natural and obvious. As unwooed women unearth more of our tradition, we can begin to hear and understand our own oracles, which have been caricatured as the "screeching" of "old crows."

Hag-ographers perceive the hilarious hypocrisy of "his" history. At first this may be difficult, for when the whole is hypocrisy, the parts may not initially appear untrue. To put it another way, when everything is bizarre, nothing seems bizarre. Hags are women who struggle to see connections. Hags risk a great deal—if necessary, everything—knowing that there is only Nothing to lose. Hags may rage and roar, but they do not titter.

Webster's defines *titter* as follows: "to give vent to laughter one is seeking to suppress: laugh lightly or in a subdued manner: laugh in a *nervous, affected, or restrained* manner, especially at a high pitch and with short catches of the voice [emphasis mine]." Self-loathing ladies titter; Hags and Harpies roar. Fembots titter at themselves when Daddy turns the switch. They totter when he pulls the string. They titter especially at the spinning of Spinsters, whom they have been trained to see as dizzy dames. Daddy's little Titterers try to intimidate women struggling for greatness. This is what they are made for and paid for. There is only one taboo for titterers: they must never laugh seriously at Father—only at his jokes.

There is nothing like the sound of women really laughing. The roaring laughter of women is like the roaring of the eternal sea. Hags can cackle and roar at themselves, but more and more, one hears them roaring at the reversal that is patriarchy, that monstrous jock's joke, the Male Mothers Club that gives birth only to putrefaction and deception. One can hear pain and perhaps cynicism in the laughter of Hags who witness the spectacle of Male Mothers (Murderers) dismembering a planet they have already condemned to death. But this laughter is the one true hope, for as long as it is audible there is evidence that someone is seeing through the Dirty Joke. It is in this hope that this Hag-ography is written.

## The Silencing of Women and Silent Spring

This is an extremist book, written in a situation of extremity, written on the edge of a culture that is killing itself and all of sentient life. The Tree of Life has been replaced by the necrophilic symbol of a dead body hanging on dead wood. The Godfather insatiably demands more sacrifices, and the fundamental sacrifices of sadospiritual religion are female.

The sacrificing of women requires the silencing of women, which takes place in myriad ways, in a maze of ways. A basic pattern of these ways is Self-splitting, which is initiated by the patriarchally powerful and which the victims internalize and continue to practice within the caste of women. Women are silenced/split by the babble of grammatical usage. Subliminal and subtle Self-splitting is achieved by the very pronouns we are trained to use to designate our Selves. Julia Stanley and Susan Robbins have written of the peculiar history of the pronoun *she,* which was introduced into Middle English as a late development. During the Middle Ages, *he* had come to be both the female and the male pronoun. After *she* was introduced, it referred only to females, while *he* became "generic," allegedly including women. This transition in the history of the pronoun *he* was hardly insignificant:

> Since the female pronoun always designates females—while the male pronoun designates all humans as well as all males, patriarchal language, as manifested in the pronominal system of English, extended the scope of maleness to *include* humanity, while restricting femaleness to "the Other," who is by implication nonhuman. Any speaker internalizing such a language unconsciously internalizes the values underlying such a system, thus perpetuating the cultural and social assumptions necessary to maintain the patriarchal power structure.[31]

When women become aware of the manipulable ambiguity of the pronoun *he,* we have perceived only the foreground of grammatical silencing techniques. Just as it would be a mistake to fixate upon the pseudogeneric *man* and assume that terms such as *people* and *person* are "real" generics (a falsehood disclosed by such expressions as "people and their wives") so it is a mistake to fixate upon the third person singular. As Monique Wittig has shown, the pronoun *I* conceals the sexual identity of the speaker/writer. The *I* makes the speaker/writer deceptively feel at home in a male-controlled language. When she uses this pronoun, she may forget that *she* is buried in the false generic *he.* The fact is that the female saying "I" is alien at every moment to her own speaking and writing. She is broken by the fact that she must enter this language in order to speak or to write.[32] As the "I" is broken, so also is the Inner Eye, the capacity for integrity of knowing/sensing. In this way the Inner

Voice of the Self's integrity is silenced; the external voice babbles in alien and alienating tongues. And when the Self tries to speak out of her true depths, the pedantic peddlers of "correct" usage and style try to drown it in their babble.

Women are silenced/split by the embedding of fears. These contrived and injected fears function in a manner analogous to electrodes implanted in the brain of a victim ("patient") who can be managed by remote control. This is a kind of "silent" control (as silent as the pushing of a button). Women may feel that they are free from certain fears ("liberated") and then bend to the unacknowledged power of these fears with mental knee-jerk responses. A brief analysis of responses to a few of these instilled fears should unmask the methods of "silent" control which silence the voices of women's deep Selves, while allowing the "liberated" false selves to babble freely.

For example, the cliché, "She lacks a sense of humor"—applied by men to every threatening woman—is one basic "electrode" embedded just deeply enough into the fearful foreground of women's psyches to be able to conduct female energy against the Self while remaining disguised. The comment is urbane, insidious. It is boring and predictable if seen through, devastating if believed. The problem is that the victim who "sees through" this dirty trick on one level may "believe" the judgment literally on more vulnerable levels. It is perfectly consistent with patriarchal patterns that this device is used especially against the wittiest women, who are dismissed as "sharp-tongued." The Godfather is the Father of Lies and favors the most blatant lies.

In the Land of the Fathers, the more blatant the lie the greater its credibility, for it is then most consistent with the general pattern of bizarre beliefs. Our ability to overcome the power of such particular fear-instilling lies depends upon our ability to discern the pattern of the whole. Gyn/Ecology requires a constant effort to see the innerconnectedness of things. It involves seeing the totality of the Lie which is patriarchy, unweaving its web of deception. Since the totality of the patriarchal Lie is *not* integrity, since it lacks the complexity of real integrity, it tends to fall apart quickly once we see its pattern, once we dare to face "the whole thing." Moreover, since it depends entirely upon the reality which it distorts and demonically reflects, our seeing through patriarchy is at the same time learning to see the Background, our stolen integrity/energy/be-ing.

Once we are attuned to the fact of instilled fears and of how they are used to keep women in line, we can detect the patterns over and over again. As we isolate each fear and examine it, we can see that our overcoming it depends upon seeing it in context: seeing through The Whole Thing. Consider, for example, the instilled fear of becoming like one's mother (matrophobia).[33] Repeatedly we find daughters who repudiate the particular kind of victimization they see in their mothers' lives, only to live and die out an apparently opposite but really only slightly variant form of the same dis-ease (for example, the life of a Cosmo Girl as opposed to that of a staid suburban housewife). Embedded fears of being labeled "sick," "selfish," or "sexless" all function in similar ways. If the victim does not see the pattern, she will react to the particulars by becoming mindlessly "normal," murderously "self-less," moronically "sexy." In these various ways, her Self is silenced.

Fear of the label "lesbian" has driven many into matrimony, mental hospitals, and—worst of all—numbing, dumbing normality. It has driven others into heterosexist "gay pride" protests promoted by and for men, into butch-femme matings modeled on matrimony, into aping the genital fixations of porn peddlers, pimps, priests. Lesbians/Spinsters/Amazons/Survivors can defeat the embedded fears only by acknowledging the total context of deception plotted by the male supremacist script-writers. Spinning, A-mazing, Surviving is coming out of the shadows into a fullness of light which reduces the "spotlights" of the fathers' fixations to invisibility/impotence. In her own light the Self sees/says her own light/insight. She sees through the lurid male masturbatory fantasies about made-up "lesbians" who make out in *Playboy* for men's amusement. The Self expels them, together with other embedded "seminal ideas."[34] Images of the macho female prison guard, the "rejected" old maid, the bad mother, the "happy" bunny-bride, the Totaled Woman—all are interconnected implanted fears that can be silenced only when women dare to see the connections among them and to see/name our Selves.

Overcoming the silencing of women is an extreme act, a sequence of extreme acts. Breaking our silence means living in existential courage. It means dis-covering our deep sources, our spring. It means finding our native resiliency, springing into life, speech, action. Many years ago Rachel Carson published her book *Silent Spring*. She was an early prophet foretelling ecological disaster. Her book was greeted with noise and babel but despite the awards and praise, essentially it received the silent treatment. Like the mythic Cassandra, who was cursed by Apollo ("the god of truth") to be disbelieved when she prophesied truth, Rachel Carson, whose credibility was weakened by her sex, was greeted with superficial attention and deep inattentiveness.[35] Ecologists today still deny her recognition, maintaining dishonest silence.[36] Meanwhile the springs are becoming more silent, as the necrophilic leaders of phallotechnic society are carrying out their programs of planned poisoning for all life on the planet.

I am not suggesting that women have a "mission" to save the world from ecological disaster. I am certainly not calling for female Self-sacrifice in the male-led cause of "ecology." I am affirming that those women who have the courage to break the silence within our Selves are finding/creating/spiraling a new Spring. This Spring within and among us makes be-ing possible, and makes the process of integrity possible, for it puts us in touch with the intuition of be-ing which Jan Raymond has called the intuition of integrity.[37] This intuitive, dynamic integrity enables us to begin seeing through the mad reversals which have been our mindbindings. It empowers us to question the sacred and secular "texts" which have numbed our brains by implanting "answers" before we had a chance to question and to quest. Our dis-covery of the Spring within us enables us to begin asking the right questions. There is no other way to begin. The hope which springs when women's deep silence—the silence that breaks us—is broken is the hope of saving our Selves, of delivering our Selves from the Sins of the Fathers and moving on from there. Since this Spring of women's be-ing is powerfully attractive to our own kind (womankind), we communicate it even without trying. Thus by breaking the imposed silence we help to spring other prisoners of patriarchy whose biophilic tendencies have not been completely blighted and blocked.[38] The point is not to save society or to focus on escape (which is backward-looking) but to release the Spring of be-ing. To the inhabitants of Babel, this Spring of living speech will be unintelligible. If it is heard at all, it will be dismissed as mere babble, as the mutterings of mad Crones. So much the better for the Crones' Chorus. Left undisturbed, we are free to find our own concordance, to hear our own harmony, the harmony of the spheres.

## The Purpose, the Method, the Style of This Book

Writing this book is participating in feminist process. This is problematic. For isn't a book by its definition a "thing," an objectification of thinking/imagining/speaking? Here is a book in my hands: fixed, solid. Perhaps—hopefully—its author no longer wholly agrees with it. It is, at least partially, her past. The dilemma of the living/verbing writer is real, but much of the problem resides in the way books are perceived. If they are perceived/used/idolized as Sacred Texts (like the bible or the writings of chairman Mao), then of course the idolators are caught on a wheel that turns but does not move. They "spin" like wheels on ice—a "spinning" that in no way resembles feminist process.

We cannot avoid this static kind of "spinning wheel" by becoming anti-literate, anti-cerebral. "Feminist" anti-intellectualism is a mere reaction against moronizing masculinist education and scholarship, and it is a trap. We need creative crystallizing in the sense of producing works—such as books. Like crystal balls, Glowing Globes, these help us to foretell the future and to dis-cover the past, for they further the process itself by transforming the previously unknown into that which we explicitly know, and therefore can reflect upon, criticize. Thus they spark new visions. This creative crystallizing is a translation of feminist journeying, of our encounters with the unknown, into a chrysalis.[39] This writing/metamorphosing/spinning is itself part of the journey, and the chrysalis—the incarnation of experience in words—is a living, changing reality. It is the transmission of our transitions. Feminist process must become sensible (in actions, speech, works of all kinds) in order to become. The journey requires the courage to create, that we may learn from lucid criticism, that we may re-member the dismembered body of our heritage, that we may stop repeating the same mistakes. Patriarchal erasure of our tradition forces us to relearn what our foresisters knew and to repeat their blunders.

The warped mirror image of creative Hag-ography is standard patriarchal scholarship, which merely re-searches and re-covers "women's history." Insofar as this book is true to its original impulse, it is a written rebuttal of the rite of right re-search. It is part of the metapatriarchal journeying of women. Hopefully, it will not merely "survive" as a thing, a noun, but will spin as a verb, as a gynocentric manifestation of the Intransitive Verb.

Elsewhere I have advocated committing the crime of Methodicide, since the Methodolatry of patriarchal disciplines kills creative thought.[40] The acceptable/unexceptional circular reasonings of academics are caricatures of motion. The "products" are more often than not a set of distorted mirrors, made to seem plausible through the mechanisms of male bonding. On the boundaries of the male-centered universities, however, there is a flowering of woman-centered thinking. Gynocentric Method requires not only the murder of misogynistic methods (intellectual and affective exorcism) but also ecstasy, which I have called *ludic cerebration*. This is "the free play of intuition in our own space, giving rise to thinking that is vigorous, informed, multi-dimensional, independent, creative, tough." It arises from the lived experiences of be-ing. "Be-ing is the verb that says the dimensions of depth in all verbs, such as intuiting, reasoning, loving, imaging, making, acting, as well as the couraging, hoping, and playing that are always there when one is really living."[41]

Gynocentric writing means risking. Since the language and style of patriarchal writing simply cannot contain or carry the energy of women's exorcism and ecstasy, in this book I invent, dis-cover, re-member. At times I make up words (such as *gynaesthesia* for women's synaesthesia). Often I unmask deceptive words by dividing them and employing alternate meanings for prefixes (for example, *re-cover* actually says "cover again"). I also unmask their hidden reversals, often by using less known or "obsolete" meanings (for example, *glamour* as used to name a witch's power). Sometimes I simply invite the reader to listen to words in a different way (for example, *de-light*). When I play with words I do this attentively, deeply, paying attention to etymology, to varied dimensions of meaning, to deep Background meanings and subliminal associations. There are some woman-made words which I choose not to use for various reasons. Sometimes I reject words that I think are inauthentic, obscuring women's existence and masking the conditions of our oppression (for example, *chairperson*).[42] In other cases my choice is a matter of intuitive judgment (for example, my decision not to use *herstory*).[43]

At times I have been conscious of breaking almost into incantations, chants, alliterative lyrics. At such moments the words themselves seem to have a life of their own. They seem to want to break the bonds of conventional usage, to break the silence imposed upon their own Backgrounds. They become palpable, powerful, and it seems that they are tired of allowing me to "use" *them* and cry out for a role reversal.[44] I become *their* mouthpiece, and if I am not always accurate in conveying their meanings, that is probably because I haven't yet learned to listen closely enough, in the realm of the labyrinthine inner ear.

Another delicate area has been the use of pronouns, especially the choice between *we* and *they* to refer to women. Elsewhere I have stressed the importance of the pronoun *we* and avoided the "objective" *they*. Obviously, there are times when the use of *we* would be absurd—for example, when referring to the women of ancient Greece. However, there are other instances when I have to play pronoun usage by ear. As the Journey progresses, and as the extent of the risk of radical feminism becomes more evident, it becomes clear that there are women, including some who would describe themselves as "feminists," with whom I do not feel enough identification to warrant the pronoun *we*. Sometimes, since the ambiguity about whether to use *we* or *they* is not clearly resolvable, there are difficult choices. Since pronouns are profoundly personal and political, they carry powerful messages. Despite the fact that many writers and readers ignore this pronominal power, subliminal clues are transmitted and received. At times my choice of *we* or *they* is a means of realizing my identification with, or separation from, certain roles and behaviors. At other times I use these pronouns interchangeably in reference to the same subject out of a sense of balance which is simply "playing by ear."

My use of capitalization is "irregular," conforming more to my meaning than to standard usage. For example, I consistently capitalize *Spinster*, just as one normally capitalizes *Amazon*. I capitalize *Lesbian* when the word is used in its woman-identified (correct) sense, but use the lower case when referring to the male-distorted version reflected in the media.[45] *Self* is capitalized when I am referring to the authentic center of women's process, while the imposed/internalized false "self," the shell of the Self, is in lower case. In writing of the deep *Background* which is the divine depth of the Self, I capitalize, while the term *foreground*, referring to surface consciousness, generally is not capitalized. I have not created or followed rigid rules about this matter, but simply have tried to convey meaning accurately/forcefully. Thus, when I write *State of Possession*, the capitals are meant to convey that this is not only an individual or internal condition, but a kind of society. At times I choose *not* to capitalize when this would be required by standard usage. The reader will see what I mean when she encounters such an expression as *the patriarchal god* (as contrasted with *The Godfather*). I have no need to consistently capitalize *christian* or *god*, being much more inclined to capitalize *Crone* and *Goddess*. This is obviously a matter not only of "taste" but of evaluation. I generally do not bother to change proper names which are conventionally capitalized. Thus I relegate such cases as the terms *Apollo*, *Christ*, and *Zeus* to their conventional upper cases. One could spend too much energy worrying about such matters. As Gertrude Stein remarked:

> Sometimes one feels that Italians should be with a capital and sometimes with a small letter, one can feel like that about almost anything.[46]

I do not generally put the terms *feminine* and *masculine* in quotation marks. I use both of these terms to refer to roles/stereotypes/sets of characteristics which are essentially distorted and destructive to the Self and to her process and environment.[47] Thus, if the terms *feminine* and *masochist* are used synonymously this has nothing to do with the deep reality of the female Self, but with patriarchally imposed, Self-denying masks.

There is also the matter of the use of sources. The primary sources of this book are women's experiences, past and present. Its secondary sources are male-authored texts from many "fields." I use the latter in various ways. Sometimes I use them to expose their limitations, to display and exorcise their deceptions. Sometimes I use them as springboards. At all times I am acutely aware that most of these books and articles were written at the expense of women, whose energies were drained and ideas freely and shamelessly taken over. The following "acknowledgments" from Edwin Newman's *Strictly Speaking* are slightly more obvious than the average, but convey the typical situation:

> This book is dedicated to my wife and daughter. My wife's contributions have been so many and varied that it is not possible to list them. There would be no book without her. My daughter supplied many suggestions, much encouragement, and through the years, tolerance of my kind of humor above and beyond the call of duty. Jeanette Hopkins provided the impetus for the book and edited it. Carol Bok did the typing and the

> research. To both of them my deep thanks. Mary Heathcote was the invaluable copy editor.[48]

As Andrée Collard has said of male authors: "He not only copies her ideas; he also holds the copy-right."[49] Finally, I must add that in using male sources, at no point have I acted in the position of "disciple" citing an authority. I have tried, righteously, to use the materials available to me under the prevailing conditions, deploring, as scholars should, the necessity for resorting to such secondary re-sources.

## Naming the Enemy

This will of course be called an "anti-male" book. Even the most cautious and circumspect feminist writings are described in this way. The cliché is not only unimaginative but deadeningly, deafeningly, deceptive—making real hearing of what radical feminists are saying difficult, at times even for ourselves. Women and our kind—the earth, the sea, the sky—are the real but unacknowledged objects of attack, victimized as The Enemy of patriarchy—of all its wars, of all its professions. There are feminist works which provide abundant examples of misogynistic statements from authorities in all "fields," in all major societies, throughout the millennia of patriarchy.[50] Feminists have also written at length about the actual rapist behavior of professionals, from soldiers to gynecologists.[51] The "custom" of widow-burning (*suttee*) in India, the Chinese ritual of footbinding, the genital mutilation of young girls in Africa (still practiced in parts of twenty-six countries of Africa), the massacre of women as witches in "Renaissance" Europe, gynocide under the guise of American gynecology and psychotherapy—all are documented facts accessible in the tomes and tombs (libraries) of patriarchal scholarship.[52] The contemporary facts of brutal gang rape, of wife-beating, of overt and subliminal psychic lobotomizing—all are available.[53]

What then can the label *anti-male* possibly mean when applied to works that expose these facts and invite women to free our Selves? The fact is that the labelers do not intend to convey a rational meaning, nor to elicit a thinking process, but rather to block thinking. They do intend the label to carry a deep emotive message, triggering implanted fears of all the fathers and sons, freezing our minds. For to write an "anti-male" book is to utter the ultimate blasphemy.

Thus women continue to be intimidated by the label *anti-male.* Some feel a false need to draw distinctions, for example: "I am anti-patriarchal but not anti-male." The courage to be logical—the courage to name—would require that we admit to ourselves that males and males only are the originators, planners, controllers, and legitimators of patriarchy. Patriarchy is the homeland of males; it is Father Land; and men are its agents. The primary resistance to consciousness of this reality is precisely described in *Sisterhood Is Powerful:* "Thinking that our man is the exception, and, therefore, we are the exception among women."[54] It is in the interest of men (as men in patriarchy perceive their interest) and, in a superficial but Self-destructive way, of many women, to hide this fact, especially from themselves.

The use of the label is an indication of intellectual and moral limitations. Despite all the evidence that women are attacked as projections of The Enemy, the accusers ask sardonically: "Do you really think that *men* are the enemy?" This deception/reversal is so deep that women—even feminists—are intimidated into Self-deception, becoming the only Self-described oppressed who are unable to name their oppressor, referring instead to vague "forces," "roles," "stereotypes," "constraints," "attitudes," "influences." This list could go on. The point is that no agent is named—only abstractions.

The fact is that we live in a profoundly anti-female society, a misogynistic "civilization" in which men collectively victimize women, attacking us as personifications of their own paranoid fears, as The Enemy. Within this society it is men who rape, who sap women's energy, who deny women economic and political power. To allow oneself to know and name these facts is to commit anti-gynocidal acts. Acting in this way, moving through the mazes of the anti-female society, requires naming and overcoming the obstacles constructed by its male agents and token female instruments. As a creative crystallizing of the movement beyond the State of Patriarchal Paralysis, this book is an act of Dis-possession; and hence, in a sense beyond the limitations of the label *anti-male*, it is absolutely Anti-androcrat, A-mazingly Anti-male, Furiously and Finally Female.

## The Chart of This Voyaging/Writing

In traditional accounts (Eastern and Western) of the Otherworld Journey there are gates through which the soul must pass. The soul is obliged to say the correct words in order to pass the wardens at each Passage.[55] I have already suggested that in women's metapatriarchal Otherworld Journeying the wardens are the demonic powers of patriarchy, which assume ghostly forms (that is, are difficult to perceive) and function as noxious gases. Women who are able to name our Selves are thereby empowered to name the demons at each Passage. When we say their names, they—in effect—drop dead. To put it another way, the gases drop down (condense) into a merely messy puddle.

These warden-demons can be seen as personifications of the Eight Deadly Sins of the Fathers. It is significant that in the traditional listing of the "Deadly Sins," Deception is not usually named. This nonnaming is an indicator of the pervasive deceptiveness of male-constructed "morality," which does not name its own primary Deadly Sin. Deception is in fact all-pervasive. It keeps us running in senseless circles. It sedates and seduces our Selves, freezing and fixing Female Process, enabling the fathers to feed upon women's stolen energy. The Paternal Parasites hide their vampirizing of female energy by deceptive posturing, which takes the form of Processions (religious, military, judicial, academic, etc.).

For this reason, I choose to use the term *Processions* to name the deception of the fathers. At every turn, the Voyagers of this book encounter Processions of Demons wearing multiform masks. We exorcise them, expelling their deceptions from our minds, ousting these obstacles to our Ecstatic Process. Processions both display and disguise the Deadly Sins of the Fathers. The deception they engender glues the Sins into conglomerates, reversing them, re-presenting them as Virtues.

The following list, which not accidentally may resemble a sort of incantation, is a new naming of the Eight Deadly Sins of the Fathers. Although any listing is necessarily linear, it is clear that these malfunctions (Male-Functions) are interconnected, that they feed into each other.

*Processions*

The basic Sin of Phallocracy is *deception*—the destruction of process through patriarchal processions, which are frozen mirror images of Spinning Process.

*Professions*
Deadly *pride* is epitomized in patriarchal professions, which condense the process of know-ing into an inert and mystifying thing ("body of knowledge").

*Possession*
Androcratic *avarice* is demonic possession of female spirit and energy, accomplished not only through political and economic means, but, more deeply, through male myth.

*Aggression*
The malevolence of male violence (which is, in fact, usually dispassionate) is misnamed *anger*, masking the fact that women are The Enemy against whom all patriarchal wars are waged, and muting righteous female anger.

*Obsession*
Male *lust* specializes in genital fixation and fetishism, reflecting a broken integrity of consciousness, generating masculine and feminine role constructs legitimated by sadospiritual religion.

*Assimilation*
Gynocidal *gluttony* expresses itself in vampirism/cannibalism—feeding upon the *living* flesh, blood, spirit of women, while tokenism disguises the devastation of the victims.

*Elimination*
Misogynist *envy* tends inherently toward the elimination of all Self-identified women, accomplishing this end through the re-conception/re-forming of some women into Athena-like accomplices.

*Fragmentation*
Patriarchal *sloth* has enslaved women, whose creativity is confined by mandatory menial labor and by deceptively glorified subservient social activities, resulting in "busy" and enforced feminine sloth.

Each of these Sins of the Fathers is more than a sum of abstractions. Each is incarnated in the institutions of patriarchy and in those who invent, control, and legitimate these institutions. Thus women's journey of Self-centering becoming, passing through the "gates of god" which block us from our own Background, means confronting these deceptive incarnations/demons, naming them and naming their games.

Our Journeying past these watchful wardens is not linear. A-mazing their mazes involves spinning through them, at multiple times in multiple ways. Since their names are legion, there is not one simple once-and-for-all name for the demons. Their lecherous litanies are like passages of Unholy Scripture which they repeat over and over again, and which have many levels of deception, not perceptible all at once. They become more perceptible as we learn to name our Selves, become our Selves, more adequately. Concomitant with the a-mazing struggle, which is exorcism, is the ecstatic process of Spinsters dis-covering the labyrinth of our own unfolding/becoming. Passing through the male-made mazes is not simply a preliminary lap of the journey. It makes way for and accompanies the Ecstatic Labyrinthine Journey of Survivors.

In this book I will chart/describe this a-mazing and spinning voyage. That is, I will write about fundamental "blind alleys" of the masters' maze, which hide the Passages of the Labyrinthine Way of Ecstasy. I will be concerned with dis-covering the fathers' Processions and with breaking away from them. The Voyage will involve encounters with the other seven Deadly Sins/Demons as well. These encounters are re-current and in random order, as the Demons appear and re-appear at various points, attempting to block our way.

The Voyage of this book moves through three Passages. As the terrain changes so also does the style of the explorer, her movement, her language. In The First Passage there is an exuberance of dis-covery as the Voyager breaks through the barriers of obsolete myths which block vision. There is the constant surprise of seeing what is on the other side of the hill and on all sides as the scope of vision broadens and deepens.

In The Second Passage there is a soberness and focused attention as the Explorer encounters the Unnatural Enemies of Female Be-ing in their multiple postures of Indecent Exposure. There is a focused intensity as she marks the snares laid by the deadly game trappers, analyzing the archetypal atrocities in order to unmask the lethal intent of the death dealers.

In The Third Passage, having perceived the *intent* of the gynocidal gamesters, she moves deeper into the Otherworld—which is her own time/space. Her style reflects her new-found capacity to recognize their intent in its seemingly innocent and chillingly familiar manifestations (their chivalry, their help, their care, their art, their romance, their respect, their rewards, their blessings, their love).[56] This new knowing—

her Beatific Vision—encourages her to invent new modes of Be-ing/ Speaking, which are Spooking, Sparking, Spinning.

My charting and describing are inspired by many foresisters. Since all who have embarked on this journey are "contemporaries" in the only sense that matters, the century or span of decades measured by patriarchal time in which "his" history places each of us is far less relevant than our own network of communication. All women who define our own living, defying the deception of patriarchal history, are journeying. We belong to the same time and we are foresisters to each other.

Here, in this volume, my charting and describing is inspired in a particular way by the words of one foresister, Virginia Woolf, who in her profoundly anti-patriarchal book, *Three Guineas*, asks:

> What are these ceremonies and why should we take part in them? What are these professions and why should we make money out of them? Where, in short, is it leading us, the procession of the sons of educated men?[57]

In this prophetic book, published in the 1930s, she shows connections among the absurd professional processions, displaying their deception, their morbidity and meaninglessness. She advises us to "break the ring, the vicious circle, the dance round and round the mulberry tree, the poison tree of intellectual harlotry."[58] The circle of processions and of professions is linked to possession. Of women's dilemma, she writes:

> Behind us lies the patriarchal system; the private house, with its nullity, its immorality, its hypocrisy, its servility. Before us lies the public world, the professional system, with its possessiveness, its jealousy, its pugnacity, its greed. The one shuts us up like slaves in a harem; the other forces us to circle, like caterpillars head to tail, round and round the mulberry tree, the sacred tree, of property. It is a choice of evils. Each is bad.[59]

Yes, and each is part of the *same* system of patriarchal possession, whose primary property is female life.

The writing/journeying of this book passes/spins through the phallocratic maze. Yet the Other side of this Otherworld Journeying is discovered at every turn. This is the ecstatic side. It involves speaking in various modes: Spooking, Sparking, Spinning. Although there is no "one-to-one" correlation between the exorcising and the ecstatic movements, there is a kind of moving pattern, a spiraling of counterpoints, a harmony of hearing and speaking. Our acts of exorcising are Rites of Passage, by which we win the rights of passage.

In the process of encountering and naming the Male-Factors who freeze process into processions, hoard knowing within professions, and kill creativity by possession, I point out clues which, as they are recognized, disclose the living process which has been hidden, caricatured, captured, stunted, but never completely killed by the phallocentric Sins. These clues point to a force which is beyond, behind, beneath the patriarchal death march—an unquenchable gynergy. They serve as raw material for a process of alchemy. We transmute the base metals of man-made myth by becoming unmute, calling forth from our Selves and each other the courage to name the un-nameable.

15

# Secular S and M

From chapter 2 of *Gyn/Ecology*, pp. 93–96.

*Sado-Ritual Syndrome:* a set of interconnected components of sado-rituals which, when Dis-covered, can be seen by Searchers as links among seemingly unrelated atrocities, such as witchburnings, gynecological practices, lynchings, pogroms, nuclear arms buildup, the exploitation and torture of animals.
—*Wickedary*, p. 94

This short excerpt shows Daly at her most critical, but also shows the scope of the patriarchal mindset she opposed. Most shocking—to her, to her readers, and to her future audience—would be the revelations about Paul Tillich's indulgence in sadistic pornography, a fact exposed by his wife, Hannah Tillich. Given Daly's earlier extensive use of Tillich's thought and work, this revelation came as affirmation of the universal nature of the cruelty of the patriarchal mind. Linda Barufaldi, one of the editors, recalls that when she first read Hannah Tillich's *From Time to Time*, she thought that his pornographic exploits proved that "We feminists were not making this up."

Aside from the shock, though, of Tillich's pornographic understanding of the cross, Daly placed this incident among a set of appalling instances of sado-masochistic torture: from the Rolling Stones to the Nazi death camps, from early modern torture of heretics to the impregnation of the Virgin Mary, from contemporary hospitals to the torture of political prisoners. Far from being a vindictive strike against a former inspiration, her inclusion of Tillich's pornographic imagination here dramatically revealed the scope of patriarchy.
—Editors

In christendom as well as in postchristian secular society, the words/expressions of female spirit are raped, twisted, tortured, dismembered. From the witch trials, brought about by the bonding of theologians and legal specialists, to the Hearst trial, effected by the bonding of secular theologians (psychiatrists) and attorneys, the dis-spiriting process is essentially the same. Whereas the christian cross glorified suffering as a means to purification and ultimate joy in the "Afterlife," the contemporary secular sadomasochistic gospel proclaims that female suffering *is* joy. Thus even the agony of Patricia Hearst was perceived by many as "a rich girl getting her kicks."

A Rolling Stones billboard atop Sunset Strip in Los Angeles in 1976 depicted a woman with hands tied together and legs tied spread apart, accompanied by the words, "I'm 'Black and Blue' from the Rolling Stones—and I love it!" The anonymous authors of a 1977 *Time* article entitled "Really Socking It to Women" paternally discusses some gimmicks of "kings of kink" who admittedly seek revenge against women. With Timely detachment they write of the men who shoot photos of women mutilating themselves, and describes the men who design albums with pictures of women chained, women hanged, women gang-raped. Predictably, they find a woman psychiatrist who is willing to claim that all of this corresponds to masochistic fantasies of independent women.[1] Thus the rape of female mind/will, the message of the Virgin Mary's impregnation by the holy ghost, is repeated and completed in the "joyful" secular S and M resurrection of the torture cross.

I suggest that theologians have always fantasized a female hanging on the cross. Hannah Tillich, in her lucid autobiography, *From Time to Time*, describes the pornographic exploits of her husband, Paul Tillich, the famous theologian. She describes entering his room during his showing of a porn film for his own private entertainment:

> There was the familiar cross shooting up the wall. . . . A naked girl hung on it, hands tied in front of her private parts. . . . More and more crosses appeared, all with women tied and exposed in various positions. Some were exposed from the front, some from the side, some from behind, some crouched in fetal position, some head down, or legs apart, or legs crossed—and always whips, crosses, whips.[2]

Tillich was not atypical. He simply had a wife who was determined to publish the truth after his death, despite all the attempts of theologians, psychologists such as Rollo May, and other "friends" at first to stop her and later to discredit her.[3] His private life and fantasies reflected the essential symbolic content of his and other theologians' christology. Indeed, these sadomasochistic fantasies were the juice/sap of his impressive theologizing. Hannah, who after his death unlocked his drawers (supposed to contain his "spiritual harvest"), found the details of his sex-obsessed life:

> All the girls' photos fell out, letters and poems, passionate appeal and disgust. I was tempted to place between the sacred pages of his highly esteemed lifework those obscene signs of the real life that he had transformed into the gold of abstraction—King Midas of the spirit.[4]

Hannah Tillich thus helps to place the high symbolism and abstract rationalizations of christian theology of the cross in realistic perspective.

Torture for "higher causes," religious and secular has always been legitimated by christian cross-bearers. In the fifteenth century witchcraft was defined as *crimen exceptum*, removing all legal limits to torture. Thus it is not surprising that the secular sadomasochistic society which has descended from christianity by no means restricts its brutality to the realm of advertising, pornographic films, and kinky sex orgies. There is abundant evidence that systematic torture of political prisoners is carried on by many—probably most—governments. Here the rationalization is not "joy in sex" but something like "national security." In the 1970s, Amnesty International, an organization devoted to the release of all political prisoners in the world, reported evidence that brutal political torture is a worldwide practice. While this reality is not new, and while the evidence of the horrors of the Nazi death camps and of American torture of Vietnamese is easily available, it is important to see this in the context of the superrefinement and simultaneous coarsening of postchristian secular extensions of christian myth.[5]

Considering the horrors of the torture of heretics and witches in the beginnings of the patriarchal "modern" period, it would appear that the application of torture cross mythology could hardly get coarser. It does, in the sense that coarsening blends with superrefinement of technique. The most hideous/harsh/coarse torture is carried out with the sophisticated techniques of modern medicine, including "life-prolonging" machines and a variety of pharmacological means also used in hospitals. Indeed, the sadistic methods used in the Nazi death camps, in contemporary political prisons, and in hospitals, including "mental hospitals," bear striking resemblances to each other.[6] Each of these subcultures of sadism has its own hierarchy, apprenticeship, initiation rites, and its own language. The subculture of torture in Brazil is a bizarre example, with its "parrot swings," its "dragon chair," its "spiritual seance," and its "advanced school of torture."[7] Moreover, women have a special role in these subcultures as subservient token torturers of other women. The "bitch of Buchenwald" and female torturers of female political prisoners in such countries as Argentina are illustrations of this traitor-token syndrome.

My point here is not that the sadosymbolism of christianity is the unique source for worldwide S and M. Sadomasochism is the style and basic content of patriarchy's structures, including those antecedent to and outside christianity. Rather, christianity, with its torture cross symbolism, has been one expression of this basic pattern. I am contending, however, that within Western culture this symbolism has provided legitimation and impetus for subsequent refinements/coarsenings of sadomasochism. Virtually all of modern patriarchal society has been influenced/shaped profoundly by the West, becoming a sort of Total Westworld. Thus, the ever more deceptively refined/coarsened/extended tentacles of the torture cross syndrome pervade the planet.

16

# African Genital Mutilation

## *The Unspeakable Atrocities*

Chapter 5 of *Gyn/Ecology*, pp. 153–77.

*sado-rituals:* rituals which recreate and reinforce the primordial patriarchal mythic event—the murder/dismemberment of the Goddess within women and all be-ing; rituals devised to accomplish and legitimate the dis-spiriting and devastation of the Wild; rituals designed to destroy the integrity of Life and creative divine powers in women.
—*Wickedary*, p. 94

This chapter is included in its totality because of the ongoing debates concerning genital mutilation, and the controversies surrounding *Gyn/Ecology* at the time of its publication. The atrocities described in this chapter are difficult to read, but they are much more difficult to endure. While some have re-termed this practice "genital modification," it would be Daly's position that this distorts and masks the cruelties of the practice.

Daly's methods and sources in the chapters she names "The Second Passage"—detailing patriarchal practices such as widow-burning, footbinding, and the development of American gynecology—have been critiqued by numerous feminists as not exhibiting scholarly rigor, or due suspicion of colonial sources. Daly's defense was always to focus ethical anger and outrage at the practices themselves rather than to be worried about methods and sources in the face of these crimes.

Audre Lorde's famous "Open Letter to Mary Daly" largely concerned this very chapter; Lorde accused Daly of portraying African women only as token torturers. While the "Open Letter" has become a staple in anthologies in women's studies, the full text of Daly's chapter has not been widely read. Whatever the merits of Lorde's argument, or Daly's responses, the reader owes it to herself to read the original documents. For more on the controversy with Lorde, see chapter 44 in this volume.

Daly's deepest contention—and insight—concerned the universal nature of patriarchy. What is happening in the case of African genital mutilation is happening everywhere under patriarchy:

> Erasure of all this on the global level occurs when leaders of "advanced" countries and of international organizations overlook these horrors in the name of "avoiding cultural judgment." They are free of responsibility and blame, for the "custom" must be respected as part of a "different tradition." By so naming the tradition as "different" they hide the cross-cultural hatred of women.

When Daly spoke of this "cross-cultural hatred of women," she meant that women have been denied the ability to define themselves as autonomous beings. One key aspect of this erasure of women's selves drew forth an explicit comparison later in the Second Passage: the removal of the clitoris in both African genital mutilation and American gynecology. As Daly pointed out, this "removal of her specifically *female*-identified organ, which is not necessary for the male's pleasure or for reproductive servitude," is the means by which, in an androcentric society, one "becomes a woman."[1]

Another issue that has caused Daly to be widely criticized, concerning transgender people, appears here in the footnotes. Daly's position is best understood in its historical context. At that time very few people knew much about the trans world; there weren't many visible or known transfolk at the time. It was also a time in the movement when male-to-female transgenders were experienced by many lesbian-feminists as reluctant to surrender male privilege. That was a long time ago, and much has changed.

—Editors

Have you ever risen in the night
bursting with knowledge and the world
dissolves toward any listening ear
into which you can pour

whatever it was you knew
before waking
Only to find all ears asleep
or drugged perhaps by a dream of words
because as you scream into them over and over
nothing stirs
and the mind you have reached is not a working mind
please hang up and die again? The mind
you have reached is not a working mind
Please hang up
And die again.
—Audre Lorde, from "A Sewerplant Grows in Harlem,
or I'm a Stranger Here Myself When Does the Next Swan
Leave," *New York Head Shop and Museum*

If a woman ignores these wrongs, then may women as a sex continue to suffer them; there is no help for any of us—let us be dumb and die.
—Elizabeth Barrett Browning, *Letters of Elizabeth Barrett Browning*

I have gained many sisters.
And if one is beaten,
or raped, or killed,
I will not come in mourning black.
I will not pick the right flowers.
I will not celebrate her death
& it will matter not
if she's Black or white—
if she loves women or men.
I will come with my many sisters
and decorate the streets
with the innards of those
brothers in womenslaughter.
No more can I dull my rage
in alcohol & deference
to *men's* courts

I will come to my sisters,
not dutiful,
I will come strong.
—Pat Parker, from "Womanslaughter," *Womanslaughter*

There are some manifestations of the Sado-Ritual Syndrome that are unspeakable—incapable of being expressed in words because inexpressibly horrible.[2] Such are the ritual genital mutilations—excision and infibulation—still inflicted upon women throughout Africa today, and practiced in many parts of the world in the past.[3] These ritualized atrocities are unspeakable also in a second sense; that is, there are strong taboos against saying/writing the truth about them, against *naming* them. These taboos are operative both within the segments of phallocracy in which such rituals are practiced and in other parts of the Fatherland, whose leaders cooperate in the conspiracy of silence. Hags see that the demonic rituals in the so-called underdeveloped regions of the planet are deeply connected with atrocities perpetrated against women in "advanced" societies. To allow ourselves to see the connections is to begin to understand that androcracy is the State of Atrocity, where atrocities are normal, ritualized, repeated.[4] It is the City of Atrophy in which the archetypal trophies are massacred women.

Those who have endured the unspeakable atrocities of genital mutilation have in most cases been effectively silenced. Indeed this profound silencing of the mind's imaginative and critical powers is one basic function of the sado-ritual, which teaches women never to forget to murder their own divinity. Those who physically survive these atrocities "live" their entire lifetimes, from early childhood or from puberty, preoccupied by pain. Those women who inhabit other parts of the planet cannot really wish to imagine the condition of their mutilated sisters, for the burden of knowing is heavy. It is heavy not merely because of the differences in conditions, but especially because of similarities which, as I will show later in this Passage, increase with the march of progress of phallotechnology.

The maze of lies and silences surrounding the genital mutilation still forced upon millions of young girls in many African countries continues to be effective. Yet it is becoming the subject of increasingly widespread attention.[5] Fran P. Hosken presents the following important definitions of the practices usually lumped under the vague and misleading expression, "female circumcision":

1. Sunna Circumcision: removal of the prepuce and/or tip of the clitoris.
2. Excision or Clitoridectomy: excision of the entire clitoris with the labia minora and some or most of the external genitalia.
3. Excision and Infibulation (Pharaonic Circumcision): This means excision of the entire clitoris, labia minora and parts of the labia majora. The two sides of the vulva are then fastened together in some way either by thorns . . . or sewing with catgut. Alternatively the vulva are scraped raw and the child's limbs are tied together for several weeks until the wound heals (or she dies). The purpose is to close the vaginal orifice. Only a small opening is left (usually by inserting a slither of wood) so the urine and later the menstrual blood can be passed.[6]

It should not be imagined that the horror of the life of an infibulated child/woman ends with this operation. Her legs are tied together, immobilizing her for weeks, during which time excrement remains within the bandage. Sometimes accidents occur during the operation: the bladder may be pierced or the rectum cut open. Sometimes in a spasm of agony the child bites off her tongue. Infections are, needless to say, common. Scholars such as Lantier claim that death is not a very common immediate effect of the operation, but often there are complications which leave the women debilitated for the rest of their lives.[7] No statistics are available on this point. What is certain is that the infibulated girl is mutilated and that she can look forward to a life of repeated encounters with "the little knife"—the instrument of her perpetual torture. For women who are infibulated have to be cut open—either by the husband or by another woman—to permit intercourse. They have to be cut open further for delivery of a child. Often they are sewn up again after delivery, depending upon the decision of the husband. The cutting (defibulation) and re-sewing goes on throughout a woman's living death of reproductive "life."[8] Immediate medical results of excision and infibulation include "hemorrhage, infections, shock, retention of urine, damage to adjacent tissues, dermoid cysts, abscesses, keloid scarring, coital difficulties, and infertility caused by chronic pelvic infections."[9] In addition, we should consider the psychological maiming caused by this torture.

Yet this is an "unmentionable" manifestation of the atrocity which is phallocracy. The World Health Organization has refused for many years to concern itself with the problem. When it was asked in 1958 to study this problem it took the position that such operations were based on "social and cultural backgrounds" and were outside its competence. This basic attitude has not changed.[10] There has been a conspiracy of silence:

> International agencies, the U.N. and U.N. agencies, especially the WHO and UNICEF (both devoted to health care), development agencies (such as U.S. Agency for International Development), non-governmental organizations working in Africa, missionaries and church groups concerned with health care, also women's organizations including World Association of Girl Guides and Girl Scouts, Y.W.C.A., and the Associated Country Women of the World, and others working in Africa, all know what is going on. Or they have people in Africa who know. This quite aside from the Health Departments and hospitals in African countries and the M.D.s, especially gynecologists, who get the most desperate cases. . . . The doctors know all. But they don't speak.[11]

It is important to ask why such a variety of organizations and professions have other priorities. Why do "educated" persons babble about the importance of "tribal coherence" and "tradition" while closing their eyes to the physical reality of mutilation? We might well ask why "female circumcision" was reinforced in Kenya after "liberation" and described by President Kenyatta, in his book *Facing Mount Kenya*, as an important "custom" for the benefit of "the people."[12] Hosken maintains that in the socialist countries in Africa clitoridectomy and infibulation are practiced on a vast scale without comment from the governments or health departments. Again, one must ask why. Why do anthropologists ignore or minimize this horror? Why is it that the catholic church has not taken a clear position against this genital mutilation (which is practiced upon some of its own members in Africa)? Why do some African leaders educated in the West continue to insist upon the maiming of their own daughters?

These questions are profoundly interconnected. The appearance of disparateness among these groups and of their responses (or nonresponses) masks their essential sameness. Even the above-named organizations whose membership is largely female are androcratic since they are willing to participate in the conspiracy of silence. Socialists, catholics, liberal reformers, population planners, politicos of all persuasions—all have purposes which have nothing to do with women's specific well-being unless this happens to fit into the "wider" aims.

## I

The components of the Sado-Ritual Syndrome are present in African excision and infibulation. The obsession with purity is evident. The clitoris is "impure" because it does not serve male purposes. It has no necessary function in reproduction. As Benoîte Groult points out, hatred of the clitoris is almost universal, for this organ is strictly female, for women's pleasure.[13] Thus it is by nature "impure," and the logical conclusion, acted out by the tribes that practice excision and infibulation, is purification of women by its removal. Furthermore, it is believed that excision encourages fidelity, that is, moral "purity," for there is a "decrease in sensitivity from the operation."[14] The term *decrease*, here, is a euphemism for *loss*. These women have been de-sensitized, "purified" of the capacity for sexual pleasure. The ideology among some African tribes which explains and justifies this brutal robbing from women of their clitoris—the purely female organ—displays the total irony of the concept of purity. There is a widespread belief among the Bambaras and the Dogons from Mali that all persons are hermaphroditic and that this condition is cured by circumcision and excision. Since they believe the boy is female by virtue of his foreskin and the girl is male by her clitoris, the sexes are purified (that is, officially distinguished) by the rites of puberty. Thus the removal of the purely female clitoris is seen as making a woman purely female. In fact, its purpose is to make her purely feminine, a purely abject object.

Infibulation goes even further, displaying yet other dimensions of the androcratic obsession with purity. For the "sewn women" are not only deprived of the organ of pleasure. Their masters have them genitally "sewn up," in order to preserve and redesign them strictly for their own pleasure and reproductive purposes. These women are 100 percent pure because 100 percent enslaved. Their perpetual pain (or the imminent threat of this) is an important condition for their perpetual purity, for pain preoccupies minds, emotions, imaginations, sensations, prohibiting presence of the Self.

## II

The second component of the syndrome, erasure of male responsibility, is present by virtue of male absence at the execution of the mutilation. In most cases, it is not males who perform the brutal operation, although male nurses and surgeons now do it in some modern hospitals.[15] Moreover, there are comforting myths, ideologies, and clichés which assure political leaders and other males that they are blame-free. Together with the hermaphroditic myth, described above, there is the justification that "this is a way of teaching women to endure pain." There is also the belief among the Bambaras that a man who sleeps with a nonexcised woman risks death from her "sting" (clitoris). The Mossis believe that the clitoris kills children at birth and that it can be a source of impotence among men. A basic belief that justifies all, erasing all responsibility, is of course that these rites keep women faithful.[16] What is erased is the fact that these "faithful" wives have been physically reconstructed for male purposes. They have been deprived of their own sexuality and "tightened up" for their masters' pleasure—tightened through devices like wounding and sewing and through the tension of excruciating pain.[17] Erasure of all this on the global level occurs when leaders of "advanced" countries and of international organizations overlook these horrors in the name of "avoiding cultural judgment." They are free of responsibility and blame, for the "custom" must be respected as part of a "different tradition." By so naming the tradition as "different" they hide the cross-cultural hatred of women.

## III

The massive spread of female genital mutilation throughout Africa has been noted by responsible Searchers. Accurate statistics are impossible to obtain, since the operation is usually performed in secret. Nevertheless the ritual, which is of ancient origin, is known to be widespread from Algeria in the north to the Central African Republic in the south, and from Senegal and Mauritania in the west to Somalia in the east.[18] Doctors working in Africa are in a position to know what is going on, since women suffering from complications connected with the operations are sometimes brought to them. Two physicians have given lists of countries in which female genital mutilation, in one form or another, is still practiced.[19] Fran Hosken, using these and other sources, and relying also upon her own personal investigations, concludes that some form of female circumcision is probably practiced in all countries of Africa today in at least some tribal groups.[20] Hosken believes that the practice started historically in Africa and was taken on by Arab conquerors and later islam.[21] Ashley Montagu maintains that infibulation and the successive operation—defibulation—are practiced among some Indian tribes in Peru and possibly elsewhere in South and Central America.[22] Montagu also holds that genital mutilation is still practiced in Australia.[23] It will require a massive effort to obtain detailed and accurate information. One point is certain: this ritual spread rapidly over a large geographical area, involving the torture and maiming of millions of women, condemning them to a living death, deadening the divine spark of be-ing, the Goddess within.[24]

In discussing the phenomenon of the spread of sado-rituals, in the "cases" of Indian *suttee* and Chinese footbinding, I have shown that there is a pattern of proliferation from an elite to the upwardly aspiring lower echelons of society. The case can be argued that this pattern has also existed in female genital mutilation. According to Strabo's *Geography*, Pharaonic Egypt was characterized by clitoral excision, meaning the cutting off of sections of the clitoris and of the labia minora.[25] Inspection of royal female mummies has led some authorities to conclude that these high-caste women of Egypt had been excised. Huelsman claims that in ancient Egypt, female genital surgery was performed between the ages of fourteen and fifteen years. He remarks brightly that "it seems probable that even the amorous adventures of Cleopatra may have been conducted *sans* clitoris."[26] Shandall suggests that genital surgery on ancient Egyptian women was limited to the female relatives of rulers and priests. He speculates that women from these social and economic classes may not have been able to inherit property unless they had first undergone some form of genital surgery.

Indeed, a large number of Pharaonically circumcised mummies have been discovered.[27] Since the privileged classes were mummified, it would appear that excision was a feature of female life among the royalty. Benoîte Groult claims that the mummies of both Cleopatra and Nefertiti lack clitorises.[28] Although Ashley Montagu seems to think that all girls in ancient Egypt were excised, there really is not much evidence to back this up.[29] The evidence points to the existence of rites of passage involving genital mutilation of upper-class girls. Since we know that at the present time it is practiced upon girls at all levels of society among many African tribes (and most likely in other parts of the globe)[30] it is logical to think that it did spread from royalty to lower strata of society, as well as expanding outward geographically. The spread of this atrocity was condoned, legitimated, demanded by the World Religion which is patriarchy. Although such sects as islam and christianity did not invent it, neither did they effectively stop it. More ancient than islam, it was practiced by pre-islamic Arabs. The "custom" was prevalent in widespread areas of the globe, in Aboriginal Australia, South America, India, Pakistan. Today it still massacres the bodies and spirits of millions of women in Africa, women living in poverty, far removed from the palatial splendors that surrounded Cleopatra and other royal victims of sado-ritual.

## IV

The use of women as token torturers is horribly illustrated in this ritual. At the International Tribunal on Crimes Against Women the testimony of a woman from Guinea was brought by a group of French women. The witness described seeing "the savage mutilation called excision that is inflicted on the women of my country between the ages of 10 and 12." In the instance she describes, which she saw with her own eyes, six women were holding down the victim, intoning prayers to drown her screams:

> The operation was done without any anesthetic, with no regard for hygiene or precautions of any sort. With the broken neck of a bottle, the old woman banged hard down, cutting into the upper part of my friend's genitals so as to make as wide a cut as possible, since "an incomplete excision does not constitute a sufficient guarantee against profligacy in girls."

> The blunt glass of the bottle did not cut deeply enough into my friend's genitals and the exciseuse had to do it several more times.
>
> . . . When the clitoris had been ripped out, the women howled with joy, and forced my friend to get up despite a streaming hemorrhage, to parade her through the town.[31]

The witness goes on to describe the "parade," in which the mutilated girl, dressed in a loin-cloth, her breasts bare, is followed by a dozen or so women singing:

> They were informing the village that my friend was ready for marriage. In Guinea, in fact, no man marries a woman who has not been excised and who is not a virgin, with rare exceptions.

This last sentence unmasks the male-centeredness of the entire ritual. It is men who demand this female castration, and possession in marriage is required in *their* society for survival. The apparently "active" role of the women, themselves mutilated, is in fact a passive, instrumental role. It hides the real castrators of women. Mentally castrated,[32] these women participate in the destruction of their own kind—of womankind—and in the destruction of strength and bonding among women. The screaming token torturers are silencing not only the victim, but their own victimized Selves. Their screams are the "sounds of silence" imposed upon women in sado-ritual.

The extent to which female token torturers have been used to mask the male master-minds of female genital mutilation is suggested in an account given by Montagu of female infibulation as practiced among tribes immediately south of the First Cataract of the Nile. Part of the procedure involves a visit to the bridegroom before the marriage by one of the women who performs the infibulation. The purpose of the visit is to obtain exact measurements of his "member." The following activity ensues:

> She then makes to measurement, a sort of phallus of clay or wood and by its aid she incises the scar for a certain distance and leaves the instrument wrapped round with a rag—in the wound in order to keep the edges from adhering again.[33]

Thus the master has his bride made to order to suit his "member." Montagu gives a similar account of a ceremony that was practiced among the Conibos of the Rio Ucalayi of Peru. He first describes the incision. Then:

> The old sorcerers rubbed some medical herbs into the bleeding parts, and after a while introduced an artificial penis, made of clay, into the vagina of the maiden, the thing being exactly the same size as the penis of the man betrothed to her. Thereafter she was considered properly prepared to marry, and was given over to her future husband.[34]

Again, the master is assured of a snug and pleasurable fit. The fact that "women did it—and still do it—to women" must be seen in this context. The idea that such procedures, or any part of them, could be woman-originated is only thinkable in the mind-set of phallocracy, for it is, in fact, unthinkable.[35] The use of women to do the dirty work can make it appear thinkable only to those who do not wish to see. Yet this use of women does effectively blunt the power of sisterhood, having first blocked the power of the Self.

Most horrifying is the fact that mothers insist that this mutilation be done to their own daughters. Frequently it is the mother who performs the brutal operation. Among the Somalis, for example, the mother does the excising, slicing, and final infibulation according to the time-honored rules. She does this in such a way as to leave the tiniest opening possible. Her "honor" depends upon making this as small as possible, because the smaller this artificial aperture is, the higher the value of the girl.[36]

An indication of the strength of the stranglehold which tradition has upon the mother-daughter relationship is the fact that some women who by academic and professional standards would be considered educated also insist upon excision. The case is cited of a young Egyptian woman physician who was expecting a baby and was asked by a Danish scholar, Henny Harald Hansen, about the reasons for these mutilations. She informed him that "if the child she was expecting should be a girl she would circumcise her herself." The young woman gave several reasons. The first was religious: she was a muslim. The second was cosmetic: she wanted "to remove something disfiguring, ugly and repulsive." Third, the girl should be protected from sexual stimulation through the clitoris. The fourth reason was tradition. "The young doctor argued in support of her intention to respect tradition that the majority of husbands preferred their wives to be circumcised."[37] The fact that this woman was a physician might at first seem startling. Yet further reflection suggests that there is not such inconsistency as one might suppose, particularly in view of the facts of gynecological mutilation in present-day America, which will be discussed later in this Passage.

## V

The fifth component of the syndrome, compulsive orderliness which misfocuses attention away from the fact of evil, is manifested even in the most primitive environment. Although the "surgical instrument" may be as crude as broken glass or a kitchen knife, the performance is itself highly ritualized. The "ceremony" in the Sudan is described by Montagu as "preceded with food and merriment."[38] Certain women are chosen to perform the rite. Often it is a relative who does the excising. The procedures differ among different tribes, but they always follow certain rules that have been handed down, which constitute "the way it has always been done." Thus, among the Nandi in Africa, there is a two-part horror show. The first day, stinging nettles are applied to the clitoris, so that it swells and becomes unimaginably large. The second day, an old woman chars it off with glowing coals. The mutilated girl is then sent to a convalescent hut, having been converted into property for her husband.[39] Another manifestation of the ritualized orderliness is the age of the victims: The mutilating rite takes place at different ages in different tribes, but the point is that each has its prescribed age, which often does not correspond to the individual girl's onset of puberty. It is claimed that some Arabs do it several weeks after birth, that the Somalis fix the age of mutilation at 3–4 years, that in southern Egypt it is done at 9–10 years, that in Abyssinia it is at 8 years or else 80 days after birth. Among the Malinkes and Bambaras the age is 12–15 years.[40] All of this indicates that the order imposed is the contrived order of ritual, having nothing to do with the physiological stage of development.

There are various ritual prescriptions in various places, but the obsessive repetitiveness and fixation upon minute details are clearly present.

Thus, van Gennep describes some details of the ritual among the Masai of Tanganyika:

> The rites for the girls differ [from the boys'] in the following respects: several are excised at a time; their heads are shaved; they remain at home until scar tissue forms on the wound; they adorn their heads with grasses, among which they place an ostrich feather, and smear their faces with white clay; all of the women of the kraal eat a communal meal; and the marriage takes place as soon as the fiancé is able to pay what he owes on the dowry.[41]

Other tribes have other versions of this sado-ritual.[42] There are rules for the stages in the mutilation process, rules about festivity, about timing, about dress and "cosmetics," about seclusion, about relation of the maiming to marriage. These distract the attention of the participants (and of foreign specialists such as anthropologists) from the victimized women's physical agony, mutilation, life-long deprivation, deformity, pain, and premature death from complications.

## VI

The sado-ritual of excision and infibulation bestows acceptability upon gynocidal behavior—even to the extent of making it normative. This is illustrated in the precept of the president of Kenya, Jomo Kenyatta, that "no proper Gikuyu would dream of marrying a girl who has not been circumcised," since this operation "is regarded as the *conditio sine qua non* for the whole teaching of tribal law, religion, and morality."[43] With these words, one chief in the Higher Order of phallocratic morality dictates its chief lesson: that women should suffer. Typically, the justification for the atrocious ritual under the reign of phallic morality involves a reversal in which the unnatural becomes normative. Only a mutilated woman is considered 100 percent feminine.[44] By removal of her specifically *female*-identified organ, which is not necessary for the male's pleasure or for reproductive servitude, she "becomes a woman." At first the reversal might seem astonishing, if one hears the term *woman* as representing a state of natural integrity. But if we understand this term to refer to an embodiment of the feminine, which is a construct of phallocracy, then the meaning of the expression becomes clear.[45]

In *La Cité magique*, Jacques Lantier reports a conversation about clitoridectomy with a tribal chief and magician. The latter illustrates the way in which atrocious, sadistic behavior has come to be regarded as normative. According to this sage:

> [God] has given the clitoris to the woman so that she can use it before marriage in order to experience the pleasure of love while still remaining pure. . . .
>
> The clitoris of very little girls is not cut off because they use it for masturbating. The clitoris of girls is sliced off when they are judged ready for procreation and marriage. When it has been removed, they no longer masturbate. This is a great hardship to them. Then all desire is transferred to the interior. Thus they then attempt to get married promptly. Once married, instead of experiencing dispersed and feeble sensations, they concentrate all [desire] in one place, and the couples experience much happiness, which is normal.[46]

So much for brutish and monodimensional male wisdom and romance, the purpose of which is to negate the complexity of female experience. It is perfectly obvious who "god" is in this de-lightful tale (which has a number of variants). The legitimating myth not only erases pain and mutilation, but turns it all into the right, good, and fit. It is god's (man's) plan. Even the fact that "they feel deprived" is made to seem a marvelous prelude for the "great happiness" to come. By now we are in a position to guess the nature of this "happiness."

But it is not necessary to guess. Dr. G. Pieters, a gynecologist who worked in a hospital in Somalia (1966–1968) explains that defibulation—the opening of the scar of the infibulated girl—is performed with a knife when she is married. The same author says that intercourse takes place immediately and it must be frequent during the first weeks of marriage, because otherwise the wound might close again.[47] The deception inherent in the magician's tale of female sexuality and marital bliss boggles the mind. Yet we should not fall into the trap of allowing ourselves to think that such religious/mythic legitimation is entirely foreign to "our"

Western society. As Fran Hosken points out, the medical profession and especially Freud in the West "are enthralled by the same male-created misconception: that of vaginal orgasm."[48] This is the universal test of the "normal" woman. Moreover, the logical acting out of this misconception, brutal and unnecessary gynecological surgery, including clitoridectomies, is not unknown in nineteenth- and twentieth-century American medicine (a point to be discussed in Chapter Seven).

As I have shown in analyzing other ritual atrocities, the acceptability and normative character of the monstrous rite becomes so ingrained that it continues even after the circumstances of its original performance appear to have changed drastically. Thus "practical *suttee*," as we have seen, has continued to take place in India for more than a century after it was legally abolished. In the case of African genital mutilation, in some countries the practice has moved from the arena of old women with broken bottles and kitchen knives in the forest to sterile rooms of modern hospitals. This is the case in the Sudan, in Egypt, and throughout Somalia—but only, of course, for a small number of girls. According to Dr. Pieters, the wealthy do not use the hospitals, but have private surgeons. It does not require great imagination to realize that the medical profession, rather than rejecting these horrors, has even made a specialization out of them, to its own economic benefit.

Dr. Pieters, whose article I have cited above, observed these operations in a hospital of the European Common Market in Mogadishu, the capital of Somalia. It is clear that no religious rituals (in the commonly accepted sense of the term *religious*) are involved in the hospitals, although moslem leaders and parents oppose stopping the atrocity. What has happened is that the barbarous rites of religion have been replaced (for those "privileged" few) by the barbarous rites of modern medicine. In the latter, male nurses wear surgical gloves and gowns, and use disinfectants, (insufficient) local anesthetic, surgical scissors (for cutting off the labia minora and excising the clitoris), catgut (for suturing), silk (for sewing), and sometimes penicillin.[49] As in other parts of the world, refined, "white" destruction by the practice of "medicine" perpetuates and "purifies" the religious rituals of gynocide.

## VII

Finally, we find the legitimation of the sado-ritual by the last rites of "objective" scholarship. Thus, for example, Felix Bryk, in a book entitled *Dark Rapture: The Sex Life of the African Negro*, introduces his telling description of female genital mutilation with a maze of deceptive expressions and manifestations of crass indifference. Alluding to the "gallant fight" being put up by missionaries to stop this "custom," he writes:

> It is hoped that the barbaric custom, *which is no less cruel than that of circumcision of the male* [!] may be gradually abolished through education and punishment. Personally I do not believe that punishment and education will do any real good in this instance because the custom is primarily practiced for erotic reasons [emphasis mine].[50]

Hags may well ask: "*Whose* erotic reasons?" The author's use of the expression "no less cruel" can be recognized as totally mendacious, when one compares excision and infibulation to the relatively minor operation of male circumcision. Had he written that male circumcision is "no less cruel" than female mutilation, this simply would have been a blatant lie. Instead, he performs a semantic trick, giving an illusion of justice or even of generosity toward the female sex in his assessment of the situation. Given the fact that this author himself presents a horrifying description of excision among the Nandi, it might seem astonishing that he can erase its reality in the same book. However, we have encountered this sort of gross contradiction in works of re-search concerning *suttee* and footbinding. The use of sensational materials, combined with erasure/denial of their significance, is a familiar pattern in patriarchal scholarship.

Bryk, who at the end of his foreword irrelevantly informs us that he is writing on Mount Elgon, "2,350 meters above sea level," is so high above the subject of his book, apparently, that he can give the de-tached opinion that "punishment and education" will not "do any real good"—a perspective which the physically and mentally mutilated women are in no position to refute. It is from this lofty perspective that he is able to interpret the Nandi bride's wedding night plea, "Let me be!" This comes,

Bryk explains, "more out of passion than dread."[51] A few lines down we read a description of the scene to which she protests "more out of passion than dread":

> During the first night, among the Nandi, some of his friends wait to hold her down in case she refuses to obey her husband. If the hymen happens to be too tough for ordinary defloration, the husband pierces it with a knife *without letting her know* [emphasis mine].

Despite his bird-like perspective when writing the book on Mount Elgon, this scholar, in doing his re-search, was not above endangering the life of one of these young victims, whom he describes as "the poor, mutilated child." He writes:

> I recall how once, *driven by curiosity*, I crossed the door of the sacred sanctuary [where the recently circumcised girl was confined], in spite of all restrictions, at a time when no woman was around [emphasis mine].[52]

In that society, his seeing the child was a violation of taboo, and could have resulted in the girl's death—a fact of which he was aware.

It is important to note Bryk's views on sex differences and on race. One can imagine him looking down upon the earth from Mount Elgon with his telescope as he utters the following bit of wisdom about "woman" and "man":

> Woman is forever woman, and man everywhere man; independently of race or color of skin—white, black, yellow, or copper-red; whether ugly or beautiful; despite youth or age; beyond good and evil.[53]

The universality of the patriarchal role-defined society is thus described and legitimized. It is "beyond good and evil." On the next page we read about racial differences:

> They [Blacks] like to lie—particularly to the whites—just as children do, because, like children, they cannot comprehend the moral necessity for truthfulness.[54]

It is obvious, then, that Blacks are different from the author, who is a paragon of truthfulness. Women are also "forever" different from him, but all women of all colors are alike. It would be helpful if women of all races could hear this message of patriarchy with the deep understanding/hearing of the labyrinthine inner ear, for it describes succinctly the sexual caste system, pointing to its fundamentally same view of all women.

There is a danger presented by such unabashedly racist books that the underlying, universal misogyny will go unnoticed. Haggard criticism should enable women who have been intimidated by labels of "racism" to become sisters to these women of Africa—naming the crimes against them and speaking on their behalf—seeing through the reversal that is meant to entrap us all. It is truly *racist* to keep silent in the face of these atrocities, merely "studying" them, speaking and writing deceptively about them, applying different (male-created) standards to them, failing to see and name the connections among them. Beyond racism is sisterhood, *naming* the crimes against women without paying mindless respect to the "social fabric" of the various androcratic societies, including the one in which we find our Selves imprisoned.

Among the most mystifying practitioners of sado-ritual scholarship legitimating female genital mutilation are "noted" anthropologists, for example Arnold van Gennep. First of all, the subject is erased in the index, having been lumped together with male circumcision under the single entry, *circumcision.* If one looks up this topic, one finds excision of the clitoris discussed incidentally. The following statement sums up the author's views:

> The length of the clitoris varies with individuals and races. In certain cases, the object of the excision may be to remove the *appendage* by which *the female resembles the male* (a view which is *correct* from an anatomical point of view), and the operation is nothing more than a rite of sexual differentiation on the *same order* as the first (ritual) assigning of *dress, instruments, or tools* proper to each sex [emphases mine].[55]

It might seem to require a special talent to assemble this much misinformation/deception in one brief footnote. In what sense is the idea that the clitoris is an "appendage" by which the female "resembles" the male "correct"? According to Merriam-Webster, the term *resemble* means: to be like or similar to. Leaving aside the fact that many women would consider this not only absurd but insulting, one might ask what the author could possibly have in mind in this "anatomical point of view." Would he agree that cutting off the penis is "nothing more" than a rite on the same order as "assigning of dress," et cetera? One can safely assume that he would not, and this throws some light on the implications of his use of the term *resembles* in this context. Van Gennep apparently sees the clitoris precisely *not* from an "anatomical" perspective, but for what it symbolizes/signifies: the potential in females for the independence, power, and prerogatives which are preserved exclusively for males by all the phallocratic "rites of sexual differentiation." For this reason he can minimize and erase the physical reality of female pain and mutilation.

We should not be surprised to read on the very next page not only the familiar remark that excision will "*diminish* sexual excitability," but also his inclusion of the clitoris among the organs which "because of their histological constitution undergo all sorts of treatment without harming an individual's *life* or *activity* [emphases mine]."[56] The other organs which van Gennep compares to the clitoris are the ear and nose, but of course the "treatment" is not at all comparable. Our scholar has in mind such operations as "cutting off the ear lobe" or perforating it. He is of course not discussing the total removal of both ears or slicing off the nose, which would be comparable to total removal of the clitoris. Finally, the author fails to mention infibulation, which is the most horrifying part of female genital mutilation. This erasure completes his contribution to the vast body of ignorance about his subject, "the rites of passage."

The Freudian psychoanalyst, Maria Bonaparte, also muddies matters in her famous "Notes on Excision" in her book, *Female Sexuality*. In this academic treatise she takes issue with Bryk's theory that "the Nandi males, in this way, seek to maximally feminize their females by doing away with this penile vestige, the clitoris, which, he adds, must result in encouraging the transfer of orgastic sensitivity from the girl's infantile erotogenic zone, the clitoris, to the adult erotogenic zone of the woman, which must necessarily be the vagina at puberty."[57] Bonaparte concludes that the Nandi men may have had such a wish, but that even such cruel excision would not achieve this aim. To support her response she cites cases of excised women who continued to refuse to "internalize [their] sexuality." Although she recognizes the cruelty of excision, Bonaparte's attitude toward these women is de-tached; she "studies" them.

Her analysis, moreover, is couched in the falsifying jargon and framework of freudian/fraudian theory, which assumes the reality of the "vaginal orgasm." Her language contains absurd phrases, such as "physical *intimidation* of the girl's sexuality by this cruel excision . . . [emphasis mine]."[58] The term *intimidation* is hardly accurate in this context. More freudian than Freud, Bonaparte lacks not only social perspective but the sensitivity and imagination to even begin to relate to the situation of these women outside the doctrinaire freudian framework. Thus she declares in passing that the "mutilations . . . are delegated to the old women who doubtless enjoy thus revenging their age on the young."[59] Such terms as *doubtless*, *enjoy*, and *revenging* reflect the male-identified ignorance/arrogance of father Freud's acolyte and disciple. To say the least, they are not based upon evidence. Bonaparte's poverty of imagination about the feelings of other women is damning evidence of the mind mutilation of women in phallocracy.

Mircea Eliade also contributes generously to the body of ignorance in his book, *Rites and Symbols of Initiation*, which has a section entitled "Initiation of Girls." He is perfectly silent about genital mutilation, making no reference either to excision or infibulation. He does note that "female initiatory rites—at least so far as they are known to us—are less dramatic than the rites for boys."[60] If we take the term *dramatic* to mean "showy," this is probably true. There is generally more ceremony surrounding the circumcision of a boy—more sound and fury. In the case of millions of mutilated girls, there is less "show" and far more reality in the initiation rites—horrible reality. This Eliade chooses to ignore (genuine ignorance in this case would seem to be impossible). He mentions that girls are "isolated" at menstruation and refers to dietary taboos. Focusing upon some Australian tribes, he points out signs which mark the *end* of female initiation, such as tattooing and blackening of the teeth. He writes: "The essential rite, then, is the solemn exhibition of the girl to the entire community."[61] Since this is written as a general statement, giving the impression that it applies generally to the initiation of girls in "ancient" stages of culture, it is essentially deceptive (skipping over excision and infibulation), erasing by its deceptiveness the essential patriarchal rite: dismemberment of female be-ing.

Just as Eliade fails to convey the physical/psychological mutilation which is the sado-ritual of "initiation of girls" into androcracy, so also he fails to see/name the ecstatic reality which is initiation and process in gynocentric be-ing. Yet, oddly and obtusely, he points to some clues. Thus on the symbolic level he gives information whose Background meaning must be lost on most of his readers, as it is on himself. He writes of the periods of seclusion which are part of girls' puberty rites, and remarks that they often learn such skills as spinning and weaving. Discussing the symbolism of these crafts, he says:

> The moon "spins" Time and "weaves" human lives. The Goddesses of Destiny are spinners. We detect an occult connection between the conception of the periodical creations of the world (a conception derived from a lunar mythology) and the ideas of Time and Destiny, on the one hand, and on the other, nocturnal work, women's work, which has to be performed far from the light of the sun and almost in secret. In some cultures, after the seclusion of the girls is ended they continue to meet in some old woman's house to spin together.[62]

Spinsters reading such works of re-search can search and find lost threads of connectedness. Thus when Eliade goes on to say that "spinning is a perilous craft," which can be carried on only in special houses during particular periods and until certain hours, we hear the meaning of this peril in the deep recesses of the labyrinthine inner ear. And when he says that "in some parts of the world spinning has been given up, and even completely forgotten, because of its magical peril," we recognize the peril as our own, and know that we have neither given up nor forgotten. Indeed, in the face of the atrocities associated with phallocratic female initiation into femininity, we must respond not only with exposé. Nor is feminist analysis enough. Most importantly, we must live through the genuine initiation, which is not into femininity but into Self-centering female integrity. This means exorcising the atrocities not only by seeing/naming/acting against them, but also by refusing to remain fixated upon them, and by exercising our new and ancient craft of spinning. This is the initiation of Spinsters, our heritage and new beginning.

The words of Eliade convey something of this woman-centered quality of spinning:

> In some places—Japan, for example—we still find the mythological memory of a permanent tension, and even conflict, between the groups of young spinning girls and the men's secret societies. At night the men and their Gods attack the spinning girls and destroy not only their work, but also their shuttles and weaving apparatus.[63]

The members of "the men's secret societies" throughout patriarchy have never ceased to fear and envy the gynaesthetic gift for Spinning.[64]

In the following chapters we will come to understand more deeply the perils which must be faced by women who have the talent and courage to Spin. We shall see how attackers destroyed the work and "weaving apparatus" of the women in "renaissance" Europe who were/are our foresisters, the witches.

17

# Prelude to the Third Passage

Reprinted from "Prelude to the Third Passage" of *Gyn/Ecology*, pp. 315–20.

*Spinster:* a woman whose occupation is to Spin, to participate in the whirling movement of creation; one who has chosen her Self, who defines her Self by choice neither in relation to children nor to men; one who is Self-identified; a whirling dervish, Spiraling in New Time/Space.
—*Wickedary*, p. 167

*Gyn/Ecology* presented an explicit threefold structure, with three parts, labeled "Passages." The Second Passage focused on atrocities committed against women by patriarchal males. The Third Passage focused on female strategies, tactics, and energies. In the "Prelude to the Third Passage," Daly warned her readers against remaining mired in the horrors of the Second Passage. While "know-ing of this deadly intent has been necessary for our a-mazing process of exorcism," it is also necessary to look away, to look to the positive, to avoid being a woman who is "'spinning her wheels' instead of spinning on her heel and facing Other directions."

Sparking, Spinning, Spiraling, Speaking, Spooking, Whirling—these words that imply limitless and unpredictable movement become key entry points to understanding Daly's philosophic intent. She created an open ontology for women—a group denied even the most basic freedoms by patriarchal society. The poetry she spun carries an infectious exaltation: "The force of Spinsters' Spinning is the power of spirit spiraling, whirling. As we break into The Third Passage we whirl into our own world. Gyn/Ecology is weaving the way past the dead past and the dry places, weaving our world tapestry out of genesis and demise."

The anger generated by the Second Passage, though, returned as a now self-assured universalization of patriarchy. The Second Passage had shown the necrophilic intent of the fathers in a variety of settings. But there are some readers who have, and will, find Daly's language too Manichean.
—Editors

In the course of The Second Passage, Crone-ographers who have survived dis-covering the various manifestations of Goddess-murder on this patriarchal planet have become aware of the deep and universal intent to destroy the divine spark in women. We have seen that the perpetrators of this planetary atrocity are acting out the deadly myths of patriarchy and that this ritual enactment of the sado-myths has become more refined with the "progress of civilization." This refinement includes an escalation of violence and visibility and at the same time a decrease of visibility to those mesmerized by the Processions of fathers, sons, and holy ghosts.

The know-ing of this deadly intent has been necessary for our a-mazing process of exorcism. It is equally necessary for moving on the Labyrinthine Journey of Ecstasy, for this process is damaged/hindered by not knowing/acknowledging the dangers, traps, deceptions built into the terrain. As long as "knowledge" of the horrors of androcracy is fragmented, compartmentalized, belittled, we cannot integrate this into our know-ing process. We then mistake the male-made maze for our Self-centering way.

Since we have come through the somber Passage of recognizing the alien/alienating environment in which woman-hating rituals vary from *suttee* to gynecological iatrogenesis, we can begin to tread/thread our way in new time/space. This knowing/acting/Self-centering Process is itself the creating of a new, woman-identified environment. It is the becoming of Gyn/Ecology. This involves the dis-spelling of the mind/spirit/body pollution that is produced out of man-made myths, language, ritual atrocities, and meta-rituals such as "scholarship," which erase our Selves. It also involves dis-covering the sources of the Self's original movement, hearing the moving of this movement. It involves speaking forth the New Words which correspond to this deep listening, speaking the words of our lives.

Breaking out of the patriarchal processions into our own Gyn/Ecological process is the specific theme of this, The Third Passage. In a general sense, our movement through the preceding Passages has all been and is Gyn/Ecological Journeying. Moreover, since our movement is not linear but rather resembles spiraling, we continue to re-member/re-call/re-claim the knowledge gained in the preceding Passages, assuming this into our present/future. Hence, there is no authentic way in which the preceding Passages can be dissociated from the Third. Thus, Gyn/Ecology is not the climax or linear end point in time of the Journey, but rather it is a defining theme/thread in our Labyrinthine Journey of the inner ear, in the course of which we constantly hear deeper and deeper reverberations from all of the Passages and learn to be attuned to echoes, subtleties, and distinctions not attended to before. Yet, Gyn/Ecology is the proper name for The Third Passage, for it names the patterns/designs of the moving Female-identified environment which can only be heard/seen after the Journeyer has been initiated through The First and The Second Passages.

As the Spinster spins into and through this Passage she is en-couraged by her strengthened powers of hearing and seeing. By now she has begun to develop a kind of multidimensional/multiform power of sensing/understanding her environment. This is a Self-identified *synaesthesia*: it is woman-identified *gynaesthesia*. It is a complex way of perceiving the interrelatedness of seemingly disparate phenomena. It is also a pattern-detecting power which may be named positive paranoia. Far from being a debilitating "mental disease," this is strengthening and realistic dis-ease in a polluted and destructive environment. Derived from the Greek terms *para*, meaning beyond, outside of, and *nous*, meaning mind, the term *paranoia* is appropriate to describe movement beyond, outside of, the patriarchal mind-set. It is the State of Positively Revolting Hags.

Moving through all three Passages is moving from the state of anesthesia to empowering gynaesthesia, as dormant senses become awake and alive. Since, in The Second Passage, the Voyager became more aware not only of the blatancy and interconnectedness of phallocratic evil, but also of its reality, she is enabled to detect and name its implicit presence and therefore to overcome roadblocks in her dis-covery of being. Empowered with positive paranoia she can move with increasing confidence.

We have seen that this is the age of holy ghosts, with particular reference to gynecology. It is an age of manipulation through/by invisible and *almost* insensible presences. Some of these might be called physical, such as radiation and "white noise." Others more properly may be said to belong to the realm of the spirit, of "ghost." We are dealing here with the realm of implicit or subliminal manipulation, of quiet, almost indiscernible, intent on the part of the manipulators and quiet, unacknowledged acceptance of their ghostly presences and messages by their victims. Hence, the first chapter of this Passage will be concerned with Spooking. The Haggard Journeyer will not be astonished to find that Spooking is multi-leveled. Women are spooked by patriarchal males in a variety of ways; for example, through implicit messages of their institutions, through body language, through the silences and deceptive devices of their media, their grammar, their education, their professions, their technology, their oppressive and confusing fashions, customs, etiquette, "humor," through their subliminal advertising and their "sublime" music (such as christmas carols piped into supermarkets that seduce their listener into identifying with the tamed Goddess who abjectly adores her son).

Women are also spooked by other women who act as instrumental agents for patriarchal males, concurring, with varying degrees of conscious complicity, in all of the above tactics. To the extent that any woman acts—or nonacts when action is required—in such complicity, she functions as a double agent of spooking, for politically she *is* and *is not* functioning as a woman. Since Hags/Witches have expectations of her—righteous expectations which are almost impossible to discard without falling into total cynicism and despair—she spooks us doubly, particularly by her absences/silences/nonsupport. Finally, Spinsters are spooked by the alien presences that have been inspired (breathed into) our own spirits/minds. These involve fragments of the false self which are still acting/nonacting in complicity with the Possessors. They also take the shape of nameless fears, unbearable implanted guilt feelings for affirming our own being, fear of our newly discovered powers and of successful use of them, fear of dis-covering/releasing our own deep wells of anger, particularly fear of our anger against other women and against ourselves for failing our Selves. Spinsters are spooked by fear of the Ultimate Irony, which would be to become a martyr/scapegoat for feminism, whose purpose is to release women from the role of martyr and scapegoat.

Faced with being spooked, Spinsters are learning to Spook/Speak back. This Spinster-Spooking is also re-calling/re-membering/reclaiming our Witches' power to cast spells, to charm, to overcome prestige with prestidigitation, to cast glamours, to employ occult grammar, to enthrall, to bewitch. Spinster-Spooking is both cognitive and tactical. Cognitively, it means pattern-detecting. It means understanding the time-warps through which women are divided from each other—since each woman comes to consciousness through the unique events of her own history. It means also seeing the problems caused through space-warps—since Hags and potential Hags are divided from each other in separate institutional settings, disabled from sharing survival tactics in our condition of common isolation, spooked by our apparent aloneness. Tactically, Spooking means learning to refuse the seductive summons by the Passive Voices that call us into the State of Animated Death. It means learning to hear and respond to the call of the wild, learning ways of en-couraging and en-spiriting the Self and other Spinsters, learning con-questing, learning methods of dispossession, specifically of dis-possessing the Self of possession by the past and possession by the future. It means a-mazing the modern witchcraze, developing skills for unpainting the Painted Birds possessed through the device of tokenism, exposing the Thoroughly Therapeutic Society.

Since Spooking cannot always be done alone, and since it is a primary but not complete expression of Gyn/Ecology, the second chapter of this Passage is concerned with Sparking. In order to move on the con-questing Voyage, Spinsters need fire. It is significant that witches and widows were burned alive, consumed by fire. For fire is the course and symbol of energy, of gynergy. It is because women are known to be energy sources that patriarchal males seek to possess and consume us. This is done less dramatically in day-by-day draining of energy, in the slow and steady extinguishing of women's fire. Sparking is necessary to re-claim our fire. Sparking, like Spooking, is a form of Gyn/Ecology. Sparking is Speaking with tongues of fire. Sparking is igniting the divine Spark in women. Light and warmth, which are necessary for creating and moving, are results of Sparking. Sparking is creating a room of one's own, a moving time/spaceship of one's own, in which the Self can expand, in which the Self can join with other Self-centering Selves.

Sparking is making possible Female Friendship, which is totally Other from male comradeship. Hence, the Spinster will examine male comradeship/fraternity, in order to avoid the trap of confusing sisterhood with brotherhood, of thinking (even in some small dusty corner of the mind) of sisterhood as if it were simply a gender-correlative of brotherhood. She will come to see that the term *bonding*, as it applies to Hags/Harpies/Furies/Crones is as thoroughly Other from "male bonding" as Hags are the Other in relation to patriarchy. Male comradeship/bonding depends upon energy drained from women (its secret glue), since women are generators of energy. The bonding of Hags in friendship *for* women is not draining but rather energizing/gynergizing. It is the opposite of brotherhood, not essentially because Self-centering women oppose and fight patriarchy in a reactive way, but because we are/act for our Selves.

The term *comrade* is derived from a Middle French word meaning a group of soldiers sleeping in one room, or roommate. The concept of room here is spatial, suggesting links resulting from physical proximity, not necessarily from choice. The space is physical, not psychic, and it is definitely not A Room of One's Own. To the degree that it has been chosen, the choice has been made by another. The comrades do not choose each other for any inherent qualities of mind/spirit. Although this accidental and spatial "roommate" aspect does apply to all women insofar as all women are oppressed/possessed, it does not apply to the deep and conscious bonding of Hags in the process of be-ing. Since the core/the soul-spark of such deep bonding is friendship, it does not essentially depend upon an enemy for its existence/becoming.

At first, it is hard to generate enough sparks for building the fires of Female Friendship. This is particularly the case since patriarchal males, sensing the ultimate threat of Female Sparking, make every effort to put out women's fires whenever we start them. They try to steal the fire of Furies in order to destroy us in their perpetual witchcraze. Like Cinderellas, Hags stand among the cinders, but we know that they are cinders of our burned foresisters. We know that the cinders still Spark.

Sparking means building the fires of gynergetic communication and confidence. As a result, each Sparking Hag not only begins to live in a lighted and warm room of her own; she prepares a place for a loom of her own. In this space she can begin to weave the tapestries of her own creation. With her increasing fire and force, she can begin to Spin. As she and her sisters Spin together, we create The Network of our time/space.

Gyn/Ecological Spinning is essential for entry into our Otherworld. The Voyager who does not Spin is in mortal danger. She may become trapped in one of the blind alleys of the maze which has been uncovered in The Second Passage. That is, she may become fixated upon the atrocities of androcracy, "spinning her wheels" instead of spinning on her heel and facing Other directions. Or the nonspinner may make the fatal mistake of trying to jump over the atrocities into pseudo-ecstasy. As a result of this escapism, this blind "leap of faith," she can only fall into a tailspin.

The force of Spinsters' Spinning is the power of spirit spiraling, whirling. As we break into The Third Passage we whirl into our own world. Gyn/Ecology is weaving the way past the dead past and the dry places, weaving our world tapestry out of genesis and demise.

18

# Newspeak versus New Words

From chapter 8 of *Gyn/Ecology*, pp. 329–33.

*New Words:* words Heard in a new semantic context and arising from qualitatively Other experience; words of Gynocentric communication—many of which are not "new" in the old sense (materially) but New in a New sense, having different meanings because they are Heard and Spoken in New ways.
—*Wickedary*, p. 86

Many twentieth-century intellectuals grappled with the writings of George Orwell, particularly his two novelistic fables, *1984* and *Animal Farm*. For Mary Daly, the importance of *1984* grew from its perceptive analysis of the dumbing-down of language. This excerpt takes off from a critique of feminist reshapings of the language that compared feminist efforts to Orwellian Newspeak. Daly then demonstrated how Newspeak reflects patriarchal values, using language instrumentally, rather than transformatively or evocatively.

Daly's insistence on the logical priority of women's oppression finds no more blunt statement than this: "All male-instigated degradation of victims and enemies has as its hidden paradigm the female as Other, as victim."
—Editors

The struggle against semantic spooking is essential for Hags escaping/overcoming the State of Possession. The courage to *try*, to risk ridicule, is essential for our encounter with the demons of timidity and other-directed "correctness." This is especially the case since a basic weapon in the arsenal of spookers is ridicule. The spookers make those who challenge their deception appear laughable, sometimes even to ourselves. They also make the Deep Background, which they hide and belittle through their spooking, seem unreal. This is an important tactic of the ghostly deceivers, for it serves their purposes to stop women who are coming close to the entry of the Labyrinth, the Background of our Selves.

Predictably, boringly, feminists who begin unspooking language are compared by linguistic "purists" to the originators of "Newspeak" in Orwell's *1984*. A classic example, on the *Time* magazine level, is a cutely titled article, "Sispeak: A Msguided Attempt to Change Herstory."[1] The author, Stefan Kanfer, compares feminist critiques and language changes to Orwell's "Newspeak," which, of course, is not recognized as prototypical Malespeak. Kanfer deserves to be nominated for Reversal of the Century Award. In his caricature of women's efforts to break the bonds of rapist language, he equates our new words to the "breakdown of language" exemplified in the rapist film, *A Clockwork Orange*. Kanfer uses the power of "humor" to spook his female readers:

> As they [feminists] see it, William James' bitch-goddess Success and the National Weather Service's Hurricane Agnes are products of the same criminal mind.[2]

This weaponry is effective, because most readers "know" that naming a hurricane "Agnes" is not criminal, and at the same time do not know deeply enough that both naming and such ridicule are, on a psychic level, at least as destructive to women as a hurricane. The spirit of deceptive mockery blasts into the minds of the intended victims; its aim is to destroy the balance of the novice Voyager.

Another *Time*-grimed trick exemplified in this essay is naming the problem in such a correct but at the same time deprecating way that its reality is erased in the reader's mind. Thus, Kanfer writes: "It is pathetically easy to spy in this [traditional] vocabulary a latent slavery, a cloaked prejudice aimed at further subjugating women in the name of language." This statement is exactly correct. However, the choice of such words as "pathetically easy," "spy," and "cloaked," manages to belittle and lampoon the women who have lucidly pointed out that it is pathetically easy to see through traditional language.

The same author is not above accusing feminists of crime:

> The feminist attack on social crimes may be as legitimate as it was inevitable. But the attack on words is only another social crime—one against the means and the hope of communication.

Thus feminists are permitted to "attack social crimes," but we must stop short of attacking the more insidious social crime of sexist language.

To break the spell of such revelatory reversals, Crone-ographers should remind our Selves that the Newspeak of Orwell's negative utopian tale is patriarchal Oldspeak. Since his "prophecies" are descriptions of what has already happened, we can follow through on his clues, naming the Missing Links/Agents overlooked by Orwell. He writes: "Newspeak was designed not to extend but to diminish the range of thought . . ."[3] This applies to male-controlled language in all matters pertaining to gynocentric identity: the words simply do not exist. In such a situation it is difficult even to imagine the right questions about our situation. Women struggling for words feel haunted by false feelings of personal inadequacy, by anger, frustration, and a kind of sadness/bereavement. For it is, after all, our "mother tongue" that has been turned against us by the tongue-twisters. Learning to speak our Mothers' Tongue *is* exorcising the male "mothers."

Orwell writes that "the special function of certain Newspeak words . . . was not so much to express meanings as to destroy them."[4] We need only think of such words as *feminine*, *unfeminine*, *womanly*, *unwomanly*, to recognize how certain words, particularly those that are supposed to name us, not only fail to express who we are but also destroy our identity. Moreover:

> These words . . . had had their meanings extended until they contained within themselves whole batteries of words which, as they were sufficiently covered by a single comprehensive term, could now be scrapped and forgotten.[5]

The doublebinding, falsely opposite words for women contain a great number of pejorative meanings, which the spooking speaker need not spell out. A single mystifying term will do the trick.

The crippling of thinking—mindbinding—by lack of words is expressed in another way:

> In Newspeak it was seldom possible to follow a heretical thought further than the perception that it *was* heretical; beyond that point the necessary words were nonexistent.[6]

Haggard Heretics are familiar with this thought-stopping aspect of the male-mothered tongue. Often Hags are worn down by this stupefying resistance of those who are unable to follow our thoughts further than the perception that they are heretical/heterodox/unacceptable. When we create New Words, re-call our Old Words, these are perceived/named Newspeak (read: trite, gimmicky, pretentious, nonintellectual) by the Newspeakers/spookers themselves.

In Orwell's *1984*, some words were euphemisms, such as *joycamp*, meaning forced-labor camp. Women can think of such haunting euphemisms as *homemaker, rest cure, finishing schools, intensive care, beauty parlor, the natural look, emotionally disturbed women.* Furthermore, in Orwell's dystopia, which we recognize as the patriarchal present, emphasis was placed upon short clipped words "which could be uttered rapidly and which roused the minimum of echoes in the speaker's mind."[7] In other words:

> Ultimately it was hoped to make articulate speech issue from the larynx without involving the higher brain centers at all. This aim was frankly admitted in the Newspeak word *duckspeak,* meaning "to quack like a duck."[8]

Applying this ideal of political language to the realm of sexual politics, which are the most basic politics of patriarchy, we note the similarities between duckspeak and male obscenity: Words like *fuck*, *prick*, *cock*, *cunt*, *gash*, *slopjar*, *slut*, illustrate the point.

We should note that such mindless "duckspeak" is also used by certain professionals, particularly members of the military and medical professions, to refer to their enemies/victims. Thus American soldiers referred to the Vietnamese as *gooks*. Women spooked by false inclusion in the "we" of patriotic Americans have been prevented from seeing that the female sex is the hidden paradigm for such naming of "gooks." Indeed, male identifying of femaleness with *gook* (defined in Merriam-Webster as "sticky or gooey stuff") is shamelessly illustrated in existentialist philosopher Jean-Paul Sartre's long discussion of "the slimy," which he identifies with the Other, the female.[9] As Peggy Holland has demonstrated, Sartre's identification of women with "the hole" and "the slimy"—his proclamation of "the obscenity of the female sex"—is a philosophical "NO to women." In short: "Aligned with the slimy, the hole, and a precipice, she represents nothingness."[10] It can also be illuminating for Hags to consider the slang/"duckspeak" of modern medicine. Thus the staff of some hospitals refer to unconscious patients as *gorks* and "difficult" patients as *turkeys*. Female doctors and nurses haunted by the illusion of inclusion in male medicine are hindered from seeing that "normal" women are the primordial "gorks," that deviant women are the archetypal "turkeys." All male-instigated degradation of victims and enemies has as its hidden paradigm the female as Other, as victim.

Finally, there is "doublethink." Winston Smith, after torture in the Ministry of Love, came to understand that:

> . . . if you want to keep a secret you must also hide it from yourself. You must know all the while that it is there, but until it is needed you must never let it emerge into your consciousness in any shape that could be given a name. From now onwards he must not only think right; he must feel right, dream right.[11]

We have seen many examples of doublethink in the preceding Passage. In order to understand spooking as it occurs in the environment of common, everyday gynocide, we should note that the broad aim of doublethink includes forcing us also to feel and dream right. The manipulation of feelings is accomplished through methods as seemingly varied as those of the psychotherapeutic establishment and of subliminal advertising. The "prolefeed" (which we might translate as "femfeed"), dished out by television, films, magazines, and best-sellers, programs women's dreams, setting up ghostly walls within the mind that block out the messages of the deep Background.

19

# Sparking

## *The Fire of Female Friendship*

From chapter 9 of *Gyn/Ecology*, pp. 382–84.

*Sparking:* speaking with tongues of Fire; igniting the divine Spark in women; lighting the Fires of Female Friendship; encouraging women to become sister Pyrotechnists; building the Fire that is fueled by Fury—the Fire that warms and lights the place where we can Spin and Weave tapestries of Crone-centered creation.
—*Wickedary*, p. 165

This culminating encomium to female friendship establishes three philosophic principles in a brief space. First, lesbian relations, being outside the heteronormative, are asserted to be outside "social approval," and thus "we are free to seek Self-approval. We are free to follow our passion for Self-centering." Historically, in 1978, the active LGBT political movement was not even a decade old, and lesbians were, indeed, quite far outside social approval; very few feminists of that time expected the direction that the movement has taken in areas like same-sex marriage and employment protections. Whether Daly would have considered this progress, though, is unknown.

Second, in a theme that she would develop using Thomistic angelology in *Pure Lust*, she said that Amazon searchers need "not haggle over 'equality,' for we know there is no equality among unique Selves." This contribution to discussions of diversity has been overlooked by Daly's supporters and critics alike; while it can tend to individualism, even exceptionalism, it also offers an opportunity for understanding difference as a creative force. She quoted Jan Raymond as saying that what feminists ask of each other is to "be equal to the task at hand."

Third, in the penultimate paragraph, in a poetic passage about Fury, Daly implied that this "uprising of Amazon Fire" does not exist to destroy

patriarchy: that may be its effect, but it exists for itself, as an emanation of "gynergy for its own sake."
—Editors

Whereas discussion of relations between men and women eulogize the so-called complementarity of opposites, an Amazonian analysis of female friendship/love dis-covers the fact that the basis of woman-identified relationships is neither biological differences nor socially constructed opposite roles. As Jan Raymond has observed, rather than accepting a standardized "difference" (femininity), Lesbians/Spinsters find in our authentic likeness to each other the opportunity to exhibit and develop genuine differences.[1] Rather than relying upon stereotypic role relationships, Amazon friends/lovers/sisters cast our Selves into a creative variety of developing relationships with each other. Since there are no models, no roles, no institutionalized relationships to fall back upon, we move together and apart in ever-varying patterns of relating. As each friend moves more deeply into her own Background she becomes both her earlier and her present Self. At times this re-membered integrity makes her appear Strange to her friends, and since the latter are also re-membering, the encounters of these older/younger Selves can be multiply Strange. This Dreadful Strangeness is part of the terrain of the Otherworld Journey. It is essential to Amazon adventure.

Women who have the courage to travel can see the absence of standardized roles as an asset, for such roles inhibit our struggle for truthfulness and fidelity. Heterosexist society does not reward Lesbians for friendship and fidelity to each other. Therefore, the way is clear for honest Amazon bonding. Since we know that our friendships will not in the final analysis yield social approval, we are free to seek Self-approval. We are free to follow our passion for Self-centering. As de Beauvoir correctly points out, men and women are always playing a part before one another. In contrast to this, Lesbians need not pretend. As she observes: "They [these liaisons] are not sanctioned by an institution or by the mores, nor are they regulated by conventions; hence they are marked by especial sincerity."[2]

Such sincerity involves risks. Since woman-identified relationships are unrestrained by mystification over biological and role-defined differences, there is often great intensity and turbulence in be-ing together. It has been observed that sisterhood involves stages when one seems to be stepping off a cliff, and that, mysteriously, the ground rises under the Journeyer's feet.[3] That ground is the Self's own confrontation with her reality, her truth—a confrontation made possible and unavoidable by her unprotected situation. Having defied the patriarchal protection racket, she finds her Dreadless Self.

Paradoxically, then, it is the likeness of women that makes room for our otherness, our wildness, our strangeness. The creation of separate female-identified psychic, mythic, semantic, physical spaces is necessary for likeness and wild otherness to grow. Each individual Amazon must have such room of her own, and she must be free to communicate the light and warmth generated in the privacy of her own room to the hearts/hearths of other Hags, and to receive their luminous energy.

Isolation of female-identified women from each other—a basic tactic of patriarchy—does not quench the individual woman's Spark, but contains it in a dampening environment. Each such woman, locked into the damp dungeon assigned to her by the misogynistic State, must struggle to maintain her own sense of reality against the prevailing lies. When she makes contact with even one other Sparking Self, the combination is conflagration. Each woman sees her own knowledge of reality confirmed in her sister. The possessors' spell is broken. Their prisons are reduced to ashes as these Sparking Selves energize and re-energize each other, giving each other the incendiary incentive.

Crones kindle the Fury of our own kind against the god-fathers who burned our foremothers. The uprising of Cinderellas from the cinders/ashes of our mothers is the righteous Renaissance. In our rising together, Hags affirm the true identity of our foremothers who were burned as witches during the alleged "renaissance." We affirm the reality hidden by the "wicked stepmother" image[4]—the reality of the women of Wicce, whose fire still burns in every Haggard heart. This uprising of Amazon Fire, our life-loving, be-ing, is the hellfire deserved and dreaded by the Grand Inquisitors. If its purpose were merely to consume them it would be less effective. In fact, it is simply the expression/expansion of gynergy for its own sake, and this transcendence of Fury itself is the Renaissance of Fire. In its light, the patriarchal male is forced to see his history of holocausts, to re-view the multitudes of women sacrificed as burnt offerings to his gods. This is his unbearable "beatific vision," his Last End.

As this Sparking communication occurs, Hags do not haggle over "equality," for we know there is no equality among unique Selves. Noting that one definition of the term equal is "capable of meeting the requirements of a situation or a task," Jan Raymond observes that what each asks of the other is that she be equal to the task at hand.[5] Crones expect and en-courage each other to become sister pyrotechnists, building the fire that is fueled by Fury, the fire that warms and lights the place where we can each have a loom of our own, where we can spin and weave the tapestries of Crone-centered creation.

## 20

# The Dissembly of Exorcism

From chapter 10 of *Gyn/Ecology*, pp. 418–19, 422–24.

*Naming:* Original summoning of words for the Self, world, and ultimate reality; liberation by Wicked Women of words from confinement in the sentences of the fathers; Truth-telling: the only adequate antidote for phallocracy's Biggest Lies; exorcism of patriarchal labels by invoking Other reality and by conjuring the Spirits of women and of all Wild natures; re-calling the Race of Radiant Words.
—*Wickedary*, p. 83

Roseanne Barr describes this uproarious conclusion to *Gyn/Ecology* as the best comic material ever written, and indeed, the images and the intent are fantastical, humorous while also being deadly earnest. The Dissembly of Crones unmasks and melts the evil demons of patriarchy. The wild beasts, within and without, are freed, until the final mystical/paradoxical paragraph:

> In the beginning was not the word. In the beginning is the hearing. Spinsters spin deeper into the listening deep. We can spin only what we hear, because we hear, and as well as we hear. We can weave and unweave, knot and unknot, only because we hear, what we hear, and as well as we hear. Spinning is celebration/cerebration. Spinsters Spin all ways, always. Gyn/Ecology is Un-Creation; Gyn/Ecology is Creation.

—Editors

At our Un-Conventions, Crones cackle at the crude Deceptions of the Demons who persist in trying to blend their voices into our Hearings. A-musing Amazons unravel the twisted tales of androcratic "Argonauts" who allegedly sailed with Jason on a ship named *Argo* in quest of the Golden Fleece. Furies fume at the fact that these misnamed imposters tried to kill Amazons. Crone-ographers crack up reading that the term *Argonaut* is used specifically to name those men "who went to California in 1849 in search of gold." The whole gathering of Gyn/Ecologists agrees that the Processions of deceptive demons must be woven into disposable tapestries to be made visible/tangible. Once distinguishable, they will be extinguishable, and can be consumed in the Flames of our Fury.

As the convocation unweaves more deceptions, the Procession of demons comes ever more glaringly into view. We recognize them, having encountered all of them numerous times in the course of our Voyage. We perceive ever more distinctly that they are ghostly personifications (masks) of the Deadly Sins of the Fathers.[1] Since we are ready for them now, we invoke them by weaving their previously hidden presences into visibility/audibility. We contain our cackles as more demon wardens appear in our labyrinthine conference chamber. More than once the Chaircrone finds it imperative to call the dissembled Hags back into Dis-order, since many are tempted to tweak the noses and twist the tails of the dissembling demons. Some of the more spirited Harpies have to be hindered from clawing the invoked visitors before the latter have had ample opportunity to expose themselves. A few Furies must be restrained from setting fire to the costumes and uniforms of the ghastly guests. As the Amazonian Dissembly is hushed into readiness, the final contingent of infernal infiltrators materializes in the filled chamber. Suddenly seeing where they are, the demons react with routinized reflexes. Pompously approaching the Chaircrone in groups, they offer to address and advise the Dissembly. The calculating Crone accepts the entertaining offer of the unsuspecting spooks. Each group is allotted three moments of Crone-time. It is noticeable that the Infernal Imposters wear a variety of uniforms, but that each group includes some wearing business suits and/or casual sportswear.[2] [ . . . ]

[The demonic types present themselves.]

[. . . T]he members of the [ . . . ] demonic delegations attempt a quick escape, but the roaring of the Revolted Hags engulfs them, stopping them dead. Instead of running, they begin to unravel. The black and red robes, the white coats, the academic gowns, the police uniforms, the business suits—all unravel rapidly. The demons try to cling to each other for support, but each is more unsolid than the next; each has Nothing to hang on to. The Un-Convention gazes in a-mazement, noticing that the unraveling costumes contain Nothing. The Watching Witches and Hearing Hags realize that the demons will re-materialize. But no one present will ever forget this scene. We will tell it on the mountains and in the valleys. We will tell it to the Daughters of the Daughters of Crones, who will re-member our history and how the spell of the Demons is broken. In the times of storms and earthquakes we will re-member the story of The Great Unraveling.

## The Celebration of Ecstasy

Having seen, heard, and understood the Rite of Unraveling, the Gyn/Ecologists re-gather gynergies. Furies rush forth and collect the shreds of the deadly deceivers' costumes. We throw the threads and shreds into a heap. We toss onto the pile the combustible samples displayed by the Obsessors, such as magazines and bras. We set the pile afire with the flames of our combined Fury. Harpies fan the fire with our great wings. The fire crackles and roars. In the Background of its roaring can be heard the voice of Fore-Crone Woolf howling: "Let it blaze, Daughters! Let it blaze!" [ . . . ]

Sounds of joy echo through the chamber, and reverberate through other and deeper chambers of the labyrinth. The Voyagers glimpse our Paradise that is beyond the boundaries of patriarchal paradise, the Playboys' Playground. We hear the call of our wild. We play games to end their games. Those who have been called bitches bark; pussies purr; cows moo; old bats squeal; squirrels chatter; nags whinny; chicks chirp; cats growl; old crows screech. Foxy ladies chase clucking biddies around in circles.[3]

The play is part of our work of unweaving and of our weaving work. It whirls us into another frame of reference. We use the visitation of demons to come more deeply into touch with our own powers/virtues. Unweaving their deceptions, we name our Truth. Defying their professions we dis-cover our Female Pride, our Sinister Wisdom.[4] Escaping their possession we find our Enspiriting Selves. Overcoming their aggression we uncover our Creative Anger and Brilliant Bravery.[5] Demystifying/demythifying their obsessions we re-member our Woman-loving Love.

Refusing their assimilation we experience our Autonomy and Strength. Avoiding their elimination we find our Original Be-ing. Mending their imposed fragmentation we Spin our Original Integrity.

As we feel the empowerment of our own Naming we hear more deeply our call of the wild. Raising pairs of arms into the air we expand them into shells, sails. Splashing our legs in the water we move our oars. Our beautiful, spiral-like designs are the designs/purposes of our bodies/minds. We communicate these through our force-fields, our auras, our O-Zones. We move backward over the water, toward the Background. We gain speed. Argonauts move apart and together, forming and re-forming our Amazon Argosy. In the rising and setting of our sister the sun, we seek the gold of our hearts' desire. In the light of our sisters the moon and stars we rekindle the Fore-Crones' fire. In its searing light we see through the fathers' lies of genesis and demise; we burn through the snarls of the Nothing-lovers.

In the beginning was not the word. In the beginning is the hearing. Spinsters spin deeper into the listening deep. We can spin only what we hear, because we hear, and as well as we hear. We can weave and unweave, knot and unknot, only because we hear, what we hear, and as well as we hear. Spinning is celebration/cerebration. Spinsters Spin all ways, always. Gyn/Ecology is Un-Creation; Gyn/Ecology is Creation.

21

# Daly on Matilda Joslyn Gage

From foreword to *Woman, Church and State: The Original Exposé of Male Collaboration against the Female Sex*, by Matilda Joslyn Gage, edited by Sally Roesch Wagner (reprint, Watertown, MA: Persephone, 1980), pp. vii–x.

*Foresister:* Great Hag whom the institutionally powerful but privately impotent patriarchs found too threatening for co-existence and whom historians erased.
—*Wickedary*, p. 126

The great nineteenth-century feminist writer, activist, and theorist Matilda Joslyn Gage (1826–1898) was one of the most stunning rediscoveries of second wave feminist compensatory history. Daly's encounter with Gage's unsparing critique of religion, and with the maddening story of Gage's erasure by her erstwhile feminist allies in the late nineteenth century, felt like a mirror, confirming Daly's own sense of her trajectory and her work. Furthermore, Gage's unabashed use of terms like "patriarchate" corroborated Daly's analysis.

This brief foreword to the 1980 reprint of Gage's monumental *Woman, Church and State* also witnessed to the feminist friendship between Daly and the Gage scholar and advocate Sally Roesch Wagner. Wagner has now established the Matilda Joslyn Gage Foundation in Fayetteville, New York.[1]

This edition of *Woman, Church and State* has been out of print for decades, and access to this distilled evaluation of Gage by Daly has remained virtually unknown. Daly's excitement and rage here extended the tone of *Gyn/Ecology*, while also transitioning to her envisioned trans-historical sisterhood of radical feminists prominent in her last two books, *Quintessence* and *Amazon Grace*.
—Editors

Matilda Joslyn Gage is a major radical feminist theoretician and historian whose written work is indispensable for an understanding of the women's movement today. Her great work, *Woman, Church and State*, is as timely as it was at the date of its original publication in 1893.

Gage is one of the great foresisters of contemporary feminists. In her writing she transcends the boundaries of time and becomes our contemporary. The qualities which make this possible are the depth of her daring and the a-mazing scope of her analysis. She made the connections which others feared to make. She prophesied, and she named the enemy. Consequently, of course, her stature has never been acknowledged.

*Woman, Church and State* was published when Gage was a Crone of sixty-seven. Her understanding had transcended the fixations upon suffrage and "equal rights" which stunted the imaginations of others. Like Virginia Woolf, who finally came to know that women must join the "Outsiders' Society" (see *Three Guineas*), Gage the Crone cast caution to the winds. She became a voyager in new woman-identified time/space. In her words:

> Woman herself must judge of woman. The most remote feminine personality is not less incomprehensible to man than the woman of to-day; he now as little understands the finer qualities of her soul or her high intuitive reasoning faculties as in the past. . . . Although the course of history has given many glimpses of her superiority, and the past few decades have shown in every land a new awakening of woman to a recognition of her own powers, man as man is still as obtuse as of yore.

Indeed. Perhaps as a young activist she had not fully known this, but Crone Gage had exorcised timidity. Unlike male authors, who generally become more conservative with age (after about thirty) she followed the route of all true Spinsters, becoming radical and free.

The effect upon me of re-reading *Woman, Church and State* in 1980 (together with Sally Roesch Wagner's clear and beautiful Introduction to the Persephone Press edition) was one of cumulative admiration, grief, rage, and hope. I will try to explain each of these responses, although of course they did not surface in a linear way.

First, this work is, in my estimation, extraordinarily admirable. It is a vast compendium of information; its breadth is breath-taking. It brings together apparently disparate phenomena, unveiling an astonishingly coherent pattern, giving the reader what Virginia Woolf called "a great delight to put the severed parts together." The book ranges from a discussion of the ancient matriarchate and the Goddess to a scathing analysis of christian priestly celibacy and its effects upon the sexual enslavement of women. It moves on to expose Canon law as a primary means of enforcing a double code of morals (for the holy sex and the unholy one). The fourth chapter then follows with one of the most moving exposés of female sexual slavery ever written, ranging from a discussion of the medieval custom of "Marquette" (according to which women were the rightful prey of their feudal lord) to a horrifying account of the organized kidnapping and imprisonment of young girls in the "dens" (brothels) guarded by bloodhounds in the lumber camps of Michigan and Wisconsin.

By the time the reader reaches the classic fifth chapter, "Witchcraft," which itself is worth the price of the book, it is more than evident that Gage's method is not merely chronological but Crone-logical. The madness in her method will appeal to every witch who reads the work (and for "witches," as Gage suggests, we can read "women," in order to gain fuller comprehension of the cruelties inflicted by the church upon women). This is followed by potent chapters on "Wives" and on "Polygamy." Nor does the book lose its momentum as it moves toward its end. The chapter "Woman and Work" is a poignant and informative treatise on the subject of the brutal exploitation of women's labor in christian countries. This is followed by "The Church of To-day," which can be recognized as absolutely timely by women who have followed such media events as the 1979 papal visit to the United States and the woman-hating crusades of Jesus-enthusiasts like Anita Bryant, Marabel Morgan, and Ruth Carter Stapleton.

The final chapter, "Past, Present, Future," explicitly names the threads of connectedness that have run through this monumental work. Gage points out that, while other scholars have examined separate parts of women's history, "hardly anyone has attempted to outline them into a whole and ascertain the way they are connected with each other." She *has* outlined them into a whole:

> The most stupendous system of organized robbery known has been that of the church towards woman, a robbery that has not only taken her

> self-respect but all rights of person; the fruits of her own industry; her opportunities of education; the exercise of her own judgment, her own conscience, her own will.

A second strand in my experience of re-reading *Woman, Church and State* in 1980 was profound grief. Those of us who in this century have written analytical/historical studies of the rape, murder, and dismemberment of women legitimated by patriarchal religion can feel deeply connected with the passionate writing of Gage. It is a case of "the more you see the more you see." This is not a despair-laden grief, however. My experience of re-encountering these horrors as depicted on the tapestries of Gage's work has not been paralyzing but empowering. One reason for this empowering power of her book is, I think, that its clear focus elicits creative rage.

Rage, then, is my third response to this book: rage at the multifarious atrocities she exposes; fury at the erasure of Gage's work. It is infuriating that her place in the nineteenth century feminist movement was erased/minimized by women historians—but this is, in a sense, of minor import. Matilda was not obsessively concerned about "credit" for her role as an activist in the annals of history. She was too much alive for that kind of concern. However, she did care that the ideas and information she put together in her writings be known and understood by women. She obviously wanted women to have these ideas and this information and thus be enabled to *move* to "a brighter day." It is the erasure of Gage's written work—our rightful heritage—that is ultimately enraging. The fact that this book has been out of print, the fact that most women who have passed through years of undergraduate and graduate university education are ignorant of its contents and even of its existence—all of this is ineffably enraging. However, the focused, clarifying rage thus elicited can fuel creative feminist hope.

Hope is the primary motivation and product of *Woman, Church and State*. The book was obviously created by Gage in a spirit of passionate hope. She wrote of "the wide psychic under-current which seething through women's souls, is overthrowing the civilizations built upon the force principles of the patriarchate and will soon reinstate the reign of truth and justice."

Of course, one could respond with cynicism that this book was first published almost ninety years ago and that "the reign of truth and justice" hardly seems to have been reinstated. I think that such cynicism misses the point, however. Gage knew that truth and justice first have to reign in women's psyches in the form of creative vision. It was because of its tough creative vision that this book was erased, and it is precisely for this same reason that it is surfacing again. As Matilda wrote:

> The world is full of signs of the near approach of this period; as never before is there an arousing sense of something deeper, holier in religion than the christian church has given.

"Near approach" must be measured not chronologically, but Crone-logically. The threads of connectedness between Gage and radical feminists of the 1980s are here, strong and spinning. Spinsters' rage at our affliction of apparent amnesia, which has been inflicted upon us by the patriarchal mind-controllers and lobotomists, will help to ensure that we will not allow the pattern to be lost again.

Like that great twentieth century Hag, Elizabeth Gould Davis (author of *The First Sex*), Gage knew that women are *not* "the second sex." The strength of this knowledge and conviction enabled her to stride past the traps and snares set for the faint-hearted. In her Cronehood she discovered uncompromising vision. Overcoming the cautions of those who thought they could reach "all women" by overlooking the essentially woman-destroying nature of christianity she demonstrated that "the fashions of the christian world have changed but not its innermost belief." Fittingly, *Woman, Church and State* is "Addressed to all Persons, who breaking away from custom and the usage of the ages, dare seek Truth for the sake of Truth."

*Dare* is a good verb to describe what Matilda does. In the 1980s when the word *feminist* is being tamed to include almost everyone, a dose of her daring is what she might call a much needed "tonic." In this decade, when women are being seduced by the right and seduced by the left in the name of feminism, when millions of women cheer the Pope and "radical feminists" expend their energies crusading for the ordination of women to the christian priesthood, when women are persuaded in the name of feminism that they should be drafted into military service, when hundreds of thousands are conned into believing that dulled out depression caused by therapeutic treatment is bliss and that gynecologists know what is good for them—in the name of feminism, and when the work of radical Hags like Gage is hidden, erased, re-covered in Women's Studies courses, it is indeed high time that Matilda's work be re-introduced to us and that we re-member her.

Finally, at this time, when the creative rage of Revolting Hags is surfacing, when our network is expanding, when Spooking, Sparking, and Spinning are intensifying, when more and more women are understanding that this is the age of ultimate warfare between principalities and powers, when nuclear holocaust can be seen as the logical and technological embodiment of christian doctrine, those women who intend to survive are very close in spirit to Matilda Joslyn Gage. It is good that in 1980 Persephone Press is bringing out *Woman, Church and State.*

## 22

# On Lust and the Lusty

From introduction to *Pure Lust*, pp. 1–12.

*Elemental:* ["characterized by stark simplicity, naturalness, or unrestrained or undisciplined vigor or force . . . CRUDE, PRIMITIVE, FUNDAMENTAL, BASIC, EARTHY"—*Webster's*]: This definition has been awarded *Websters'* Intergalactic Seal of Approval.
—*Wickedary*, p. 72

Six years separate the publication of *Gyn/Ecology* (1978) and *Pure Lust* (1984), during which time the controversies surrounding *Gyn/Ecology*, as well as changes in the women's liberation movement, created feminist polarization around the figure of Mary Daly. Under these circumstances, the fact that *Pure Lust* (in the opinion of one of the editors, Daly's strongest work philosophically) emerged as a nearly perfect blending of the righteous anger of *Gyn/Ecology* with the ontological, cosmological dimensions of *Beyond God the Father* is nothing short of astonishing.

Take, for example, this paragraph from the introduction:

> Elemental female Lust is intense longing/craving for the cosmic concrescence that is creation. It is charged, tense, in tension with the tenses of fabricated "father time." Incensed, it burns through the shallow impressions of insipid senses, sensing the Sources, Astral Forces, Angels and Graces that call from the Deep. This Lusting is divining: foreseeing, foretelling, forecasting. Unlike the dim divines and divinities, the deadheads of dead-land whose ill-luminations blind us, Lusty women portend with luster, our radiance from within that radiates from and toward Original Powers of creation.

Words are used for their resonance, their pinpoint accuracy, their multivalence, their sound, their cadence and incantatory power, while the dialectic tension between achieving a living union with be-ing and struggling against the non-being of patriarchy takes on cosmological rather than historical or political significance. Daly makes this explicit when she says that "women dis-cover our Original Race through the release of deep ontological Fury."

However, the controversies had to be addressed, and Daly tried to counter the questions about her racial presumptions by defining "Race" differently, as an active verb rather than as a noun. Whether one agrees or disagrees with her perspective on this, it seems clear that she refused to address race within the existing parameters of the discussion.

The section explaining the title of the book features an analysis of a Pauline text. Daly uses Paul's hatred of this world, and of any elemental beings or philosophies, to give the clearest positive assessment of the feminist elemental spirituality she champions: "The joy of Elemental women, then, is Earthy, and so also is our philosophic quest." Going beyond the false dichotomy of transcendence and immanence, Daly articulates "the essential unity and intelligence of spirit/matter, the inherent telos of spirit/matter." This culminated in the rich term "Nag-Gnostic" to describe those who assume the existence of "transcendental knowledge" but "never cease to Nag our Selves and others with recurrent awareness and uncertainty."

—Editors

*Eye-beam:* "archaic: a radiant glance of the eye."
—*Webster's Third New International Dictionary of the English Language*[1]

*I-Beam:* "Archaic: a radiant glance of the I/Eye."
*Websters' First New Intergalactic Wickedary of the English Language*[2]

This book focuses upon and Spirals off from the traditional Deadly Sin of lust, which is treated here in an untraditional way. Phallic lust is seen as a fusion of obsession and aggression. As obsession it specializes in genital fixation and fetishism, causing broken consciousness, broken heartedness, broken connections among women and between women and the elements. As aggression it rapes, dismembers, and kills women and all living things within its reach. Phallic lust begets phallocratic society, that is sadosociety, which is, in fact, pseudosociety. The Lusty women who rage and roam through the Realms of this book wield the Labryses of our lustrous minds—our double-axes of divination—to defeat this obsession/aggression.

## The Title of This Book

The title *Pure Lust* is double-sided. On one side, it Names the deadly dispassion that prevails in patriarchy—the life-hating lechery that rapes and kills the objects of its obsession/aggression. Indeed, the usual meaning of *lust* within the Lecherous State of patriarchy is well known. It means "sexual desire, especially of a violent self-indulgent character: LECHERY, LASCIVIOUSNESS."[3] Phallic lust, violent and self-indulgent, levels all life, dismembering spirit/matter, attempting annihilation. Its refined cultural products, from the sadistic pornography of the Marquis de Sade to the sadomasochistic theology of Karl Barth, are on a continuum: they are essentially the same. This lust is *pure* in the sense that it is characterized by unmitigated malevolence. It is *pure* in the sense that it is ontologically evil, having as its end the braking/breaking of female being.[4] Its goal is the obliteration of natural knowing and willing, of the deep purposefulness which philosophers have called *final causality*—our innately ordained Self-direction toward Happiness.[5]

The word *Lust* has utterly Other meanings than this, however. It means "VIGOR, FERTILITY (the increasing lust of the earth or of the plant—Francis Bacon)." It means "an intense longing: CRAVING." It means "EAGERNESS, ENTHUSIASM." The word, then, derived from the Latin *lascivus*, meaning wanton, playful, is double-edged. Wise women wield our wits, making this word our wand, our Labrys. For it Names not only the "thrust of the argument" that assails women and nature on all levels (mythic, ideological, institutional, behavioral) but also the way out—the vigor, eagerness, and intense longing that launches Wild women on Journeys beyond the State of Lechery.

Primarily, then, *Pure Lust* Names the high humor, hope, and cosmic accord/harmony of those women who choose to escape, to follow our hearts' deepest desire and bound out of the State of Bondage, Wanderlusting and Wonderlusting with the elements, connecting with auras of animals and plants, moving in planetary communion with the farthest stars. This Lust is in its essence astral. It is pure Passion: unadulterated, absolute, simple sheer striving for abundance of be-ing. It is unlimited, unlimiting desire/fire. One moved by its magic is Musing/Re-membering. Choosing to leave the dismembered state, she casts her lot, life, with the trees and the winds, the sands and the tides, the mountains and moors. She is Outcast, casting her Self outward, inward, breaking out of the casts/castes of phallocracy's fabrications/fictions, moving out of the maze of mediated experience. As she lurches/leaps into starlight her tears become tidal, her cackles cosmic, her laughter Lusty.

The struggle Named by the Labrys of this title is between reality and unreality, between the natural Wild, which is be-ing, and man-made fabrications that fracture her substance, simulate her soul. It is between the desire, eagerness, vigor, enthusiasm of/for expanding be-ing, which philosophers have called final causality, and blockage/blockers of this reaching of be-ing. Such blockage *is* the State of Lechery, in which longing for participation in transcendent Be-ing is reified, displaced, plasticized, rehabilitated.

Elemental female Lust is intense longing/craving for the cosmic concrescence that is creation. It is charged, tense, in tension with the tenses of fabricated "father time." Incensed, it burns through the shallow impressions of insipid senses, sensing the Sources, Astral Forces, Angels and Graces that call from the Deep. This Lusting is divining: foreseeing, foretelling, forecasting. Unlike the dim divines and divinities, the deadheads of deadland whose ill-luminations blind us, Lusty women portend with luster, our radiance from within that radiates from and toward Original Powers of creation.

The word *luster* is itself a double-edged word, a Labrys, having quite opposite definitions. It means, on the one hand, "a glow of reflected light: GLOSS, SHEEN," and "a coating or substance that gives luster to a surface." On the other hand, it means "a glow of light from within: LUMINOSITY, SHINE: (luster of the stars)" and "an inner beauty: RADIANCE." These opposed definitions give clues concerning the condition of women and of words.

When reflecting the artificial lights of patriarchal prisons, words help us recognize the superficial coatings, the flashy phoniness of the fathers' foreground falsifications. Thus, for example, the word *woman* Names the alienating archetype that freezes female be-ing, locking us into prisons of "forever feminine" roles. But when we wield words to dis-close the inner beauty, the radiance of the Race of Lusty Women, we/they blaze open pathways to our Background/homeland. Thus *woman*, wisely wielded, Names a Wild and Lusty Female claiming wisdom, joy, and power as her own.

In their double-edged dimensions, then, words wield/yield messages about the tragedy of women and all Wild be-ing confined within imprisoning patriarchal parameters. Besides/beyond this, they radiate knowledge of an ancient age, and they let us know that they, the words themselves, are treasures trying to be freed, vibrations whose auras await awakening ears.

Breaking the bonds/bars of phallocracy requires breaking through to radiant powers of words, so that by releasing words, we can release our Selves. Lusty women long for radiant words, to free their flow, their currents, which like our own be-ing have been blocked and severed from ancestral Memory. The Race of Lusty Women, then, has deep connections with the Race of Radiant Words.

## Re-Calling the Elemental Race

A basic thesis of this book, implied in the title, is that women who choose biophilic be-ing belong to the Race of Lusty Women, which participates in the Race of Elemental be-ing. For we are rooted, as are animals and trees, winds and seas, in the Earth's substance. Our origins are in her elements. Thus, when true to our Originality, we are Elemental, that is "of, relating to, or caused by great force of nature."

Under the conditions of patriarchy, women dis-cover our Original Race through the release of deep ontological Fury. By *Fury* I do not mean an agitated state of chronic or acute anger that immobilizes, or that misfires at the wrong target. Rather, I mean a focused gynergetic will to break through the obstacles that block the flow of Female Force. Female Fury is Volcanic Dragonfire. It is Elemental breathing of those who love the Earth and her kind, who Rage against the erasure of our kind. It is the Rage of those who choose this, our own Race of Elemental be-ing over all man-made, male-designed divisions and categories, Naming our Selves and all truly life-loving creatures as priority, refusing to be e-raced, to be severed from our deep roots—refusing the effacement of our Race.[6] Lusty women experience great diversity, and know that we belong to many tribes.[7] Dis-covering radical female-identified diversity, we decline confinement in man-made racetracks.[8]

A primary meaning of *race* is "the act of rushing onward: RUN." This definition describes the movement of women who have dis-covered our original, Elemental Lust. Another definition is "a strong or rapid current of water that flows through a narrow channel." Elemental life must often flow through narrow channels, for in the State of Lechery options are narrowed. Yet, under these conditions, force and focus can be intense. *Race* also means "a heavy or choppy sea; especially one produced by the meeting of two tides." This definition indeed applies, for the Race of Women is Wild and Tidal, roaring with rhythms that are Elemental, that are created in cosmic encounters.

The principalities of the Phallic State continually connive to eradicate the Elemental Race, to reduce us to the state of possession by pulling us up by our roots, making us rootless. Their goal is our *deracination*, which is "detachment from one's background (as from homeland, customs, traditions)." Thus women and other Elemental creatures on this planet are rendered homeless, cut off from knowledge of our Race's customs and traditions. To the extent that such tactics are successful, we are *deracinated*, that is, "physically, mentally, or emotionally separated from [our] racial, social, or intellectual group: free from racial characteristics or influence (as deracinated migrants from another country)." In this way, our Racing is blocked, tracked into repetitive, circular movements. Cut off from our origins, we are disoriented.

Many women sense that we have been physically, mentally, and emotionally separated from our Original, Elemental Race, made "free"—that is, purified—of our own native characteristics and influence. We sense that we are "migrants from another country." Yet that country seems to be nowhere: it seems to be only a feminist utopian's dream.

Together with Virginia Woolf, feminists moan: "As a woman I have no country." And together with her we may add: "As a woman I want no country. As a woman my country is the whole world."[9] But there is something poignant about this brave assertion, for "the whole world" is groaning under phallic rule. It must be, then, that it is in some other dimension that "the whole world" is the country, the homeland of the

Race of Women. This is not to say that a woman should cease struggling for survival within, or rather, on the boundary of, phallocracy. But that struggle is inadequate without Pure Lust, the active longing that propels a woman into her own "country," that is, into the Realms of Elemental Reality, of ontological depth.

As the oppression and depression of the eighties increases, women are indeed pressured to be free from our "racial characteristics or influence." Subsumed under the fathers' spheres of influence women have forgotten that *influence* means "the exercise of a power like the supposed power of the stars: an emanation of spiritual or moral force." Afflicted with amnesia, women have been subliminally seduced into forgetting the emanations of spiritual/moral power that are the influence characteristic of this Race.

This book is an invitation to women to unforget our potentialities—to re-call the Elemental potency asleep in our ancestral Memory. This requires entering Elemental Realms, and encountering the Race of Radiant Words, that is, dis-covering Elemental feminist philosophy.

## The Subtitle of This Book: Elemental Feminist Philosophy

In scribing the words *Elemental feminist philosophy* I intend to Name a form of philosophical be-ing/thinking that emerges together with metapatriarchal consciousness—consciousness that is in harmony with the Wild in nature and in the Self. The force of this philosophy has its source in women breaking out of the tamed/tracked modes of thinking/feeling of phallocracy. It is the force of reason rooted in instinct, intuition, passion.

Several meanings of the word *Elemental* converge for the conjuring of Elemental feminist philosophy. An "obsolete" definition is "material, physical." The philosophy here unfolded is material/physical as well as spiritual, mending/transcending this deceptive dichotomy. Another definition is "characterized by stark simplicity, naturalness, or unrestrained or undisciplined vigor or force: not complex or refined: CRUDE, PRIMITIVE, FUNDAMENTAL, BASIC, EARTHY." Elemental feminist philosophy is crude (in a natural state), primitive (original, primary), fundamental, basic, and, especially, Earthy. Its stark complexity spurns contrived simplicity.

*Elemental* also means "SPIRIT, SPECTRE, WRAITH." The sixteenth-century alchemist, physician, philosopher Paracelsus used this word to name the spirits of the elements, the "administrators of the processes of the elements." Since, according to his own admission, Paracelsus learned everything he knew about healing from the Witches, we can surmise who were the true sources of his naming of Elementals.[10] Following sources from Greece, Egypt, India, and China he divided these into four groups: the gnomes (earth spirits), undines or nymphs (water spirits), salamanders (fire spirits), sylphs (air spirits).[11] Elementals, thus understood, provide Radiant Words for Naming our spiritual connections with the elements.

*Elemental* also means "a first principle: RUDIMENT." Wonderlusting women seek understanding of first principles. Sensing deeply that officially condoned knowledge has been on the wrong track, a Wild woman yearns to return to beginnings, to rudiments, to the original questions of her childhood, of her ancestral/racial Memory.[12] She recognizes that these have a special aura, that they are imbued with a sense of deep Wonder, which as Aristotle noted is the beginning of the philosophical quest.[13] For Wonderlusters, this is the quest for Elemental Wisdom, which is knowledge of first principles.

Clues about the nature of Elemental Wisdom can be gleaned from statements attributed to the apostle Paul—arch-hater of life in general and women in particular—concerning elements and Elementals. He wrote:

> See to it that no one makes a prey of you by philosophy and empty deceit, according to human tradition, according to the elemental spirits of the universe, and not according to Christ. (Col. 2:8 [R.S.V.])

It is evident that Paul experienced distaste for philosophy which is associated with Elemental spirits. The antithesis of such Wild Worldly Wisdom is Christ. The extent of the necrophilic lust motivating these words becomes even more evident later in the same chapter:

> If with Christ you died to the elemental spirits of the universe, why do you live as if you still belonged to the world? (Col. 2:20 [R.S.V.])

Elemental philosophy *is* of the world. It is for those who love and belong to this world, who experience Be-Longing in this world, who refuse the horror of Self-loss implied in dying "with Christ" to the Elemental spirits of the universe. In case there could be any delusions concerning the element-hating thrust of christian ideology, which seeks to kill Earthy wisdom, Paul drives home the point:

> Set your minds on things that are above, not on things that are on earth. For you have died, and your life is hid with Christ in God. (Col. 3:2–3 [R.S.V.])

In contrast to this, Elemental women experience our Selves, and, therefore, our philosophy, as rooted in love for the earth and for things that naturally are on earth. This Elemental Earthy Lust was expressed by Emily Brontë in *Wuthering Heights*, in the words of Catherine:

> "If I were in heaven, Nelly, I should be extremely miserable. . . . I dreamt once that I was there . . . that heaven did not seem to be my home; and I broke my heart with weeping to come back to earth; and the angels were so angry that they flung me out into the middle of the heath on the top of Wuthering Heights; where I woke sobbing for joy."[14]

The joy of Elemental women, then, is Earthy, and so also is our philosophic quest.

The lust to kill this philosophical quest is expressed in yet another pauline text, which provides further clues for understanding the perversion/reversal of primal Wonderlust:

> When we were children, we were slaves to the elemental spirits of the universe. But when the time had fully come, God sent forth his Son, born of woman, born under the law, to redeem those who were under the law, so that we might receive adoption as sons. And because you are sons, God has sent the Spirit of his Son into our hearts, crying "Abba! Father!" . . . But now that you have come to know God, or rather be known by God, how can you turn back again to the weak and beggarly elemental spirits, whose slaves you want to be once more? (Gal. 4:3–9 [R.S.V.])

Elemental women who have learned to recognize the technique of reversal will be suspicious of the word *slave* in this context. We do not wish to be redeemed by a god, to be adopted as sons, or to have the spirit of a god's son artificially injected into our hearts, crying "father." Having seen the horror of such phallocratic "spirituality," we indeed *can* "turn back again," re-membering our Selves as strong and proud "Elemental spirits," and using this expression as Metaphor to Name our Sources, Sisters, Muses, Friends, as well as our Selves. As we turn back, re-membering, we understand ever more deeply the war continually waged against Elemental life by the fathers and sons.

The logical outcome of the war against Elemental be-ing that is legitimated by such "spirituality" was expressed in the second epistle of Peter:

> But the day of the Lord will come like a thief, and then the heavens will pass away with a loud noise, and the elements will be dissolved with fire, and the earth and the works that are upon it will be burned up. (2 Pet. 3:10 [R.S.V.])

As self-fulfilling prophecy and manifesto of necrophilic faith, this "inspired" text is one among many that have paved the way for modern technological war against the elements, which takes such forms as nuclearism and chemical contamination. Understanding/moving through and beyond this war is the work of Elemental feminist philosophy of life.

Women who have not died to the Elemental spirits of the universe naturally do live as if we still belong to this world, which is the Otherworld in relation to the sadostate legitimated by Peter and Paul, Tom, Dick, and Harry. Naturally, we Lust for more re-membering of the elements and of Elemental spirits.

## Re-membering Elements

Unwittingly, biblical scholars have provided some helpful hints for Earthy Hags concerning the Greek word *stoicheia* as used in Paul's letters, which is translated sometimes as "elemental spirits" and sometimes simply as "the elements." It means: (1) the spoken letters of the alphabet; (2) the fire, air, earth, and water of which the world was thought to be constituted; (3) the elements of the universe, the larger cosmos, including the sun, moon, planets, and stars; (4) "the spirits, angels, and demons which were believed to ensoul the heavenly bodies, traverse all space, and inhabit every nook and cranny of earth, particularly tombs, desert places, and demented persons."[15] These multiple meanings not only name the targets of the life-haters who control sado-society. They can also aid adventurous Amazons to cut through the foreground films of deception into our Elemental Realms. These meanings can be examined separately.

First, *elements,* defined as the spoken letters of the alphabet, suggests—if a Wondering woman listens with her Third Ear—the primal Race of Words: their cosmic sounds, meanings, rhythms, and connections. The fathers, sons, and holy ghosts attempt to annihilate this Archaic alphabet, replacing these sounds with meaningless noises, with verbiage and verbigeration. Women Naming our own experience awaken our Powers to hear the Elemental sounds.

Second, *elements* as fire, air, earth, water constitute the deep Realms of reality with which our senses are naturally and Wildly connected. These Realms are masked by the mediators who produce substitutes for the natural components of this world. Women Naming this world for our Selves re-member our relations with these Earthy realities.

Third, *elements* as the larger cosmos describe the vast context within which primal powers must be understood. They also describe the context in which Elemental philosophy is woven and suggest the scope of the Wanderlust/Wonderlust that motivates exploration/creation. The lords of lechery hide this context by embedding unnatural limitations in minds, senses. Muses melt these blinders with the Fire of desire. We break them with the winds and waters of Wild Words, Racing free.

Finally, *Elemental spirits/angels/demons* may be understood as Metaphors manifesting the essential unity and intelligence of spirit/matter, the inherent telos of spirit/matter. They Name Intelligence ensouling the stars, animating the processes of earth, air, fire, water, enspiriting the sounds that are the elements of words, connecting words with the earth, air, fire, water and with the sun, moon, planets, stars. The Metaphoric language of "Elemental spirits" is crucial for the empowering of women, for this conjures memories of Archaic integrity that have been broken by phallic religion and philosophy. The task of reclaiming this integrity demands *Stamina*—the threads of life spun by the Fates. The Spinning of these threads is the task of Elemental philosophy. Also it is the work of Graces, the work of natural, Elemental Grace.

## Traveling Companions

Readers of *Gyn/Ecology* will recall that its Journey was/is a work of Hagography, a whirl through the time/space of Hag-ocracy, the Otherworld (Background) inhabited by Hags, Crones, Harpies, Furies, Amazons, Spinsters. As the Spooking, Sparking, and Spinning Voyagers continue to move, our Wanderlust/Wonderlust intensifies. The heat of our battles is heightened. The Force of our Fire is volcanic/epiphanic. The expanse of our Journey is Astral/Archaic and the Voyagers are Archelogians whose Lust is fueled by the influence of the stars.[16]

Archelogians are neither religious nor irreligious; we are Nag-Gnostic. One meaning of the verb *nag* is "to affect recurrent awareness, uncertainty, need for consideration, or concern; make recurrently aware of something (as a problem, solution, situation)." One meaning of the adjective *gnostic* is "believing in the reality of transcendental knowledge." Nag-Gnostic Archelogians sense with certainty the reality of transcendental knowledge. At the same time, we never cease to Nag our Selves and others with recurrent awareness and uncertainty.

The Nags who blaze the paths of *Pure Lust* are characterized by rich diversity. Fired by Dreadful Desire, we battle the butchers/blockers/stoppers. Reeling through new Realms, Nags conjure forth Sister-Nagsters, all fueled with Elemental Fury. The following list will Name and summon forth a few. We are: Augurs, Brewsters, Dikes, Dragons, Dryads, Fates, Phoenixes, Gorgons, Maenads, Muses. We are Naiads, Nixes, Gnomes, Norns, Nymphs. We are Oceanids, Oreads, Orishas, Pixies. We are Prudes, Salamanders, Scolds, Shrews, Sibyls, Sirens. We are Soothsayers, Sprites, Stiffs, Sylphs, Undines. We are Viragos, Virgins, Vixens, Websters, Weirds.

As the crowd increases, the diversity intensifies. Our power is not of numbers but of astral force.

23

# Metaphors of Metabeing

From introduction to *Pure Lust*, pp. 24–30.

*First Philosophy* ["*Aristotelianism*: a study of being as being. . . . *Aristotelianism*: a study of supersensible immutable being"—*Webster's*] *1: Elemental Feminist Philosophy:* a study of be-ing as be-ing *2: Elemental Feminist Philosophy:* a study of Super Sensible Shape-shifting be-ing.
—*Wickedary*, p. 76

This section from the introduction to *Pure Lust* elucidates Daly's philosophic approach, in particular her embrace of language and wordplay to re-call dimensions of existence, life, and the archaic past that have been buried by patriarchy. In presenting her reasons, though, Daly went beyond the metaphors to three key ontological claims that are axiomatic for her.

The first concerns her development of God-the-Verb, now Goddess-the-Verb. This dynamic sacred, first introduced in *Beyond God the Father*, now was described with explicitly metaphoric language, so that naming the Verb with a noun becomes not a stagnant limitation but an intentionally self-aware means of describing another manifestation of Be-ing: "When I choose to use such words as *Goddess* it is to point Metaphorically to the Powers of Be-ing, the Active Verb in whose potency all biophilic reality participates."

Second, Daly bounced off of a description of ontological wonder she encountered in Tillich (though it goes back, ultimately, to Heidegger). Tillich faces the "shock of possible nonbeing" by asking, "Why is there something instead of nothing?" Daly, after acknowledging the (seeming) profundity of this question, asserted that such a question would not "arise spontaneously" in a biophilic setting, where the question is why patriarchal nothingness wants to project itself into Be-ing.

Third, Daly explicitly engaged an ancient tension in any dynamic and monistic/pluralistic philosophic system: how can we describe unity and diversity simultaneously? Daly explicitly cast the question of the One

and the Many as part of the debate around diversity within the women's movement. It likely convinced no one to change their perspectives, but ultimately its importance may emerge as a means to understanding her ontology rather than her ethics or historical context.
—Editors

At this point it is important to discuss briefly the role of symbols and metaphors in Elemental feminist philosophy, particularly since this mode of discourse traditionally has been disdained by philosophers in general and metaphysicians in particular. Since this work describes/unfolds a deviant philosophy—and a philosophy for deviants—the reader might jump to the facile conclusion that the use of metaphor is "understandable" or even "excusable" in the absence of an adequate philosophical/metaphysical tradition to express woman-identified thought. The point is, however, that symbols and "mere" metaphors are required, not because of some deficiency or lack in the sphere of abstract conceptualization, but because of the demanding, rigorous nature of the work itself.

Symbols, in contrast to mere signs, participate in that to which they point. They open up levels of reality otherwise closed to us and they unlock dimensions and elements of our souls which correspond to these hidden dimensions and elements of reality. As Tillich pointed out, they cannot be artificially produced, but rather grow out of the unconscious. "They grow when the situation is ripe for them, and they die when the situation changes."[1] There is no way that Elemental feminist philosophy can speak adequately to the realms of Wild be-ing without symbols. In dis-covering these, we must pay particular attention to the task of "sounding out" symbols. Of course, there can be no One Absolutely Right symbol for all Lusty women, for we belong to different tribes and have great individual diversity. Despite this fact, and also because of it, Prudes prudently heed our intuitions about which symbols ring true, listening to the sounds of their names and to the rhythms of the contexts in which this Naming occurs.

When I use the word *metaphor* I intend this to include the qualities attributed above to symbols. However, there is more involved. As theologian Nelle Morton has explained, metaphors evoke action, movement. They Name/evoke a shock, a clash with the "going logic" and they introduce a new logic.[2] Metaphors function to Name change, and therefore they elicit change. When, for example, I write of women using double-edged words as *Labryses* to cut through mazes of man-made mystification, the word *Labrys* is not a static symbol; rather, it is associated with transforming action. Thus the very arduousness of the task of Naming and calling forth Elemental be-ing requires metaphors.[3]

The word *metaphor* is derived from the Greek *meta* plus *pherein*, meaning to bear, carry. Moreover, *metapherein* means to transfer, change. Metaphors of Muses carry us past the unnatural being/things that are simulations of be-ing, leaving these in the past. Metaphors of Soothsayers carry us toward knowledge of our future as they connect us with our Racing memories. They transform/transfer our perceptions of reality, enabling us to "break set" and thus to break out of linguistic prisons.

Metaphors are necessary for Elemental feminist philosophy, for this is about and *is* transformation, movement. It is philosophy in the basic sense of "love or pursuit of wisdom: search for the underlying principles and causes of reality." This Lust/pursuit is Racing; it is Musing. An Archaic meaning of the verb *muse* is "to become astonished: WONDER, MARVEL." Women who Lust for wisdom become astonished/astonishing, Wondering. As Muses of our own creation, Wonderlusters remember our Original Powers. Unlike the frozen "philosophy" that is packaged and stored within academic refrigerators, Wonderlust moves us always. Our vehicles are often Metaphors. Our destinations are the Realms of Metabeing.

The word *Metabeing* is used here to Name Realms of active participation in the Powers of Be-ing.[4] Be-ing, the Verb, cannot without gross falsification be reified into a noun, whether that noun be identified as "Supreme Being," or "God," or "Goddess" (singular or plural). When I choose to use such words as *Goddess* it is to point Metaphorically to the Powers of Be-ing, the Active Verb in whose potency all biophilic reality participates.

A problem that is implicit in such Naming is the classic philosophical problem of "the one and the many." For it is clear that Lusty women are profoundly different from each other. Not only are there ethnic, national, class and racial differences that shape our perspectives, but there are also individual and cross-cultural differences of temperament, virtue, talent, taste, and of conditions within which these can or cannot find expression. There is, then, an extremely rich, complex Diversity among women and within each individual. But there is also above, beyond, beneath all this a Cosmic Commonality, a tapestry of connectedness which women as Websters/Fates are constantly weaving. The weaving of this tapestry is the Realizing of a dream, which Adrienne Rich has Named "The Dream of a Common Language."[5]

The word *Metabeing* is a metaphysical way of Naming forth and Naming faith in this common bonding of Lusty women. For *Metabeing* Names the Elemental participation in Powers of Be-ing which is the source of authentic female bonding. By choosing the plural—*Powers* of Be-ing—I intend to affirm our Diversity within Commonality.[6]

*Metabeing* conveys multiple meanings, since the prefix *meta* has several senses. First, it means "occurring later." This aspect is important since, under patriarchal conditions, knowledge of participation in Elemental Powers of Be-ing is experienced as an existential breakthrough *after* a woman has understood that the blockage of her powers within phallocracy, that is, the reduction of these to mere things/beings, is insufferable. The second meaning of *meta*, which is "situated behind," is also essential, for Lusty women's dis-coverings of our be-ing are not experienced as entirely new. In breaking through the man-made reifications of Be-ing, women enter Realms that are situated behind these reifications—the Realms of our ancestral memories. These memories can move women out of the passive state of things/nouns, cut off from our own be-ing.

The third sense of *meta*, that is, "change in, transformation of," thus follows logically, for dis-covering Metabeing means transforming release of lives that have been fragmented and frozen into stagnant bits of being. Since this transformation is not "once and for all," but rather a continuing process, the fourth meaning of *meta*, that is, "beyond, transcending," is also essential. The Realms of *Metabeing* are times/spaces of continuing transcending of earlier stages of shedding the shackles of body/mind that fix women as targets of phallic lust.

Metaphors of Metabeing awaken Muses, awaken in Muses memories that transform us, transfer us to these Realms of continuing transcending. Once partially awake, Muses awaken more Metaphors. We live in a veritable sea of sleeping Metaphors. Philosopher Susanne Langer referred to "faded" metaphors and suggested that "our literal language is a very repository of 'faded metaphors.'"[7] Explaining this, she wrote:

> . . . if a metaphor is used very often, we learn to accept the word in its metaphorical context as though it had a literal meaning there. If we say: "The brook runs swiftly," the word "runs" does not connote any leg-action, but a shallow rippling flow. If we say that a rumor runs through the town, we think of neither leg-action nor of ripples; or if a fence is said to run around the barnyard, there is not even a connotation of changing place. Originally they were probably all metaphors but one (though it is hard to say which was the primitive literal sense).[8]

Like Langer, Shrews are aware of apparently faded metaphors, but unlike Langer's theory, Shrewish analysis dis-covers a sexual politics of fading. Powerful old words whose Metaphoric force has "faded" under the reign of phallicism include *Spinster*, *Witch*, *charm*, *spell*, *Weird*, *Goddess*. In fact, these words have not lost their vitality but have been covered under rubble heaps of bore-ocratic verbiage. Dis-covering them is a Wonder-full Work for Websters, yielding endless riches. Like Gnomes who know how to find buried treasures, we unearth these riches and share this abundance with friends. To snools,[9] of course, the treasures remain invisible, "faded."

Carried by Metaphors to the Realms of Metabeing, Musing women encounter/uncover our own First Questions and hence find our First Philosophy. Since Prudes are occupied with our own priorities, making biophilic participation in Be-ing our ultimately intimate concern, it is imperative that we Weave a First Philosophy of the First Sex. Implicit in this Naming of the first sex is a conjuring of such visionary Foresisters as Elizabeth Gould Davis—the bold ones, the uncompromising Crones.[10]

In the classic philosophical tradition, *first philosophy* means ontology, the "philosophy of being." In the Elemental transition, *first philosophy* Names the philosophy of be-ing. It is first in the sense that it is Elemental, for elements are first principles. Since this first philosophy is about Elemental be-ing, it is radically metaphysical, concerned with ontological potency, knowledge, passion, virtue, creation, transformation. Given this complexity, our thinking must be not only imaginatively intense and concrete, but also intellectually extensive and abstract. The deep Spinning power of Metaphor is essential, and so is the honed logic of traditionally rational discourse. To Wonderlusters, these are as inseparable as the edges of the Labrys.

A standard definition of *ontology* is "the science or study of being; that department of metaphysics that related to the being or essence of things, or to being in the abstract" (*O.E.D.*). Traditionally, it has attempted to deal with the most primary philosophical questions. Yet the questions have been framed/confined within parameters that fail to express biophilic intuitions. They are framed by the word *being* itself. Theologian/philosopher Paul Tillich exemplifies these limitations.[11] He wrote, for example:

> The ontological question, the question of being-itself, arises in something like a "metaphysical shock"—the shock of possible nonbeing. This shock often has been expressed in the question, "Why is there something; why not nothing?"[12]

Readers who have subjected themselves to philosophical "discipline" are familiar with such language. One of the positive things that can happen when biophilic women read such words is the eliciting of a memory of an intuition of be-ing. The situation is complex, however. As a result of the intellectual deprivation inflicted upon all women, those who can still feel a deep thirst for philosophy are often too respectful of such "masters" and overlook their fundamental fallacy—phallicism. Thus, when reading the question "Why is there something; why not nothing?" a Wonderlusty woman might imagine that the question thus posed corresponds to her own ontological experience, to her Lust for Be-ing. She might imagine that the ontological question thus posed expresses an attitude identical with her own Wonder and gratitude that things *are*. Caught up in this Wonder, she might fail to notice anything suspect about the second half of Tillich's question: "why not nothing?" Musing women would do well to ask ourSelves whether this question would arise spontaneously in biophilic consciousness.

Thought that starts with the noun, *being*, cannot go behind it—cannot transform/transfer itself into Realms of Metabeing. Such thought is stuck, fixated, fixed and thus does not actively participate in Powers of Be-ing. It is terrified of these Powers. Tillich reveals his terror:

> Thought is based on being, and it cannot leave this basis; but thought can imagine the negation of everything that *is*, and it can describe the nature and structure of being which give everything that is the power of resisting nonbeing.[13]

The philosophers of phallicism, huddling behind the bastions of reified *being*, unable to leave this basis, can well imagine the negation of these bastions of boring thought, for they know that they are living, as it were, in a house of cards. The implications of such ontology are the antithesis of Wonderlusty, Elemental philosophy, the quest for Be-ing. The fact of the antithesis must be evident to Nag-Gnostic Archelogians.

The quest of Wanton women is not preoccupied with terror of "the negation of everything that *is*." Rather it is rooted in the intuition that Powers of Be-ing are constantly unfolding, creating, communicating—Be-ing more. And it is rooted in the experience of active potency to move behind the Foreground of fathergods and other fabrications, fictions, fixed questions and answers, entering the Radiant Realms of Metabeing.

## 24

# Beyond the Sado-Sublime

## *Exorcising Archetypes, Evoking the Archimage*

From chapter 2 of *Pure Lust*, pp. 102–13, 116.

> *Arch-Image:* Mary: vestige of the Goddess symbol that has been preserved in christianity as a hook for the Heathen masses; tamed Goddess symbol which, although it is intended to conceal the Background Memory of the Archimage, functions at times to evoke Archaic Active Potency in women
> *Archimage 1:* the Original Witch within *2:* Power/Powers of Be-ing within all women and all Biophilic creatures *3:* Active Potency of Hags *4:* Metaphor pointing toward Metabeing, in which all Elemental Life participates.
> —*Wickedary*, p. 63

Mary Daly, by virtue of both her own name and her intellectual training in catholic institutions, retained an interest in Mariology, reinterpreting catholic dogma as an elaborate rape, burial, and plasticization of the Goddess. In this excerpt, she develops the categories of Arch-Image and Archimage—one of her less successful neologisms—to contrast the rage of authentically living women (Archimage) with the "impotent priests' hatred of Female Power" and "their attempt at ontological castration" of the Virgin Mary.

This section also includes an analysis of tokenism and exceptionalism, as exemplified in the Virgin Mary. Tokenism gives an "illusion of progress" that breaks solidarity among women, "taming the radical impulse with false hope." The token comes to believe in her own exceptional status, and therefore accepts her sponsorship by the patriarchy. Daly offers an important counterbalance to the process of tokenism in endnote 9 of this excerpt, where she asserts the ontological existence of a Self, regardless of the oppressive attempts to erase it.

Few passages better capture the ecstasy of the intellectual life as Daly lived it than this one:

> Such study requires Stamina, staying power, which is also Straying Power—ability to Stray off the tracks of traditions that betray women and nature. Straying is sparked by E-motion, that is, passion that moves women to thinking and acting The Way Out. E-motion is ecstatic, delirious. *Delirium* is derived from the Latin *de* (from, off) plus *lira* (track). Deliberate delirium keeps us off the tracks of trained responses, traditional expectations. Since the word *learn* is also derived from *lira,* it is clear that Lusty women's delirium should be a matter of Studied Unlearning. The word *studied* is important here, for one must know the tracks well in order to break out of them, without sliding back into them. To be truly truant requires study/training and untiring untraining. The process is unnarrowing, harrowing. Ultimately, its motivating E-motion is Wonderlust/Wanderlust. Its scope is vast, visionary, planetary. The wonderings/wanderings of Straying women are wayward, earthward, skyward. Witches long and learn to fly.

—Editors

## The Immaculate Conception

It is Crone-logically significant that although belief in the "Immaculate Conception" of Mary was part of popular piety for centuries, it was not made an official dogma of catholic faith until 1854. For this coincides with the period when the so-called "first wave" of feminism was beginning to crest. The year 1848 marked the first Women's Rights convention in America, in Seneca Falls, New York. From 1848 on, American feminists increasingly voiced their grievances. Susan B. Anthony, Matilda Joslyn Gage, Angelina and Sarah Grimké, Elizabeth Oakes Smith, Elizabeth Cady Stanton, Sojourner Truth, and Emma Willard—to name a few—were beginning to find their voices.

Moreover, the killer instinct of the patriarchal males responded immediately. The impotent priests of the medical profession aimed their weapons directly at the female genital area, creating the gynocidal field of gynecology.[1]

The rise of feminism and the anti-feminist backlash were occurring more or less simultaneously in Europe.[2] Throughout Europe, ministers and journalists as well as politicians denounced female independence. In England, distinguished male writers in the late 1840s were protesting against the exercise of intellect in women—for example, Benjamin Disraeli in *Sybil* (1845) and William Thackeray in *Pendennis* (1848–50). It is within this context that Crone-ologists should analyze the proclamation in 1854 of the dogma of the "Immaculate Conception" by pope Pius IX, in the Bull *Ineffabilis Deus*. This bull signaled an advanced stage of chicanery, beautifully parodied in the title of Suzanne Arms' book on childbirth, *Immaculate Deception*.[3]

This dogma is a baffling phenomenon. It presents for belief a concept which is quite inconceivable, as we shall presently see. According to the dogma, Mary was conceived in her mother's womb without "original sin." Of course, it might seem that there is really nothing remarkable about such a conception, especially if one does not accept the concept of "original sin."[4] Thus the very fact that such a conception would be proclaimed, and proclaimed as unique, is already mind-boggling. This, however, is only the beginning of the boggle.

The doctrine of the "Virgin Birth" of Jesus—a doctrine that should not be confused with the "Immaculate Conception"—is also subversive of ancient myths of the parthenogenetic goddess.[5] Since parthenogenesis would produce only female offspring, the story of the "Virgin Birth" of a male savior should be eminently suspect. Or, to put it another way, the birth of Jesus was *indeed* a miracle, as Martha Yates has pointed out.[6] However, in comparison with the immaculate conception, the virgin-birth-of-Jesus story is but a pale perversion. The greater deception, the deeper mythic undermining of the Originally Parthenogenetic Goddess required the erasure of her own Self, prior to her role as mother-of-god.

Such mythic erasure of Mary's Self was attempted through the immaculate conception doctrine. According to this inconceivable doctrine, Mary was "preserved" from original sin by the grace of her son immediately at the moment of her conception—not only in advance of *his* birth, but also in advance of her own. Nor was she merely "purified" as an embryo in the womb of her mother.[7] Indeed, according to this astonishing doctrine, Mary never had a moment of life, even of embryonic life, without being "full" of the "grace" merited by her son through his death on the cross. Thus she was purified of autonomous be-ing before ever experiencing even an instant of this.

The doctrine certainly can be read as an expression of the impotent priests' hatred of Female Power. Indeed it represents their attempt at ontological castration of the Arch-Image, and, through her, of the Archimage.[8] Mary is so "full of grace" that she is de-natured, destined to become the mother of a god-son who bestows upon her his pseudo-nature, this "grace." In this pornographic mythic mirror-world, the son totals his virgin-mother-victim. The immaculate conception is the ultimate depiction of (pre-natal) woman-battering, a mythic model of incestuous assault. It is the primal rape of the Arch-Image. Within the mad ill-logic of dogmatic constructs, it is logically prior to the rape of the Virgin that takes place at "The Annunciation," when the adolescent Mary is told by the angel Gabriel that she is to be the mother-of-god and gives her fictitious assent. To put it in other words, as a consequence of her initial rape ("grace") Mary has been totaled, made totally unable to resist divine aggression/lust/rape. At "The Annunciation," then, the already raped Mary "consents" to further rape.

In the world of christian symbols, then, the immaculate conception exhibits a kind of ultimacy in undermining women—going far beyond the rape, killing, and dismemberment of the full-grown parthenogenetically conceived Goddess. Its target is her parthenogenetic (woman-identified) origin, and thus it undermines her original Power of Self-Naming, and Creation.[9] Since the Original Source, the Archimage, cannot be defiled, she has been symbolically simulated and this simulation has been defiled and therefore called "Immaculate." Such rape of Female Archaic Power is appropriately named the "Immaculate Conception" since it is a purely phallic (mis)conception, a purification/purge of conceptions/memories of Elemental female be-ing. As Anne Dellenbaugh has remarked, this resonates with women's common experience of rape—one effect of which is the blockage of thoughts, the breaking/interruption of the thinking process.[10] Rape "purifies" women's conceptions, making these conform to phallic norms. Thus the doctrine is a mythic model for the thought/memory-stopping dimensions of rape.

Through its subliminal messages, then, the doctrine of the "Immaculate Conception" sets forth the image of Mary as model rape victim. From the moment of her conception she is ineffably undermined by this sublime spiritual rape. Later, by her inevitable acceptance of Gabriel's message, she seeks salvation by the rapist. In "real life," it is also often the case that once raped, a woman finds it difficult to forget the horrible event; she is continually trying to undo it. Conditioned to believe that she is to blame for the rape, she seeks to undo it by seeking male approval, for she no longer trusts the power of her own judgment. Believing that, through her own fault, a male has succeeded in degrading/defiling her, she concludes that only a male can save her. Thus rape implies the need of a male savior. This is one reason for the hold of christian myth upon women's raped psyches. The myth itself, of course, reinforces the self-blame of victimized women.

The immaculate conception thus illustrates and legitimates the ineffable circularity of rapism. Already violated at her conception, Mary affirms at the annunciation her need of male acceptance. Her initial violation made the later one—when "she conceived of the Holy Ghost" in order to become the mother-of-god—unavoidable. Pure rapism is inconceivably circular.[11]

Mary's victimization is astonishing. She was totaled across time. Anne Dellenbaugh has remarked that as "Virgin" she is a reminder to women of their destiny to be raped, for in the patriarchal system, a virgin is a future rape victim.[12] Since she is "forever virgin" (despite her maternity), she is forever future rape victim. The message is even exacerbated by the extremity of her tantalizing purity.[13] Moreover, as archetypal "Mother," she is past rape victim. Encompassing all time, her rape is the perpetual entombment of her life-time.

By their subliming of this monstrous mythic disguise for the Archimage, the impotent priests produced an archetype who could not have had a Divine Daughter because she had been purified of her Self, and indeed never had been herSelf. Such a being would be inconceivable to herself. Totally de-natured of her Powers as parthenogenetic Goddess, she was set up as model for patriarchal women. And indeed patriarchally possessed women cannot have Daughters, although they may have female offspring. Patriarchal women cannot create, for they have been made unable to conceive of themselves—of their Selves. Thus an Elemental Female tradition within patriarchal structures is inconceivable.

Faced with this mythic and lived out boggle/baffle, Musing women can choose to exorcize the patriarchal myth through Naming and Living our own lives—which is to breathe forth the Archimage within. Only women who choose to participate in the Archimage can conceive of our Selves, creating our Selves and our tradition.[14] As more Websters find the Original Witch within, we obliterate the raped replacement and make ancestral Memories more available. It is by Self-identified creating that women can crack the archetypal mirrors, finding Archai/Beginnings, becoming Verbs, unleashing our Powers.

## The "Immaculate Conception" and the Strategies of Tokenism

We have seen that the doctrine of the immaculate conception appeared much later in christian myth and theology than did the virgin birth. Many centuries of preparation were required for acceptance of *this* belief.

To put the matter bluntly, symbolically speaking the Goddess had to be totally done in, in order to be an appropriate mother-of-god. The fact that the church could not get around to this tidying up of the Goddess-murder program until recently would seem to have been a matter of political strategy. For, as we have seen, the power of the Arch-Image had been needed in order to convert the "pagans," even at the risk that this power might get out of hand. Moreover, it is Crone-logically significant that the proclamation of this dogma followed the European Witchcraze, for the mass murder of women and its deep psychic impact paved the way for the deceptively degrading dogma.

The promulgation of the dogma was equivalent to an advanced refining/subliming of the Arch-Image—a further battering of Female Power into archetypal shape—purifying the intuition of Elemental female being to such a degree that this became inconceivable, inaccessible, while pretending that under christianity women are "on a pedestal," and, of course, Sublime.[15]

Shrewds who reflect upon this phenomenon will be able to see some interesting clues concerning the strategies of tokenism. Since the tokenizing of strong women is a primary feature of anti-feminist politics at this time, it is useful to consider in what ways the dogma may throw light upon the dilemmas posed by such politics. Bearing in mind that myths often function as self-fulfilling prophecies, we might well ponder the message of this mythic development. I suggest that the "news" is not cheering, but that the worst mistake would be refusal to know it.

We have seen that on the symbolic level the immaculate conception fosters a delusion of advancement of women's position while it undermines the possibility of conceiving any image of autonomous female transcendence. In this respect it resembles tokenism. Indeed, the case can be made that the proclamation of this dogma in 1854 ushered in the Age of Female Tokenism and subliminally contained prophetic messages concerning the ways in which the tactics of tokenism would be developed.

Since women have been incorporated (in limited numbers) into the professions in the nineteenth and twentieth centuries, the phenomenon of tokenism warrants close attention.[16] Hags might ask our Selves forthright questions, for example: Will there be a second Witchcraze? If so, what form will it take? There is, of course, a perpetual Witchcraze in patriarchy, and I have discussed some of its forms elsewhere. For example, gynecology and psychotherapy are gynocidal weapons of the patriarchs. My precise concern here, however, is to find the most deceptive and Modern Mode of gynocide, succeeding the European Witchcraze (which terminated in the mid-eighteenth century), in Western industrialized society. My method is to look at the recent Marian dogmas [ . . . ] as mythic paradigms disclosing and foretelling social reality.

There are clues in the fact that the Witchcraze in Western Europe was fostered and fueled by the rising professional power block. Not only priests and ministers, but members of the legal and medical professions had an active role and vested interest in the killing of the Witches. Looking at the professions today, we can see a continuation of this vested interest and overt violence against women, for example, by the medical profession. The phenomenon that I intend to focus on here, however, is the false inclusion of women within the professions as a means of destroying female integrity and powers. There are several points to be considered.

*First*, looking at the immaculate conception and at the tokenizing of women—in the professions and, by extension, in various men's/boys' clubs, such as male-led political groups—we find that both promote an *illusion of progress*. Both Mary and tokens are "raised up." What is obliterated from memory is the knowledge of *who put them down* in the first place. The fact of the sexual caste system is disguised, or at least the impression is created that if it ever existed, it has now been overcome—or is well on the way to being overcome. Of course, nothing could be further from the truth. The immaculately conceived/deceived woman is being prepared for the ultimate Self-destruction—the selling out of her Self and of her sisters. As Judith Long Laws points out, she is appointed to the role of hatchetman to her sisters.[17] Like Mary, she has been prepared to assent to the spiritual rape that will reproduce the myth of male divinity.

This delusion of progress inhibits radicalism. Some insight concerning the strategy operative in this production of delusion can be gleaned from Ralf Dahrendorf's critique of Marxian theory. He makes the following point:

> A class composed of individuals whose social position is not an inherited and inescapable fate, but merely one of a plurality of social roles, is not likely to be as powerful a historical force as the closed class Marx had in mind. Where mobility . . . is a regular occurrence, and therefore a legitimate expectation of many people, conflict groups are not likely to have either the permanence or the dead seriousness of caste-like classes composed of hopelessly alienated men [*sic*].[18]

The point is that the appearance of social mobility, or progress, squelches the instinct to revolt and create radical change. Tokenism provides this appearance/illusion for women (and all oppressed groups), taming the radical impulse with false hope.

A *second* point of comparison between the dogma and the strategy of tokenizing women is the employment of the *delusion of exceptionalism*. The immaculate conception worked a symbolic transformation, rendering Mary an exception, free of "original sin." As Laws shows, "the self-attribute of exceptionalism . . . is central to the psychology of the Token."[19] If we ask: "Exception to what?" the answer is clear. The token woman believes herself to be an exception to the alleged incompetency and array of weaknesses ascribed to women in general, that is, to the "original sin" of being a woman. If the tokenized woman in this situation is a woman of color, or Jewish, or lesbian, or elderly, or of working class background, or belongs to any other stigmatized group, her self-attribution of exceptionalism is, of course, multiplied.

*Third*, Mary is exceptional because she is full of grace, that is, full of male-identification, bestowed by her son, who is her "Savior." Likewise, the token is in a *role partnership with a male sponsor/savior* who legitimates her male-identification. However, as Judith Long Laws points out:

> Once the Token is confirmed in her role, her interaction with the larger group is facilitated and need not be mediated by the Sponsor.[20]

Like a brain surgeon after performing a lobotomy, the sponsor knows when his work is done. The token has lost a great deal of her capacity to cause trouble. She has been groomed to deny her autonomous Self.

*Fourth*, the immaculately conceived Mary is immaculately deceived—*emptied of autonomous intellect and will.* She can have no memory of woman-identified consciousness. Her mind is, as it were, a clean slate. Similarly, the token "is more unaware of her stigma [of being a woman] than any member of the dominant class."[21]

What does all of this tell us about the strategies of the contemporary Witch-killers? Following through on the mythic paradigm employed here, I suggest that the strategy of tokenizing women is ultimate purification from society, or, more precisely, from women's consciousness, of woman-identified Elemental/Original thinking and passion. The perfect token is the perfect traitor, betraying her Self and womankind. She gives her assent to rapism. The spectacle of her betrayal feeds the patriarchally embedded hatred of women in women.

I suggest that the mythic paradigm of the immaculate conception carries the war against female Elemental be-ing beyond earlier stages. This is not simply physical massacre of women. It is killing of consciousness and integrity in women. In this Second Coming of the Witchcraze, the chief character of the story is missing. There is no Witch to be crazed/razed. Moreover, this mythic model goes far beyond the symbol of the twice-born Athena, who was born, male-identified, from the head of Zeus. For a born-again might have some memory of her previous life. After all, Athena's mother, with Athena in her womb, was swallowed by father Zeus. Athena is tokenized and she betrays women, but the myth itself reminds us of her original parthenogenetic mother, Metis, the Goddess of Wisdom. In contrast to this, the immaculately conceived

Mary has no memory of a Divine Mother. She is not a Daughter. In the age of the second Witchcraze, Memory of Gynocentric Origins is obliterated. Tokens, having memorized male words and uncritically copied male texts, become complicit in the destruction of Memory. The token, detached from her Self, filled with gratitude to her sponsors, destroys the Source, which would have been her only recourse. Moreover, she knows not what she does. The Pure Token is an Immaculate Conception, freed from all knowledge of the stain of Original Female Nature, freed from consciousness of stigma.

To put it starkly and simply, the Second Coming of the Witchcraze will employ different methods. This time, women are trained and legitimated to do it to each other. Women have been coached by the impotent priests to destroy each other.

A particularly lethal instrument of this training is man-made and male-controlled pseudofeminism. One of the most deadly effects of pseudofeminism is the manufacture and spread of disillusion among women, who have been tricked into believing that the "illusion" is feminism itself. Thus the illusion-makers create the illusion that feminism is an illusion. Since this causes deceived and discouraged women to turn to the phallic sponsors for support in their crisis of feminist faith, the further spread of tokenism is achieved.

In the process of embedding this confusion, the master tricksters rely upon the unexorcised mechanisms of horizontal violence.[22] Their success is measured by the degree to which they are able to erase women's Archaic Elemental Memory. Since men cannot by themselves completely erase Memory from women, they must channel women into effecting the erasure ourselves, of our Selves. The most effective means employed by males to induce women to perform this dirtywork has been and continues to be the manufacture of illusions which trigger the mechanisms of Self-hate and horizontal violence among women. Thus programmed and activated in the direction of Self-destruction, women actively will *not* to re-member deep Memory, for woman-identified knowledge has been made to seem repugnant. Fixed by the pushers of pseudofeminism, women are "purified" of even the desire to re-member. Filled with the "grace" of false knowledge of "feminism," women turn to their saviors/sponsors, cooing, "Let it be done to me according to your will." Thanks to the purifying effects of phallic lust, this immaculate conception is achieved. Bored by the stimulations of female be-ing, women retreat further into the amnesic state of totaled tokens. Complicit in their own brainwashing, women thus totaled become intellectual scrub-women, fanatically cleansing the minds of others. The fanaticism reaches fantastic proportions, especially when a woman is consumed with the Need not to know her Self. Immaculately conceived, women often have a zeal that can only rarely be ascribed to males—for this is Elemental vigor turned against its Source.

The only hope for Overcoming this Second Coming of the Witchcraze is to risk be-ing the Crazed Witch, re-calling Rays of Elemental Memory. This involves facing the blinding light of the mythic paradigm of female assimilation/tokenism—seeing through the conception of deception, Undeceiving ourselves, Believing our Selves. [ . . . ]

[. . . This] requires Stamina, staying power, which is also Straying Power—ability to Stray off the tracks of traditions that betray women and nature. Straying is sparked by E-motion, that is, passion that moves women to thinking and acting The Way Out. E-motion is ecstatic, delirious. *Delirium* is derived from the Latin *de* (from, off) plus *lira* (track). Deliberate delirium keeps us off the tracks of trained responses, traditional expectations. Since the word *learn* is also derived from *lira,* it is clear that Lusty women's delirium should be a matter of Studied Unlearning. The word *studied* is important here, for one must know the tracks well in order to break out of them, without sliding back into them. To be truly truant requires study/training and untiring untraining. The process is unnarrowing, harrowing. Ultimately, its motivating E-motion is Wonderlust/Wanderlust. Its scope is vast, visionary, planetary. The wonderings/wanderings of Straying women are wayward, earthward, skyward. Witches long and learn to fly.

25

# Restoration and the Problem of Memory

From chapter 3 of *Pure Lust*, pp. 136–39.

*foreground:* male-centered and mono-dimensional arena where fabrication, objectification, and alienation take place; zone of fixed feelings, perceptions, behaviors; the elementary world: FLATLAND.
—*Wickedary*, p. 76

This short excerpt poses the question of pre-patriarchal history. Daly chose a strong figure to voice the argument that women have never had a history and have always been subject to men: Simone de Beauvoir in *The Second Sex*. While Daly did not spin an entire feminist prehistory here, she provided the groundwork for doing so, in women's intuition of Be-ing, and in feminist research. For Daly, the motivating question had to do with memory, in particular what she would come to call Deep Memory, of realms beyond the patriarchal foreground.

Readers should note that Daly used the terms "elementary" and "elemental" as opposites here, in which elementary:elemental::patriarchy :Be-ing.
—Editors

Restoration, the product of sado-sublimation, conceals the real nature of the breakdown it pretends to mend and thus distracts women's minds/hearts from the quest to know Elemental integrity. It does this in part by misnaming the dis-ease inflicted upon women and nature. To tell a woman who has been sickened and mutilated that her major task is to regain "femininity and desirability" is to distract her from her deep Self's search, her final causality. It distracts her from re-membering her powers. In order to comprehend her breakdown and therefore be enabled to heal her Self, she would have to intuit what a woman *can be*. The problem is how to be in touch with such intuitions, when they have been obscured by restorationist ideology.

So colossal has been this concealment that even the French feminist philosopher Simone de Beauvoir, in her monumental work, *The Second Sex*, actually reaffirms the discouraging assumption that underscores all of the other assumptions of androcracy, namely, that women have always been "second." This is suggested in the title of her book. One could, of course, argue that the title is factually accurate since women have been relegated to the status of "the second sex." However, de Beauvoir is more patriarchal in her assumptions than that.[1] In the Introduction, she writes:

> Throughout history they [women] have always been subordinated to men, and hence their dependency is not the result of a historical event or a social change—it was not something that *occurred*. The reason why otherness in this case seems to be an absolute is in part that it lacks the contingent or incidental nature of historical facts.[2]

This premise is repeated in the book. De Beauvoir introduces her chapter on the nomads, for example, with the cliché that "this has always been a man's world."[3] And again in the following chapter she repeats this assumption:

> From humanity's beginnings, their biological advantage has enabled the males to affirm their status as sole and sovereign subjects.[4]

Many feminists today find it hard to believe that de Beauvoir could have written of women:

> They have no past, no history, no religion of their own; and they have no such solidarity of work and interest as that of the proletariat.[5]

It is not unusual, of course, to hear such assumptions/clichés from the mouths of women's erasers. That the author of such an important feminist work as *The Second Sex*—first published in 1949—accepted them so uncritically is evidence of the memory-covering effects of restorationist "knowledge."[6]

Within the context of such unexamined assumptions it is extremely difficult to guess what a woman *can be*. Within such a context personal hope is muted, undermined. Despite all the positive values of de Beauvoir's work, the woman who accepts this context is mired in the suspicion that the situation is immutable.

Of course, other feminist scholars writing before and after the publication of *The Second Sex* have brought forth mountains of evidence to support the idea/intuition that this has *not* always been "a man's world." These scholars include Matilda Joslyn Gage in *Woman, Church and State* (1893) and Elizabeth Gould Davis in *The First Sex* (1971).[7] Women who have not read such books but have maintained a sense of Self have done so because on some level we have known with profound certainty that this has not always been "a man's world," and that reality in the deep sense—Elemental be-ing—has never been such. For the man's world, patriarchy, is the Foreground, which, since it is derivative, contains countless subliminal messages about the deep spheres of meaning—Archespheres—which its myths are intended to mask. The power to decode its myths is the natural power of Lusty women to hear the messages of the elements, the Elemental Words—to recognize these and remember them.

One suggestive term which we might use to name the incarnations that constitute the Foreground, the "this" world that has "always been" patriarchy is a word used by Paracelsus: *elementary*. According to his theory:

> . . . the elementary is an artificial being, created in the invisible worlds by man himself. . . . Most elementaries seem to be of an evil or destructive nature. They are generated from the excesses of human thought and emotion, the corruption of character, or the degeneration of faculties and powers which should be used in other, more constructive ways.[8]

I will use the term *elementary* here to Name a number of phenomena which mediate/distort our experience of elements, and which are largely invisible by reason of being all-pervasive. Elementaries include not only the poisonous fumes and radioactive emissions of phallic technology, but also the popular media and the specialized fields (the -ologies that mediate knowledge), as well as traditional assumptions, spoken or unspoken. All of these artificial beings are filled with fallacies invisible to those manipulated by means of them. In mediating experience they modify memory; they mummify memory.[9]

It is through acts of Elemental creation that Lusty women unblock/unlock our deep memories. Therefore, in sado-sublimated society, women must be prevented from such acts, not only by the embedding in the female psyche of elementary images and words of which women are unwitting recipients, but especially by the cooptation of women into elementary speech and action. Insight can be gained from knowledge of the fact that according to traditional christian theology the image of the (all-male) trinity is to be found especially in the acts of the soul.[10] In keeping with this tradition, possessed women are converted into images of artificial beings by being trained to act/operate like elementaries even on the level of internal thoughts and desires. Pre-occupied with elementary concerns, a woman becomes a memory-blocker.

In order to understand how women are caught on the wheel of elementary thinking and acting, it is important to face the fears and embedded sense of vulnerability which are the foreground conditions of phallocracy afflicting all women—since all are threatened perpetually by the phallic lust that rapes, kills, and dismembers women and nature. There can be no genuine doubt about this situation, which has been demonstrated and documented in many books and in the individual histories of women. So terrible is the lust, the intent, to destroy female nature, that women commonly attempt to erase their Selves in order to be spared.

26

# Phallic Power of Absence

From chapter 3 of *Pure Lust*, pp. 146–52.

*Nag-Gnosticism:* the philosophy of those who Sense with certainty the reality of transcendental knowledge and at the same time never cease to Nag ourSelves and Others with recurrent awareness of questions and uncertainties; the philosophy of those who overcome the pseudodichotomy between transcendence and immanence, between otherworldliness and worldliness.
—*Wickedary*, p. 83

Showing the influence of Aquinas on the very structure of her thought, Daly, in *Summa* fashion, elaborated a full set of logical possibilities around the words "absence" and "presence." She chose these words for both their philosophical resonance and their applicability to the women's liberation movement, in which women's presence to each other was perceived by men as absence.

This passage culminated in her research on the etymological root of the word "sin," which derives from the Indo-European root *es-*, meaning "to be." This dis-covery that what dogmatic religions consider cosmically wrong, is actually cosmic existence itself, confirmed all of Daly's suspicions about patriarchy, and about the hidden powers in words. She would draw on this etymology and the implications of reversing Sin for the remainder of her life.

Later Daly would embrace this etymology as license for reversing patriarchal logic, expressed in the phrase (which we endorse) "Sin Big!"[1]
—Editors

Since patriarchal male omnipresence is in reality an omniabsence that depends upon women for its incarnations, it is totally unlike the power of Presence of Elemental women. In *Beyond God the Father* I have discussed this Presence:

> The power of presence that is experienced by those who have begun to live in the new space radiates outward, attracting others. . . . For those who are. . . . threatened, the presence of women to each other is experienced as absence.[2]

Such power of Presence is individual, original, creative. It is participation in Powers of Be-ing. In contrast to this, patriarchal power of presence is institutional power. This power requires absence of genuine individuality, of true deviance. Whereas Elemental female power of Absence is a consequence of our Presence, the patriarchal male's (or female's) institutional presence is derived from ontological absence; it is elementary presence.

When this elementary presence is not denied access to our psyches by women—when it is allowed to insinuate itself in the form of myths, ideologies, or emotional responses—women become its vessels, vehicles, carriers. Pregnant with it, women perpetuate its incarnations. Vampiristic, the elementary patriarchal presence is forever fetal. Women who are pre-occupied by it are not only de-energized; they are spooked. For this is both *presence of absence* and *absence of Presence.*

Phallic *presence of absence* is experienced by women as a growth of nothingness, an expansion of emptiness that fills the mind. The meaninglessness of male-centered myths and ideologies is experienced as mental/spiritual bloat. It is "stuff" that packs the mind, which becomes a garbage heap of details without a focus. The glut of non-sense can be experienced watching television, reading newspapers, or attending an ordinary university. It is decentralized mass without organic purpose; it expands like a tumor of the soul. It is a parade of images and "facts" that are not facts because the context is a lie. The emotional responses that it elicits also pre-occupy the mind, weighing it down with guilt, anxiety, despair. Its victim becomes absent to her Self.

Phallic *absence of Presence* is lack of content and purpose. It is negation of meaning in a conversation, lack of affection or of intelligence in a face, nonresponse to a question, to an act of love. It is absence of soul.

This double-edged absence has power insofar as it prevents women from being Really Present. It accomplishes this through the double method of deception and discouragement. For it is nonbe-ing that poses as Presence, and that blunts the hope of dis-covering Presence. Therefore, Wonderlusters should consider further the meaning of Real Presence.

## Real Presence

First of all, Gnomic Nags should note that Real Presence implies being presentient—"feeling or perceiving beforehand." When a woman's consciousness is captured and filled with phallic absence, to be presentient is to be filled with foreboding about a coming ill or misfortune, that is, to have anxiety. When women are Present to our Selves, however, to be presentient is to be animated with hope. This presentient Presence is Positively Powerful, for it implies our capacity to *presentiate*, that is, "to make or render present in place or time; to cause to be perceived or realized as present" (*O.E.D.*). Real Presence of the Self, then, which is participation in Powers of Be-ing, implies powers to Realize as present our past and future Selves. Augurs, Sibyls, Soothsayers, Muses, Actualize/Realize these powers.[3]

The primary meaning of the verb *realize* is "to make real: change from what is imaginary or fictitious into what is actual: bring into concrete existence: ACTUALIZE." The Real Presence of Lusty women is Realizing Presence. It is active potency/power to create and to transform, to render present in place and time.

The elementary omnipresence/omniabsence of phallocracy obstructs Elemental Realizing Presence. Therefore, a Lusty woman uses her Labrys, her double ax of exorcism and ecstasy to extricate her Self from its ghostly manifestations. These are the *presence of absence* and *absence of Presence* that frustrate her Lust, distracting her from her deep *telos,* her purpose.

The elementary *presence of absence* that blunts and bloats our minds with messages of unreality requires expulsion, exorcism. Elemental women expel such pseudopresence, achieving the *Absence of absence.* By acts of daring, Prudes prune away this pseudospirit/pseudomatter. We know that *exorcism* traditionally means "to drive out or drive away (an evil spirit) by adjuration, especially by use of a holy name or magic rites." As Dragons/Dryads women drive away the phallic presence of absence, not by use of a holy name/noun, but by Wholly Naming actions, ideas, symbols, feelings, that is, by Naming these events in Gyn/Ecological context. We do this in Archimagical Rites that include clear reasoning rooted in deep intuition and verified by direct experience. Prudish, Shrewish reason burns away the expanded vapors of non-sense, freeing the places, spaces, that have been occupied, possessed.

The elementary *absence of Presence* that is the normal nothingness of bore-ocracy, the routinized rule in snooldom, is expelled through the expansion of our own reality. Yet this absence *is* difficult to face and Name. As Orwell expressed the problem in *1984*:

> The only evidence to the contrary was the mute protest in your own bones, the instinctive feeling that the conditions you lived in were intolerable and that at some other time they must have been different.[4]

Since all women born and bred in the Restored Society that is patriarchy have spent most of our lives in conditions of overt and/or subliminal states of intellectual, emotional, and sensory deprivation, it requires Amazonian Acts of imagination and courage to continue feeling the mute protest, and to attend to the signals of Real Presence. Indeed, many women coming to real consciousness can identify with the experience of Winston as described in *1984*:

> He was a lonely ghost uttering a truth that nobody would ever hear.[5]

The truth is that there are millions of women who feel like "lonely ghosts" in the endless "1984" that is phallocracy. Imagining that nobody will ever hear her truth, a woman can feel the elementary absence of Presence and feel helpless. Yet the fact of feeling it is, of course, a signal of potentiality for something more. When this signal is heard, a woman has the chance to begin Realizing/Actualizing her potentiality. Her Realizing Presence radiates to other "lonely ghosts" who recognize their own truth in her expression/expansion. This *Presence of Presence* is increasingly contagious. It is ecstasy. *Ecstasy* is derived from the Greek *existanai*, meaning "to put out of place." Realizing Presence puts/pulls Wild women out of the places/times of absence, releasing our be-ing. Refusing false assumptions, unassumed and unassuming Elemental women are of the Earth, Earthy. Together with winds, seas, trees, sands, fires, rains, thunder, moon, sun, stars, we are Present. Unfathered/Unfettered, we are Sisters and Daughters of the Radiant Array of the Elements.[6]

## Presentiating Our Selves: The Courage to Sin

When Prudish/Shrewish women first uncover our presentient and presentiating powers, our unleashed Sparking, Spinning speech and action may appear to those possessed by restored reason as pixilated, that is, "BEMUSED, under or seeming to be under a magic spell: ENCHANTED, BEWITCHED." In fact, the ontological presentiating powers of Elemental women make us BE-MUSED, BE-WITCHED, casters of Archimagical spells from our depths of be-ing. Small wonder that we also appear to be *Pixie-led*, that is "led astray by Pixies" *(O.E.D.)*. The term *astray* is derived from a Middle French word (*estraier*) meaning to roam about without a master. The *Pixie-led*, then, would seem to be moving in a promising direction. This insight is confirmed by the following definition of *astray*: "into a wrong or mistaken way of thinking or acting: in or into error: WRONG: away from a proper or desirable course of development." As women roam about without masters, breaking the rules of snools, the statutes of studs, the decrees of drones, the canons of cocks, the precepts of prickers, we are indeed "in error: WRONG." Wandering away from "a proper or desirable course of development," we presentiate our Selves.

Self-presentiating women—being WRONG according to the prevailing assumptions—may be said to Sin. It is pixilating to find that the word *sin* is probably etymologically akin to the Latin *est*, meaning (s)he *is*, and that it is derived from the Indo-European root *es-*, meaning *to be* (*American Heritage Dictionary*). Clearly, our ontological courage, our courage to be, implies the courage to be WRONG. Elemental be-ing is Sinning; it requires the Courage to Sin.

Rather than confessing the creeds of cockocracy, which implies eternal confessions of guilt, Lusty women Sin in the most major way, by be-ing Really Present and presentient. This implies becoming Soothsayers. As Soothsayers we presentiate, making our future *be* present, as we prognosticate, presage, portend. Moreover, as we foreshow the future we are mindful of the past.

The word *sooth* (which means truth)—like the word *sin*—is derived from the Indo-European root *es*-. Ironically, so also is the word *suttee*. As one authority has put it, *suttee* (from the Sanskrit *sari*) means "a true or virtuous wife, a term applied to a widow who immolates herself on the funeral pile of her husband. . . . Sanskrit *sati* is the feminine of *sant*: being, existing, true, right, virtuous; present participle of *as*, to be."[7] Joseph Campbell, then, was etymologically correct when, apparently with no sense of irony, he wrote:

> Sati . . . is the female who really *is* something inasmuch as she is truly and properly a player of the female part: she is not only good and true in the ethical sense but true and real ontologically. In her faithful death, she is at one with her own true being.[8]

Nag-Gnostic Soothsayers will not forget this and other massive crimes against female be-ing. The memory is embedded in the history of the very words we use to speak of truth and be-ing.

The Courage to Sin, to be Elemental through and beyond the horrors of The Obscene Society, is precisely about being true and real ontologically, about refusing to be "a player of the [patriarchal] female part." It is about moving away from elementary pseudoreasoning to Elemental reason. To Sin against the society of sado-sublimation is to be intellectual in the most direct and daring way, claiming and trusting the deep correspondence between the structures/processes of one's own mind and the structures/processes of reality. To Sin is to trust intuitions and the reasoning rooted in them. To Sin is to come into the fullness of our powers, confronting now newly understood dimensions of the Battles of Principalities and Powers. To Sin is to move deeper into the Archespheres, overcoming the ghosts of sado-sublimination, Realizing Elemental potency.

## 27

# Realizing Reason

From chapter 6 of *Pure Lust*, pp. 160–78.

*Realize:* ["to make real . . . bring into concrete existence: ACCOMPLISH . . . to bring from potentiality into actuality: ACTUALIZE. . . . to conceive vividly as real: be fully aware of"—*Webster's*]: These definitions have been awarded *Websters'* Intergalactic Seal of Approval.
—*Wickedary*, p. 92

This chapter of *Pure Lust* shows Daly at her most philosophic. She returned to the ancients—Plato and Aristotle—to establish the contrast between their realism and later philosophic schools of nominalism. She then stated, categorically, that "Elemental philosophy is not compatible with nominalism and its claim that only the individual has reality, for this negates participation."

The opening of this chapter is a near-mystical embrace of the life of the mind, and the love of wisdom that is philosophy. In the words of one of the editors, this is a description of how living biophilically feels:

> Lusty women Realizing our Presence reclaim the original force of words. For presentiating our Selves requires Self-conscious participation in ontological Elemental reason. By living our Real Presence beyond the confines of the State of Lechery, then, Wonderlusting women Realize reason. This is not simply "taking a philosophical position," such as classical realism. . . . Rather, the living of our Real Presence is the *process* of Realizing the meaning that is behind the prevailing meaninglessness by thinking and acting passionately out of Lust for Wild Wisdom. Realizing reason is both dis-covering and participating in the unfolding, the Self-creation, of reason.

Daly considered philosophizing a necessity for women. Under patriarchy women's reasoning has been castrated, she maintained, meaning its potency has been silenced. The way to recover that potency is through the

memory of Moments of Being, a phrase and a set of examples that she takes from Virginia Woolf, and develops in the latter part of this excerpt.
—Editors

In the classical philosophical tradition, reason (logos) has multidimensional meanings and implications: thought about the universe; the rational structure of the universe, that is, its intelligibility; and the source of this structure. The question of *how* these aspects are related, especially the question of how minds are related to that which they know, or can know, has preoccupied philosophers in the West for thousands of years, and the varying responses to the questions are well known.

The "answer" or approach known as "realism" formerly referred to the doctrine that universals have a real existence outside the mind. According to Platonic realism, this meant that universal ideas exist prior to things. The mind remembers these pre-existent forms (ideas). Memory is stirred by experiences of the material world, which is made up of mere reflections of the ideas. According to Aristotelian realism, universals exist in things (treeness is in the tree). All knowledge comes through the senses, and the intellect attains a knowledge of universals through the process of abstracting these from the "phantasms" perceived through the senses.[1]

The doctrine of nominalism stands in sharp contrast to classical realism. A common dictionary definition of *nominalism* conveys its deficiencies quite adequately: "a theory . . . that universal terms such as indicate genus or species and all general collective words or terms such as *animal, man, tree, air, city, nation, wagon* have no objective real existence corresponding to them but are mere words, names, or terms or mere vocal utterances and that only particular individual things and events exist." As one author put it, "nominalism empties out the big words."[2] As Orwell has shown, the world of *1984* (which Crones recognize as having been around for a long time) *requires* the destruction of words.

Elemental philosophy is not compatible with nominalism and its claim that only the individual has reality, for this negates participation. Tillich accurately criticizes the nominalist rejection of participation. He writes:

> But pure nominalism is untenable. Even the empiricist must acknowledge that everything approachable by knowledge must have the structure of "being knowable." And this structure includes by definition a mutual participation of the knower and the known. Radical nominalism is unable to make the process of knowledge understandable.[3]

I would add that it also renders incomprehensible the sense of Wonderlust, the desire that is Wanderlust, the Journey through Archespheres, the ontological bonding that is female friendship, the connection with elements that is at the heart of Gyn/Ecological, Elemental be-ing and thinking.

The negation of any deep ontological Elemental sense of creative participation of the knower and of the known in Be-ing, whether this negation is called "nominalism" or "modern realism" or simply "science," is indeed an emptying out of big—that is, meaning-full—words. It is verbicide/logocide in the fundamental sense that it is an expression of the will to stop reasoning. In this Stopped State words are reified, disconnected things, reproducing themselves endlessly. Their Metaphoric powers, which characterize them as Messengers of Metabeing, are suffocated. They become embodiments of that glut which we recognize as *presence of absence*. They also become vessels of the sado-subliminal messages which massage our minds into deeper and deeper amnesia.

Lusty women Realizing our Presence reclaim the original force of words. For presentiating our Selves requires Self-conscious participation in ontological Elemental reason. By living our Real Presence beyond the confines of the State of Lechery, then, Wonderlusting women Realize reason. This is not simply "taking a philosophical position" [ . . . ]. Rather, the living of our Real Presence is the *process* of Realizing the meaning that is behind the prevailing meaninglessness by thinking and acting passionately out of Lust for Wild Wisdom. Realizing reason is both dis-covering and participating in the unfolding, the Self-creation, of reason.

Many times, women coming to consciousness of reason that transcends the elementary assumptions introduce discussions of their previous condition with remarks such as: "I just didn't realize . . ." The statements are often more accurate than the speaker realizes. For elementary thinking, feeling, acting does not Realize, that is, actualize understanding which is latent, potential. The speaker is of course also expressing astonishment that what she now sees as self-evident was not previously obvious, but somehow masked. It is important at this point that she know clearly that Realizing reason is not a supernatural revelation, but an Elementally natural process/unfolding that will continue.[4] The correspondence between her mind and deep reason has always been there. It has not been "there" merely as a thing fits into a place, however.

To understand this dynamic connection, it is helpful to think of the word *correspond*, derived from the Latin *con-*, meaning together, and *respondere*, meaning to answer, which in turn is from *spondere*, meaning to promise. The correspondence between the minds of Musing women and the intelligible structures of reality is rooted in our *promise*, that is, our potential and commitment to evolve, unfold "together," in harmony with each other and with all Elemental reality. This promise is answered/echoed in the promise of others. This is why the experience of Realizing reason, after what seems to have been aeons of amnesia, often feels like coming home.

In the process of Realizing reason, women realize that the restored world is an artificial product resulting from the forced compliance of "reality" to the patriarchal male's perception of and designs upon "reality."[5] This "creativity" of restoration results in the embedding of layers of unreality in minds and over the surfaces of things which, like plastic coatings, insulate/isolate minds from Elemental reality, breaking the threads of connectedness, and requiring attitudes of "grasping-and-shaping." In contrast to sado-pseudocreativity, Realizing reason elicits the natural Wild correspondences among minds and other realities. This Realizing, which is active participation in Wild reality, makes possible the deep connections among Realizing women.

When analyzing conflicts and misunderstandings in women's relationships/friendships with each other, it helps to know that Realizing does not happen "all at once," for Realizing is a verb. No woman is/has completely Realized. So long as the sadostate is supported and legitimated by the (unreal) world-building activities of subliming, sublimation and sublimination, generating the elementary covers/veils that disconnect our minds from Elemental reality, and so long as women's minds/passions are still contaminated/laminated with these coatings, we will continue to be haunted by mixed messages, false feelings, aphasic namings, apraxic actions. All of these are forms of possession paralyzing the Archimage.[6] Pure Lust, then, is not a suddenly arrived at state; it is unfolding, questing, Realizing.

Women who are risking Realizing soon realize that this event is not at all a passive reception of a revelation. The latter is inevitably a re-veiling, for active participation is essential to true dis-covering. Realizing is a "creative political ontophany."[7] It is continuing manifestation of be-ing; it is participation in creation, overcoming the reason-blocking elementary constructs, unfolding the potentialities of be-ing.

Women are universally trained not to Realize, especially in those institutions that proclaim that they are offering a "higher education." Andrea Dworkin describes this phenomenon as she experienced it when a student in the sixties at academically prestigious Bennington College (which at that time was still a college for women). She conveys a sense of rage and irony as she recalls that the students did not know they had been "consigned from birth to that living legal and social death called marriage." Moreover:

> We imagined, in our ignorance, that we might be novelists and philosophers. . . . We did not know that our professors had a system of beliefs and convictions that designated us as an *inferior gender class*, and that that system of beliefs and convictions was virtually universal—the cherished assumption of most of the writers, philosophers, and historians we were so ardently studying.[8]

Despite the two-decade interval, during which the feminist movement has flourished, the situation described above still prevails. The "cherished assumptions" of the sixties were subliminal, undermining the unsuspecting students. In the 1980s, despite the large body of feminist writings and the re-emergence of the feminist movement, and despite the presence of a few genuinely feminist women on faculties, the sadosublimination continues, incorporating into its multiple multifarious messages distorted ideas about feminism—for example, the lie that the goals of the movement have been achieved, and the depiction of feminists of the seventies as bitter, "old" women.

Since the lecherous "cherished assumptions" are subliminal, they constitute an elementary presence of absence, and they are also experienced as absence of Presence. The presence of Mark Twain and the absence of Harriet Beecher Stowe—or again the presence of James Joyce and the absence of Gertrude Stein—in literature courses typify this presence of absence and absence of Presence. So also does the presence of the christian triune god and the absence of the Triple Goddess in religion courses. Since the "inferior gender class" assumptions, or what I call the Touchable Caste assumptions, are subliminal, so also under these conditions female Presence is rendered subliminal. Only the process of Realizing Elemental ontological reason can break through the smog of sado-sublimination, actualizing the natural, Elemental relation between women's minds and the structures of our own reality.

The training of a woman not to Realize begins, of course, many years before she reaches the age when, if she is among the "privileged," she can receive the advanced subliminal indoctrination of a Bennington College, a Vassar College, UCLA, or the University of Notre Dame. From her earliest years, a woman is dependent for elementary information upon the assumers, who engender lack of confidence in her own perceptions. The cliché "Women (or girls) are not logical" is an assumed "truth." When properly programmed, a woman becomes an avid consumer of mediated "knowledge." She becomes herself a propagator of mediated "knowledge," a male-ordered missionary fueled by the zeal that characterizes the "selfless." In short, she becomes a walking, talking subliminal message, cajoling women to accept defeat. Psychically castrated, she is a master-minded medium for male presence of absence. Fortunately, *perfect* programming is rare. There is always the hope that women will Realize. In order to understand this process better, it is helpful to consider the meanings of *potency* and of *act*.

## Potency and Act: Realizing Potency

In Aristotelian and medieval philosophy, *potency* can mean either passive potency, or capacity to receive a perfection (called "act"), that is, capacity to be acted upon, or it can mean active potency, meaning capacity to act. To put it another way, whereas passive potency is a capacity to receive something from something else, active potency is the ability to effect change. It is power.[9] Clearly, phallic lust assigns/confines women to the arena of passive potency, as vessels/vehicles for males, who have reserved what they believe to be active potency for themselves. Moreover, its intent is the castration of women both on the level of passive potency and of active potency.

The reversal involved in the epithet "castrating bitch" has been recognized, at least in its more obvious dimensions, by feminists for years. The physical castration of women has taken place on a vast scale through genital mutilation of millions of women, especially in African countries and through modern gynecology. One of the dictionary definitions of the verb *castrate* is worth re-viewing: "to deprive of vigor or vitality (intelligence is *castrated*—John Dewey): weaken by removal of the most effective or forceful elements: EMASCULATE (the bill was castrated by removal of the enforcement provisions)." Although *Webster's* does grant (in another definition) that *castrate* can also mean "to deprive of the ovaries" (while ignoring clitoridectomy), it is significant that this definition is confined to the purely physical level. *Webster's* does not connect female physical castration with "to deprive of vigor or vitality," and "weaken by removal of effective or forceful elements." The subliminal message is that vigor, vitality, and effective or forceful elements are "masculine." Thus the very definition functions to castrate the minds of women, who are thus conned once again into a negative self-image, injected with the assumption that effective and forceful elements are not female.

The castration of women's reason is a collective and not merely an individual phenomenon. One definition of the noun *castration* is "a depriving of vigor: WEAKENING (mass persecution of most eminent scientists, a castration of science—A. G. Mazour)." Never has any dictionary acknowledged and legitimated the fact that the mass persecution of women, for example through the European Witchcraze, Chinese footbinding, American and European gynecology, has been a castration of female reason. For, first of all, these historical facts are not acknowledged as atrocities. Second, it is not admitted that female reason—the minds of women and the memories, ideas, products engendered by our minds—even has an identity, to say nothing of vigor and vitality, that is capable of being castrated. The assumption is that there are no "effective or forceful elements" to be removed.

Moreover, if one substitutes "feminist scholars" for "eminent scientists," the conditions of women's culture can be moved from a subliminal to an overt state in the reader's mind. Thus, we might read *Webster's* chosen example as follows: "mass persecution of most feminist scholars, a castration of women's studies." The first phrase immediately seems absurd, because, unlike the quantity of (male) scientists, the number of feminist scholars has not been allowed to reach "mass" proportions. Indeed the persecution of feminist scholars happens on a level of "Immaculate Conception." It is done to women from earliest infancy, so that girl children's minds are purified of positive conceptions of "feminist" and "female scholar," and certainly of "feminist scholar" before these can be conceived as possible. That is, the persecution/execution takes place on the level of potency/potentiality before this can begin, in most cases, to be actualized. Thus persecution is on the level of passive potency—on the basic level of capacity to receive information/inspiration that would move the female Self to active potency. It is therefore persecution that is difficult to perceive; it is subliminal persecution.

The problems inherent in the expression "castration of women's studies" are less obvious, more subliminal. For many women assume that "women's studies" is a "field" that freely thrives in universities and that is already vigorous, unhindered, strong. If one's analysis is at this stage, it could seem plausible that "women's studies," big and strong, is already "all there," capable of being castrated. However, the fact is that it, too, is often destroyed/persecuted in the stage of early infancy, on the level of passive potency—on the basic level of the students' and teachers' capacity to receive the information and inspiration that would move them to active potency. Thus women's studies, not allowed truly to develop, has become in some situations "immaculately conceived."[10] Here, too, the purification/persecution is difficult to perceive. It is subliminal persecution/castration.

Lusty Searchers should reflect also upon the following definition of *castration*: "the deletion of a part of (a text) especially for purposes of expurgation: *also*, a part deleted." If we apply this definition to the majority of women's texts, we again find that the word *castrate* just barely begins to name the horror of the violence against women's potency. For it is hardly adequate to say that a "part" of the texts of women has been deleted by primal sado-silencing. Nor does the term "deleted" fully describe what has been done. *Delete* means "to reduce to nullity as (a) *archaic*: DESTROY, ANNIHILATE; (b) to reject by physically obscuring (as by blotting out, scratching out, or cutting out) or by excluding or marking for exclusion during further processing." This is indeed a sufficiently powerful word to name some of the everyday atrocities perpetrated against women's writings, and, indeed, against women's active potency in all spheres. However, to be deleted, something has to have some actual existence. It is true that in countless cases the actual texts of women have been deleted, and this has discouraged both the deleted writers and other women, who are then deprived of our tradition, of historical memory, of knowledge that women can and did produce important works. But the *primal* deletion is the blotting out of what might have been, of the texts—philosophical, theological, literary, scientific—that were *not* conceived, composed. It is the cutting out of the potency/capacity to receive inspiration and therefore of the active potency to create.

The purpose of this kind of castration/deletion is named in the last part of the definition: "for purposes of expurgation." *Expurgation* means "purification from something morally harmful, offensive, sinful or erroneous." Knowing the intent of patriarchal morality, and being familiar with its strategy of reversal, Nags know that the "morally harmful, offensive, sinful, and erroneous" object of its acts of castration is our biophilic potency. [ . . . ]

Realizing potency, then, is interacting with the Elemental world, and not merely re-acting/re-enacting in the elementary "world." Ontological interacting is participation in Be-ing. Insofar as women's interacting is still contaminated with elementary re-acting/re-flecting, this participation is diluted, weakened. This is not to say that fighting in the Foreground is unnecessary. It is to say that the motivation of such fighting must come from re-membering levels that are deeper than the attack itself. It is deep Elemental rootedness/connectedness that wards off the elementary invasions. In order to Realize potency in truly radical participatory ways, then, and to get through and beyond the subliminal side-tracks and set-ups that distract women from Realizing, it is necessary to encounter the meaning of memory, both elementary and Elemental.

## Potency and Memory

As Louky Bersianik has pointed out, the memory of a woman within patriarchy is such that "she can't see the first in the second."[11] That is to say, she usually does not see the cause of her suffering. She forgets the identity of her torturer—and often the fact that there was/is a torturer—who gave her the problem she now seeks to solve. For example, as Denise Connors has demonstrated, many women cannot remember that physicians have caused the complications, the unnecessary mutilations, and the diseases from which they now seek relief.[12] Women often deeply forget who they were before the destruction inflicted upon them in rapist society and they forget the destruction. This forgetting, interlaced with partial memory, debilitates, and it is rooted in fear. [ . . . ]

[. . . In contrast] there are explosions of foreground/elementary memories that originate in stirrings of deep, internal potency. This is sometimes experienced as comparable to the eruption of a volcano. Recalling the definition of the word *volcano* can be helpful here: "a vent in the earth's crust from which molten or hot rock and steam issue." Volcanic eruptions and women's deep re-memberings are Elemental, breaking through vents in the crust. Although they may be experienced as sudden, their Elemental force has been brewing in deep, natural cauldrons. All Lusty women are Brewsters, actively potent. One meaning of the verb *brew* is "to bring about (something troublesome or woeful) as if by brewing magical potions or spells (brewing mischief)." The bringing forth of Original Memory by Brewsters is indeed troublesome to the torturers of women. It also *troubles* Brewsters, especially in the sense "to put into confused motion: cause to become turbulent or turbid through moving." For Elemental Memory stirs deep Passion. It is E-motional, generating movement out of the Foreground.

Virginia Woolf knew about E-motional Memory. She wrote:

> In certain favorable moods, memories—what one has forgotten—come to the top. . . . Will it not be possible, in time, that some device will be invented by which we can tap them? I see it—the past—as an avenue lying behind; a long ribbon of scenes, emotions. . . . I feel that strong emotion

> must leave its trace; and it is only a question of discovering how we can get ourselves again attached to it, so that we shall be able to live our lives through from the start.[13]

Other women have had a sense of what Virginia Woolf here describes, have known moments when memories "come to the top." An old Jewish woman, quoted by Barbara Myerhoff, described this experience after participating in a storytelling session:

> But finally, this group brought out such beautiful memories, not always so beautiful, but still, all the pictures came up. It touched the layers of the kind that it was on those dead people already. It was laying on them like layers, separate layers of earth, and all of a sudden in this class I feel it coming up like lava. It just melted away the earth from all those people. It melted away, and they became alive. And then to me it looked like they were never dead. . . .
>
> The memories come up in me like lava. So I felt I enriched myself. And I am hoping I enriched somebody else. All this, it's not only for us. It's for the generations.[14]

Yet in pondering "how we can get ourselves again attached to it" (past strong emotion), many women would empathize with the question posed by Frances Theoret: "How can this (explosion of memories) happen without destroying the woman?"[15] For memories do come in ribbons/chains and, as we have seen, many of these—if a woman allows herself to really feel them—are excruciating. As Muriel Rukeyser has written:

> What would happen if one woman told the truth about her life? The world would split open.[16]

Many women are consciously afraid that if they tell themselves the truth about their lives they themselves will split open. Within the sadostate then, elementary memory functions as eraser and censor, preventing deep E-motional Memory from "coming to the top."

In the passage cited above, Virginia Woolf wonders whether it is possible that "some device will be invented by which we can tap them [deep memories].” She is being whimsical, perhaps. She knows very well that her own “device” is writing. The profound importance of writing to Virginia Woolf for “getting ourselves again attached” to what I choose to call E-motional Memory has to be understood in relation to her remembered experiences of “sudden violent shock.” Most of these initially engendered a feeling of powerlessness:

> I only know that many of these exceptional moments brought with them a peculiar horror and a physical collapse; they seemed dominant; myself passive.[17]

She explains, however, that this was not always the case, describing her experience of an intuition, a shock, when she suddenly perceived a flower and understood that the flower itself was part of the earth, “and that was the real flower, part earth, part flower.” The intuition was expressed in the words “That is the whole.” This was a different experience from the others, in which the horror held her powerless, as when she discovered that people hurt each other. In the moment of experiencing the flower she was not powerless, for, as she writes, “I had found a reason.”[18]

She goes on to suggest that as one gets older one has a greater power to provide explanations through reason. Virginia Woolf understood that there is a design behind the “cotton wool of everyday life.” For her, these “moments of being,” as she calls them, or “shocks,” were “scaffolding in the background . . . the invisible and silent part of my life as a child.”[19]

This Great Shrewd had a particularly acute “shock-receiving capacity,” which was essential to her greatness as a writer. Since the way of access to the Background was very explicit for her, she was able to provide passages to deep Memory. It is clear from the sections I have cited that she understood profoundly the experience of powerlessness and the empowerment that comes through reason, through what I am identifying here as Realizing reason—and which is re-membering reason.[20] Having experienced volcanic explosions, and having learned the connecting power of reason as Memory, she was a Brewster. Needing to know connections, she was a Gnostic Nagster, Nagging her Self, and consequently others toward the knowledge of deep re-membering. Intuitively, she knew that the shocks from the Background which she had felt as a child were ontological. Their Elemental force singled them out as "moments of being . . . embedded in many more moments of non-being."[21] She was a Webster, dis-covering the hidden connections and weaving them into audibility, visibility, with words. She was/is a Muse, singing other women into conscious Memory, a Soothsayer whose creative pursuit of the past overcame impotence and paralysis, actualizing potency. Intuitively she knew that the passive potency to hear/see/receive knowledge of the Background is interconnected with active potency to Name, for "it is only by putting it into words that I make it [reality] whole."[22]

Writing actualizes Memory in an especially potent way. The process of writing, and of seeing/hearing the words come forth on the page, is journeying. The dis-covering of one connection, this lifting it out, lifts out others. A complex tapestry is found, woven. The writer becomes more energized as the process continues, as she seeks, says, and finds more. As Woolf wrote: "The pen gets on the scent."[23]

One might turn into an "objection" the obvious fact that Virginia Woolf was a professional writer, and claim that such a "device" is inaccessible to most women. There can be no question that in addition to courage and genius she had privilege. But the fact is that nearly all women have the potency "to put it into words," in their own unique ways. It is possible to write letters, journals, notes. Women can talk to each other, sharing stories, dis-covering through Spinning conversations, beginning "to put the severed parts together."[24]

To affirm this possibility is not to underestimate the enormous difficulties—the unspeakable oppression—of countless women, especially women of color and all poor women. Alice Walker writes:

> How was the creativity of the Black woman kept alive, year after year and century after century, when for most of the years Black people have been in America, it was a punishable crime for a Black person to read or write? And the freedom to paint, to sculpt, to expand the mind with action, did not exist. Consider, if you can bear to imagine it, what might have been the result if singing, too, had been forbidden by law. Listen to the voices of Bessie Smith, Billie Holiday, Nina Simone, Roberta Flack, and Aretha Franklin, among others, and imagine those voices muzzled for life. Then you may begin to comprehend the lives of our "crazy," "Sainted" mothers and grandmothers. The agony of the lives of women who might have

> been Poets, Novelists, Essayists, and Short Story Writers (over a period of centuries), who died with their real gifts stifled within them.[25]

Knowledge of this horror, rather than stopping the possibility for creativity, must be channeled—together with Unrelenting Rage, into creation now, whenever, wherever, this is possible. Gloria Anzaldúa has written of the struggle of women of color to write:

> The problems seem insurmountable and they are, but they cease being insurmountable once we make up our mind that whether married or childrened or working outside jobs we are going to make time for the writing.
>
> Forget the room of one's own—write in the kitchen, lock yourself up in the bathroom. Write on the bus or the welfare line, on the job or during meals, between sleeping and waking. I write while sitting on the john. No long stretches at the typewriter unless you're wealthy, or have a patron—you may not even own a typewriter.[26]

Women, particularly those who are multiply oppressed, are silenced.[27] The struggle to break the silence can call forth further possibilities. The chains of silencing are broken by continuing acts of creativity, inspired by Pure Lust.

What women find by Naming—through writing, speech, all forms of art—is something like a stream that runs deep within the soul. Its sounds are musical, rhythmic. Significantly, the word *stream* is etymologically connected with *rhythm*. Both are rooted in the Greek *rhein*, meaning "to flow." Underneath the elementary unrhythm of mediated, master-full memories flow rhythms of empowering Memory. One meaning of *rhythm* is "an ordered recurrent alternation of strong and weak elements in the flow of sound and silence in speech." Although women who are Muses for our Selves do not measure "strong" and "weak" elements by the rules of the masters, there is definite Diversity among experiences re-membered, and among Nagsters re-membering. Diversity is essential to proud and positive Potency.

The rhythms of Naming deep Memory are quite unlike the tidy, tedious tick-tock of patriarchal clocks and watches. The rhythms of re-membering are Tidal. They are in harmony with the elements within and around us, and they are expressed in Elemental sounds. The complexity of these rhythms can be intuited when we think of tides. Rachel Carson explains:

> The tides present a striking paradox, and the essence of it is this: the force that sets them in motion is cosmic, lying wholly outside the earth and presumably acting impartially on all parts of the globe, but the nature of the tide at any particular place is a local matter, with astonishing differences occurring within a very short geographic distance.[28]

When Muses re-membering enter the rhythms of Tidal Memory we experience a connectedness with the cosmos that had been broken. Our reason/passion connects with the most distant of the stars, yet the astonishing differences within short distances make re-membering difficult. Although Crones do experience synchronicity, there is also the sense of being broken-hearted/broken-souled as we break from the mazes of delusion. As Gnostic Nags break from the stable-world of pseudomemory, we become Unstabled. This is pixilating at first—the striving for new and ancient equilibrium. [ . . . ]

When racing with the rhythms of Tidal Memory, women are focused. [ . . . ] Concentrating, re-membering, women bring light, heat, and sounds together and send them forth again with intensified intent. [. . . A]ccord (being of one heart) and unanimity (being of one mind/soul) can be genuine only when Dreadful and Daring Diversity is recognized. When women break into Naming this concord and this difference, the consequence can be a cosmic *concento*, the Crone-logically simultaneous sounding of the tones of a chord.

Certainly this dream of a gynaesthetic concert/concordance often can seem "far out." It is. As Jan Raymond has movingly written:

> It is not enough for feminists to dissect the corpse of patriarchal pathologies. Women have not always been for men. We need to know the genealogy of women who did not and who do not exist for men or in pivotal relation to them. And we need to create a vision of the future of Gyn/affection. What women search for can be as important as what we find.[29]

The search itself is part of the process of presentiating our past and future concordance.

When feeling unfocused, out of contact with the rhythms of Tidal Memory, it is important to realize that this Memory *is*, needing only to be Realized. Perhaps we can take heart from Rachel Carson's description of a very small green worm known to marine biologists as *Convoluta roscoffensis*, who lives in the sea sand, rising when the tide has ebbed and sinking into the sand when the tide returns. Sometimes scientists transfer a whole colony of these worms into an aquarium, where there are no tides. Rachel Carson writes:

> But twice each day Convoluta rises out of the sand on the bottom of the aquarium, into the light of the sun. And twice each day it sinks again into the sand. Without a brain, or what we would call a memory, or even any very clear perception, Convoluta continues to live out its life in this alien place, remembering, in every fiber of its small green body, the tidal rhythm of the distant sea.[30]

[ . . . ] Women consenting can sense that be-ing sane *is* making our Selves heard in the only way that matters. Be-ing of sound mind, a woman participates in the flow of sound and silence that is the Tidal Rhythm of Empowering Memory. Actively potent, she makes sense of things, inspiring her sisters to trust their own senses. Putting her memories into words, she Nags others to find and weave their wholeness, to Race with Tidal rhythms and to know in the Gnomic Present—the present that is experienced when one is backed and moved by the past, by E-motional Memory, and therefore presentient. Thus she comes to understand more about principalities and powers.

28

## The Raging Race

From chapter 6 of *Pure Lust*, pp. 257–59.

*Rage:* transformative focusing force that awakens transcendent E-motion; Passion that unpots the potted passions and melts down the plastic ones; Passion which, when unleashed, enables Furies to sever our Selves from the State of Severance, breathe Fire, and fly into freedom.
—*Wickedary*, p. 91

Distancing herself from real-world issues of race, Daly instead used the term "race" to reinforce her dynamic, open ontology, doing this through the glowing poetry of an ode to raging movement. This style of accumulated neologisms, wordplay, and intellectual ecstasy marked her writings—and her public appearances—for the remainder of her life.
—Editors

Women sever our Selves from the State of Severance by the force of righteous Fury, unleashed Rage. This passion unpots the potted passions and melts down the plastic ones. Potted love, desire, joy, hate, aversion, and sorrow, as well as potted fear, daring, hope, despair, and anger shoot forth, shattering the confining pots. Extending their roots and branches, they reach for their Elemental connections with Earth, Air, Water, Fire. Touched by the sweet earth, wild winds, rich rain, warm sun, they expand unendingly.

Righteous Rage makes love, desire, and joy realistic, unsentimental. Unsatisfied with the appeasing sops/slops fed to imprisoned plants, loving, desiring, rejoicing women—that is, Lusty women—allow no limits to the qualitative expansion of our Lust. Disdaining the dainty morsels served in the Severed State of Domestication, we drink deeply of Wild elements and thrive, grow.

Freed Fury makes hate, aversion, and sorrow biophilic. No longer twisted inward, devouring women's Selves, these passions purge our souls of horizontal violence. Our hate and aversion—moving past the token torturers who are also victims—stir us to end the cruel rule of agents of aggression. Applying our Selves to Naming the real agents, Furies fueled by these passions are unappeasable. Our Fire is unallayed, unassuaged by Rites of Appeasement.

Our grief is for the Earth, our Sister, as well as for the Fore-crones of our Race. It melts/unfreezes frozen tears, tearing open Eyes to see what has been hidden and denied. Touching ancient scars, uncovering wounds, we wash away infections of Self-hate. The healing waters of our weeping give us strength. Our words of wailing wash our souls with truth that cleanses while it clears the air we breathe.

Rage-fueled fear and daring combine in forming focused ferocity. Furies know that the Ultimate Fearful Thing is loss of Lust for Life, and that this Lust is lost/killed by compromise, by crumbling before our fears of lesser evils. The righteous fear of compromise is one Source of Haggard Dreadful Daring. Furies dare also to reverse the reversal contained in this word—*compromise*—itself. For in its roots this does not mean "selling out" but simply "promising together." Promising together to spurn the spurious promises of our would-be procurers and appeasers, Raging women learn anew the meanings of faith, of Fate. Faithful to our promises to each other, we can dare to re-create our Fates, to be Spinners of Stamina, the threads of Life.

Hope and despair are sharpened also by Righteous Rage. Furies dispense with potted hopes, such as hopes for equality within patriarchy, recognizing this to be a contradiction in terms. In this sense we despair, that is, turn our energies away from what had formerly been perceived as "good" and which was an illusion. Rage at having been deceived/duped into expending energy in the pursuit of false hopes emboldens women to reach/hope for more arduous and ultimately more real Goods. Rage, then, as a forceful reaction to realistic assessment of our caste's conditions, releases pent up gynergy which can then express itself as original, creative hope.

Anger is unpotted and transformed into Rage/Fury when the vast network that constitutes the context of our oppression is recognized. It is further transformed when the positive network of Elemental be-ing is glimpsed behind the Foreground. As the Realm of Pyrospheres is Realized, anger bursts forth as Creative Rage.

In this Realm, passions are truly movements, verbs. We experience the melting down of noxious nouns embedded in our psyches, which are the plastic passions. Depression is converted into expression. Guilt, anxiety, frustration, and the other lumps of fixated feelings are broken into their real components—the hate, aversion, sadness, fear, despair, and Rage that really move. Full-fillment melts down simply into Nothing. This process cannot happen "all at once," of course, but each movement of be-ing is experienced as an epiphany/ontophany.

Pyromancers learn to live simultaneously in many dimensions. Thus the passions that have evil as their object, such as sorrow, fear, and daring, do not and should not disappear. As powerful forms of E-motion, they have a place within a realistic, biophilic context. The same principle applies to Rage.

Pyromantic, creatively Raging women are Racy women. *Racy* means "having the distinctive or characteristic flavor, quality, or excellence of a race or kind." *Racy* also means "full of life, zest, or vigor: LIVELY, SPIRITED." Racy, Raging women, then, are Lusty, having the distinctive qualities of the Race of Women.

To comprehend raciness we can recall that the Race of Women is many-dimensional. We have seen (in the Introduction) that *race* means "act of rushing onward: RUN."[1] The distinctive flavor, quality, and excellence of Racy Women, then, implies movement—the act of rushing onward. Moreover, *race* means "a strong or rapid current of water." The raciness of the Race of Women involves strength, speed, and focus. Also, *race* means "a heavy or choppy sea; especially one produced by the meeting of two tides." The Elemental raciness of the Race of Women involves Wild and roaring movement, and Tidal meetings and encounters. Clearly, then, the Racy Raging Race of Women will require the Realizing of Volcanic Virtues, as we move deeper into Pyrospheres.

29

# From "Justice" to Nemesis

From chapter 7 of *Pure Lust*, pp. 274–85.

*Nemesis 1:* Virtue beyond justice, acquired by Inspired Acts of Righteous Fury; Virtue enabling Seers to unblindfold captive Justice *2:* participation in the powers of the Goddess Nemesis; Elemental disruption of the patriarchal balance of terror; Passionate Spinning/Spiraling of Archaic threads of Gynergy.
—*Wickedary*, p. 84

Mary Daly's own fighting spirit surfaces here, both philosophically and in the tale of the Furious Fighting Cow. She drew an important distinction between justice and nemesis. Justice is seen as too small a goal, too accommodating, to be worthy of Amazons. By contrast, the goddess Nemesis does not negotiate with oppression, but pursues transformation instead. Daly even defined Nemesis as "a relevant mysticism which responds to the tormented cries of the oppressed, and to the hunger and thirst for creative be-ing."

Perceptively, Daly understood justice as embedded in economic rather than transformative metaphors: "Even the expression 'fighting (or working) for justice' suggests a commodity to be gained through active struggle. It does not convey the object of this striving as *something that women create.*" Justice is revealed as a finite object, and thus another limitation that Daly is determined to break through.

The story of the Furious Fighting Cow held great significance for Daly because of the singularity of the cow's rebellion; one must fight even when one is alone in that fight. She made clear that

> Sin-full Courage does not of its essence rely upon sisterly support. To recognize this is not to fall into "blaming the (other) victim." What embattled woman (or animal) has energy to squander on that? To recognize this is to cultivate the Self-reliance so prized by [Elizabeth Cady] Stanton and other sturdy souls—who of course have Given Heart beyond measure.

Perhaps this indicates that Daly saw herself, more and more, in a situation parallel to that of the Furious Fighting Cow: struggling with or without the sisterly support that had seemed so abundant in the mid-1970s.
—Editors

The first of the moral virtues, *justice*, has been defined as "the perpetual and constant will to render to each one his right."[1] Barring the masculine/pseudogeneric pronoun, the definition would appear to have some merit. It becomes more problematic, however, when a woman asks what rights the "just" person judges that "each one" has. It is hardly necessary to review here in detail the long struggle of women to obtain "equal rights" within patriarchy in order to know that the patriarchal devisers of this definition of *justice* had in mind something substantially less than "right" when they created the device of such a concept. Since, moreover, the moral virtue of justice was believed to be situated in the will and thus to require the intellectual virtue of (virile) prudence to direct its acts, it is clear that much, too much, is askew in phallic theories of justice. The "just" king, president, pope, physician, boss, husband, father knows with certainty the proper place and "rights" of the touchable caste.

Nor does the patriarchally defined "vice" of *injustice* throw much light upon the predicament of women. For the Droningly Dictated Dichotomy of justice-injustice is chiefly concerned with the making and breaking of Boys' Club rules. The situation of women—both the oppression and the a-mazing authentic aspirations—is ineffably outside the sphere of petty paternal disputes that is reflected in this dreary semantic dichotomy. The pair, justice-injustice, is too pallid to Name the Righteous Virtue of Raging women.

More accurate to name the object and the process of Racy Righteousness is the term *Nemesis*. As Goddess of divine retribution, the Nemesis within Pyrosophical women wills to act/live the verb which is the root of her Name: *nemein*, meaning to deal out, to dispense retribution. Unlike "justice," which is depicted as a woman blindfolded and holding a sword and scales, Nemesis has her eyes open and uncovered—especially her Third Eye. Moreover, she is concerned less with "retribution," in the sense of external meting out of rewards and punishments, than with an internal judgment that sets in motion a kind of new psychic alignment of energy patterns. Nemesis, thus Named, is hardly irrelevant mysticism. Rather, this Names a relevant mysticism which responds to the tormented cries of the oppressed, and to the hunger and thirst for creative be-ing.

Certainly, women have always cried and struggled for "justice." The thwarting of this longing and struggling gives rise to the birth pangs of radical feminist awareness. But only when the knowledge that something is not "right" evolves into uncovering the invisible context of gynocide and, beyond this, into active participation in the Elemental context of biophilic harmony and power can there be great and sustained creativity and action. To Name this active Elemental contextual participation, which transcends and overturns patriarchal "justice" and "injustice," Other words are needed. Nemesis is a beginning in this direction.

The thirst for what has been perceived as attainable "justice," as well as the longing to overcome "injustice," has driven women into the arms of the male left and of the male right. Women of the left have sought Justice through male-approved methods of "revolution." Women of the right have sought justice (though they often cannot articulate even this word) through tears, self-deprecation, insistence on their place in heaven, militant anti-feminism, vicarious living. Women swing to the left and to the right when captured within the confines of patriarchally controlled imagination—expressed in the words "justice" and "injustice."

Understandably there is often a passivity in women's hope for justice, as for a commodity long overdue. Even the expression "fighting (or working) for justice" suggests a commodity to be gained through active struggle. It does not convey the object of this striving as *something that women create*. This may in part be related to the passive condition of women as oppressed. I suggest, however, that the problem has to do also with the word *justice*, which is not sufficiently inspiring/Firing. It has the flavor, texture, and odor of a hand-out which women deserve, and which presumably could ultimately be bestowed by or wrenched from the prevailing order. But the prevailing order/ordure does not have the capacity to bestow or even to have wrenched away from it the sought-after treasure. It would be more fruitful to engage in the proverbial fruitless task of trying to obtain blood from a stone.

If a woman experiments with changing her discussion of justice from the nominal to verbal forms, she will quickly hit upon the verb *rectify*. For justice, after all, is said to be about "the right." Consistent with this is the fact that *rectify* suggests that the task is to straighten out, correct, redress, remedy, reform a situation, that is, to re-turn it to a previous condition that is understood on the same level as the "problem." The procedure sounds like correcting an error in arithmetic; it appears to be correcting an imbalance, restoring balance. There is nothing in this language that stirs the imagination beyond a patriarchal future and past, a regainable status quo.

Recognizing on some level the stagnation inherent in the dichotomy justice-injustice, theologians such as Paul Tillich have tried to write of "creative justice." Yet this effort is so alien to Pyrosophical awareness and analysis, so reinforcing of submission and of what can be called the feminine imperative, that it will make a feminist's flesh crawl. Tillich writes, for example:

> Creative Justice demands . . . that he be accepted who is unacceptable in terms of proportional justice. In accepting him into the unity of forgiveness, love exposes both the acknowledged break with justice on his side with all its implicit consequences and the claim inherent in him to be *declared* just and to be *made* just by reunion [emphases mine].[2]

Certainly, acts of forgiveness are necessary in any deep relationship. But this is not all that Tillich is arguing for.

In order to savor the true flavor of this text, the reader could try the following exercise: Imagine a priest, rabbi, or minister reciting this text to a woman who has been repeatedly battered by her husband, or whose husband has sexually assaulted their daughter. Imagine the woman trying to find moral support for her decision to leave. Clearly, *declaring* the offender/criminal "just" and reuniting with him will not make him "just." Rather, what happens in such a case is that the woman is "morally" bullied into forfeiting her right to judge. She is "morally" intimidated into Self-castration, into breaking her own Naming process. She is duped, guilt-tripped into separation from her own powers as Nemesis, blocked from re-claiming her life. Tillich's moral verbiage in such a case, then, is worse than useless. It serves structures of oppression—

notably those of the sexual caste system—which are not even taken into consideration.

I am suggesting, then, that *justice* is not an adequate name for that which Canny, Raging women create. The new psychic alignment of gynergy patterns associated with Nemesis is not merely rectifying of a situation which the term *unjust* could adequately describe. Nemesis is Passionate Spinning/Spiraling of new/ancient forms and connections of gynergy. It is an E-motional habit acquired/required in the Pyrospheres. It demands Shrewd as well as Fiery judgment and is therefore a Nag-Gnostic/Pyrognostic Virtue. Nemesis is a habit built up by inspired acts of Righteous Fury, which move the victims of gynocidal oppression into Pyrospheric changes unheard of in patriarchal lore.

Some women have always known about active desire that reaches beyond the confines of "justice." In 1852, in a political speech at the Woman's Rights Convention, Elizabeth Oakes Smith asked:

> My friends, do we realize for what purpose we are convened? Do we fully understand that we aim at nothing less than an entire subversion of the present order of society, a dissolution of the whole existing social compact?[3]

Assessing the twentieth-century American scene, Florynce Kennedy, commenting from her vantage point as Black feminist activist and attorney, wrote:

> Every form of bigotry can be found in ample supply in the legal system of our country. It would seem that Justice (usually depicted as a woman) is indeed blind to racism, sexism, war, and poverty.[4]

The specific functioning of blindfolded "justice" in the legal mind (the patriarchal mind *par excellence*) has been expressed by Joyce Carol Oates in her description of a defense lawyer:

> . . . he believed in the justice of his using any legal methods he could improvise to force the other side into compromise or into dismissals of charges, or to lead a jury into the verdict he wanted. Why not? He was a defense lawyer.[5]

As archetypally cast into the role of "the other side," women know about the self-righteous sense of "justice" of professional defenders of the sadosystem, who use every method to force those who are pleading for justice "into compromise or into dismissal of charges," and to lead the "jury" of patriarchally possessed peers to pronounce the destroyers of women "not guilty." And women know that the nefarious methods of gynocide are legal.

E-motionally propelled beyond the inadequate naming expressed in the dichotomy "justice-injustice," Pyrosophical women begin to live in dimensions of that which, transitionally at least, can be called Nemesis. The Virtue of Nemesis may be perceived as *sinister*, for it is creativity that is utterly Other than the righteousness of the sadorulers. It is *sinister*, not merely in the sense of choosing left as opposed to right, for this would be mere opposition of opposites on the same plane. Rather, Nemesis moves within a different context, and creates such a context as it moves. The Otherness of this context is not "complementary" to the prevailing order of sadosociety, for it *is* Other. Women participating in the powers of Nemesis, Spinning gynocentric ways of be-ing, are not caught in reactive rage, but are Actively Raging, Racing. [ . . . ]

[ . . . ] Nemesis is engendered by Rage. Pyrographers will note that Nemesis as divine vengeance often has been envisioned as a visitation in the form of Elemental phenomena. Inspired by the Muses of Rage, a woman coming into touch with Nemesis becomes awakened to Elemental powers of Geomancy, Aeromancy, Hydromancy, Pyromancy. Her "visitations," or her influence upon situations, arises from Realizing her harmony with the elements. She becomes more at home in the world of dimensions uncaptured by the Phallic State.

Awareness of these dimensions gives the Canniness necessary to Spin new/ancient gynergy patterns that transform oppressive states. Sometimes this implies moving out of an old environment physically; always it implies transforming the conditions where/when one lives.

To imagine that women who choose Creative Nemesis are therefore insensitive to the reality of oppression is to miss the point. For it is Visionary Creation that carries Women's Movement foreward (upward, downward, aroundward) and that sustains the woman warrior. Maxine Hong Kingston vividly illustrates the sustaining power of feminist vision, in relating how the stories of women warriors, told to her by her mother, aided her in the struggle of growing up female and Chinese in American society.[6] Monique Wittig's feminist classic, *Les Guérillères,* has inspired thousands of women with Amazonian Imagination.[7] Indeed, numerous Crones have been engaged in the process of conjuring Nemesis through re-membering the lore of our fore-mothers and through Spinning Original tales.[8] It is precisely such transcendent vision that makes possible acute sensitivity to the common facts of oppression, for in the light of what might be and perhaps once was, an A-mazed woman sees/feels the horror of each fact, each event of the Possessed State of her sex and of nature on this planet. This vision fires her to fight back.

Unlike blindfolded, static patriarchal "justice," a woman inspired by Nemesis sharpens her senses, sharpens her Labrys. As her axe, this can cut back barriers. As her wings, it carries her on the wind. Better than a broom, it bears her beyond the foreground fortresses.

Nemesis is not about casuistry, nor about cautiously measured rewards and punishments. It is about flying through the badlands, badtimes. It is about creating new cacophony, new concord, countering destruction with creation. For such symphonic soaring, a woman needs Outrageous Courage.

## Outrageous, Contagious Courage

I have attempted to show that Racy women Sin in the most colossal and cosmic way by be-ing Elemental. Ontological Courage, then, the Courage required for Pyrosophical be-ing, is a Sin-full Virtue. Derived from the Latin *cor,* meaning heart, *Courage* signifies a heartfelt, passionate strength. Sin-full Courage is the core/heart of all the Volcanic Virtues.

The Courage of Pyromantic Crones is necessarily Outrageous. One meaning of *outrageous* is "exceeding the limits of what is normal or tolerable." It means "not conventional or matter-of-fact: EXTRAVAGANT, FANTASTIC." An Outrageously Courageous Crone, since she is Pyrogenetic and therefore not conventional or matter-of-fact, risks being perceived as *outrageous* in the sense of "extremely offensive: showing a disregard for decency or good taste." Of course, as her taste becomes more and more discerning she is more and more subjected to foreground labeling as "tasteless." Such deprecations should be treated as en-couraging/heartening signs that she has made progress in reversing the reigning reversals.

At the core/"heart" of the maze of reversals which Raging, Outrageous women must reverse, are the sado-ideology and sado-symbolism of the heart itself. The heart is said to symbolize "the centre of being, both physical and spiritual; the divine presence at the centre."[9] The symbol of the heart as center has been spoiled for countless women, however, by the sickening sado-sophism that "man is the head, and woman is the heart." For the cliché is intended to legitimate women's condition of subjection as entombed in the touchable caste.

The sadosages speak euphemistically of the heart as representing the "central wisdom of feeling" as opposed to the "head-wisdom" of reason.[10] The clue to the ensuing deceptions is in the dichotomy/opposition itself. No matter how highly patriarchal propagandists extol what they call "the heart," their ascribing of this to women says it all. The "central wisdom of feeling" is intended to signify mush-headed sentimentality requiring control by The Head.

By the symbolic dissociation of "the heart" from Intellectual Courage, from "head-wisdom," the decapitators have attempted the symbolic castration of women (the "hearts") cutting us off from our Active Potency. It is only by Taking Heart again, by Courage-ing the Sin of reuniting her passion and intellect, that a woman can Realize her powers. Pyrosophical Crones, wrenching the Heart back into our own semantic context, make Courage the core of Women's Movement. Taking Heart, then, becomes a Metaphor of Metabeing, carrying a woman into the Pyrospheric Realm, where she transforms, transvalues virtues, desiring, acquiring Volcanic Virtue.

Taking Heart is an essential feminist task. In 1851, Elizabeth Cady Stanton wrote movingly of the need for Courage:

> The manner in which all courage and self-reliance is educated *out* of the girl, her path portrayed with dangers and difficulties that never exist, is melancholy indeed. Better, far, suffer occasional insults or die outright, than live the life of a *coward*, or never move without a protector. The best protector any woman can have, one that will serve her at all times and in all places, is *courage*; this she must get by her own experience, and experience comes by exposure.[11]

Here Stanton Names the problem—the breeding out of courage from women under the guise of protection—the breeding out that breaks the hope of Breaking Out. Yet, some have never been thoroughly broken in, and these, less broken, hearten others. As Millicent Garrett Fawcett put it, in 1920:

> Courage calls to courage everywhere, and its voice cannot be denied.[12]

This is a Naming of the Contagiousness of Outrageous Courage, of its Pyromagnetic propensity. It is a Naming of the basic calling of Nagsters, who by Taking Heart, Give Heart.

A woman who Takes Heart and Gives Heart moves to the heart of the matter, becoming Self-centering. Having known heartbreak over the dis-memberment of her kind, she now heartens her Self and her Sisters. Her Taking Heart is the magic Self-woven carpet that carries her to Metabeing, the place of her heart's Desiring/Firing. Heartened, she engages in Pyromachy, fighting with Fire, with the fullness of luminous intelligence, the Radiance of Realizing reason. Her words/actions are Outrageous simply because they are beyond the proscribed limits of the familiar Flatland. She judges and *acts* according to Pyrometric standards.

Such Taking Heart is essentially that which can Give Heart to another woman, in the sense of en-couraging her to re-claim her own heart/head. I am not suggesting that an Outrageous woman acts Courageously chiefly in order to inspire others. Rather, her Taking Heart is essential to her own Elemental be-ing. It is contagious, but not always in an immediately perceivable way. Yet Crones know that Courage is the Elemental Lifeline.

## The Furious Fighting Cow, and How She Escaped

Courage is a bond between Outrageous women and other Wild creatures, especially those who in some dimensions, at least, escape the sadorule. In a remarkable travel book, *The Sea and the Jungle* (a favorite book of Rachel Carson), H. M. Tomlinson describes the brutal taking aboard ship of sixty head of cattle—each being hauled on board by a rope around her horns, the rope being attached to a crane, so that all of each cow's weight was on her horns. Each was hoisted up, bumping against the ship's side, and then dumped on the deck. All were subdued by this treatment but one, a small black heifer. Tomlinson describes the resistance of this "implacable rebel":

> The cattlemen, as punishment for the trouble she had given them ashore, kept her dangling over the deck, and one got level with her face and mocked her, slapping her nose. She actually defied him. . . . She was no cow. She was insurrection, she was the hate for tyrants incarnated. They dropped her. She was up and away like a cat. . . . She put everybody on that deck in the shrouds or in the forecastle head as she trotted round with her tail up, looking for brutes to put them to death. None of the cows (of course) helped her. By a trick she was caught. . . . Then she tried to kick all who passed. If the rest of the cattle had been like her none would have suffered. Alas! They were probably all scientific evolutionists, content to wait for men to become kindly apple-lovers by slow and natural uplift; and gravely deprecated the action of the heifer from which, as peaceful cows, they disassociated themselves.[13]

During the voyage, though her head was fixed unmovably, unlike the others, the black heifer kept her unabated Fury. Recalling this, Tomlinson wrote, "What a heart!" But the story does not end here. After the journey the men had to unload the cattle:

> We waited for the turn of the black heifer. . . . She made a furious lunge at the men when her nose was free, but the winch rattled, and she was brought up on her hind legs, blaring at us all. In that ugly manner she was walked on two legs across the deck, a heroine in shameful guise, while the men laughed. She was hoisted, and lowered into the river. She fought at the waiting canoe with her feet, but at last the men released her horns from the tackle. With only her face above water she heaved herself, open-mouthed, at the canoe trying to bite it, and then made some almost successful efforts to climb into it. The canoe men were so panic-stricken that they did nothing but muddle one another's efforts. The canoe rocked dangerously. This wicked animal had no care for its own safety like other cattle. It surprised its tormentors because it showed its only wish was to kill them. Just in time, the men paddled off for their lives, the cow after them. Seeing she could not catch them, she swam ashore, climbed the

bank, looking around then for sight of the enemy—but they were all in hiding—and then began browsing in the scrub.[14]

This story, which could be called "The Furious Cow and How She Escaped," depicting the triumphant escape of the heifer who did not have the support of her subdued sisters, might be taken from its context and read as a poignant parable for weary and dis-couraged feminists—the moral being: Take Heart. If the brave heifer had been able (or willing) to read, she certainly would have agreed with Stanton's words: "Better, far, suffer occasional insults or die outright, than live the life of a coward." In any case, she demonstrated her knowledge of the fact that Sin-full Courage does not of its essence rely upon sisterly support. To recognize this is not to fall into "blaming the (other) victim." What embattled woman (or animal) has energy to squander on that? To recognize this is to cultivate the Self-reliance so prized by Stanton and other sturdy souls—who of course have Given Heart beyond measure.

Tomlinson's account can be read by feminists as a parable also on another level—critically, looking at it within the context of his telling it. For this story of the brave heifer and the fifty-nine who were subdued leaves something to be desired. His playful description of the "peaceful cows," as "gravely deprecating" the action of the heifer, erases the fact that it was the torture endured by the animals that had subdued them. Tomlinson did acknowledge this, of course, but seems immediately to have forgotten the significance of his own information in his delighted admiration of the solitary rebel. For, as he writes, the cows had *all* been "wild things, which had been collected in the campo with great difficulty."[15] He writes, as we have seen, "None of the cows (of course) helped her. . . . If the rest of the cattle had been like her, none would have suffered." The Outraged reader might ask: Did Tomlinson even protest? As an honored passenger he could have tried to intervene in the face of extraordinary cruelty. The context of his account does not suggest that this was his reaction.

Tomlinson does record the "great joy" which he and his companion, the ship's doctor, experienced at watching the tortured heifer's efforts to free her horns. But "great joy" at seeing the struggle of one "implacable rebel" does not strike the critical reader as an adequate response to this spectacle of suffering and bravery.

In short, the self-description of Tomlinson portrays/betrays the attitude of the liberal who by his passivity legitimates the Lecherous State. He legitimates this State also by his propensity for singling out the singularly courageous victim/escapee for his admiration, while sustaining contempt for the other Others. The subliminal association with women and other oppressed people is not hard to detect, nor are the applications. In contrast to this "sympathetic liberal observer" stance, the position of the Self-reliant, Outrageous Courageous Crone implies refusal to erase the history of oppression of those Sisters who were subdued and conquered. The Furiously Focused re-calling of the history of oppression of all women is essential to the identity of a feminist and for sustaining the Pyrosophical Vision, even under conditions of seeming desertion and isolation.

30

# The "Soul" as Metaphor for Telic Principle

From chapter 10 of *Pure Lust*, pp. 344–47.

*Telic Focusing Principle 1:* All-pervasive principle within an organism, entirely present in all parts of the organism; Source of deep purposefulness, which makes possible growth, adaptation, creation 2. Re-membering and Metapatterning principle in Metamorphosing women.
—*Wickedary*, p. 97

Mary Daly's philosophy, manifest in from *Beyond God the Father* to *Pure Lust*, explicitly connects ontological and political dimensions. In this brief excerpt, she returned to that sense of purpose—"telos"—that provided the dynamism in her system. She called attention to how her thought had hologrammatic qualities, meaning the whole is present in every part. What she meant here by Unfolding is cosmological: the world is not a static or humming monism, but a constant and unpredictable movement of change. Here she named this by the deliberately paradoxical formula of "unfolding integrity" that "is changing in harmony with the universe." This implies an integrity that cannot be observed externally, but only experienced internally, for which change is a quality of virtue, rather than a blemish on perfection.
—Editors

One traditional way of naming the principle of telic focus has been to call this the "soul." Shrewds can use this as a starting point for our analysis. Since my intent is to wrench this concept out of its traditional context, using it in a Nag-Gnostic context, I am employing it not simply as an analytic concept but also as Metaphor.

*Soul*, as springboard word, then, refers here to the animating principle of an organism. Specifically, it means the "substantial form" of a living body, as this is understood in Aristotelian philosophy.[1] Soul, then, as the word is used here, is not intended in a Platonic sense, as if it were a distinct entity loosely connected with the body, or imprisoned in the body. Certainly I do not mean it in any sort of Cartesian sense, as if it were "mind" or *res cogitans* vaguely connected with matter. Rather, I use the word *soul* to mean an animating principle that is intimately united with/present to the body, in a union that traditionally has been called a "hylomorphic union." According to this theory, in human beings the "intellectual principle" is united to the body as the body's form.[2]

To speak of the soul in this sense, then, is not to convey the naïve, dualistic notion that soul and body are two united entities. The soul, conceived as the animating and unifying principle of the organism, is the radical source of life functions and activities. It is the source of telic centering—of the purposiveness of the organism.

The soul, understood in this tradition, is wholly present in each part of the body.[3] It is not a mere quantitative whole. An example of the latter would be a house, which is composed of foundation, walls, and roof. (Obviously, the entire house is not in each of its parts.) Moreover, the soul is not just a generic or logical whole, as a whole definition is made up of all of its parts. Rather, it is a "potential whole." Explaining this concept, Aquinas wrote that the whole soul is divided into "virtual parts." That is:

> The whole soul is in each part of the body, by totality of perfection and of essence, but not by totality of power. . . . with regard to sight, it is in the eye; and with regard to hearing, it is in the ear, and so forth.[4]

Since this concept of unity (of essence) at the root of multiplicity (of parts/powers) was not comprehended by all philosophers, Aquinas had to refute the position that "besides the intellectual soul there are in man other souls essentially different from one another."[5]

This seemingly simple position, namely, that there are not many souls in one person, but rather one soul, wholly present everywhere within that person, can be a Metaphoric springboard for Metamorphosing women. It can function as an aid to Amazons seeking the meaning of our Be-Longing in the face/faces of the fear-full fragmentation of women that is inflicted in the fatherland. Some of the implications may be more obvious if the Searcher substitutes the word *Self* for *soul*, thereby constructing the statement: There are not many Selves in one woman, but rather, one Self, wholly present in that woman. I am not asserting here that Self and soul are precisely equivalent terms; in fact, they are not. My point is that one obvious consequence of the idea that a woman has one soul wholly present in all of her "parts," is that there is an essential integrity at the very core of her Self.

Be-Longing implies the Unfolding, the Realization, of this inherent integrity. It is Realized as a woman becomes wholly Present in all of her activities. The phenomenological manifestation of this integrity and pervasive Presence of her soul is a radical consistency in her behavior. She does not seem to be "one person one day and someone else the next." This is not to say that she lacks complexity and variety of skills, activities, and experiences. Quite the opposite is the case; she manifests a high degree of differentiation. Moreover, she is spontaneous. This is possible because her energy is focused; it is not dissipated in the maintenance of masks, of fragmented false selves—splintered personae parading on the periphery of her Self.

The Unfolding/Realizing of this integrity is be-ing beyond such reified beings, the solidified pseudo-selves. It is participation in Metabeing. The Lust for this intensely focused ontological activity, or Be-Longing, is the Lust for Happiness.

## Souls and Holograms/Holographs

The concept of the unity of the soul, as presented in Aristotelian philosophy and developed in the doctrine of Aquinas, can not easily be dismissed as completely absurd and irrelevant. To one who has long been familiar with this doctrine, it is both fascinating and funny to find contemporary scientific thinkers using language that in some ways is reminiscent of this idea, when they write of the universe and of the mind as "holograms."

According to David Bohm, for example, who often uses the holographic analogy, the information of the entire universe is contained in each of its parts. As Larry Dossey describes holograms:

> A hologram is a specially constructed image which, when illuminated by a laser beam, seems eerily suspended in three-dimensional space. The

> most incredible feature of holograms is that any *piece* of it, if illuminated with coherent light, provides an image of the *entire* hologram. The information of the whole is contained in each part.[6]

Dossey—and others before him—asks whether, as part of the universe, we have holographic features ourselves that permit us to comprehend a holographic universe. Stanford neurophysiologist Karl Pribram has answered the question in the affirmative, proposing the hologram as a model of brain function.[7] Putting together the ideas of Bohm and Pribram, Dossey suggests that the brain is a hologram "that is part of an even larger hologram—the universe itself."[8]

The holographic analogy is, of course, just that—an analogy.[9] It has provided a language for these scientists to speak of an idea of the mind and of its relation to the universe that is really not entirely new. Comparable themes have recurred in the history of philosophy.[10] Bearing this in mind, Brewsters may wish to use holograms/holographs as variant metaphors pointing to integrity/wholeness. This is not to suggest that contemporary scientific jargon legitimates the classical philosophical language, concerning the soul, for example. It may be, however, that the holographic metaphor can render more accessible some of the potentially helpful concepts that are contained/captured within the contexts of philosophical treatises.

The holographic metaphor, moreover, as applied to the idea of the soul, can suggest a telic centering principle which is an unfolding potential whole—one that is changing in harmony with the universe. Prudes can use this combination of metaphors to point to the internal source of the unfolding integrity of meta-patriarchal women. Such integrity is manifested in the whole spectrum of a woman's activities and characterizes her presentiating Presence.

31

# Be-Friending

## *The Lust to Share Happiness*

From chapter 11 of *Pure Lust*, pp. 373–79.

*Be-Friending:* [*befriend* "to act as a friend to: show kindness, sympathy, and understanding to (befriend a helpless person)"—*Webster's*]: radically active transcending of the need for the belittling "befriending" bestowed upon women by their many "protectors" in the state of helplessness/Selflessness which is patriarchy; overcoming the unnatural separation of women from our Selves and each Other imposed by phallocracy; weaving a context/atmosphere in which the Acts/Leaps of Metamorphosis can take place; Realizing the Lust to share Happiness.
—*Wickedary*, p. 63

Daly's three most significant books—*Beyond God the Father, Gyn/Ecology,* and *Pure Lust*—all end with positive appreciations of the shared power of women who participate in Be-ing. The Sparking possibilities of female friendship were crucial to Daly, both philosophically and in her own life. Female friendship and its mutual sparking were not limited by time or space—Daly nurtured her connection to her favorite feminists of the past, like Sojourner Truth and Matilda Joslyn Gage. And while feminist friendship en-Couraged women, it also became a place to share our rage. As she wrote, "Women require the context of Be-Friending both to sustain the positive force of moral Outrage and to continue the Fury-fueled task of inventing new ways of living." This moral Outrage, coupled with the striving for transcendent knowledge, is another example of how Daly combines mysticism and activism. In one of her most famous formulations—"Rage is not 'a stage'"—found in this chapter, she pointed out that the horrors that motivate us to fight for women are not small problems to be resolved in order to achieve space for spiritual development.
—Editors

## Be-Friending: Weaving Contexts, Creating Atmospheres

Spinsters, who have experienced something of the process/activity of Happiness, Lust to share such Realization of participation in Be-ing. The actualization of this desire requires *Be-Friending. Be-Friending* is the creation of a context/atmosphere in which acts/leaps of Metamorphosis can take place. Websters Weaving this context are inspired to do so by our knowledge of female potential. That is, it is not the supposition that women are "weak" that inspires the Weaving. Rather, it is certain knowledge of the potency of women—a potency that needs to be actualized—that emboldens us to continue the work.

While the knowledge of female potency is certain, it is far from certain that this will be Actualized/Realized by many women under the prevailing conditions of the State of Separation. Therefore, quantum leaps of Fate-identified faith, hope, and Lust are in order. These leaps are part of the process itself of Weaving. They are acts of Metamorphosis, for they strengthen and actualize spiritual capacities. As Lusty Leapers, women carry the threads of connectedness ever further, beyond already Realized limits. That is, we are actualizing psychic and physical ultimacy. This Leaping/Weaving is a continuing act of sharing Lust for Happiness.

In choosing/inventing the word *Be-Friending* to Name such Webster-identified activity, I do not mean to suggest that every woman, or even every feminist, can "be a friend with" every other woman. It is clear, first of all, that there are limitations of time and energy. Second, there are serious differences of temperament and circumstances which make it impossible for some women to be friends with each other, no matter how well intentioned each may be. There are also, as Jan Raymond has pointed out, women who hate their Selves and other women, and there are histories of "unfulfilled expectations, betrayal, lack of real caring, and the wall of entrenched differences between friends that become insurmountable."[1] Moreover, a genuine friendship between any two women develops over a long period of time, and it requires basic creative harmony between the friends and a firmness of commitment to each other.

Although friendship is not possible among all feminists, the work of Be-Friending can be shared by all, and all can benefit from this Metamorphospheric activity. Be-Friending involves Weaving a context in which women can Realize our Self-transforming, metapatterning participation in Be-ing. Therefore it implies the creation of an atmosphere in which women are enabled to be friends. Every woman who contributes to the creation of this atmosphere functions as a catalyst for the evolution of other women and for the forming and unfolding of genuine friendships.

An example of Be-Friending will illustrate this process. In the late 1940s the publication of Simone de Beauvoir's great feminist work, *The Second Sex*, made possible dialogue among women about their own lives. For many years this work functioned as an almost solitary beacon for women seeking to understand the *connections* among the oppressive evils they experienced, for they came to understand the fact of otherness within patriarchal society. There were other feminist works in existence, of course, but these were not really accessible, even to "educated" women. *The Second Sex* helped to generate an atmosphere in which women could utter their own thoughts, at least to themselves. Some women began to make applications and to seek out less accessible sources, many of which had gone out of print. Most important was the fact that de Beauvoir, by breaking the silence, partially broke the Terrible Taboo. Women were Touched, psychically and e-motionally. Many such women, thus re-awakened, began to have conversations, take actions, write articles—even during the dreary fifties.

It could not accurately be said that de Beauvoir was a personal friend to the thousands of women awakened by her work. It can be said that she has been part of the movement of Be-Friending and that she has been a catalyst for the friendships of many women. The atmosphere to which her work contributed could not remain stagnant. The "air" was invigorating—a stimulant encouraging women to make those quantum leaps that bring us into Metamorphospheres.

Similarly today, any woman who makes leaps of metapatterning, whether these be in a personal relationship, in political activity, in a work of theory or of art, in spiritual understanding, or in all of the above, is a weaver of the network of Be-Friending. So also have been the Fore-Spinsters who have preceded us, Spinning and Weaving the context that makes our friendships possible.

## Be-Friending, Be-Longing, and Rage

Be-Friending is radically connected with Be-Longing. The latter is that which metapatriarchal women wish for each other and en-courage in each other, for only the longing/Lusting for be-ing can bring about Happiness. Be-Friending arouses and awakens in a woman her Be-Longing, her telic focus. Be-Friending is both the flowering of Be-Longing and an important condition for the arousal and sustaining of this ontological Passion.

Be-Friending provides the context in which the low-grade multiple-personality disorder which I have suggested is the "contrary" of Rage can be confronted and overcome. The manner in which the context of Be-Friending functions to overcome this affliction of dissociation is analogous to the action of a magnet. That is, it attracts the telic focusing powers of be-ing in a woman. For, as we have seen, everything that IS is connected with everything else that IS. Only be-ing can call forth be-ing. Only confirmation of one's own Reality awakens that Reality in another.

As she is drawn into the Spiraling movement of Be-Friending, a woman becomes a friend to the be-ing in her Self, which is to say, her centering Self. The intensity of her desire focuses her energy, which becomes unsplintered, unblocked. This focusing, gathering of her dissociated energy, makes possible the release of Rage. The Metamorphosing Sage rides her Rage. It is her broom, her Fire-breathing, winged mare. It is her spiraling staircase, leading her where she can find her own Kind, unbind her mind.

Rage is not "a stage." It is not something to be gotten over. It is transformative, focusing Force. Like a horse who streaks across fields on a moonlit night, her mane flying, Rage gallops on pounding hooves of unleashed Passion. The sounds of its pounding awaken transcendent E-motion. As the ocean roars its rhythms into every creature, giving birth to sensations of our common Sources/Courses, Rage too, makes senses come alive again, thrive again.

Women require the context of Be-Friending both to sustain the positive force of moral Outrage and to continue the Fury-fueled task of inventing new ways of living. Without the en-couragement of Be-Friending, anger can deteriorate into rancor and can mis-fire, injuring the wrong targets. One function of the work of Be-Friending, then, is to keep the sense of Outrage focused in a biophilic way.

## The Context of Outrage

The knowledge woven through acts of Be-Friending is characterized by the woman-identified recognition of connectedness that inspires and sustains the Weavers. Websters do not flinch from seeing the complicity of women as token torturers. At the same time, we struggle always to see who in fact holds the institutional power that man-ipulates and damages the consciousness/conscience of women who oppress other women. Examples of such complicity are legion. Crones know the horrifying history of mothers used as token torturers of their daughters. Crones born and brought up in America can hardly be unaware of the compounded complicity involved when phallocratic racial oppression further desensitizes and dissociates the woman who has "power" from her more oppressed sister.

The history of Black slavery in the United States illustrates this situation most tragically. A testimony of Sarah M. Grimké, abolitionist from South Carolina, published in 1839, concerns the torture of a young woman "whose independent spirit could not brook the degradation of slavery" and who repeatedly ran away. The young woman's back was lacerated to such an extent that "a finger could not be laid between the cuts." In addition:

> A heavy iron collar, with three prongs projecting from it, was placed round her neck, and a strong and sound front tooth was extracted, to serve as a mark to describe her, in case of escape.[2]

Sarah Grimké, who personally saw this young woman, stated:

> Her sufferings at this time were agonizing; she could lie in no position but on her back, which was sore from scourgings, as I can testify from personal inspection, and her only place of rest was the floor, on a blanket. These outrages were committed in a family where the mistress daily read the scriptures, and assembled her children for family worship. She was accounted, and was really, so far as alms-giving was concerned, a

> charitable woman, and tender-hearted to the poor; and yet this suffering slave, who was the seamstress of the family, was continually in her presence . . . with her lacerated and bleeding back, her mutilated mouth, and heavy iron collar without, so far as appeared, exciting any feelings of compassion.[3]

The passive complicity of the pious bible-reading mistress illustrates one way in which hatred could work itself out. Sometimes the cooperation has been more active. In 1853 Solomon Northup described the breaking of a high-spirited young woman whose back "bore the scars of a thousand stripes . . . because it had fallen her lot to be the slave of a licentious master and a jealous mistress." Northup testified concerning the agony of this woman:

> Nothing delighted the mistress so much as to see her suffer. . . . Patsey walked under a cloud. If she uttered a word in opposition to her master's will, the lash was resorted to at once, to bring her to subjection; if she was not watchful while about her cabin, or when walking in the yard, a billet of wood, or a broken bottle perhaps, hurled from her mistress' hand, would smite her unexpectedly in the face. . . .
>
> Finally, for a trifling offense, Patsey was given a savage whipping, while her mistress and the master's children watched with obvious satisfaction. She almost died.
>
> From that time forward she was not what she had been.[4]

Black women, aware of this history and faced with the day-to-day experience of racial oppression, are faced with the dilemmas implied in bonding with white women. Together with other women of color, many are creating their own radical feminist analysis.[5] White women, especially in the United States, often feel discouraged by the knowledge of white patriarchal female indifference, racial hatred, and cruelty. In the face of such unspeakable cruelty, vividly illustrated in the accounts of the mistresses' behavior and repeated thousands of times over in the country of Reagan and Company, what can be said about Female-identified Outrage?

Considering the behavior of the slaveholders' wives described above may re-mind Hags of certain basic threads in the context of our Outrage. The bible-reading mistress of the tortured young seamstress was "supported" in her dissociation from the victimized Black woman by patriarchal religion, the patriarchal institutions of slavery and racism, and the patriarchal institution of marriage. The vicious mistress of the other young woman, whose jealousy was aroused by the fact that her lecherous lout of a husband raped his defenseless slave, was the product of these same soul-molding sado-institutions. None of these institutions were invented by women or have ever been under the control of women.

It would be not only absurd but ethically wrong to excuse the slaveholders' wives, or to excuse contemporary female racist oppressors, or to condone a Phyllis Schlafly for her gynocidal, genocidal, biocidal politics. As conscious carriers of phallocratic diseases and executors of phallocratic crimes, such women are indeed responsible. Furies, moreover, will recognize that the obvious corruption and cooptation of women under patriarchy can function to weaken Female-identified Outrage in women who are sincerely struggling to live a metapatriarchal morality. That is, token torturers function as instruments of the sadostate not only as the appointed executors of oppressive acts, but also as dis-couraging and confusing role models, driving other women into paralyzing guilt and misdirected anger. Patriarchal women, then, function as Rage-blockers/twisters.

It is predictable and already observable that as the biocidal nuclear arms race continues, as the destruction of Third World people by the United States and other powerful nations escalates, as racism and poverty "at home" worsens, many women's energy and motivation for Weaving tapestries of Female Be-Friending is undermined. This is partly traceable to disgust and horror at the increasing visibility and apparent moral bankruptcy of right-wing women and other female servants of the sadostate. It is also traceable to false guilt for putting the cause of feminism first.

Crones, then, can recognize the time-honored trick of the patriarchs efficiently operating in the eighties. This is the creation of a perpetual State of Emergency, in which some male-ordered activity is always made to appear prior in importance to the liberation of women. In the face of this onslaught, Metamorphic leaps of be-ing will be possible only if there is an intensification of intent and determination on the part of women who recognize phallocracy as the root of rapism, racism, gynocide, genocide, and ultimate biocide.

Only clearly focused Female Outrage can sustain the work of metapatterning. Only continuous Weaving of tapestries of female-identified knowledge—that is, our work of Be-Friending—can further the development of metapatriarchal consciousness and behavior. These Crone-centered tapestries can serve as magic carpets for women who choose to fly beyond the sado-state's Eternal Lie. These vehicles can also serve as maps of passages to Metamemory.

## PART IV

# Spiraling Onward (1985–2010)

## *Future and Past Piratical Coursing*

As Mary Daly's quiver of neologisms expanded with each of her books, readers were often confused if, as Daly liked to say, they joined "mid-voyage." So requests surfaced in the feminist community for a dictionary that could help newly arrived readers navigate Daly's texts. Thus was born, in 1987, *Websters' First New Intergalactic Wickedary of the English Language*. Known to most readers simply as the *Wickedary*, this work was "conjured in cahoots" with Jane Caputi, a former student of Daly's and a notable feminist in her own right.[1] The *Wickedary* contains essays on Daly's theories of language, but the editors of this volume have chosen to employ Daly's own technique of sprinkling *Wickedary* definitions as epigraphs to each chapter.

The *Wickedary* marks a transition to Daly's later writings. From this time forward, she assumed her readers' willing participation in the universe she had created. Thus, there is an inevitable insularity to these final works: they can remain opaque even to the well-intentioned but uninitiated.

In a trend that all feminists and historians should applaud, many of the key participants in the women's liberation movement have written autobiographies and memoirs. Daly, like her sometimes-rival Audre Lorde, conveyed her life in mythical terms.[2] Daly transformed the title of her friend Andrea Dworkin's scathing *Intercourse* to *Outercourse*. In the book's subtitle, Daly characterized herself as a pirate, stealing back what patriarchy has stolen from women: *The Bedazzling Voyage, Containing Recollections from My Logbook of a Radical Feminist Philosopher*. Excerpts from *Outercourse* in this book provide narrative accounts of key events in Daly's life and career.

Daly's final two books—*Quintessence* (1998) and *Amazon Grace* (2006)—represent a distinct break from the philosophic rigor that had characterized her previous work. The urgency of political and environmental crises compelled this change. Rycenga recalls frequent searing phone conversations with Daly over the ultimate manifestation of patriarchal necrophilia: the potential for environmental collapse. Women's liberation, as Daly knew it from the mid-1960s to the early 1980s, had morphed into a more diffuse set of social movements. The identity politics of the 1990s held no philosophic interest for her, but the flames of old controversies dogged Daly—race, transgender issues, and the teaching of men. This last issue led to her forced retirement from Boston College, when a lawsuit funded by a conservative think tank forced her teaching practices into public scrutiny. Daly loved teaching, and the loss of the classroom space furthered the isolation that attended advancing age.

As Daly's relevance to current feminist thought diminished in the late 1990s and early twenty-first century, she keenly felt her marginalization. She became more enamored with imagining a pre-patriarchal past and projecting a post-patriarchal future. Some critics dismissed her later works as extreme and eccentric. In typical fashion, she owned the intended aspersions, embracing "the qualitative leap toward self-acceptable deviance as ludic cerebrator, questioner of everything, madwoman, and witch." It is possible that, like the late works of many great thinkers, these final books contain material not yet fully understood. It is best not to dismiss this self-proclaimed madwoman. She has spoken prophecy more than once.

32

# Early Moments

## *My Taboo-Breaking Quest—To Be a Philosopher*

From chapter 1 of *Outercourse*, pp. 22–23.

*Strange:* foreign to phallocracy; outside the parameters of predictability: ECCENTRIC, ERRATIC, ODD, QUEER, QUAINT, OUTLANDISH, WEIRD.
—*Wickedary*, p. 169

*Outercourse*, Daly's philosophic autobiography, published in 1992, exemplified the unpredictable Spiraling she had written about. She called the place where she has now arrived the "Fourth Spiral Galaxy," using the metaphor of the Cow Who Jumped over the Moon as a Self-image:

> I have a lot in common with the cow that Jumped over the moon. Did *she* know where she was going? . . . It must have been a Strange experience for her. But she refused to be stopped just because her behavior seemed odd. So what if the little dog laughed? What did *he* know?[1]

*Outercourse* is not well-known among academics, or even in the feminist community, compared to Daly's earlier books. However, the illumination that *Outercourse* provides for the totality of Daly's social context, and the increasingly integral logic of her thought, will prove invaluable to serious students of her work. Even the full title of the book reveals that Daly's philosophy has reached a stage of completeness, while being open to future spiraling changes: *Outercourse: The Be-Dazzling Voyage, Containing Recollections from My Logbook of a Radical Feminist Philosopher (Being an Account of My Time/Space Travels and Ideas—Then, Again, Now, and How).*

The editors have chosen to include a number of brief excerpts from *Outercourse* in this compilation in order to retain Daly's own narration of crucial moments in her life. In this excerpt, she details early experiences of what she would term, following Virginia Woolf, "moments of being" (see

chapter 27 of this collection). In particular, the experience of the clover blossom informed her thinking and her cast as a philosopher.
—Editors

As a student in a small, working-class catholic high school in Schenectady, New York, I was a voice crying in the wilderness when I declared that I wanted to study philosophy. Even the sensitive and generous Sister who was always encouraging me to write for publication had no way of empathizing with such an outrageous urge.[2] Moreover, the school library had no books on the subject. Yet this Lust of my adolescent mind was such that I spun my own philosophies at home. I have no idea where I picked up that Strange propensity.

As a result of help from my parents plus winning the Bishop Gibbons scholarship (awarded on the basis of a competitive exam in religion) plus saving money from my supermarket check-out job, I managed to go to a small nearby catholic college for women. Being an inhabitant of the catholic ghetto, I had never even heard of such schools as Vassar, Radcliffe, or Smith. Even if I had heard of them, they would not have been accessible—nor would they have appeared desirable. I wanted to study "*Catholic philosophy*," and the path of my Questing Journey led logically and realistically to The College of Saint Rose in Albany, New York.

Ironically, the college did not offer a major in philosophy, although a required minor consisting of eighteen credit hours in that subject was imposed upon all students. The difference in my case was that I loved the subject. This love persisted, despite the boringness of priest professors who opined that women could never learn philosophy, and whose lectures consisted of sitting in front of the class and reading aloud from the textbook, thereby demonstrating their ability to read English. They appeared to be thoroughly mystified by my interest, and the mystification was no doubt associated with the fact that they had never experienced enthusiasm for this pursuit in themselves. While they sat and droned, I sat and wondered at the incongruity of the situation. This wondering itself became incorporated into my own philosophical questioning. I did not yet understand that for a woman to strive to become a philosopher was to break a Terrible Taboo.[3]

Although those professors contributed little to the furtherance of my philosophical Quest, my own experiences contributed a great deal. There had been shimmering Moments in early childhood. For example, there was the Time, when I was about five or six, that I discovered the big gleaming block of ice in the snow. There were no words for the experience. The air was crisp and it was late afternoon. There was a certain winter light and a certain winter smell when I came upon the block of ice—probably in our back yard. I was all of a sudden in touch with something awesome—which I would later call Elemental. It was a shock that awakened in me some knowing of an Other dimension and I felt within me one of the first stirrings that I can remember of the Call of the Wild. I know that my capacity for meeting ice in the snow in that way has never totally gone away, because recently, while working on this book, I went for a walk on a winter evening and it happened again. This encounter was Strangely familiar.

The shimmering Moments occurred with great intensity in early adolescence. There was the Moment, for example, when one particular clover blossom Announced its be-ing to me. It Said starkly, clearly, with utmost simplicity: "I am." It gave me an intuition of be-ing. Years later, studying the philosophy of Jacques Maritain, I knew that I was not alone with this intuition.[4]

Yet, of course, I was unspeakably Alone with it. It was always calling me somewhere that no one else could tell me about. It would eventually lead me to cross the Atlantic, basically, without any money, to obtain doctorates in theology and philosophy in a strange, medieval university where courses were taught in Latin and where my "fellow students" were catholic priests and seminarians.

The encounter with that clover blossom had a great deal to do with my becoming a Radical Feminist Philosopher. If a clover blossom could say "I am," then why couldn't I?

33

# The Dream of Green

From chapter 2 of *Outercourse*, pp. 47–49.

*Patriarchy 1:* society manufactured and controlled by males: FATHERLAND; society in which every legitimated institution is entirely in the hands of males and a few selected henchwomen; society characterized by oppression, repression, depression, narcissism, cruelty, racism, classism, ageism, objectification, sadomasochism, necrophilia; joyless society, ruled by Godfather, Son and Company; society fixated on proliferation, propagation, procreation, and bent on the destruction of all Life *2:* the prevailing religion of the entire planet whose essential message is necrophilia.
—*Wickedary*, pp. 87–88

This brief excerpt from the autobiographical *Outercourse* is significant for two reasons. First is the powerful effect on Daly of her "Dream of Green"—a vibrant living green. She had this dream decades before any environmental movement or her own articulation of Elemental Reality. The excerpt is also significant given the structural blocks that stopped women from philosophizing and studying philosophy formally in the 1940s and 1950s. The explicit nature of these prohibitions, and the double-bind created when one of Daly's master's thesis readers said she didn't have a "philosophical *habitus*," set the context for readers who, in a contemporary world (of at least tokenistic inclusion), might not comprehend (or even find credible) the severity of the sexism that she faced.
—Editors

## Running for My Life: The Call of the Dream . . . The Dream of Green

After I graduated from college [ . . . ], [i]nstead of simply amassing courses and credits I accumulated degrees. This was difficult to do in view of the fact that I had absolutely no money and no connections. It was also the case that I knew I had absolutely no choice. It was evident to me that my survival—my very life—depended upon climbing my way "up" the academic ladder by the exercise of my brain. As a secretary or high school teacher in Schenectady I would have perished of alienation and despair.

I knew that it was imperative that I go away to graduate school, but this decision was not easy. Since my father had died, my mother had only me, and there was very little money. The parish priest told me that I should stay at home with my mother and work in Schenectady. I knew in my core that he was wrong. Although he made me feel confused and guilty by giving bad advice—*bad* in every sense of the word—I had no choice but to go. My mother's understanding and generous spirit were, as always, extraordinary.

My survival instinct was clear and certain. I had had some experience with jobs when still in high school, so I knew what the odds would be against someone Odd like me if I stayed in Schenectady. [ . . . ]

So, after obtaining the B.A. I determined to get a master's degree in philosophy. However, there were serious obstacles thrown in my way by the system, which I still did not understand as *patriarchy*. (How could I? The word was never used by anyone in 1950—nor was the word *sexism*.) The only respectable university available to me as an inhabitant of the spiritual, intellectual, and economic catholic ghetto was The Catholic University of America in Washington D.C., which offered me a full-tuition scholarship. The hitch was that one could have a scholarship for the M.A. only in the field in which she/he had majored as an undergraduate. I mention this tedious detail because it was one more thwarting of my Quest to study philosophy. Rather than not go to graduate school at all I took the scholarship and got my M.A. in English, taking philosophy courses on the side.

Here I was once again in a coeducational environment. I experienced a lifting of the weight that I had felt at Saint Rose, which I Now understand as the heaviness of the subliminal broken Promise, the shattered dream. I didn't have to notice that feeling of inexplicable nostalgia. Catholic University was exhilarating in its own way. I was beginning to get a real taste of the intellectual life.

The other students in the graduate program in English were good companions. There was a complex wittiness about them that I liked. Of course, "the boys" became aware of my Feminist views (which couldn't be identified precisely as "Feminist" in that era) and hated these ideas. When my closest friend there, Ann Walsh, announced that she was getting married I agreed to be her "maid of honor" but was secretly appalled.

During that first year at Catholic University I had an extraordinary dream one night. I had spent tedious hours that afternoon and evening engaged in the arduous task of translating passages from Middle English into modern English. When I finally went to bed that night my brains were fried. It had definitely not been an invigorating experience. However, I fell into a deep sleep and I dreamt of something that was of absolute importance to me. There are no words that can convey the content exactly. I have always remembered it as "The Dream of Green." I dreamt of Green—Elemental Green. When I woke up, the message was clear—clear as Be-Dazzling Green. It was: "Study philosophy!" It was saying: "This tedious stuff is not what you should be doing with your life. Do what you were born to do. Focus on philosophy!"

It is possible that The Dream of Green was triggered by something in the Middle English texts I was reading, some of which were mystical and Elemental. It could have been connected with the fourteenth-century poems *Gawain and the Green Knight* and *Pearl*. But what mattered was its absolutely thunderous message. Of course, the problem remained: How *could* I, with no money?

During my second year in that program I wrote my master's dissertation in the field of literary theory.[1] It was an analysis of the theory of John Crowe Ransom. I chose that area despite unwritten rules that no master's dissertation should be done in it. It was generally reserved for doctoral work. I argued and fought to do this, because it was as close to working in philosophy as I could get. Moreover, the professor who taught literary theory was James Craig La Drière. We didn't communicate well personally, but he was a great teacher. From him I began really to learn to think. I could not then realize that his excellence was in large measure contingent upon male privilege.[2] The fact was that in comparison to him the Sisters who had taught me in college were limited and limiting—competent and committed though they were. I could not yet understand that this was one more manifestation of the tragedy of the broken Promise. The comparison was unfair, but the fact was that this privileged male professor who was at best indifferent to me was my first outstanding exemplar of a teacher who was a sophisticated scholar and systematic thinker.

Professor La Drière was my M.A. dissertation director. One priest professor, a W. J. Rooney, who was a reader, was especially discouraging. He complained that my dissertation showed a lack of a "philosophical *habitus*." I wasn't quite sure what such a *habitus* was, but I was determined to find out. The priest's criticism was cruel, since what I really wanted to study was philosophy anyway, and his institution was preventing me from doing so. However, it stung me into an even fiercer determination to obtain a doctorate in philosophy and *to be* a philosopher.

I think it was at about this time that I decided to destroy all of my poetry. I judged it to be "flabby" and lacking the rigor of a "philosophical *habitus*." This was a somewhat dramatic act, but I really decided that if I were ever to write lyrically/poetically again, my work would be strong and absolutely precise. It would be philosophically poetic.

34

# The Anti-Modernist Oath

From chapter 3 of *Outercourse*, pp. 68–70.

*Academentia* (Diana Beguine): normal state of persons in academia, marked by varying and progressive degrees; irreversible deterioration of faculties of intellectuals.
—*Wickedary*, p. 184

Mary Daly famously earned two PhDs at the University of Fribourg—one in philosophy and one in theology (see *Outercourse*, pp. 55–57). The doctorate in catholic theology presented her with both opportunities and challenges. As she related in this excerpt from *Outercourse*, her dissertation defended the speculative nature of thought, forming a continuity with her later Radical Feminist work.

One of the funniest stories in all of *Outercourse* concerns the catholic church's Anti-Modernist Oath that Daly feared she would be required to take in order to receive the degree in theology. This story is best read aloud, to underline both the bloated ecclesiastical arrogance and the preposterous humor of the situation.
—Editors

## My Doctorate in Sacred Theology: An Astonishing Phenomenon

By the end of my fourth year in Fribourg (summer 1963) I had completed my dissertation for the Doctorate in Sacred Theology and had passed my final examinations for that degree, *summa cum laude*. The whole phenomenon of my attainment of that degree is, from my Present perspective, astonishing but comprehensible. As I have already said, it can be understood only within the context of my Quest during that time, which was still before the "Second Wave" of Feminism came crashing through.

One of the astonishing aspects of that achievement was my doctoral dissertation itself, on "The Problem of Speculative Theology." Looking at that document in the Present Time—having carefully hidden it from myself for years—I Now am amazed to See what was really going on.

It was with some trepidation that I took it off the shelf in the spring of 1988, blew off the dust, and began to analyze its contents as possibly representing some preliminary Moments of the Be-Dazzling Voyage. I noted with some slight chagrin that its author was "Mary *F.* Daly." Oh, well. I then began to read. What I found in this work was a Passionate defense of the life of the mind, and especially of knowledge for its own sake, carried to the ultimate degree.

My dissertation was a fierce and intricate argument against certain Augustinians who held that theology was primarily practical, and in support of the Thomistic position that it is primarily speculative wisdom—that is, knowledge for its own sake. This is one way of describing it on a foreground level. However, reading it Now, I can clearly see what I was trying to get at. In my analysis of Thomistic texts, I had found passages suggesting that theological knowledge has a "dynamism to go beyond itself," a "tendency to overreach itself," that is, to attain understanding that is beyond reason, but in an inherently rational way. I was arguing that theology overreaches blind faith in its seeking for understanding, that it "tends to a certain participation in the vision of God." To put it simply, I was fighting for intellectual autonomy.

Of course this was written in terms that I would not use Now, but the dissertation was an elegant argument for the possibility of rational knowledge that goes beyond appearances to the very core of reality. If I were to try to explain the intellectual process that I see going on in this dissertation, I would say that I was writing and thinking in a language that could not say what I was trying to say. I detect a kind of Metaknowledge running through my arguments. I think I was functioning in what might be called "a subliminal mode." That is, I was writing in code without realizing this. Much later on, when I was writing *Beyond God the Father*, *Gyn/Ecology*, *Pure Lust*, and the *Wickedary*, this experience of having been obliged to think subliminally was very useful. Having been sensitized to this multileveled nature of discourse, I was enabled to reverse the process and decode patriarchal theological and philosophical texts, thus exposing their hidden messages.

The obtaining of my Doctorate in Sacred Theology involved many amazing events. One of the most Stunning of these had to do with the university's requirement that all doctoral candidates in theology take the "Anti-Modernist Oath" after final examinations. This involved kneeling in front of the white-robed Dominican Dean of the Faculty of Theology and putting one's hands on the bible which he held in his lap.

Since Modernism involved many ideas with which I was fully in agreement, e.g., trusting one's individual inspiration without reliance on "authority," there was no way that I could perjure myself in this fashion.[1] However, if the candidate did not take this oath, the doctoral degree would not be conferred.

The reason that I hadn't foreseen this crisis was that for the earlier degrees (the baccalaureate and licentiate) the "Anti-Modernist Oath" was taken in a group. We all stood there while one student rattled off the thing in Latin. The student chosen for this role was invariably a Spanish seminarian, because the Spaniards could rattle off Latin faster than anyone. Since I hadn't been obliged to *say* anything, I hadn't felt that I was perjuring myself on these earlier occasions.

The doctoral situation was different. I would have to say the abominable thing alone, and I could not in conscience do that. I began to wonder if, after all these years of struggle, I would not get the doctorate after all. Then at the last minute, without having any idea of what they were doing, the esteemed members of the Faculty of Theology saved me. Since I was the first woman ever to earn this degree, they were faced with a unique situation. They decided that, although they could not bar me from the degree, they did not want a woman to be allowed to take the "Anti-Modernist Oath," because the implication of taking that oath was that she would be legitimated to teach in a Pontifical Faculty of Theology (for example, at The Catholic University of America). So they forbade me to take it. I almost exploded with relief and laughter in the face of the professor who pompously announced this solemn decision. As usual, I was very Lucky.

35

# My Doctoral Dissertation in Philosophy

## *Paradoxes*

From chapter 4 of *Outercourse*, pp. 74–80.

*Gynergy:* "the female energy which both comprehends and creates who we are; that impulse in ourselves that has never been possessed by the patriarchy nor by any male; women-identified be-ing"—Emily Culpepper.
—*Wickedary*, p. 77

This excerpt from *Outercourse* contains a major historical highlight: Daly's presence as an observer at the catholic church's Second Vatican Council. But it also speaks to her growing awareness of the situation of women and to the Sparking that women could offer each other.

The writing of *Outercourse* led Daly to reread her earlier works. In reconsidering her philosophic dissertation from Fribourg, Daly recapitulates her own philosophic method, as well as naming the roadblocks that patriarchy and the church erected against her. She describes in excellent detail Jacques Maritain's "intuition of being" as she weaves past the dichotomy of reason and intuition. Readers will also note that Daly's language, perfectly adept with philosophic categories, feminist analysis, and her own neologisms, also grows saltier in *Outercourse*!

> Sickened by the downgrading and caricaturing of intuition and the relegation of this pathetically reduced "talent" to women—which of course also implied the safeguarding of "reason" as the prerogative of males—I was struggling to Name this game which had been played by academics for centuries. It was indeed one of the masters' major mind-fucks of the millennia.

—Editors

I went back to work on my doctoral dissertation in philosophy, which was entitled *Natural Knowledge of God in the Philosophy of Jacques Maritain*. This would actually be completed in the spring of 1965, in time for me to take final examinations for the doctorate in July of that year.

The experience of taking this volume off the shelf during the process of writing *Outercourse* and encountering it for the first time in many years was comparable to my recent renewal of acquaintance with my theological dissertation. The philosophical work was also written by one "Mary F. Daly," an ardent Thomist scholar, who referred to herself, in the academic convention of the time, as "we." Having already familiarized mySelf with her style in my study of her earlier dissertation, I was ready to plunge into the subject matter.

It was not surprising to see that this work too is a passionate treatise on the intellectual life. Like the theological dissertation, it is extremely technical. Of course it deals with different subject matter, and writing it involved close reading of Maritain's copious works in French. Yet the theme of knowledge that has a dynamism to go beyond itself continues like a haunting refrain. The primary concern here is the "intuition of being," which to me was a subject of intense interest. I wrestled with Maritain wherever I thought he was in danger of slipping into a kind of "soft" intuitionism. Although I agreed with him that "it is this intuition that effects, causes the metaphysical habitus," I worried that his line of thinking could fall into an easy assumption that "this quasi-mystical intuition could play the role of substitute for the *work* of philosophy."

The point is that although I cherished this intuition, and could see no use in philosophizing without it, perhaps even in living without it, I wanted a clear defense of intellectual rigor/vigor. This insistence on having it *all*—intuition *and* arduous reasoning that is rooted in intuition—was of deep importance to me. I loved both modes of knowing, which I recognized as essential to each other. Sickened by the downgrading and caricaturing of intuition and the relegation of this pathetically reduced "talent" to women—which of course also implied the safeguarding of "reason" as the prerogative of males—I was struggling to Name this game which had been played by academics for centuries. It was indeed one of the masters' major mind-fucks of the millennia.

I now realize that my work on this dissertation, as well as my theological work, had an extremely important role in preparing me to write all of my books, although, of course, I had no idea at the time that these would come into be-ing. Through my work on this dissertation I strengthened my ability to go to the heart of a problem, to make connections logically, to trust my own intuitions while demonstrating their implications rigorously, and to articulate my arguments in a way that is inherently clear in itself—which is quite a different matter from being a good "debater" who argues only to score points but does not seek the truth. Later on, as a Radical Feminist Philosopher, I would draw upon these skills and the confidence that came with them. I would need them, especially because my own free creativity, knowledge that overreaches itself, needs to be Fiercely Focused.[1] To put all of this in a somewhat oversimplified way: I had to learn the rules extremely well in order to break them with precision.

So my training as a Thomist theologian and philosopher became my Labrys, enabling me to cut through man-made delusions to the core of problems and to Dis-close the deceptive deadly devices that are used by the academics, media men, and culture controllers of patriarchy—devices such as erasure and reversal. As the challenges have become greater, my work has become Wilder and I have continued to draw upon that training in precision. An essential aim of my task has been the development of a philosophy that sustains both the daring free play of intuition and the rigor of rational analysis.

It may seem paradoxical that I went to learn from the medieval masters and their disciples and later came to the point of Realizing the necessity for overthrowing the patriarchal masters of all kinds. However, I do not experience this as inconsistent with the direction of my own Be-Dazzling Journey. There has been an inherent consistency in this Quest, which has required continual breaking through blockages, tearing off mindbindings, reversing of reversals, Dis-covering what has been defaced and erased and buried—in other words, working as a Crafty Pirate.[2] And since I am a woman-identified philosopher in a patriarchal world it makes sense that it is turning out this way, which is the way of Outercourse.

Another paradox is the fact that those years of study, culminating in my writing of the philosophical dissertation, increased my understanding of and respect for intuitive powers, including those of so-called "simple" or "uneducated" women. I became better equipped to analyze how patriarchal "education" can blunt and stunt such power. The direction in which my study was pointing me was away from academic elitism and toward Realizing our common knowledge.

This paradoxical understanding was reinforced by my gradual realization that some of my professors were less admirable than the doctrines they taught. One example stands out. An esteemed professor of new testament, who specialized in the idea of "charity" (*agapē*) in the epistles of saint Paul, took it upon himself to try to destroy the possibility of my teaching in the junior year abroad programs, which would have meant economic disaster for me, as well as the end of hope that I would be able to continue my study, and ultimately the destruction of my reputation. This much admired priest went to the director of one of the junior year abroad programs and announced to her that I was an immoral person and should not be allowed to teach. Since I was not engaged in "immoral" behavior even by his standards, the incident was bizarre.

Luckily the director politely laughed the saintly scholar out of her office. When she told me about it later, I felt a peculiar horror at the lowdown nastiness of this priest. The experience helped to prepare me for variations of the same theme of priestly christian charity that would occur later. At that time, I saw this as the grotesque behavior of one individual, and even experienced some "guilt," wondering what I had done that was bad enough to elicit this underhanded punitive behavior. Later I would come to recognize it as one manifestation of ordinary, banal, institutionalized evil, specifically, misogynism. I would also question more closely the lofty ideology of christian virtue that could legitimate such woman-hating.

Yet the attitude of the Dominican professors was not unequivocally or universally one of misogynism. Some members of both the Faculty of Theology and the Faculty of Philosophy genuinely tried to be helpful. The director of my doctoral dissertation in philosophy—M.-D. Philippe, O.P.—was a genuine scholar and a person of integrity who respected my work. I have no reason to think that he would be pleased with my Feminist books, but I would expect a more complex reaction than the predictable arrogant hostility of many others. In any case, at that time, he was a good dissertation director and a brilliant teacher.

## The Summons to Write a Book

It was during that period of working on my dissertation in philosophy that The Momentous Thing began to happen. In December of 1963, *Commonweal* magazine published an article by Rosemary Lauer, a professor of philosophy at St. John's University in New York, entitled "Women and the Church," in which she argued for the equality of women in the catholic church. That article was magical in its effect. It awakened in me the power to speak out and to Name women's oppression. That is, it awakened my sleeping Powers of Be-Speaking.

In response to that article I wrote a letter to *Commonweal* announcing that I was ashamed of my own silence—ashamed that I had not published such an article myself. After proclaiming that there should be a deluge of such essays and of scholarly books which study the history of the problem of women and the church, I wrote:

> This much I know: the beginnings of these articles and these books (how badly we need these books especially!) are already in the minds and on the lips of many of us. And—this is both a prophecy and a promise—they will come.[3]

This was before the cresting of the "Second Wave" of Feminism, and I was referring to future books by myself and other women. These words came out of my typewriter before I was even confident that I could write such a book. I did not even know that I knew such a thing until the words were right there before me.

Without realizing consciously what was happening I had leaped into the whirling movement of Moments of *Be-Speaking*, that is

> *1:* Auguring, foretelling, Speaking of what will be *2:* bringing about a psychic and/or material change by means of words (*Wickedary*).

The Momentum of that Original Moment of Be-Speaking propelled me into the writing of my first Feminist articles. One of these was published by the Swiss Feminist Gertrud Heinzelmann in her anthology, *Wir schweigen nicht länger!—We Won't Keep Silence Any Longer!*, a collection of statements by women to the "Fathers" of the Second Vatican Council.[4]

Another was "A Built-in Bias," published in *Commonweal*, in January 1965.[5] The publication of this article had Momentous consequences.

In the spring of 1965, while I was hard at work on my dissertation and teaching yet another batch of American junior year abroad students, my *Commonweal* article was having its effects—all unknown to me. A publishing consultant who worked for a London publisher (Geoffrey Chapman, Ltd.) had read the article and was trying to find me. As I wrote in the "Autobiographical Preface to the 1975 Edition" of *The Church and the Second Sex*:

> Some weeks later a letter from a British publisher in London found its way to me in Fribourg, after visiting several wrong addresses. It contained an invitation to write a book on women and the church, developing the ideas in the *Commonweal* article. . . . The letter was like a summons, and I knew clearly that the time was right for the First Coming of *The Church and the Second Sex*.[6]

Looking back at this Moment, I am struck once again by the fact that it was an Act of Be-Speaking by another woman that had triggered the chain of events that made it possible for me to actualize my own Be-Speaking Powers. The Gynergy that was released by her Courageous Act opened my (Third) Eye/I. It ripped off the blindfold that had covered my eyes and the gag that had kept my mouth shut, enabling me to See and to Name "the mystery of man."

It is in the nature of Moments that one Moment leads to another. This is because it has consequences in the world and thus Moves a woman to take further Leaps. My Act of "writing out loud" my own thoughts had real consequences. Thus the "summons" to write a book that came from the British publisher was like a Call from the cosmos itself—an unrelenting Call. The letter finally found me, after being blown through all those wrong addresses by the Great Wild Wind that had carried me this far. The phenomenon was both very Strange and very familiar. So when the letter did reach me, I understood what I had to do. Of course the Calling had been reciprocal. By writing "A Built-in Bias" I had summoned this summons. On a deeper level still, the Call of the Clover Blossom that had lured me to Fribourg was behind it all, beckoning me on to further Be-Speaking.

There followed an accelerated Spiral of Moments. In May 1965 the contract for *The Church and the Second Sex* was signed [ . . . ]. I was slightly distracted from this project by the fact that I had to complete and defend my doctoral dissertation in philosophy—a task which I did accomplish in July of that year, while wrapping up yet another semester of teaching. There remained only the problem of publication of the dissertation, which was required by the university.[7]

The completion and defense of my doctoral dissertation was the grand culmination of my Quest through the mazes of academia. I don't mean that by my acquiring of that degree I magically became a philosopher, as if that could be accomplished by conferral of a degree. Rather, it was a kind of rite of passage. Moreover, for me—although I could not yet articulate this—it established a Right of Passage on my Piratic enterprise of Plundering treasures stolen by phallocratic thieves and Smuggling them back to women within academia itself. That is, it was a patriarchal professional legitimation for my Absolutely Anti-patriarchal, Unprofessional career of seeking and Dis-covering lost/stolen knowledge and of Re-membering my own Lost Senses and Lost Senses of words. In Other words, it was a Momentous Moment on my Voyage of becoming a Radical Feminist Philosopher.

## Rome 1965: Investigating the Second Vatican Council

In the fall of 1965 I took a train to Rome in order to conduct my own personal investigation of The Second Vatican Council. I checked into a relatively bug-free *pensione* and began my wanderings of the streets of Vatican City. No one had invited me, of course. I had no official role. However, I felt quite at home among hundreds of other deviants who were there to lobby for their various causes. I bonded with other catholic Feminists and hob-nobbed with theologians and students as well as journalists. A couple of the latter were willing to loan me their identification cards so that I could sneak into saint Peter's when the council was in session and view the fantastic scene.

My visit to Rome was packed with intense, multicolored, multileveled experiences. I saw and heard the pompous cardinals, who seemed like silly old men in red dresses, droning their eternal platitudes. I engaged in intense conversations with catholic thinkers and advocates of social change. We shared an exhilarating sense of hope, an impassioned belief in the possibility of change.

Among my serendipitous encounters was one special meeting with the gentle Irish journalist, Gary MacEoin. Sitting in one of Rome's friendly restaurants, Gary very simply described to me the secret art of how to write a book. It was true that I had written doctoral dissertations, but I was mystified by the problem of how to go about beginning to write a *Book*. The project seemed massive and unmanageable. When this friendly journalist showed me how he set up the structures of his books, the mystery was cracked in one easy lesson.[8] I was ready to begin writing *The Church and the Second Sex.*

I was somewhat impoverished by the expenses of a month's living in Rome (even in my budget *pensione*) but vastly enriched in every other way. I now had countless memories of exciting encounters and conversations—of exchanges of energies that had electrified every day. My imagination also had been Sparked by a Stunning array of visual experiences. There had been the Moment, for example, when just outside saint Peter's I suddenly found myself within a few feet of a pathologically weighty cardinal in his flaming red attire literally being lifted out of his limousine by two sturdy members of the Swiss Guard who apparently had been assigned to get him to the council on time. His eminence saw me gaping and gave me a look of pure hate. I would never forget those dark beady eyes and that look of utter misogyny. Indeed, one could say that this was, in a certain way, a Moment of Inspiration.[9]

So I returned to Fribourg with clear, sure determination that I would and could and had to write this book. It was already in process, since my unconscious Self had been working away on it, Spinning and Weaving connections at every Moment.

36

# The Time of the Tigers

From chapter 7 of *Outercourse*, pp. 136–39.

*Tiger 1:* Ferocious, Fighting Feline *2:* a Fierce, Catty Woman. *Example:* A tribe of Ferocious women, known among themselves as "The Tigers," began growling together in Boston in the early 1970s and has continued to stir up Trouble throughout the world.
—*Wickedary*, p. 173

The Harvard Memorial Church Exodus remains a luminous moment in Daly's own activism. The full text of the "sermon" she gave on that occasion (November 1971) constitutes chapter 5 in this book. The inclusion of this narrative retelling of the event provides historical context. But, more than that, it illustrates Daly's prizing of women's voices, and, especially, of female friendship. The lifelong affection between Daly and the women most involved in the Exodus walkout formed the basis for her articulation of Be-Friending and Sparking. She had done her intellectual work in isolation, in institutions in which she was the only woman; the communal scholarship and cerebral play that characterized this scholarly feminist "cell" was new and exhilarating to all concerned.
—Editors

## Whirlwinds: Teaching, Speaking, Growling

The academic year 1971–1972 was the beginning of the Time of the Tigers. I taught my first Feminist classes that year. During the first semester I taught "The Women's Revolution and Theological Development" (as well as other courses, of course). This was followed in the second semester by "Women's Liberation and the Church." These were the first two Women's Studies courses offered within the consortium of theological schools known as the Boston Theological Institute (BTI). My students included Jan Raymond, who was then beginning her doctoral studies in the joint doctoral program of Boston College and Andover Newton Theological School. Also Present were three Wild Women from Harvard Divinity School—Linda Barufaldi, Emily Culpepper, and Jean MacRae. These four women, together with myself, constituted a very loosely organized but closely bonded group known among ourselves as "the Tigers."

The chief activities of the Tigers among ourselves were Spinning ideas, organizing subversive events, and, in general, having a good time. Several of us also growled frequently, particularly as a form of salutation and greeting, in person and on the telephone.

## The Harvard Memorial Exodus: A Metamorphic Moment

The fall of 1971 provided opportunities for Fiercely Focused action. One such action stands out especially as an historic Moment. It became known as the Harvard Memorial Church Exodus. This event began to brew sometime in October when I was invited to be the first woman to preach at a Sunday service in Memorial Church's three-hundred-and-thirty-six-year history. The invitation posed a dilemma. To simply accept would be to agree to being used as a token. To refuse would seem like forfeiting an opportunity. I tried to think of a creative solution.

The solution came when a group of women met at Harvard Divinity School (in Linda Barufaldi's room, to be precise) to discuss the problem. With the encouragement of these Cohorts I decided that I would accept the invitation and turn the sermon into an action. Together we planned the event, which was to be a call for a walk-out from patriarchal religion.[1] The resulting "Exodus" (on November 14) turned out to be an historic Moment of Breakthrough and Re-Calling.

In order to give the sermon, I was obliged to sit up in the sanctuary during the first part of the service. It was evident that the ministers and choir had got wind of the fact that "something" was going to happen. The pastor had delegated his assistant to conduct the service, seating himself discreetly among the congregation, and thus sparing himself some embarrassment. Some of the members of the choir were suppressing giggles of nervous excitement. Obviously "non-sexist" hymns had been judiciously selected for the occasion.

Scriptural passages were read by two women (Cohorts). Liz Rice read from the old testament (1 samuel 15:23): "For rebellion is as the sin of witchcraft." Emily Culpepper, wearing her bright red "Witch Shoes," read from the "new" testament, specifically from pauline epistles. I Re-Call the look of absolute satisfaction and glee on Emily's face as she intoned from 1 timothy 2:11: "Let the women learn in silence with all subjection," and so on, and on.

The way was thus prepared for the sermon. When the moment came I solemnly mounted the steps up into the gigantic, phallus-like pulpit. My address began: "Sisters and other esteemed members of the congregation: There are many ways of refusing to see a problem." I discussed the need for the Courage to See and to Act, affirming that "externalized action, or *praxis*, authenticates insight and creates situations out of which new knowledge can grow."

As the sermon moved toward its dramatic ending I fervently hoped that I would not have to go through the humiliation of being almost alone, accompanied by six or seven staunch comrades, stalking out of the church. But whatever the consequences, I would have to go through with it. So I went on:

> We cannot really belong to institutional religion as it exists. . . .
>
> The women's movement is an exodus community. Its basis is not merely in the promise given to our fathers thousands of years ago. Rather its source is in the unfulfilled promise of our mothers' lives, whose history was never recorded. Its source is in the promise of our sisters whose voices have been robbed from them, and in our own promise, our latent creativity. We can affirm *now* our promise and our exodus as we walk into a future that will be our *own* future.
>
> Sisters—and brothers if there are any here:
>
> Our time has come. We will take our own place in the sun. We will leave behind the centuries of silence and darkness. Let us affirm our faith in ourselves and our will to transcendence by rising and walking out together.[2]

I need not have feared the embarrassment of walking out almost alone. Hundreds of women and some men began stampeding out of the church the Moment I finished. Far from being "the leader" of a "flock" as some journalists chose to perceive it, I was caught in the middle of a stampede. By the time I managed to run down out of the enormous pulpit half of "the flock" were rushing ahead of me. So I just joined the crowd.

Some of the brightest and funniest Moments happened afterward on the steps outside the church. We roared as we heard the concluding hymn being sung by those who had chosen to remain inside for the rest of the service. It was a hymn to "the Holy Spirit"—chosen for the occasion, no doubt, because of its "inclusive" language—and it was being sung entirely, or almost entirely, by male voices. The deep voices dutifully droning the hymn on the inside contrasted sharply with the cackling and cheering of the predominantly female crowd outside. In the midst of this joyous chaos, members of the press pressed us with questions. They had been notified of the event by Feminist activist and publicist Mary Lou Shields, who also fielded their questions. Soon after that we rushed off for a self-congratulatory brunch.

The Exodus sermon was a qualitatively different Act of Be-Speaking for those of The First Spiral Galaxy. It was not Be-Speaking from within a patriarchal institution, nor was it an attempt to reform/change such an institution. It involved a Seeing of connections and a Radical Departure. Thus it was also a summons to Acts of Be-Falling.

As an event, the Exodus was a manifestation of the *Courage to Leave,* which is:

> Virtue enabling women to depart from all patriarchal religions and other hopeless institutions; resolution springing from deep knowledge of the nucleus of nothingness which is at the core of these institutions (*Wickedary*).

For some of us who walked out that day, our Act was indeed a departure from all patriarchal religions. As Linda Barufaldi wrote:

> It [the Exodus] involved admitting into my consciousness the painful fact that the Judeo-Christian tradition . . . its culture, its doctrine, and its community, is male-oriented and male-dominated. It is not mine.[3]

Not everyone who walked out experienced the Exodus in this depth or made the same commitment. Some returned to Harvard Memorial

Church or to some other church on following Sundays, presumably in the hope of changing the institution "from the inside." Certainly not everyone who heard or read about the walk-out understood it in such depth. Many perceived it as simply a "symbolic" act. Among those who reduced it in this way were some who wanted to tokenize and co-opt it. At least one minister wrote to me and asked if I would come and preach in his church and "do the same thing." Obviously he saw it as a mere repeatable performance. I responded with outrage: "No, of course not; I really *meant* it when I said I was walking out." This was incomprehensible to him.

37

# Re-Calling My Lesbian Identity

From chapter 7 of *Outercourse*, pp. 143–45.

*Lesbian:* a Woman-Loving woman; a woman who has broken the Terrible Taboo against Women-Touching women on *all* levels; Woman-identified woman: one who has rejected false loyalties to men in every sphere.
—*Wickedary*, p. 78

Daly's lesbian coming-out involved both physical and intellectual dimensions. This brief explanation from *Outercourse* connects the naturalness of lesbianism to Elemental philosophy. The desire to understand lesbianism as political, spiritual, philosophic, and physical simultaneously remains significant for lesbian-feminists; Daly's description of her own choices and intuitions makes her life paradigmatic.
—Editors

## Volcanic Taboo-Breaking: Re-Calling My Lesbian Identity

If 1971 was a Sparking year, 1972 was Volcanic. *Notes from the Third Year* contained an interview by Anne Koedt, entitled "Loving Another Woman."[1] It was a transcription of a taped interview with a woman who talked about her love relationship with another woman. Just as Rosemary Lauer's article of 1963 had Be-Spoken me into Naming and Realizing my Prophecy and Promise as a Feminist writer, awakening my Powers of Be-Speaking, this interview Be-Spoke me into Moments of Breakthrough and Re-Calling my Lesbian identity. Reading it in 1972 Be-Spoke me into Be-Falling.

In this interview the (anonymous) speaker said:

> I guess it was also a surprise to find that you weren't struck down by God in a final shaft of lightning. That once you fight through that ini-

tial wall of undefined fears built to protect those taboos, they wither rapidly, and leave you to operate freely in a new self-defined circle of what's natural. You have a new sense of boldness, of daring, about yourself.[2]

And, as the same woman emphasized:

. . . it very quickly became natural—natural is really the word I'd use for it. It was like adding another dimension to what we'd already been feeling for each other. It is quite a combination to fall in love with your friend.[3]

My friend and I read this piece together and soon sprang into action. From that Moment nothing was ever the same again. That relation ended after a few years but the transformation was permanent. I Re-Call looking out my office window at trees whose branches met and having an overwhelmingly powerful intuition that expressed itself in the words "The trees came together." I would Now call that experience "an intuition of Elemental integrity."

Enormous forces were unleashed by this Dis-covering of an Other dimension of my identity. I had already glimpsed the Promise of women together and I had written and acted boldly. Now I could live and create more boldly—even while Moving through various kinds and degrees of turmoil.

Why hadn't this possibility been obvious before? Clearly there had been a Taboo against it. When I had broken the Taboo sexually and Re-alized how very Natural/Elemental this was, I began to understand more and more explicitly the vast dimensions of what I would later Name the *Terrible Taboo*, which is also a *Total Taboo* against exercising Touching Powers.[4]

These words were Dis-covered much later, of course. But in the early seventies I knew clearly that the physical and spiritual dimensions of the Taboo were closely intertwined. The Totality of my Breaking the Taboo opened the way for Re-Calling Original Integrity—and for Spelling Out this knowledge in words and actions that would reach other women. This process would be Realized much more fully in the Third Spiral Galaxy.

Breaking the *Terrible Taboo/Total Taboo* is not a simple affair, so to speak. I did not think then, nor do I believe Now, that the fact that a woman relates sexually with another woman necessarily means that she has broken the Taboo in the most profound way. In my view, then and Now, there are many dimensions of woman-identification.

38

# Some Be-Musing Moments

From chapter 8 of *Outercourse*, pp. 152–58.

*Labrys 1:* "The double ax, 'the sign of Imperial might' . . . the symbol of gynocratic power in Crete as it was among the Lycians, the Lydians, the Amazons, the Etruscans, and even the Romans. . . . found in the graves of Paleolithic women of Europe, buried 50,000 years ago"—Elizabeth Gould Davis *2:* the A-mazing Female Mind that cuts through the double binds and doublebinding words of patriarchy; the double ax of Wild wisdom and wit that breaks through the mazes of man-made mystification, cutting the mindbindings of master-minded doublethink; Power of Discernment which divines the difference between Reality and unreality, between the Natural Wild and elementary fabrications *3:* any double-edged word or phrase that exposes the evil of phallocracy, Dis-covering its corruption and evoking the Presence of the Background.
—*Wickedary*, p. 142

During the writing of *Beyond God the Father,* Daly and her feminist community (friends, allies, and students) experienced a shared awakening. As they sensed the scope, depth, and malice of patriarchy, and its symbiotic intertwining with religious ideologies, it dawned on them that they would have to leave the church permanently. No matter how caustic history thinks Daly became toward christianity, the decision to leave was not simple: one of the Tigers recalls taking to her bed for three days over the agony of grief caused by the decision. This excerpt contains more examples of the friendships that flourished in this time of radical transformation, while documenting the sense of exhilaration admixed with trepidation that wells up during times of revolutionary change.
—Editors

## Some Be-Musing Moments

There were many Be-Musing Moments when the Tigers were together in my Cove.[1] One beautiful evening in late summer or early fall of 1972 was especially Momentous. We were all sitting in my living room (which really was a Living Room, the workshop where I was writing *Beyond God the Father*), and we were engaged in an intense discussion. It is possible that we were discussing the point which I Originally and frequently summarized in the one-liner: "If God is male, the male is God."

At any rate, Linda has reminded me that for her that evening was a Moment of Realizing that she couldn't be a christian any more. It is possible that no one made that statement out loud, but it was absolutely clear to all of us. This does not mean that this was the first Time that it had been clear. But our various Moments of Realizing now came together with explosive force. All of our eyes/Eyes met—ten Eyes. We sat in complete silence for some Time as the sun set and the room grew dark. It was a Moment of "Interface of all the Realms."[2]

With my Fourth Galactic telescope I see such Moments as immeasurable communal Movements of breaking through the Mists of the Subliminal Sea. This does not mean that all the individuals there were moving with the same speed or with equal force, but we were synchronously crossing Limen after Limen in our individual ways. We all were responding to the Call of the Wild, actively Unforgetting our participation in Be-ing. Separately and together we were on the Boundaries of many worlds.

## Turning My Soul Around

[ . . . ] Frequently I went there [Onset, Massachusetts] alone for a swim and a couple of hours on the beach. Occasionally I went with all the Tigers. Sometimes I went with Emily and Linda, and sometimes with Jan. I also visited there with a number of other good friends. In fact, I seemed to be continually introducing my friends to the wonders of Onset.

In the early 1970s the water was sufficiently unpolluted so that swimming was generally in the picture, together with picnics on the sand. Once when all the Tigers were there we trooped into the "Ladies Room" of the Onset Hotel [ . . . ] in order to change into our bathing suits. As we marched out, wearing our clothes over our suits, we were forced to go past a group of drinking bums at the bar. (These were of the variety that I would later call "snools.") One of these deadfellows slurred something like: "Have a good time in the bathroom, girls?" There was a long second of dead silence. Then Emily drawled (her Southern accent was still very pronounced, so to speak, in those days): "Why don't *you* go to the bathroom and get ahold of yourself?" There was another second of shocked silence. Then, in spite of themselves, the snool's buddies exploded in raucous laughter *at him*, and implicitly at themselves. We kept right on stalking haughtily passed them and out the door.

This kind of gleeful triumph was typical of the Time. We were in the process of learning tactics for dealing with such assaults. It is significant that the Timing was perfect and our Victory complete. This became a Memorable Moment of Tiger lore—not at all incompatible with the mystical Background Moments associated with Onset and elsewhere. One Moment flowed into the Other. The Labrys-like combination of Exorcism and Ecstasy, a major theme of The Third Spiral Galaxy, was already coming into be-ing.

[ . . . ] It is obvious that this philosophy of be-ing has not been created in isolation, but rather in a context of participation. My Quest has converged with the Quests of myriads of Sister scholars across Time. My colleagues/collaborators included/include Matilda Joslyn Gage, Jane Ellen Harrison, Mary Wollstonecraft, Simone de Beauvoir, Pauli Murray, Elizabeth Gould Davis. My Cronies while I was creating *Beyond God the Father* included not only these and countless Other Foresister Pirates of the Past, but also contemporary Cohorts such as Nelle Morton, Betty Farians,[3] Robin Morgan, and the Tigers. These Companions all cooperated in our mutual task of Dis-covering the Context.

The bonding of Sisterhood in the early seventies and conversations that ensued led to a consensus, with Nelle Morton especially, that Be-ing is a Verb.[4] To stress that Ultimate Reality is a Verb, and an intransitive Verb, I began to hyphenate it: *Be-ing*.[5]

39

# The Fathers' Follies

## *Denial of Full Professorship*

From chapter 11 of *Outercourse*, pp. 205–8.

*Her-etical:* Weird Beyond Belief.
—*Wickedary*, p. 139

This section describes Boston College's denial of Daly's promotion to full professor. While Daly was hardly alone in being punished for feminist thought, her groundbreaking work and high visibility made her case particularly noteworthy. Even as Boston College was denying her promotion, she was invited to Cardinal König's prestigious Second International Symposium on Belief.
—Editors

In the winter and spring of 1975 I continued to be buffeted by swirling energies.[1] It would be an extraordinary understatement to say that there was much excitement in the air. On the exhilarating side, there was my expectation that my Time Bomb, the New edition of *The Church and the Second Sex*, was about to be released into the atmosphere. On the draining side, there was my anticipation of Boston College's decision regarding my application for promotion to the rank of full professor.[2]

By any and all standards of academia/academentia this was a highly appropriate time to have applied for the full professorship. My qualifications were impeccable.[3] The university's decision, unbelievably, was negative. My students and many other supporters demanded an explanation, so the department chair "explained" to interviewers from *The Heights,* the Boston College student newspaper: "She has made no significant contribution to the field. In terms of achievement, Mary's case seemed to rest on *that book* [*Beyond God the Father*] and it is not a distinguished academic achievement."[4]

Significantly, Jan Raymond was denied even an interview for a faculty position in ethics at BC. Questioned by interviewers from *The Heights* as to whether Raymond's association with Daly was the actual reason for the denial of an interview, the department chair is reported to have said: "Yes, in the sense that she approaches most subjects from a basically feminist perspective." According to the same *Heights* article, "Fr. [Robert] Daly went on to say that the department would be out of balance if two people were approaching things from a feminist anti-Christian perspective."[5] (The theology faculty consisted of more than thirty members at that point.)

On February 14, 1975, a meeting was held between fr. Thomas O'Malley, then Dean of the College of Arts and Sciences, the university attorney, my attorney, and myself. The university attorney, Philip Burling, admitted that the student reports were "favorable," that the outside experts' reports were "favorable," and that the only negative report came from within the theology department.[6] I was told to go to the department to hear their reasons.

Hence there was a subsequent meeting (February 24, 1975) between a senior theology professor (fr. Richard McBrien), Burling, my attorney, and myself. Fr. McBrien stated that the department found my publications, particularly *Beyond God the Father*, to be deficient in scholarship. Also they considered them "popular theology, unworthy of consideration for promotion." My publications were compared by fr. McBrien to those of fr. Andrew Greeley, who was denied promotion at the University of Chicago because of his popularizing works. Burling then compared my case to that of Erich Segal, whose novel *Love Story* was not considered a scholarly writing entitling him to promotion in the classics department at Yale. I terminated the meeting in disgust at this point.[7]

## "Sisters, We Meet on Bloody Jesuit Ground"

A group of women students from Boston College and Feminists from various other universities organized to protest the absurd denial of my promotion. We created a Sparkling event which was a kind of Metaresponse, not only to my situation, but to the conditions of oppression of all Feminists in "higher education." This event was a "Forum on Women in Higher Education," held in Roberts Center, a gymnasium at Boston College, on February 27, 1975. Approximately eight hundred women packed the gym.

The program began with a self-defense demonstration, which was followed by a dramatic presentation in which "Quotes from the Foremothers"[8] were read Fiercely by a number of students. Dressed as Foremothers, Linda Barufaldi (Gertrude Stein), Emily Culpepper (Elizabeth Oakes Smith), and Carol Adams (Susan B. Anthony) sat and Gossiped together on stage while the audience eavesdropped.

Robin Morgan, moderator of the Forum, greeted the audience with the battle cry: "Sisters, we meet on bloody jesuit ground!"[9] After reading a poem she had written for the occasion, which was dedicated to women fighting for freedom in academe, she introduced Linda Franklin, a Boston College student, who read an article from *The Heights* outlining the history of my case.[10] Besides myself, speakers included Christiane Joust (Tufts University), Lila Karp (SUNY at New Paltz), Marcia Lieberman (University of Connecticut), Nelle Morton (Drew University), Denise Connors (Boston College), Jan Raymond (Boston College), and Adrienne Rich.[11]

The speeches constituted massive, impressive testimony to the fact that Feminists were being purged from academia.[12] Yet the atmosphere was not grim. The otherwise boring milieu of the gym was transformed by forty or so huge portraits of Foremothers. These were the creations of Boston College student Pat McMahon, who painted these splendid representations on bedsheets. It was also transformed by the event that was transpiring, so that it became a Time/Space of whirling, zinging Gynergy.[13]

The revelations of this Forum, combined with Boston College's disparagement and attempted erasure of *Beyond God the Father* as well as *all* of my work—and indeed of my very be-ing—fomented enormous explosions in my psyche. They unleashed my powers and hurled me further on my Intergalactic Voyage.

I was thrown into greater and greater freedom. Since *Beyond God the Father* had been super-scholarly and yet had been called "unscholarly" by the cynical and deceptive fathers of reversal, I was now liberated into the possibility of qualitatively Other Daring Deeds. It was not the case that I would become *less* scholarly. Indeed, I was now free to become even more so—and to leap creatively further into the Background.

Moreover, the True Horror Stories of Radical Feminists driven out of academia that year kindled my Righteous Rage, which was/is Creative Rage. I knew then, fully, that my scholarship and originality would never be adequately rewarded within the "system," and that my Rewards would be utterly Other, chiefly in the work itself and in what this communicated to other women.

40

# Classroom Teaching of Women and of Men

From chapter 15 of *Outercourse*, pp. 327–29.

*Separatism, Radical Feminist:* theory and actions of Radical Feminists who choose separation from the Dissociated State of patriarchy in order to release the flow of elemental energy and Gynophilic communication; radical withdrawal of energy from warring patriarchy and transferral of this energy to women's Selves.
—*Wickedary*, p. 96

This excerpt contains an explanation of Daly's rationale for teaching classes to women only, as well as her accommodation for those male students who wished to learn the material. This highly controversial practice eventually led to Daly's retirement, and generates discussion even today. But at the time she instituted this practice, the politics of strategies like this were widely understood, across many political movements, allowing members of oppressed groups to have a space of their own, and dismantling the overweening sense of privilege that dominant groups unconsciously enact, such as demanding access to all spaces.

Finally, it should be noted that despite her fame, Daly never advanced to become a full professor at Boston College, and suffered financially from that institution's disregard/disdain of her work. So the motto that ends this excerpt was no mere rhetoric: it represented Daly's reality:

> Since Ecstasy is its own reward, we can ask for nothing more.

—Editors

By the use of [my] Labrys [ . . . ] I was enabled to provide the needed philosophical rationale for Women's Studies as a locus for Women's Space in patriarchal universities. I wrote in *Pure Lust*:

> The history of women's struggles to provide and maintain diverse forms of "Women's Space" has been a vivid testimony to the fact that men recognize this to be a crucial issue in the war to control women's minds. . . . Particularly instructive has been the virulent and often vicious undermining by university administrators of the efforts of Feminists to reserve some Women's Studies classes for women only. Such classes can provide the occasion for true encounters with Metamemory, for perceiving and reasoning beyond the schemata of "adult"; i.e., male-authored, memories. They can provide contexts for Re-membering beyond civilization, for Metapatterning. Therefore, they must be undermined. The radical potential of freely thinking women is a threat to the very meaning of a patriarchal university.[1]

This analysis was inspired, in large measure, by my own experience of teaching Women's Studies courses in a *very* patriarchal university. It was also inspired, and reinforced, by conversations with professors of Women's Studies in many colleges and universities in the 1970s and 1980s. My experience has been that the presence of male students together with women in such classes slows down and in fact blunts the learning process for the women. This is of course in part an effect of learned responses to the presence of males—even of one male—in the class. Eventually I discussed this with the students and began holding separate sessions for women and men. Everyone has the same reading list and course requirements. Since there have been far fewer men than women in these classes, the former have received more attention. The result, of course, has been extra work for me. However, I enjoy teaching young men as well as women students, and course evaluations have indicated general appreciation of this intellectually challenging experience.[2]

My Third Galactic resolution of the third counterpoint has had a double-edged effect. First, I succeeded in creating a Space on the Boundary of a phallocentric institution where women, and not only men, could express their ideas boldly and creatively, without interference and without blockage from mechanisms of Self-censorship. In addition, by Spinning ideas whose Sources are my own books, I overcame the old academented dichotomy between theory and practice in a special way. Following Crone-logically upon my resolution of the second counterpoint, this New Leap of the third contrapuntal movement involved Acting upon the premises and conclusions of my own philosophy, exercising my philosophical *habitus*, freely exploring and Naming Reality.[3] I have Dis-covered Elemental Feminist Philosophy in the Presence of my students, Spinning further with them. By the use of this pedagogic method I have totally broken the Total Taboo against exercising the Spiritual Touching Powers of women—overcoming *apraxia* (together with *aphasia* and *amnesia*) on the Boundary of androcratic academia. This has been Dreadful Daring Action. [ . . . ]

For this Time-traveling feat [ . . . ] we receive no honors, no degrees, no legitimations. We are, however, flooded with Congratulations. Looking around, we See massive crowds of Inter-galactic Seals of Approval waving their flippers and barking in contagious Ecstasy. Since Ecstasy is its own reward, we can ask for nothing more.

# 41

## On How I Jumped over the Moon

From chapter 16 of *Outercourse*, pp. 337–41.

*Pure Lust:* The high humor, hope, and cosmic accord/harmony of those women who choose to escape, to follow our hearts' deepest desire and bound out of the state of bondage, Wanderlusting and Wonderlusting with the Elements, connecting with auras of animals and plants, moving in planetary communion with the farthest stars; pure Passion unadulterated, absolute, simple, sheer striving for abundance of be-ing; unlimited, unlimiting desire/fire.
—*Wickedary*, p. 89

This excerpt concerns the emergence of *Outercourse* itself. Daly's goal was, as always, integrity—in this case, combining the development of her philosophy with the autobiographical direction of the work, so that "the philosophic theory and the biographical events recorded here are parts of the same Quest. . . . The Weaving is not a contrived afterthought."

Daly then launched on a quick tour of the atrocities and bore-dom of the foreground in the 1990s, contrasted with her conversations with the likes of Sojourner Truth, Matilda Joslyn Gage, and her own late friend, Andrée Collard, in the Background. The rapid string of words, names, associations, and ideas in her style here, anticipated in the excerpt from *Pure Lust* that forms chapter 31 of this collection, took center stage in her writing now. But the meditation at the end shows that Daly is no longer in the midst of an active women's liberation movement, nor surrounded by feminist students and colleagues. Her despair over the conditions in the foreground illustrates that despite the ecstasy of much of her writing, she experienced visceral pain from the necrophilia of the foreground.
—Editors

The Moments of The Fourth Spiral Galaxy began when I began working on *Outercourse.* This was during the spring of 1987, after I had handed in the manuscript of the *Wickedary* to the publisher. I do not Re-Member the Moments precisely in sequence. I do Re-Call that I was puzzled about the nature of the book that was evolving. I knew that I wanted to write a philosophical work. I also gradually came to know that I wanted to write Recollections from my *Logbook of a Radical Feminist Philosopher.*

A friend from Ireland—Ann Louise Gilligan—suggested something like the latter. We were having lunch in an outdoor café in Newton Centre one day in the summer of 1987. After expressing her appreciation of *Pure Lust* Ann Louise tactfully, in her inimitable fashion, remarked that women would like to know where *Pure Lust* and my other books came from. Essentially, the questions she posed were: "How did it happen? How did you do it?" She posed these queries not so much with the expectation of an immediate response but—as I understood her—as a suggestion for a book that was wanted and needed.

This was not the first or only Time the suggestion had been planted. Various women had asked such questions, and with greater and greater frequency. But in the conversation with Ann Louise the questions of all these women came together for me. They assumed a shape, which was like a summons—or an invitation—to write the story, the autobiography, which would speak to those questions.

While I Sensed more and more that I would like to try this, there was the seemingly conflicting Call, also coming from within my psyche, to move ahead with my own philosophy. It seemed that there were two books crying to be written at the same Time.

Reflecting upon this Now, I see that I was faced with a familiar situation, that is, a dilemma. It was not easy to find the Transcendent Third Option.

In conversations with my friends and in debates with mySelf I wondered which book I should write first. The more I thought about this problem, the more deeply troubled I felt, since there was a double imperative. Then it occurred to me that there would not only have to be two books, but that these would somehow have to be one. But the question was: How to Realize this unity? There was in my mind a growing awareness of an organic unity between the two proposed works, because

I did see that the *Logbook of a Radical Feminist Philosopher* should be the primary Source for my expanded philosophizing.

At first, I thought of how I might contain these two books, or works, in one volume. The Recollections from my *Logbook* could be a lengthy appendix to the philosophical work, I thought. But that, I soon understood, was a bad idea. The work(s) would lack integrity. As Spinster/Spider I would have to do Something Else. After a short while I understood the obvious. As I wrote in the Introduction to *Outercourse*:

> The philosophical and biographical dimensions of this book intertwine through multiple "coincidences.". . . . The philosophical theory and the biographical events recorded here are parts of the same Quest.

So in this book the parts *intertwine*. They are Woven together. The Weaving is not a contrived afterthought. Rather, as Voyager on the Subliminal Sea I am Dis-coverer of the intertwining that has been there all along. The Realizing of my own philosophy and the Re-membering of the Moments in Recollections from my *Logbook* (that is, my Realizing of their significance) are the same trip.

Hence *Outercourse* is my Transcendent Third Option to the dilemma of the two books I knew I had to write at the same Time. The Voyage has been rough at times, but it has brought me Here/Now to the Beginning. It has also brought me back around to the astonishing subject of Time.

## Expanding Now

The Moment that I began the writing of *Outercourse* I entered an Expanding Now. Sometime in June 1987 I sat at my typewriter and wrote the first sentences of Chapter One. The words just came from my typewriter as the Memories of early childhood came. The Memories were rich, variegated, colorful, poignant. The words that came were simple, even childish at times. This was not like the process of writing *Gyn/Ecology*, *Pure Lust*, or the *Wickedary*. Clearly, I had entered a different Galaxy.

The writing of *Outercourse* is not the writing of "memoirs." It has been, from the beginning of The First Spiral Galaxy, a Fourth Galactic event. It belongs to Now. It swirls back, retracing the Spiraling Paths of Moments, and it whirls ahead, more and more into Now. As I sailed to the end of The Third Spiral Galaxy I came into the Moments of the Fourth.

So I find mySelf writing of the Moments of The Fourth Spiral Galaxy from a Fourth Galactic perspective. I have Realized my subliminal knowledge of the earlier Times. Now I must Realize my subliminal knowledge of Now.

No time for dawdling Now, because I am here already. I have the equipment in my Craft to expand the Now, to Presentiate the past and the future, Conjuring the Presence of Fore-Crones, Fore-Familiars, and Other Background beings.

## The Foreground Now

bad news now. the news is bad. they made a war in 1991, raised the testosterone level in american males. yellow ribbons everywhere. flags. the hollow bully victory.

the hollow bully boys' victory parades, masking the defeat of patriarchy. decoded, they were defeat-of-patriarchy parades, charades. tons of confetti, obscene, boring. tons of confetti on the victors, prickers. tons of murdered trees.

oil spills and spills. oil burns. blight his fires. hoses on the burning bush, ashes to ashes. damn them.

Anita Hill, kicked down the hill, the victim of high tech lynching. hail to the most qualified candidate for the supreme sport. and the kennedy camelot kid, with only a million to spend on his trial, dripping with innocence. dripping with seminal tears and gratitude to "the system and God"—the god/rod. the faceless victim/woman weeps. put a technological dot/chador over her face. god! damn them.

and the women fade away, fade. *The New York Times* notices. Headline: "Stark Data on Women: 100 Million are Missing."[1] kiss them goodbye. female infanticide, neglect, starvation. rape, battering, everyday murder. "put a bag over their heads and they're all the same." no one's to blame. what a shame!

kids armed with guns, killing each other. women disarmed, forgetting each other.

the Age of Dis-memberment has arrived. the media men are excited, delighted. same old story, hate and gory. win an election. have an erection, selling polygrip and cars.

this is bore-dom.

this is the foreground now. Get out, Mary, go! Get out or die. Or get out and die. But get out. Run into the Expanding Now. Come on, Cronies, come on. Dare, Dare. And at the same Time, Stand your Ground. What? Am I crazy? Yes, by definition. Ain't I a woman?

and so I choose to Stand my Ground, right Now. How? In the Now, of course, the Now of Outercourse.

## I Choose to Stand My Ground

My Ground, the Ground that I Stand, is the Background, Now. Earlier in *Outercourse* I have explained:

> I [choose] to Fight/Act (Stand my Ground) at that precise location on the Boundary between Background and foreground where the demonic patriarchal distortions of women's Archaic heritage are most visible and accessible to me, where my Craft can be most effective in the work of Exorcism—reversing the reversals that blunt the potential for Realizing Ecstasy.[2]

The theme of Living on the Boundary is hardly unfamiliar to the Voyager of *Outercourse*. The important question is: Is my Ground, in the deepest sense, on the Boundaries of patriarchal institutions? The answer is no, not Now.

Oh, yes, I still Fight/Act there, on those Boundaries. But my true Ground, the Ground of that Ground, so to speak, is farther Out, farther Back. Back in the Background. Because I have arrived at the Four, the Fourth, the Dimension that was before, the Source, the Beginning.

Here at the Beginning I have raw, constant knowledge of my Final Cause, the Good who is Self-communicating, who is the Verb from whom, in whom, and with whom all true movements move.

Sure, they can distract me, drag me into their diddling dis-course, but the pull, oh the pull of the Verb—the intransitive One, you know—is so overwhelming that I fly sometimes, fly into the Unfolding, Enfolding arms. The arms of the Spiraling Galaxies, the wings of Spiraling angels. Call them whatever you like.

And just because I said I fly don't think I'm not Grounded. I've hung around academentia long enough to avoid being caught by old word games, old sophistries. *Of course* I mix Metaphors—that's what they're for, to be mixed and rearranged, to shoot the breeze, so to speak. How could I fly if I were not Grounded? How could I be Grounded if I couldn't fly? Everything is connected with everything else.

## Fed Up

I want to blast out of bore-dom, every way, every day. "That's so extreme," they say. "It is High Time to be Extreme," I say. While we wade knee deep in the blood of women shall I chat about Freud, Derrida, and Foucault? No, I don't think so.

Better to catch a comet by the tail and soar with it. Better to jump bail. The whole foreground is a jail.

'gender studies' . . . blender studies. The men's and women's center at o.u. (Oh, you!)

"No male-bashing!" they say. "That's very bad," they say. "Bad girl."

"Patriarchy is planetary!" I howl.

"That's none of your business," they say. Their eyes are glazed, dazed. "We're not feminists anyway. That's passé."

"Can't you Sense the pain of the footmaimed Chinese women hobbling on mutilated, gangrenous stumps over hundreds and hundreds of years?" I ask.

"It was a different culture," they say.

"Can't you feel the pain of thirty million genitally mutilated African women, today?" I ask.

"It's none of your business," they say. "It's another culture. Bad girl!"

"It's the *same* culture," I say. "Can't you *feel anything*?"

They shrink away, their faces grey. "As white privileged middle-class women we can't possibly imagine . . ."

"Shut up;" I say, politely. "You bore me, you gore me. You are killing me with your academented stupidity."

"We feel invalidated by your remarks," they say.

"Well, that's good," I say. Finally.

Oh, here's Sojourner Truth. "Hi Sojourner! They never hooked *you* into postfeminism, fragmentation, or therapeutic, thought-stopping babble, did they? What's that you say?"

"Ain't I a woman?"

"Oh, thank you, Sojourner! I was just about to lose it, but Now you've made my day. My Craft has arrived at The Fourth Spiral Galaxy. But of course I still fight on the Boundaries of patriarchal institutions. Will you help me rock the boat? What? You've been doing that right along? Of course, I knew it, but my knowledge was subliminal. Sometimes I'm kind of dumb, numb, and then I gradually wake up. Anyway, I've been feeling pissed and raw, fed up with the dis-course in the deadzone, so I'm glad you're here. I'm getting things into perspective Now. Your O-Zone—your Aura—is Be-Dazzling. I can see better! And your Cronies are here—lots of them. I mean, I can see them Now. Hi Sappho! Hi Harriet! Hi Matilda! Hi Andrée!"

Sorry if I seem a little out-of-sorts. But things are *so* bad in the foreground now. The dimwit in the white house cried on television on the fiftieth anniversary of Pearl Harbor. His voice cracked and everything. He didn't mention Nagasaki and Hiroshima. No one cried about gynocide and genocide. I know it's the same old crap. But it's worse.

Yes, of course they're losing. They're all goose-stepping into oblivion. I didn't want to go with them, so I decided to Leap out of the foreground into the Background, into the Expanding Now. And to bring along as many Others as I could.

42

# Magnetic Courage

From chapter 2 of *Quintessence*, pp. 88–89, 92–97.

*Courage, Ontological:* the Courage to Be through and beyond the State of Negation which is patriarchy; participation in the Unfolding of Be-ing—continuing on the Journey always.
—*Wickedary*, p. 69

Daly's *Quintessence* could be described as her final publication of the twentieth century, and her first of the twenty-first century, due to her framing of the book as being published simultaneously in the foreground world of 1998 and the "Archaic Future" in the Biophilic Era of 2048. Parts of *Quintessence* are written as utopic fiction/philosophy from the future; the editors have not included excerpts from these sections because of the difficulties in comprehending these parallel universes in snippets out of context.

Daly's struggle to extend her thought in the political and philosophic aridity of the postmodern, neoconservative/neoliberal 1990s can be felt achingly throughout *Quintessence*. In this excerpt, concerning Courage, Daly called on women to have a courage that is ontological, not merely situational:

> Our participation in Be-ing is at its core participation in Ontological Creation [... . Our] Leaping/Expanding requires Ontological Courage, which manifests itself as the Courage to Create—to summon out of the apparent void New Be-ing. Daring Women push back the foreground, the nonbeing pompously parading as Be-ing.

Her contrast between the foreground and the Background grew more Manichean, reflecting the global environmental crisis and her repugnance at biotech. She defined patriarchy here as "nothingness—that hideous void, that bloat of nonbe-ing which attempts to insert itself into our Presence." This language addresses the question raised in *Pure Lust* (see chapter 23):

Why is there so much nothing in the middle of something? Daly responded by unmooring herself from the conventions of the foreground:

> Spinning Spinsters literally fling ourSelves into the Unknown.

—Editors

## The Courage to Create—Creative Courage

Stormy Women find our Selves whirling further along in The Fifth Spiral Galaxy. We experience ever more vividly what it means to *be* Expanding Here, in our own Element, so to speak—participating in the Elegant Wildness of Quintessence.

It has been recounted that in numerology five is the number associated with "versatility, restlessness, and adventure."[1] This describes the experience of Voyagers in The Fifth Spiral Galaxy. The more we *are* Here, the more versatile, restless, and adventurous we become. Indeed, nothing/nowhere could be less static than Expanding Here.

The following lines are suggestive:

> People whose names "reduce" to five (when mathematical ascriptions are given to each of the letters) are said to love speculation and risks, and a varied environment. They are fond of travel and resist responsibility or any other factors in their lives that would tend to tie them down.[2]

Wild Women are not concerned about whether our names "reduce to five" in a numerological sense. However, we understand our true Names when we Expand to Five in a Crone-logical sense, by moving on in The Fifth Spiral Galaxy. We Lust for speculation (on many levels) as well as risks and a varied environment, which is precisely Here. We are inordinately fond of Travel, which involves resisting the compulsively tidy foreground responsibilities that are designed to tie us down, and assuming the vast Tidal Response-ability of multidimensional Voyaging.

Our modes of Traveling are tantamount to creating more and more Here. Our participation in Be-ing is at its core participation in Ontological Creation. As we Presentiate ourSelves and others we come into our own territory, not simply by finding something that is "already there" (like the explorers who "discovered" the "wild west" in America) but by creating over and beyond the illusory world. That is, we Realize our own potential. As long as we stay on our true course, we come to Know and Name the fact—as did Susan B. Anthony—that "failure is impossible."

This Leaping/Expanding requires Ontological Courage, which manifests itself as the Courage to Create—to summon out of the apparent void New Be-ing. Daring Women push back the foreground, the nonbeing pompously parading as Be-ing. [ . . . ]

## Ultimate Pseudocreativity: "Creation" of Mutant Species and Clones

The Great Lie and Great Reversal which is phallocracy's pseudocourageous battle against Goddess/against Be-ing is also the supreme battle against women and all of nature that is occurring at the close of the twentieth century. This is manifested in the atrocities of biotechnology, which is necrotechnology.

The nectech reversal mentality was exemplified in a 1984 interview with a physicist from the Lawrence Livermore Laboratory who was questioned about the morality of working on "weapons of death." The scientist, Lawrence C. West, replied:

> I don't think I fall into that category, of working on weapons of death. . . . We're working on weapons of life, ones that will save people from weapons of death.[3]

In the *Wickedary* I cited the expression *weapons of life* as an example of a specific kind of reversal (*reversals by redundancy and contradiction*). I explained the ill logic:

> The genus *weapons* has been fallaciously expanded to include two opposing subcategories, one of which (*weapons of death*) is included in the very definition of the genus and the other of which (*weapons of life*) contradicts the definition of the genus—that is, it is falsely included. Thus the first subdivision is redundant. . . . The second subdivision is an absurd contradiction.[4]

The Stunning fact is that at the time of writing the above paragraph I believed that the speaker was talking about nuclear weapons, since he was a physicist at Lawrence Livermore. Reading the statement now reveals that he anticipated, consciously or unconsciously, the mentality of the biotechnologists. In fact, he shared the *same* mentality. It might at first seem implausible to view life as a "weapon." Now, however, it has become clear that manipulation and pseudocreation of life—turning life against itself—is a weapon against life. Its result is gross destruction of life. And, significantly, in the 1990s the national weapons laboratories, including Lawrence Livermore, have impressive genome installations.

At laboratories in the "advanced" nations, genetic engineers are busy rearranging the genetic structures of living beings, working to invent ("create") and patent thousands of novel microbes, plants, and animals. For example, pigs are engineered with human growth hormones to increase their size; tomatoes are engineered with flounder genes to resist cold temperatures; laboratory mice are encoded with the AIDS virus as part of their genetic makeup.[5]

Little attention is given to the fact that there is an enormous amount of killing taking place under the aegis of "biotechnology," "the new reproductive technologies," "genetic engineering," and of course "cloning." When Dolly was cloned by Ian Wilmut in Scotland, it was reported that prior to this "success," there had been 277 "failures." The words *deaths* and *deformities* were not used. The author of an article in *New Scientist* cites Roger Gosden, a reproductive biologist at the Leeds General Infirmary, who stated: "There were an alarming number of miscarriages and abnormalities with the technique."[6] The words *pain* and *killing* were avoided. In fact, the "wise" old adage that "animals do not suffer pain" was dragged out from its mothballs and popularized concurrently with the advent of Dolly's cloning. Clearly, the dissociation which the biotechnologists share with the nuclear weapons builders allows them to be indifferent to the suffering of the animals they "create."

Although most scientists involved in cloning announced in Spring 1997 that human cloning could not and would not happen, public opinion shifted with alarming alacrity from "horrified negation" to "let's do it" about nine months later.[7] Professor Lori Andrews, a professor at Chicago-Kent College of Law, stated: "I see a total shift in the burden of proof to saying that unless there is actually going to be harm, then we should allow it."[8]

And an important question remains unaddressed, namely: "Harm to whom?" If human cloning is the subject at issue, we are talking not only about fetuses but about *women—women's bodies are at risk.* Given the enormous number of miscarriages and abnormalities in the case of cloned animals, the threat to women's lives and well-being is alarming. But this is rarely mentioned.

It is important to notice that a large proportion of scientists involved in animal cloning have a vested interest in infertility clinics. Dr. Donald Wolf, for example, a senior scientist at the Oregon Primate Research Center, who is also the director of Oregon's only *in vitro* fertilization center, "has two federal grants to study cloning in rhesus monkeys. One will involve cloning from cells of an adult."[9]

By late 1997 it became alarmingly obvious that enormous numbers of women in the U.S. were succumbing to the massive propaganda campaign to overcome infertility and, in effect, hand themselves over as (unwitting) guinea pigs to be worked on by technodocs (Male Mothers) at infertility clinics. And this has occurred in a time of population explosion on an already overpopulated planet. Women such as Bobbi McCaughey, by having a "successful" fertility drug-induced litter of seven, served the purpose of inspiring a national paroxysm of pride in Male Motherhood. Few mentioned the fact that multiple births often involved the production of damaged fetuses. The "way out" of the dilemma offered by the "creative" fellows of the medical profession is called "selective reduction," the medical term for the *in utero* destruction of "excess" fetuses.

In January 1998, the twenty-fifth anniversary of the *Roe versus Wade* Supreme Court decision that legalized abortion in the U.S., the voices of Pro-Choice women were drowned out by the pious whining that issued from born again christian fundamentalists and other anti-abortion fanatics.

It would appear that the pseudocreative Male Mothers are winning at the end of the twentieth century. By their nefarious actions they are proclaiming the death of Goddess. By their lies/reversals they sneer: "Ding dong, the Wicked Witch is dead." Frightened little fellows [ . . . ] are overpowered by botchers/bullies such as physicist and infertility clinic entrepreneur Dr. Richard Seed (Dick Seed?), who announced that he plans to open a human cloning clinic in Chicago. On January 6, 1998 Seed proclaimed to shocked millions on National Public Radio:

> God made man in his own image. God intended for man to become one with God. We are going to become one with God. We are going to have almost as much knowledge and almost as much power as God. Cloning and the reprogramming of DNA is the first serious step in becoming one with God. Very simple philosophy.

No doubt his more sophisticated colleagues see Seed as a buffoon, perhaps as deflecting attention from themselves as they work on in their quiet ways, destroying the lives of plants, animals, women. All the same, Seed gives the show away, speaking for them, displaying the pseudo-courage to negate.

## Countering Pseudocreativity with the Wildness of Creative Courage

Metamorphosing Women recognize our participation in Nemesis as an active war against the gods, i.e., the imposters. This war is a great series of Acts of Exorcism by Wild Women. It requires Creative Courage, not because the gods (patriarchal men and their myths) are spiritually powerful, but because the lies, which function as masks for ontological impotence, constitute a miasma that functions to hide the Background.

Our Acts of Exorcising pseudoreality are at the same time Acts of Creation. We do not have to cope with any "jealousy" on the part of Goddess(es). That idea is too absurd to contemplate. Goddess *urges* Wild Women to create. Indeed *Goddess* is a Metapatriarchal Metaphor[10] for the Be-ing in which we live, love, create, and are. The impotent jealousy of "the gods" is not able to stop Be-ing. When we truly *know* this, Radical Elemental Feminists are free to Act with Contagious Courage. Our recognition of the fact that this will not be rewarded by patriarchy liberates Lusty Women to Leap on and on.

Patriarchy is still *there*, of course, whining for our attention, begging for our submission to its ludicrous laws, imploring us to play its games, beseeching us to try to overthrow it. But whenever, wherever women are

Wild enough, Wise enough simply to shift our context and our perspective, that state shrivels.

There are rumors that some Wild Women have been disturbed and disgusted by the piteous whimpering of the shriveled gods, who are offering rewards and prizes to those who will return. Most of us, however, are too busy Moving Out to notice this nothingness. We simply are not there.

Spinning Spinsters literally fling ourSelves into the Unknown. Yes, we have Concreating Companions, but we cannot always know when and where they will manifest to us. Our Presentiating powers may sometimes feel weak. Yet we are sustained by Fey Faith[11] that they are Here and participate also in our Quest for Quintessence.

In order to Name more adequately the Fantastic Reality of this process/progress it is important to grasp yet another aspect of the Courage to Create, which is that it eventually evolves into *Creative Courage*. I am suggesting that this Courage itself takes on dimensions of creativity. It is not completely distinct from the creation that it inspires. It throws us into the throes of creation. It pushes us to Touch the as yet unknown which stirs in the Subliminal Realms, to find its forms and Realize these forms as incarnate, palpable, sensible.

Creative Courage goes/grows by leaps and bounds. It cannot stop short. It participates in the Wildness of the Act of Creation. When the Courage to Create metamorphoses into Creative Courage it becomes Quintessential, that is, it is transmuted into active participation in the Quest for Quintessence. This is not to say that it ceases to be the Courage to Create, but that it also becomes something more. It is not simply the courage to *begin* a work, but to continue the process, daring to forge on.

This Metamorphosed/Metamorphosing Virtue causes New forms to burst forth in and from the maker's mind. It permeates her aura. It is contagious, spreading from woman to woman. It expands our Presence throughout the world.

Creative Courage, then, is the Quintessential ingredient in Elemental Feminist Genius. It moves/stirs creating Crones to Realize in the material world the forms/exemplars that are taking shape in our minds. In this way, our creative Realizing Presentiates Nemesis.

Our Radical Elemental Feminist creations are specific to us as individuals. For one at one time it may be a book, for another a piece of music, for yet another a work of sculpture, and for still another organizing a massive protest against violence. All of our acts of developing friendships are manifestations of Creative Courage. As Concreators we work in harmony. At times this harmony/accord is conscious. Sometimes it is subliminally sensed.

What such Crone-logical creations have in common is that they are works of Elemental Feminist Genius. Insofar as they are fired by Creative Courage, they expand Be-Dazzling Presence/Here. They are reckless works. Smashing in the face/faces of patriarchy they reveal its nothingness—that hideous void, that bloat of nonbe-ing which attempts to insert itself into our Presence.

43

# Quintessence

## *The Music of the Spheres*

From chapter 5 of *Quintessence*, pp. 228–30.

*Genius 1:* an attendant Spirit of a Musing woman *2:* a woman in Touch with Tutelary Deities, Elemental Spirits, and Demons; a woman of extraordinary native intellectual power and capacity for creative activity; a Dangerous Woman, whom the patriarchs attempt to stifle, thwart, destroy, erase.
—*Wickedary*, p. 127

A surprising new/old voice entered the cosmic harmony of Mary Daly's world when she cited the life and work of Hildegard of Bingen (1098–1179), whose genius spanned many fields, including writing, music, visual arts, healing, science, and mysticism. The rediscovery of Hildegard by feminist scholars stands as a supreme example of compensatory history. The inspiration of Hildegard's vision led to one of the more beautiful metaphoric restatements of Daly's adroit combination of joy and anger, mysticism and ethics:

> Journeying Women living ever more consciously in harmony with the Music of the Spheres cannot conveniently block out our knowledge of evil. Our intensified sensate and intellectual abilities enable us to understand atrocities and their interconnections on deep levels. Our sadness and rage are Alive and are assumed into the Quintessential Focus of Fierce Women.

—Editors

The multiple synchronicities experienced by beings in the Fifth Dimension constitute a symphony of the cosmos. The twelfth century Wise

Woman and Mystic Hildegard of Bingen, Abbess of Rupertsberg, testified most eloquently to the reality of this cosmic harmony. Hildegard was a Genius of the first order. A gifted poet, composer, artist, doctor, preacher, and scientist, she wrote books on theology, medicine, science, and physiology, as well as seventy poems. She created a language of her own consisting of nine hundred words and an alphabet consisting of twenty-three letters, both of which have been lost to us.[1]

At the age of forty-two Hildegard began having visions, which were represented by her in thirty-six pictures or "illuminations." In one of these illuminations are painted seven rings. In the top ring she depicted Mary, Queen of Heaven, with the star-filled sky in the background. In the vision, which was also an auditory phenomenon, she heard "a sound resembling the voice of a multitude making harmony . . . a symphony of Holy Mary." She heard Mary praised as "the most brilliant gem and bright glory of the sun," and as "translucent matter."[2]

Since for many Nag-Gnostic Women the image of Mary suggests *Goddess* (albeit dethroned Goddess, tamed and possessed by the fathers), Hildegard's description of her vision, with its accompanying sounds, is of special interest. Discerning Women do not think of the word *Goddess* as Naming one individual deity with only one name. In fact, the words traditionally used to describe Mary are derived from descriptions of ancient Goddess images.[3] Moreover, Her-etical Hags do not think hierarchically, as if there were "one on top," especially if we think of *Goddess* not as a noun, but as a Verb.

The words used by Hildegard to convey her vision are suggestive of Quintessence, which in ancient Greek philosophy has been described as celestial clarity from heaven, as the fiery upper atmosphere of the sun and stars, and as scarcely material in form.[4] This is not to say that *Goddess* equals *Quintessence*, but that both words point to the same realm. *Goddess* is a Metaphor for the constantly unfolding Verb of Verbs—Be-ing. *Quintessence* also is a way of Naming Be-ing the Verb, with specific emphasis on its manifestation as source of integrity, harmony, and luminous splendor of form.

The joy of participation in Quintessence continually unfolds. This Sense of Be-Longing in the Universe sometimes feels like being part of a cosmic symphony. Our synchronistic communications are marked by rhythm, melody, harmony, and even counterpoint.

Journeying Women living ever more consciously in harmony with the Music of the Spheres cannot conveniently block out our knowledge of evil. Our intensified sensate and intellectual abilities enable us to understand atrocities and their interconnections on deep levels. Our sadness and rage are Alive and are assumed into the Quintessential Focus of Fierce Women.

Nothing that we do is small when it is seen in the Light of Quintessence. Size does not matter, nor does distance between separate beings participating in this Cosmic Concordance.[5] In Touch with Quintessence, Elemental Women become more than ever like trees and like angels. Extending our roots deeper, we are free to expand and participate in the creation of the universe.[6]

44

# A Heightened Experience of Losing and Finding (Response to Audre Lorde)

From chapter 3 of *Amazon Grace*, pp. 22–26.

*Hag-ography:* the history of women who are on the Journey of radical be-ing; the lives of Witches, of Great Hags (past and present), which are deeply intertwined; history uncovered and created by women as we live/write our own stories.
—*Wickedary*, p. 138

In this excerpt, Mary Daly gave her perspective on the highly public conflict between her and Audre Lorde. In the interests of encouraging readers to form their own analysis, the editors have included the entire chapter on African genital mutilation to which Lorde took particular exception (chapter 16). Also included here is Daly's letter to Lorde, which was written at the time, before Lorde published her open letter. The existence of this letter from Daly to Lorde was known to only a few until the letter was discovered in Lorde's papers after her death by Lorde's biographer, Alexis De Veaux. Courageously, De Veaux included the letter in her book *Warrior Poet.* When this evidence emerged, affecting the major controversy that had surrounded Daly's name in feminist circles for the better part of twenty-five years, Daly was quite hopeful. However, the existence of this letter, as significant as its rediscovery was, never repaired Daly's public image as much as Lorde's denial of its existence had damaged it.
—Editors

## An Alarming Example of the Heightened Experience of Losing and Finding

In my book *Outercourse: The Be-Dazzling Voyage* I discussed my experiences of the publication of *Gyn/Ecology* (1979):

> I [wrote and] have always seen *Gyn/Ecology* as part of a Movement, including my own Voyage, which has continued since that writing and continues, because I am not a noun but a verb. When I set it free so it could *be* in the world, I did not see it as a work of perfection. For some women it could be an Awakening shock, for others a Source of information, or a springboard from which they might Leap into their own A-mazing Searches, Words, Metaphors.
>
> Above all, I was acutely aware that I had not done or written everything. I had not written the Last Word. (Otherwise, how could I ever write again?) Rather, I had set free this book, this Thunderbird, in the hope that its Call would be Heard. I hoped that it would soar together with the works of Other women, which were coming and would come from different Realms of the Background. I looked forward to the profusion of New Creation, which I believed could emerge from women of all races, cultures, classes—from all over this planet—speaking/Be-Speaking out of our various and vital heritages.
>
> From my Fourth Galactic perspective I see that this has happened and is happening, because our Time has come. Particularly Moving to me, personally, is the work of women of Ireland, that Treasure Island which I recognize deeply as the wellspring of my Background, my ancestral home. Especially Gynergizing on a global scale is the New abundance of creation from women of color.
>
> Explosions of Diversity do not happen without conflict, however. One of the responses to *Gyn/Ecology* was a personal letter from Audre Lorde, which was sent to me in May 1979. For deep and complex personal reasons I was unable to respond to this lengthy letter immediately. However, when Lorde came to Boston to give a poetry reading that summer, I made a special effort to attend it, and spoke with her briefly. I told her that I would like to discuss her letter in person so that we would have an adequate opportunity to understand each other in dialogue, and I suggested places where we might meet for such a discussion. Our meeting

did in fact take place at the Simone de Beauvoir Conference in New York on September 29, 1979. In the course of that hour-or-so-long meeting we discussed my book and her response. I explained my positions clearly, or so I thought. I pointed out, for example, in answer to Audre Lorde's objection that I failed to name Black Goddesses, that *Gyn/Ecology* is not a compendium of goddesses. Rather, it focuses primarily on those goddess myths and symbols which were direct sources of christian myth. Apparently Lorde was not satisfied, although she did not indicate this at the time. She later published and republished slightly altered versions of her originally personal letter to me in anthologies as an "Open Letter."

It continues to be my judgment that public response in kind would not be a fruitful direction. In my view, *Gyn/Ecology* is itself an "Open Book." . . . The writing of *Gyn/Ecology* was for me an act of Biophilic Bonding with women of all races and classes, under all the varying oppressions of patriarchy. Clearly, women who have a sincere interest in understanding and discussing this book have an obligation to read not only the statements of critics but also the book itself, and to *think* about it. . . .[1]

## Letters: The Surge of Biophilic Bonding

Throughout the horrors of the academented witchcraze the letters responding to *Gyn/Ecology* came to me. They came to me like healing balm. Reading many of them was and continues to be like sampling an almost infinite variety of exquisite wines. They renewed/Re-New my Spirit.

The letters conveyed many complex things. Simply stated, they poured out love and gratitude, and they told me that the long struggle had not been in vain. They gave me something back—renewed Hope, Courage, and Strength. They surged up from the Subliminal Sea, with messages of Biophilic Bonding.[2]

Profoundly differing in tone and intent from these letters is Audre Lorde's piece ("Open Letter") which, as I wrote in *Outercourse*, has continued to be assigned

as required reading by not a few professors in academentia to students in classes where *Gyn/Ecology* itself has not been assigned, or a mere handful of pages of this book have been required reading. This kind of selectivity is irresponsible. It imposes a condition of self-righteous ignorance upon students, often within the setting of "Women's Studies." This is, in my view, a worst case scenario of pseudoscholarship. It is, even if "well-intentioned," divisive, destructive. It functions, at least subliminally, as a self-protective statement about the purity and political correctness of the professor. It can be analyzed in further detail as a manifestation of the seven-point Sado-Ritual Syndrome, as described in *Gyn/Ecology* (pp. 130–33).[3]

## *My Lost and Found Letter to Audre Lorde*

On September 22, 1979, I wrote to Audre Lorde responding to her letter of May 6, 1979, to me. She denied ever receiving this, insisting throughout the years, as she altered and republished her original letter to me, that I had never responded to her initial correspondence. Nearly a quarter of a century later, my "lost letter to Audre Lorde," with my last name written in Lorde's handwriting in the left bottom corner, was found amid her personal papers posthumously by her biographer, Alexis De Veaux, and documented in De Veaux's *Warrior Poet: A Biography of Audre Lorde.*[4]

The text of my letter is as follows:

September 22, 1979

Dear Audre,

First I want to thank you for sending me *The Black Unicorn.* I have read all of the poems, some of them several times. Many of them moved me very deeply—others seemed farther from my own experience. You have helped me to be aware of different dimensions of existence, and I thank you for this.

My long delay in responding to your letter by no means indicates that I have not been thinking about it—quite the contrary. I did think that by putting it aside for awhile I would get a better perspective than at first reaction. I wrote you a note to that effect which didn't get mailed since I didn't have your address. Then there was a hope of trying to get to Vermont in August, but the summer was overwhelmingly eventful.

Clearly there is no simple response possible to the matters you raise in your letter. I wrote *Gyn/Ecology* out of the insights and materials most accessible to me at the time. When I dealt with myth I used commonly available sources to find what were the controlling symbols behind judeo-christian myth in order to trace a direct line to the myths which legitimate the technological horror show. But of course to point out this restriction in the first passage is not really to answer your letter. You have made your point very strongly and you most definitely do have a point. I could speculate on how *Gyn/Ecology* would have been affected had we corresponded about this before the manuscript went to press, but it doesn't seem creativity-conducing to look backward. There is only *now* and the hope of breaking the barriers between us—of constantly expanding the vision.

I wonder if you will have any time available when I come to New York for the Simone de Beauvoir conference? Since I have a lot to do here, I had thought of just flying down Friday morning and returning that night. Are you free Friday afternoon or evening? Or will you be in Boston any time soon? I called and left a message on your machine. My number is. . . . Hope to see you and talk with you soon.

[Handwritten:] I hope you are feeling well, Audre. May the strength of all the Goddesses be with you—Mary

I wrote this letter with the intention of communicating from one Feminist to another, without thinking about publishing it or preserving it for archives. So I did not focus on making a copy or saving it to prove its existence. In 1979, I saw no need to make a carbon copy or go out to a copy shop before mailing my letter to Audre Lorde.

Imagine my surprise nearly a quarter of a century later, when, on June 9, 2003, I was contacted by Alexis De Veaux, who was asking my permission to quote from my unacknowledged and apparently "lost" letter of September 22, 1979. It was astonishing after all these years to see someone—in fact, Audre Lorde's own biographer—say that she had seen my letter among Lorde's personal papers. It was gratifying to read that De Veaux felt it was essential to publish my letter to Lorde in order to do justice to the historical record—especially in light of the widespread public accusations and attacks resulting from Lorde's "Open Letter." De Veaux was also determined to correct the prevailing belief that I had not answered Lorde's letter and to honor the truth of my reply.[5]

45

# What Terrific Shock Will Be Shocking Enough?

From chapter 5 of *Amazon Grace*, pp. 43–54.

*Starchase:* a Nag-Gnostic Intergalactic Gallop; an Amazonian Astral Voyage.
—*Wickedary*, p. 169

Daly's final work, *Amazon Grace*, published in 2006, sings with voices from the feminist past, present, and future, as well as from Daly's own panoply of influences. One theme that was new to her—and of deep conversational interest to her in her last decade—concerned "morphic resonance." In this excerpt, she wants that deep background connection that is morphic resonance to carry across time and space. Thus in her capacious Background, Daly found room—and she admitted this was odd—for Susan B. Anthony and Jacques Maritain to Spark together. The shock that is shocking enough turned out to be Realizing Be-ing.
—Editors

The extent and depth of damage inflicted by phallocracy on Self-consciousness is ineffable and unfathomable. To begin to See this, and then to Name it and Act consistently with this Seeing and Naming, women may require an experience of great shocks which can move us into a state of shock. Our Foresister Susan B. Anthony believed this. In 1870 she wrote:

> So while I do not pray for anybody or any party to commit outrages, still I do pray, and that earnestly and constantly, for some terrific shock to startle the women of this nation into a self-respect which will compel them to see the abject degradation of their present position; which will force them to break their yoke of bondage, and give them faith in themselves, which will make them proclaim their allegiance to women first;

> which will enable them to see that man can no more feel, speak, or act for women than could the old slaveholder for his slave.[1]

In the first decade of this century Susan B. Anthony's prayer of 1870 might seem to have been partially answered. G. W. Bush and his sordidly submissive Environmental Protection Agency delivered a "terrific shock" to this nation by abandoning all attempts at denying that climate change is real, ongoing, and man-made, and then, without missing a beat, continuing to insist on NO CHANGE in US policy that would deal with this horrendous threat. Bush & company even suggested that we can "adapt" and rely upon "voluntary efforts" to reduce US emissions of carbon dioxide and other air pollutants.[2]

The "shock" of this ongoing travesty is experienced not only by some women, of course, but also by some men, many of whom have been outstanding opponents of environmental destruction. So how does this connect with Susan B. Anthony and her prayer for a shock that would startle women, specifically? To work our way toward an answer to this complex question, consider the implications of the fact that the successive heads of the EPA appointed by G. W. have conveniently functioned as token torturers of our Sister the Earth and her nonhuman and human inhabitants.

What feelings and thoughts does this simple fact elicit in a woman who identifies as a Feminist and who cares profoundly about the fate of the Earth and its inhabitants? There is a sense of disappointment and horror. But often this is blended with a bland, matter-of-fact, sophisticated acceptance of "reality": "Of course," says our bland feminist, "they're Bush appointees, so what can you expect?"

Over a quarter of a century ago I published in *Gyn/Ecology* an analysis of assimilation, psychic numbing, token torturers, and the state of total tokenism. It may be that in the expanding state of total tokenism in this century most women have become incapable of experiencing great shocks. Perhaps the worse the shocks women have had to endure, the greater our susceptibility to psychic numbing. In the early twenty-first century the media's portrayals of everyday atrocities against women and nature all over the globe have given heightened meaning to Hannah Arendt's expression "the banality of evil."

This observation leads to the thought that in the state of shock we are knocked into an unshockable state.

The self-contradiction and dilemma attached to the condition of "shock" would seem to put a damper on Susan's famous prayer for a "terrific shock." Was she praying for the wrong thing? Not exactly; I believe that her use of the word "shock" is an indication that she was on the trail of Something Big.

Although Susan could not then adequately articulate the Wondrous Positively Shocking Reality which can hurl us beyond the self-contradiction, she intuited its existence. Indeed, her heroic life is itself a manifestation of this Reality.

The dilemma arises from hearing and saying the word *shock* only from a foreground perspective. Shocks that are caused by the deadbeat daddies of daddyland are simply not Terrific enough. Since they are mere foreground phenomena, they inevitably keep us stuck in a maze of contradictions. The "outrages" of fatherland, no matter how hideous and destructive, cannot of themselves be the answer to Susan's prayer. They cannot Shock us Out of the phallocentric foreground and into the Magnificent and Infinitely Shocking Background. For this, something Other is needed.

## The Shock of Be-ing

All Wild creatures and Other realities participate in Be-ing, by which I mean "Ultimate/Intimate Reality, the constantly Unfolding Verb of Verbs which is intransitive, having no object that limits its dynamism."[3] The Terrific Shock of encountering and Realizing Be-ing is utterly unlike the foreground shocks which keep us imprisoned and circling the masters' mazes. The Shock of meeting Be-ing is simple and direct. It is absolutely surprising and joyous. It is Self-transformative and changes Everything. It is unforgettable. It opens pathways that go on and on. It makes one Realize how Lucky she is. The Prayer that comes to mind is "Thank you! Thank you!"

Be-ing manifests in natural creatures. A clover blossom announces: "I am." The girl or woman sitting on the grass who just "happens" to Hear these words is astonished but not afraid. The simplicity and naturalness of the event—its ordinariness—does not conflict with its extraordinariness. It simply Is, and subtly everything changes.[4]

This means that the woman who has met the ontologically articulate clover blossom (or pebble or blade of grass or tree or piece of ice in the snow) gradually is enabled also to meet the foreground shocks in a different way. Having encountered Background Reality that is everywhere in nature, Be-Speaking in the Chorus of Be-ing, she becomes more Adventurous. She is surrounded by Natural Friends, as she follows her own path. She is a creator. When it is necessary she confronts the evil foreground world, taking on the attackers and oppressors of women and nature with confidence and Daring.

She is aided always, all ways by Amazon Grace, which manifests as an ontological experience.

## The Intuition of Be-ing

In a footnote in *Beyond God the Father* I commented on Jacques Maritain's analysis of his "intuition of being":

> Although he was hardly a feminist or social revolutionary, Maritain had an exceedingly fine sensitivity to the power of this intuition, which, if it were carried through to social consciousness, would challenge the world.[5]

And, I now add, it could be an answer to Susan's Prayer. On the face of it, linking Jacques Maritain and Susan B. Anthony might seem a bit odd. The result of this linkage might appear to be an Odd Couple. So? We live in an odd world.

The origin of this "marriage" is my own experience and intellectual history as a Radical Feminist philosopher. My own existential encounter with a clover blossom happened when I was about fourteen years old. I was lying on the grass after a dip in a local swimming hole in Schenectady, New York. Suddenly the clover blossom spoke two words. It said: "I am." I recall being shocked and amazed, but the experience was not heavy. Rather it was apparently casual and it was gentle. I had the impression that the clover blossom was making a statement about itSelf—not trying to show off or overwhelm me but simply making a point. Despite the astonishing speech it had made, which would change my life, it appeared to be, well, just blossoming.

I couldn't ever forget this experience. I'm not sure whether I told anyone about it at that time. I had never heard of an intuition like this and had no words for this event. But my life was suffused with it. It guided me on paths I was supposed to follow. I know that it was connected with my ever-growing conviction that I wanted to become a philosopher, even though I couldn't know exactly what that word meant. Certainly it would never have occurred to anyone in those times at Saint Joseph's Academy, the parochial high school I attended during the 1940s in Schenectady, New York, to speak to a teenage girl about the call to become a philosopher. But it didn't matter. The clover blossom had taken care of all that.

Then there was my brief but everlasting affair with a hedge on the campus of Saint Mary's College, at Notre Dame, Indiana. I was about twenty-three and was studying for my doctorate at the School of Sacred Theology, which had been established by the poet Sister Madeleva Wolfe, then president of Saint Mary's, who wanted to do something about the fact that women were not allowed to study catholic theology for a Ph.D. anywhere in the US.

One morning I happened to walk past a hedge on my way to class. It spoke two words to me. These words were: "Continued existence." I realized eventually that this was a companion intuition to the earlier one, making explicit the duration of the verb "I am," which refers to participation in Be-ing. It Announced a Now that always Is.

By the time I encountered Maritain's work in the early sixties (while studying for my doctorate in philosophy in Fribourg, Switzerland), I was ready for his books on the intuition of being. His work was useful and inspiring. However, with the surging of the Women's Revolution in the late sixties, and especially in the seventies, eighties, nineties, and—yes—in the twenty-first century, it has become ever more obvious to me that the ontological intuition is about Be-ing the Verb and that it must be "carried through to social consciousness, which will challenge the world."[6]

The word *being*, of course, can function both as a verb and as a noun. When people speak of "the Supreme Being" this refers to a noun. One cannot participate in this. It just hangs "up there." My use of the hyphen in Be-ing is intended to indicate that I am referring exclusively to the

Verb, which is Ultimate/Intimate Reality in which we (all creatures) participate by be-ing ourSelves.

The Terrific Shock that Susan B. Anthony was praying for could not come from encountering the "supreme being" (supreme block). Blocks cannot Shock. Be-ing, on the Other hand, Unblocks/Shocks. It opens the way for infinite possibilities.

Bearing this in mind, we revisit Susan's pertinent words (cited earlier) for further revelations.

In her remarkable passage Susan describes the reasons for praying for the shock. First, she wanted it "to startle the women of this nation into a self-respect which will compel them to see the abject degradation of their present position." The first consequence of the "terrific shock," then, is that women are startled into self-respect. This would not be an immediate effect of a foreground shock (for example, being molested). Indeed, when we consider the array of feelings associated with such an atrocious event—shame, fear, anger, disappointment, horror—it is unlikely that Self-respect would leap out, since this is precisely what is under attack.

However, if we think about the reaction of a woman who experiences the gift of an Intuition of Be-ing, Susan's choice of words clearly fits very accurately. The recipient of this revelation has experienced Depth Hearing (Nelle Morton's expression). She senses that she is Lucky and is honored to have received this grace, and is therefore startled into Self-respect.

Moreover, Susan is completely accurate in her observation that it is such Self-respect that will compel women to see the abject degradation of their present position and give them faith in themselves.

The Self-respect which is elicited when a woman experiences an Intuition of Be-ing naturally compels her to see the grotesque inappropriateness of her degraded position and that of all women. The contrast is glaringly obvious, intolerable, and wrong—so wrong that it forces her to break her insufferable "yoke of bondage." She is driven to break out, and she is enabled to do this because she has begun to Dis-cover Faith in herSelf. Moreover, her Acts of Seeing and Breaking Out of bondage and gaining faith in herself constitute a continuing Spiraling process, with each Act leading to another. This is the way the dynamism of the

Intuition of Be-ing works to recharge the Spiraling of consciousness and action.

Moreover, this Spiraling movement works communally as well as individually. Anthony, a Feminist Activist, wrote this passage in the plural. The use of the plural is particularly interesting to note as a theme: Communal movement is not merely collective. Rather it is interactive. As participants in Be-ing women act upon each Other. The actions of each participant not only spur her on to further Acts: e.g., of Seeing, Breaking Out, and Gaining Faith in herSelf. But also, by these further Acts each woman Gynergizes each other woman. These interactive movements constitute a complex Cosmic Dance of Be-ing. They are participation in the Creative work of the Goddess (or, as some would say, "Goddessing").

The next Leap in Susan's analysis of the effects upon women of the "terrific shock" is that (because it will give them faith in themselves) it "will make them proclaim their allegiance to women first." This is the dramatic Leap to the Core of Radical Elemental Feminism. It is the taboo-breaking, threatening Leap, at the mention of which the faint-hearted tremble and turn back. It is at this point that Susan reveals her true identity as Wild Woman, Positively Revolting Hag, Powerful Crone. In the Light and Wind of these words we See/Hear that she is no mere "equal rights feminist." She is actively participating in the powers and work of the Goddess Nemesis, Elementally disrupting the patriarchal balance of terror, Passionately Spinning/Spiraling Archaic Threads of *Gynergy*.

Susan is uncompromising: Women who proclaim their allegiance to women first See that "man can no more feel, speak, or act for woman than could the old slaveholder for his slave." Her speech crescendos:

> The fact is, women are in chains, and their servitude is all the more debasing because they do not realize it. O, to compel them to see and feel, and to give them the courage and conscience to speak and act for their own freedom, though they face the scorn and contempt of all the world for doing it![7]

It is Time Now for our Deep Hearing of this Great Hag's Defiant Howl!

## The Morphic Resonance of the Prayers and Other Acts of Great Foresisters

Great Foresisters are Be-Speaking to us Now. They are Auguring, Foretelling, Speaking of what will be. They are bringing about psychic/material change by means of words. They are Be-Speaking us further and further into Be-ing.

They are Naming our interconnectedness, which involves Transtemporal/Trans-spatial Consciousness, Communication, Sisterhood, Conversations, Synchronicities, Syn-Crone-icities, Telepathic Travels.

Women who are Trivial enough to Sense and Act upon the messages of our Foresisters can confront the nothingness of the nothing-loving technomaniacs and Realize our Hope in our Selves. We do not feel unfamiliar with the interconnectedness of the quantum universe. Nor are we alienated by the thought that, instead of being empty, space is filled with unseen connections. Indeed, this is our common experience, and it makes possible Faith in the worth of our particular works and acts, which have wide-ranging effects.

While Re-Calling the words and works of our famous Foresisters, we also Sense and acknowledge the achievements of those whose names and creations have been stolen and erased in patriarchal history (even as our own names and creations are being stolen and erased in fatherland today). The influence of our Forgotten Foresisters is felt by Wild Women, who note that in astrology *influence* means "an emanation of occult power held to derive from stars" (*Webster's*). These Foresisters are indeed like Stars whose Light and Spiritual Force flow to us/through us, producing Gynergy. They are our Hidden Power Sources, hurling Secret Weapons to Amazons, pouring into us our true Archaic Heritage, which is the Abundance of Amazon Grace.

As Wild Women actively receive this Heritage we become transmitters as well as creators. We participate in Foresisterhood, passing on the torches of our own tradition. We actualize the answer to Susan's prayer and to the prayers of all the Foresisters by Seeing, Feeling, Couraging, Speaking, and Acting for our own freedom. By Be-Speaking beyond the scorn and contempt of the fathers' world, we become the answer.

We also become like Stars, emanating Occult Power, influencing our Sisters. So it is that Trivial Women's experiences of unseen connectedness also inspire Fantastic Daring and increasing Self-confidence. As Travelers and Weavers in a participative universe we increasingly trust our own judgment even when our reasons are not evident to others.

This progress happens especially when we learn to Sense the presence of morphogenetic fields. Weird Searchers proclaim that through the influence of Prayers and Dreams of all our Foresisters the evolution of Feminist consciousness continues, and these influences do not fall off with distance in space or time. They are Here Now.

## So What Is Different about the Early Twenty-First Century?

The sense of all-pervasive nightmare-ishness did not come all at once. The creepy sense that "something is out of joint" had been present for years/decades/centuries, but it had somehow been possible to tune out the horror, at least enough to relax at times.

By the first decade of the twenty-first century, for some of us at least, the collusion/collision of seemingly disparate horrors had become increasingly obvious. Looking at the first page of *The New York Times* (or any first page of almost any newspaper) can be a way of getting the big picture "in your face."

The effect of this barrage of bad news is overwhelming. Typically our reader seeks escape, feeling a sense of helplessness and meaninglessness, perhaps to the point of nausea. Her Rage is somehow blocked, because of an apparent inability to know what connections exist among these disastrous events. Who or what is the source of them? Specifically, no one—certainly not the newspaper—Names the overriding cause of such evils.

Something is missing. It appears that "no one" is able to find a connecting thread among these horrors. Yet thirty years ago (and twenty years ago, and ten years ago, and even ten minutes ago) *many women* have seen the blatant thread. We have Named it in our multiple and powerful expressions of Gynergy—our books, our classes, our workshops, our speeches, our conversations, our political activism, our mutual support and loyalty to each other. We Named/Name it with the Wicked Old Word *patriarchy*. For the sake of clarity and convenience to the readers of this book, I will Here and Now Howl Out again the meaning of this word, which I have elaborated upon in *Beyond God the Father*, in all my books, and definitively defined in the *Wickedary* as follows:

> *1:* society manufactured and controlled by males: FATHERLAND; society in which every legitimated institution is entirely in the hands of males and a few selected henchwomen; society characterized by oppression, repression, depression, narcissism, cruelty, racism, classism, ageism, [speciesism,] objectification, sadomasochism, necrophilia; joyless society, ruled by Godfather, Son, and Company; society fixated on proliferation, propagation, procreation, and bent on the destruction of all Life *2:* the prevailing religion of the entire planet, whose essential message is necrophilia.[8]

*Patriarchy*, discredited as passé and associated with the "jargon" of dated "seventies feminism" and the rhetoric of loathsome *Radical Feminism*, is often looked upon in academic circles as less than unworthy of notice. It is too embarrassingly obvious to deserve mention by the erudite professors and sophisticated graduate students of feminist theory. That foolish term *patriarchy* MUST BE KEPT BURIED, they assume, together with bustles and bloomers, in the attics of women's history.

So what sort of Revolting Hag would dig up this threadbare term and haul it out for display in this decade of this century?

I, MARY DALY, AM THE SORT OF EMBARRASSING AND POSITIVELY REVOLTING HAG WHO WOULD DO SUCH AN INAPPROPRIATE ARCHEOLOGICAL DIG, AND I AM DOING IT HERE, NOW!

So the question then arises: Who or what caused (and continues to cause) the discrediting and erasure of a word, such as *patriarchy*, that so aptly Names the enemy of women and all of the oppressed, including our planet herSelf? Whose interest is served by this discrediting of language that enables women to Be-Speak important connections and subsequently to think and articulate coherent and liberating thoughts? Could it be that such word-suffocation benefits those who also discredit expressions like *Radical Feminism*? And could it be that such word-obliteration serves the purposes of those who wish to discredit and disappear our Foresisters themselves, thus destroying the possibility of Wild Women connecting with each Other and ourSelves? AND WE

DO KNOW THAT FURIOUS FEMALE BONDING COULD OBLITERATE PATRIARCHY ITSELF, DON'T WE?

SO LET'S DO IT!

I leave it to the Courageous reader to answer these questions, trusting that the morphic resonance of our Foresisters of the Past will carry her through the maze of lies, distortions, and silences of the foreground now and into a truly Archaic Present and Future.

# NOTES

## PREFACE

1 See chapter 39 for Daly's telling of this story.

## INTRODUCTION

1 See epigraph for chapter 33 of this collection, from *Wickedary*, pp. 87–88.
2 See chapter 6 of this collection, from *Beyond God the Father.*
3 See chapter 27 of this collection, from *Pure Lust.*
4 See chapters 6 and 7 of this collection, from *Beyond God the Father.*
5 See chapter 28 of this collection, from *Pure Lust.*
6 See chapter 28 of this collection, from *Pure Lust.*
7 See chapter 22 of this collection, from *Pure Lust.*
8 See chapter 14 of this collection, from *Gyn/Ecology.*
9 See chapter 19 in this collection, from *Gyn/Ecology.*
10 Mary Daly, *Beyond God the Father* (Boston: Beacon, 1973), p. xii.
11 This quote is from Daniel Berrigan's poem "The Verdict," in *The Trial of the Catonsville Nine*, by Daniel Berrigan, Robin Andersen, and James L. Marsh (New York: Fordham University Press, 2004).
12 See chapter 6 of this collection, from *Beyond God the Father.*
13 See chapter 6 of this collection, from *Beyond God the Father.*

## PART I. WINDS OF CHANGE (TO 1971)

1 Mary Daly, *Outercourse: The Bedazzling Voyage, Containing Recollections from My Logbook of a Radical Feminist Philosopher* (San Francisco: HarperSanFrancisco, 1992), pp. 78–79; see chapter 35 in this collection.

## CHAPTER 2. CHRISTIAN HISTORY

1 Mary Daly, "The Problem of Speculative Theology," *Thomist* 29 (1965): 177–216.
2 Origen, *In Lucam homilia* VIII (*Patrologia Graeca* 13, 1819 C).
3 Augustine, *De fide et symbolo*, 4 (*Patrologia Latina* 40, 186).
4 Augustine, *Sermo* 232, 2 (*PL* 37, 1108).
5 Jerome, *Comm. in epist. ad Ephes.*, III, 5 (*PL* 26, 536).
6 Peter the Lombard, *Collectanea in epist. D. Pauli in epist. ad Cor.*, cap. XI, 8–10 (*PL* 191, 1633).
7 Thomas Aquinas, *Summa Theologiae*, I, 92, 1, ad 1. Albert the Great also wrote that woman is misbegotten: in II P. *Sum Theol.* (Borgnet), tract. 13, q. 80, membrum 1.

8 *Summa Theologiae*, I, 92, 1 c.
9 *Ibid.*, II-II, 26, 10 c.
10 *Ibid.*, II-II, 26, 10, ad 1.
11 *Ibid.*, Suppl., 64, 3 c.
12 *Ibid.*, Suppl., 39, 1 c.
13 *Ibid.*, I, 92, 1, ad 2.
14 *Ibid.*, I, 92, 1 c.
15 [Editors' note: "Bi-sexuality" here means that there are two genders in the human species. It is not here defining a type of sexual orientation, as in twenty-first-century common usage.]
16 Thomas Aquinas, *Summa Theologiae*, I, 93, 4, ad 1.
17 *Ibid.*, I, 93, 6 c.
18 [Editors' note: Thomistic theology had been given pride of place in twentieth-century Catholic thought, particularly by Pius X and Vatican II. One of Daly's favorite thinkers, Jacques Maritain, was a prominent neo-Thomist.]

## CHAPTER 3. THE PEDESTAL PEDDLARS

1 F. X. Arnold, *Woman and Man: Their Nature and Mission* (Freiburg: Herder, 1963), p. 148.
2 Very Rev. James Alberione, S. S. P., S.T.D., *Woman: Her Influence and Zeal as an Aid to the Priesthood,* translated by the Daughters of St. Paul (Boston: St. Paul Editions, 1964), p. 40.
3 André A. Devaux, "Le féminin selon Teilhard de Chardin," *Recherches et débats* (Paris: Librairie Arthème Fayard), cahier n. 45, décembre, 1963, p. 134.
4 J. Galot, S.J., *L'église et la femme* (Gembloux: J. Duculot, 1965), p. 6.
5 *Ibid.*, p. 57.
6 *Ibid.*
7 *Ibid.*, p. 200.
8 *Ibid.*, p. 79.

## PART II. FROM GOD TO BE-ING (1972–1974)

1 Mary Daly, "Autobiographical Preface to the Colophon Edition," in *The Church and the Second Sex: With a New Feminist Postchristian Introduction by the Author* (New York: Harper Colophon, 1975), p. 11.
2 In the kind of synchronicity that would have pleased Daly herself, two major studies of these incidents were issued in 1973, soon after the Harvard Memorial walkout. Richard Allen and Absalom Jones, free Blacks living in Philadelphia in the years after the American Revolution, walked out of the parish to which they belonged, St. George's Methodist Church, to protest racism and segregation in the congregation. This 1787 protest eventually led to the establishment of the African Methodist Episcopal (AME) denomination by Richard Allen. See Carol V. R. George, *Segregated Sabbaths: Richard Allen and the Emergence of Independent Black Churches, 1780–1840* (New York: Oxford University Press, 1973); the

Abolitionist "Come-outer" movement staged protests that challenged ministers, then walked out of churches where the clergy would not take a strong public anti-slavery position. One of the key leaders of that movement was the fiery feminist Abby Kelly Foster. See Lewis Perry, *Radical Abolitionism: Anarchy and the Government of God in Antislavery Thought* (Ithaca: Cornell University Press, 1973), pp. 92–128. In an interesting moment in the Spiritualist movement of the mid-nineteenth century that helped liberate women's spiritual energy from institutional religions, one noted medium had a spirit-induced vision that may have predicted the Harvard Memorial walkout:

> Lizzie Doten thought the [lecture] platform superior to the pulpit not only because it admitted women but also because it was a better vehicle for spiritual enlightenment. In a trance lecture on the biblical text "It is a shame for women to speak in the church," Doten exclaimed, "It is indeed a shame for woman to speak in the *Church;* and woman ought to be ashamed . . . of the church. Let woman come out from the church; and, when she comes out, the minister and all the congregation will go out with her."

*Banner of Light*, February 11, 1860, p. 5, cited in Anne Braude, *Radical Spirits: Spiritualism and Women's Rights in Nineteenth-Century America* (Boston: Beacon, 1989), p. 5.

## CHAPTER 6. THE PROBLEM, THE PURPOSE, THE METHOD

1 Gerald D. Berreman, "Caste in India and the United States," *American Journal of Sociology*, LXVI (1960–61), pp. 120–27. In the same volume see Berreman's "Rejoinder," pp. 511–12. See also Helen Mayer Hacker, "Women as a Minority Group," *Social Forces*, XXX (1951–52), pp. 60–69.

2 See Gordon Zahn, Letter to the Editor, *Commonweal*, XCV (February 18, 1972), pp. 470–71. Professor Zahn strongly objects to my use of the term "caste" as inaccurate for describing the male-female situation, and yet in the same paragraph refers to legalized abortion as "oppression" of "a human being."

3 Jo Freeman, "The Legal Basis of the Sexual Caste System," *Valparaiso University Law Review*, V (Symposium Issue, 1971), pp. 203–36.

4 See Robin Scroggs, "Paul and the Eschatological Woman," *Journal of the American Academy of Religion*, XL (September 1972), pp. 283–303. A shorter and more popularized version of the article is "Paul: Chauvinist or Liberationist?" in *The Christian Century*, LXXXIX (March 15, 1972), pp. 307–09. Although Prof. Scroggs' articles are sensitive attempts to distinguish Paul's own views from the pseudo-epigraphical works attributed to him, I do not think that they confront the issues raised by the women's movement.

5 Karl Barth is of course well known for this approach to theology, which implicitly holds as sacred the presuppositions of patriarchy.

6 Male authors who are now claiming that they can write accurately "about women" give away the level of their comprehension by the use of this expression. The new consciousness of women is not mere "knowledge about," but an emotional-

intellectual-volitional rebirth. An example of inauthentic male claims is Donald McDonald, "The Liberation of Women," *The Center Magazine,* V (May-June 1972), pp. 25–42.

7 Paul Tillich's method is one of correlation. Although I find it less inadequate than the methods of other systematic theologians of this century, it clearly does not offer the radical critique of patriarchal religion that can only come from women, the primordial outsiders.

8 See Josiah Royce, *The World and the Individual,* 2 vols. (New York: Macmillan, 1900–1901).

9 See Paulo Freire, *Pedagogy of the Oppressed* (New York: Herder and Herder, 1970). Freire wrote acutely on the namelessness of the oppressed without even acknowledging in this book the prototypic namelessness of women.

10 Nelle Morton gives a profound and moving analysis of this in her article "The Rising Woman Consciousness in a Male Language Structure," *Andover Newtown Quarterly* 12: 177–90 (March 1972). [Editors' note: Virginia Woolf also uses this phrase; "New Words" was the name of the feminist bookstore in Boston co-founded by Daly's friend and student Jean MacRae.]

11 This is the sense in which "exodus" was applied to the walkout from Harvard Memorial Church called for in my sermon of November 14, 1971. See my article, "The Women's Movement: An Exodus Community," which contains the sermon and some letters from women who participated in the event, reflecting upon its meaning for them. [Editors' note: See chapter 5 in this book.]

12 The Harvard Exodus and its continuing aftermath exemplify the process. So also did the takeover by women students of a Harvard Divinity School course which supposedly dealt with liberation but failed to take into account women's liberation. See *Newsweek,* December 6, 1971, p. 58. The slick article, called "Pronoun Envy," distorts and trivializes, of course.

13 Women who were present at the seven days of exploring theology at Grailville, Loveland, Ohio (June 18–25) describe the experience somewhat in these terms. A packet of stimulating articles, "Women Exploring Theology at Grailville," is available from Church Women United, 475 Riverside Drive, Suite 243, New York, N.Y. 10027. [Editors' note: This organization is still in operation, with this same address. Its website can be found at www.churchwomen.org.]

14 Susanne Langer, *Philosophy in a New Key* (New York: New American Library, 1951), p. 19.

CHAPTER 7. AFTER THE DEATH OF GOD THE FATHER

1 [Editors' note: The distance between the time when Daly wrote this and the present can be gauged in part by the increase in the number of women in high positions. But whether or not these women are still "tokens" bespeaks a larger question.]

2 Alice Rossi, "Sex Equality: The Beginning of Ideology," *Masculine/Feminine,* edited by Betty Roszak and Theodore Roszak (New York: Harper and Row, 1969), pp. 173–86. Rossi points out some inadequacies of assimilation into male models.

3 See Jean Piaget, *Structuralism* (New York: Basic Books, Inc., 1970).

4 Arnold Toynbee, *Christianity among the Religions of the World* (New York: Charles Scribner's Sons, 1957), p. 19.

5 See Robert N. Bellah, "Civil Religion in America," *Daedalus,* XCVI (Winter 1967), pp. 1–21. Bellah points out that the inauguration of a president is an important ceremonial event in American civil religion. It involves religious legitimation of the highest political authority. At Nixon's inauguration in 1973, Cardinal Cooke of New York was reported to have used the expression "heavenly Father" approximately seven times (conversation with Janice Raymond, who counted, January 20, 1973).

6 Rabbi Louis Finkelstein, in *White House Sermons,* edited by Ben Hibbs (New York: Harper and Row, 1972), p. 68. This sermon was delivered June 29, 1969. Similar sentiments have been expressed by the Rev. John McLaughlin, S.J., "the Catholic Billy Graham." See *National Catholic Reporter,* October 6, 1972, p. 9.

7 Charles Henderson, *The Nixon Theology* (New York: Harper and Row, 1972). See also Henderson's article "The (Social) Gospel according to 1) Richard Nixon 2) George McGovern," *Commonweal,* XCVI (September 29, 1972), pp. 518–25.

8 Dr. Paul S. Smith, in *White House Sermons,* pp. 82–83.

9 Cited in Henderson, *The Nixon Theology,* p. 175.

10 *Ibid.*, p. 176.

11 This is exemplified in a statement of John L. McKenzie, S.J., in *The Two Edged Sword* (New York: Bruce, 1956), pp. 93–94: "God is of course masculine, but not in the sense of sexual distinction. . . ."

12 See Mary Baker Eddy, *Science and Health* (Boston: Published by the Trustees under the Will of Mary Baker G. Eddy, 1934). Eddy wrote what she believed to be the "spiritual sense" of "The Lord's Prayer." It begins: "Our Father-Mother God, all-harmonious . . ." (p. 16). In the same work she uses the image of God's motherhood a number of times. Ann Lee's ideas have been studied by sociologist Henri Desroches. See, for example, *The American Shakers: From Neo-Christianity to Presocialism,* translated and edited by John K. Savacool (Amherst: University of Massachusetts Press, 1971).

13 See Karl Barth, *Church Dogmatics,* edited by G. W. Bromiley and T. F. Torrance (Edinburgh: T. & C. Clark, 1956–1962), III/4, pp. 116–240. Barth goes on and on about woman's subordination to man, ordained by God. Although he goes through a quasi-infinite number of qualifications, using such jargon as "mutual subordination," he warns that we must not overlook the "concrete subordination of woman to man" (p. 175). He writes: "Properly speaking, the business of woman, her task and function, is to actualize the fellowship in which man can only precede her, stimulating, leading, and inspiring. . . . To wish to replace him in this, or to do it with him, would be to wish not to be a woman." In case the point is not clear, he adds the rhetorical question: "What other choice has she [than to be second] seeing she can be nothing at all apart from this sequence and her place within it?" (p. 171). This is justified as being the divine order, according to Barth. See also Dietrich Bonhoeffer, *Letters and Papers from Prison,* edited by Eberhard

Bethge, translated by Reginald H. Fuller (New York: Macmillan Paperback, 1966), p. 47: "You may order your home as you like, save in one particular: the woman must be subject to her husband, and the husband must love his wife." See also Reinhold Niebuhr, *The Nature and Destiny of Man: A Christian Interpretation,* Vol. 1 (New York: Charles Scribner's Sons, 1941), p. 282. Niebuhr writes: "A rationalistic feminism is undoubtedly inclined to transgress inexorable bounds set by nature. On the other hand, any premature fixation of certain historical standards in regard to the family will inevitably tend to reinforce male arrogance and to retard *justified efforts* [italics mine] on the part of the female to achieve such freedom as is not incompatible with the *primary function of motherhood* [italics mine]." As for Teilhard de Chardin, his writings are replete with spiritualized androcentrism. For examples, see Henri de Lubac, S.J., *The Eternal Feminine: A Study on the Text of Teilhard de Chardin,* translated by René Hague (New York: Harper and Row, 1971). The sexism is of course unrecognized by de Lubac. See also André A. Devaux, *Teilhard et la vocation de la femme* (Paris: Editions universitaires, 1963).

14 Gregory Baum, *Man Becoming* (New York: Herder and Herder, 1970), p. 195.

15 I would agree with Gordon Kaufman that Tillich himself does not completely escape hypostatization in his God language. The "Unconditioned" and the "Ground" are almost reified. See Gordon D. Kaufman, "On the Meaning of 'God,'" in *Transcendence,* edited by Herbert W. Richardson and Donald R. Cutler (Boston: Beacon Press, 1969), pp. 114–42.

16 Paul Tillich, *The Courage to Be* (New Haven: Yale University Press, 1952), pp. 32–63. See also Michael Novak, *The Experience of Nothingness* (New York: Harper and Row, 1970).

17 [Editors' note: We believe this to be the first use of the term "feminist revolution" in the published works of Mary Daly.]

18 See Richardson's essay "Three Myths of Transcendence," in *Transcendence,* edited by Richardson and Cutler, pp. 98–113. Richardson is more explicit on the problem of sex roles in his recent book *Nun, Witch, Playmate* (New York: Harper and Row, 1971).

19 See James Cone, *A Black Theology of Liberation* (Philadelphia: Lippincott, 1970).

20 [Editors' note: Daly rejected the word "androgynous" in her work quite soon after this; see chapter 13 of this volume, "Preface to *Gyn/Ecology.*" The full rationale of this rejection is in an article Daly wrote between the publication of *Beyond God the Father* and the publication of *Gyn/Ecology* for a collection of essays in response to the process theologian John Cobb. Daly's entry, "The Courage to Leave," not only discusses this shift, but also reveals her connections to Whiteheadean process thought. See "The Courage to Leave: A Response to John Cobb," in *John Cobb's Theology in Process*, ed. D. R. Griffin and T. J. J. Altizer (Philadelphia: Westminster, 1977), pp. 84–98.]

21 Enlightening on this point of positive ontological experiences is the work of Abraham H. Maslow, *Toward a Psychology of Being* (Princeton, New Jersey: Van Nostrand, 1962).

22 This was illustrated a few years ago in Michael Novak's book, *The Experience of Nothingness.* In various ways it has been expressed in writings and music of the counterculture.

23 This problem is acute in the work of Wolfhart Pannenberg. See, for example, his *Theology and the Kingdom of God* (Philadelphia: The Westminster Press, 1969). It is evident also in Jürgen Moltmann, *Theology of Hope,* translated by James W. Leitch (New York: Harper and Row, 1967). These theologians, of course, handle philosophical questions in a sophisticated and knowledgeable fashion, but the perspective is so biblical that it alienates "nonbelievers."

24 Unfortunately, in the Christian theological tradition this "image" was recognized as existing unambiguously only in the male. While Augustine saw the male as being to the image of God, he conceded that woman is restored to the image only where there is no sex, that is, in the spirit (*De Trinitate,* XII, 7). Aquinas was a little more generous, granting that the image of God is in both man and woman, but adding that in a special sense it is only in the male, who is "the beginning and end of woman, as God is the beginning and end of every creature" (*Summa theologiae* I, 93, 4 ad 1).

25 Bonhoeffer, *Letters and Papers from Prison,* p. 190.

26 Peter Berger, *The Sacred Canopy: Elements of a Sociological Theory of Religion* (New York: Doubleday, 1967), pp. 53–80. Berger, however, does not recognize implications of this from the standpoint of radical feminism.

27 Peter Berger, *A Rumor of Angels: Modern Society and the Rediscovery of the Supernatural* (New York: Doubleday-Anchor Books, 1970), p. 12. Unfortunately, however, Berger goes rather far in "liquidating" the work of theologians whose views are less orthodox than his own.

28 Max Weber, *The Sociology of Religion,* translated by Ephraim Fischoff (Boston: Beacon Press, 1963), p. 198.

29 *Ibid.*, pp. 198–99.

30 Johannes Metz, "Creative Hope," *New Theology No. 5,* edited by Martin E. Marty and Dean G. Peerman (New York: Macmillan, 1968), pp. 130–41. See also Metz, *Theology of the World,* translated by William Glen-Doepel (New York: Herder and Herder, 1969).

31 Jacques Maritain, *Existence and the Existent,* translated by Lewis Galantiere and Gerald B. Phelan (New York: Doubleday-Image Books, 1956). Although he was hardly a feminist or social revolutionary, Maritain had an exceedingly fine sensitivity to the power of this intuition, which, if it were carried through to social consciousness, would challenge the world. See also *Distinguish to Unite: The Degrees of Knowledge,* translated from the fourth French edition under the supervision of G. B. Phelan (New York: Charles Scribner's Sons, 1959).

32 Paul Tillich, *Systematic Theology,* 3 vols. (Chicago: University of Chicago Press, 1951), v. I, p. 74: "Whenever technical reason dominates, religion is superstition and is either foolishly supported by reason or rightly removed by it."

33 Maritain, in *Existence and the Existent*, p. 76, remarks: "When a man [*sic*] is awake to the intuition of being he is awake at the same time to the intuition of subjectiv-

ity. . . . The force of such a perception may be so great as to sweep him [*sic*] along to that heroic asceticism of the void and of annihilation in which he will achieve ecstasy in the substantial existence of the *self* and the 'presence of immensity' of the divine Self at one and the same time. . . ."

34 Max Weber, in *The Sociology of Religion,* p. 25, points out that "a power conceived by analogy to living persons may be coerced into the service of man." This means that whoever has the requisite charisma "is stronger even than the god." He also indicates that such a god can be conveniently blamed when things go wrong (p. 32).

35 Conversations with Linda Barufaldi, Boston, August 1972. Buckminster Fuller has referred to God as a verb.

36 It is clear that from such an experiential context there is not likely to come much rapport with language about God as "ultimate Limit" or Limiter.

37 Some of Sartre's thinking consequent to this rejection is in Jean-Paul Sartre, *Being and Nothingness: An Essay on Phenomenological Ontology,* translated by Hazel E. Barnes (New York: Philosophical Library, 1956).

38 Karl Jaspers and Rudolf Bultmann, *Myth and Christianity* (New York: Noonday Press, 1958), p. 14.

39 Metz, *Theology of the World*, p. 104.

40 See Mircea Eliade, *Patterns in Comparative Religion*, translated by Rosemary Sheed (New York: Sheed and Ward, 1958). See Jay J. Kim, "Hierophany and History," *Journal of the American Academy of Religion*, September 1972, pp. 334–48.

41 Tillich, *Systematic Theology*, v. III, p. 310.

42 *Ibid.*, pp. 309–10.

43 *Ibid.*, pp. 308–9.

44 The *National Organization for Women,* the *Women's Equity Action League,* and the *Saint Joan's International Alliance* (Catholic feminists) are organizations with dues-paying members. While these have important functions, the movement as I use the term is not reducible to membership in these organizations. It is far more widespread, complex, and immeasurable than the concept of organizational membership can encompass.

45 Janice Raymond, "Beyond Male Morality," a paper delivered at the International Congress of Learned Societies in the Field of Religion, Los Angeles, September 1–5, 1972. Published by the American Academy of Religion (University of Montana) in *Proceedings of the Working Group on Women and Religion, 1972,* edited by Judith Plaskow Goldenberg, pp. 83–93.

46 Leslie Dewart made the point that relative atheism is probably more indicative of an open consciousness than absolute theism. See *The Future of Belief* (New York: Herder and Herder, 1966), pp. 52–76.

47 Roger Garoudy, *From Anathema to Dialogue,* translated by L. O'Neill (New York: Herder and Herder, 1966), p. 94.

48 See William James, *The Will to Believe* (New York: Dover Publications reprint, 1956). See also *A Pluralistic Universe* (New York: Longmans Green, 1909).

49 See Alfred North Whitehead, *Process and Reality* (New York: Macmillan, 1929).
50 Well-known sources for these are treatises attributed to Denis the Areopagite, including *On the Divine Names* (*De divinis nominibus*) and a short treatise *On Mystical Theology* (*De mystica theologia*). Thomas Aquinas used the "three ways" for deriving the divine attributes in his *Summa theologiae*.
51 See Huston Smith, "The Reach and the Grasp: Transcendence Today," in *Transcendence*, edited by Richardson and Cutler, pp. 1–17.
52 See for example Thomas Aquinas, *Summa theologiae*, I, q. 6.
53 For a brief discussion of this see Etienne Gilson, *History of Christian Philosophy in the Middle Ages* (New York: Random House, 1955), pp. 368–72. See also Maritain, *Distinguish to Unite: The Degrees of Knowledge*.
54 Thomas Aquinas, *Summa theologiae*, I, 13, 2.
55 Martin Buber, *I and Thou*, translated by Ronald Gregor Smith (New York: Charles Scribner's Sons, 1958), p. 6.
56 Tillich, *Systematic Theology* I, especially pp. 71–81.
57 [Editors' note: It is another sign of the distance between the early 1970s and the present that women's studies programs are not faring as well as Daly here reports.]
58 Conversation with Emily Culpepper, Boston, November 1972.
59 *Ibid.*
60 [Editors' note: The necessary rage to continue can also be heard in Daly's phrase "rage is not 'a stage,'" found in chapter 31 of this collection.]

## CHAPTER 8. BEYOND GOOD AND EVIL

1 Albert Camus, *The Rebel*, translated by Anthony Bower (New York: Alfred Knopf, 1957), p. 4.
2 [Editors' note: See Daly's later reconsideration of "sin" in its etymological roots, in the excerpt from *Pure Lust* in chapter 26 of this compilation.]
3 Mircea Eliade, *The Sacred and the Profane: The Nature of Religion*, translated by William R. Trask (New York: Harper and Row, 1961), p. 213.
4 Felix Morrow, Foreword, in Montague Summers, *The History of Witchcraft and Demonology* (Secaucus, New Jersey: Citadel Press, 1971 [©1956, University Books]), p. xiii. Summers, a Catholic priest, was totally convinced that the church was justified in its means of persecuting witches. It is fascinating to read the dedication of his book, indicating an extraordinary devotion to the Blessed Virgin Mary. Summers in his studies of witches, of the tortures to which those accused of practicing witchcraft were subjected, apparently found nothing disconcerting about the church's inhumanity to concrete, existing women.

## CHAPTER 9. THE SECOND COMING OF WOMEN AND THE ANTICHRIST

1 See Simone de Beauvoir, *The Second Sex*, trans. and ed. by H. M. Parshley (New York: Vintage, 1974); Elizabeth Gould Davis, *The First Sex* (New York: G. P. Putnam's Sons, 1971); Daly, *The Church and the Second Sex*.

2 Jules Michelet, *Satanism and Witchcraft*, trans. by A. R. Allinson (New York: The Citadel Press, 1939), p. x.

### CHAPTER 10. THE BONDS OF FREEDOM

1 [Editors' note: The 1972 election's use of religious rhetoric seems quite tame by comparison to later, religious-right-inflected/infected campaigns. A brief analysis can be found in Brian T. Kaylor, *Presidential Campaign Rhetoric in an Age of Confessional Politics* (Lanham, MD: Lexington, 2011), pp. 25–26.]

2 Ernst Troeltsch, *The Social Teaching of the Christian Churches,* translated by Olive Wyon (2 vols.; New York: Harper and Row, 1960), I, p. 338.

3 *Ibid.*

4 *Ibid.*, p. 287.

5 See the works of Simone de Beauvoir, Kate Millett, *Sexual Politics* (Garden City, N.Y.: Doubleday, 1970), and Davis, *The First Sex.*

6 Emile Durkheim, *The Elementary Forms of Religious Life*, translated by Joseph Ward Swain (New York: The Free Press, 1965), p. 101.

7 *Ibid.*

8 Berger, *The Sacred Canopy*, p. 27.

9 Robin Morgan, *Monster* (New York: Vintage Books, 1972), p. 85.

10 Berger, *The Sacred Canopy*, p. 27.

11 Mircea Eliade, *Cosmos and History: The Myth of Eternal Return*, translated by Willard R. Trask (New York: Harper and Row, 1959), especially pp. 141–62. See also Eliade, *The Sacred and the Profane.*

12 Berger, *The Sacred Canopy*, p. 40.

13 Friedrich Nietzsche, *The Birth of Tragedy and the Genealogy of Morals,* translated by Francis Golffing (New York: Doubleday, 1956), pp. 192–93.

14 See Gordon Zahn, *Chaplains in the R.A.F.: A Study in Role Tension* (Manchester, England: Manchester University Press, 1969).

15 Morgan, *Monster,* p. 84.

16 Marcuse, *One-Dimensional Man* (Boston: Beacon Press, 1964), p. 7.

17 *Ibid.*, p. 5.

18 *Ibid.*, p. 4.

19 Linda L. Barufaldi, Letter in *Religious Education* LXVII (September–October 1972), p. 334.

20 Mary Rodda, Letter in *Religious Education* LXVII (September–October 1972), p. 335.

21 Emily Culpepper, "Something of, by, and for Women" (unpublished paper delivered at Boston College, February 9, 1972).

22 Susanne Langer wrote of "generative ideas," *Philosophy in a New Key*, p. 19.

23 Maslow, *Toward a Psychology of Being*, p. 136.

24 *Ibid.*, p. 148.

25 *Ibid.*, p. 132.

### CHAPTER 11. ANTICHURCH AND THE SOUNDS OF SILENCE

1 Durkheim, *The Elementary Forms of Religious Life*, p. 437.

2 [Editors' note: For research on Australian Aboriginal women, which largely confirms Daly's hunch here, see Diane Bell, *Daughters of the Dreaming* (Melbourne: McPhee Gribble; Sydney: Allen and Unwin, 1983).]

3 Morgan, *Monster*, p. 85.

4 Langer, *Philosophy in a New Key*.

### CHAPTER 12. THE FINAL CAUSE, THE FUTURE, AND THE END OF THE LOOKING GLASS WAR

1 Conversation with Linda Barufaldi, Boston, December 1972.

2 See Aristotle, *Physics* II, 7; *Metaphysics* I. For a medieval exposition and commentary on these texts, see Thomas Aquinas, *In Octo Libros Physicorum Aristotelis Expositio* (Rome: Marietti, 1954), and *In Duodecem Libros Metaphysicorum Aristotelis Expositio* (Rome: Marietti, 1950).

3 This identification is clear in the medieval synthesis of Aquinas. See his *Summa theologiae*, I, q. 5, a.1: "Hence it is clear that goodness and being are the same really. But goodness presents the aspect of desirableness, which being does not present."

4 *Ibid.*, I, q. 45, a.1 and 2.

5 *Ibid.*, q. 9, a.1; q. 44, a.4. For Aquinas God is an agent who is in no way a patient. That is, God does not act to acquire anything but to communicate the divine goodness, which is the final cause of all things.

6 Pannenberg, *Theology and the Kingdom of God*, pp. 134–35.

7 *Ibid.*, p. 142.

8 [Editors' note: Extreme Unction was rebranded as "Last Rites" by the Catholic Church in 1972.]

### CHAPTER 13. PREFACE TO *GYN/ECOLOGY*

1 See Mary Daly, *Beyond God the Father: Toward a Philosophy of Women's Liberation* (Boston: Beacon Press, 1973).

2 See Daly, *The Church and the Second Sex*, 1975.

3 Daly, *Beyond God the Father*, pp. 41–42. [Editors' note: See chapter 7 in this volume.]

4 Marilyn Frye, "Some Reflections on Separatism and Power," *Sinister Wisdom* 6 (Summer 1978).

5 *Sinister Wisdom* is available at feminist bookstores, and by writing to P.O. Box 30541, Lincoln, Neb. 68503 [Editors' note: This information is no longer accurate, but *Sinister Wisdom* is still publishing; check its website at www.sinisterwisdom.org.]

6 See Simone de Beauvoir, *The Ethics of Ambiguity*, trans. by Bernard Frechtman (Secaucus, N.J.: The Citadel Press, 1972), pp. 82–83. She points out that "if all it [life] does is maintain itself, then living is only not dying."

7 Virginia Woolf writes of the delight and rapture she experienced in putting the severed parts together. See her *Moments of Being: Unpublished Autobiographical Writings*, ed. by Jeanne Schulkind (New York: Harcourt Brace Jovanovich, 1976), p. 72. I owe the idea of "threads of connectedness" to Fran Chelland, who has developed many threads in her thinking and writing, particularly in an unpublished paper entitled "Mind over/versus Matter: The Spiritual Reversal."

8 There are continuing efforts by academic bureaucrats to reduce Women's Studies to "basket weaving," through the usual devices of tokenism, legal intimidation (e.g. accusations of "reverse discrimination"), economic sanctions, psychological harassment of women who are "too extreme."

9 WARNING: This book contains Big Words, even Bigger than *Beyond God the Father*, for it is written for big, strong women, out of respect for strength. Moreover, I've made some of them up. Therefore, it may be a stumbling block both to those who choose downward mobility of the mind and therefore hate Big Words, and to those who choose upward mobility and therefore hate New/Old Words, that is, Old words that be-come New when their ancient ("obsolete") gynocentric meanings are unearthed. Hopefully, it will be a useful pathfinder for the *multiply mobile*: the movers, the weavers, the Spinners. [Editors' note: Originally a footnote, p. xiv.]

10 Since the number of feminist journals can hardly begin to be adequate as outlets for the flood of creativity, feminists—Lesbian feminists in particular—are devising alternative methods of distributing and sharing our works. One such enterprise is *Matrices: A Lesbian/Feminist Research Newsletter.* Subscriptions to *Matrices* are available by writing to: Julia P. Stanley, Department of English, University of Nebraska-Lincoln, Lincoln, Nebraska 68588. A number of valuable articles and papers by subscribers are available for subscribers.

11 Virginia Woolf, *Three Guineas* (New York: Harcourt, Brace & World, Inc., 1938; Harbinger Books, 1966), p. 80.

12 See Veronica Geng, "Requiem for the Women's Movement," *Harper's*, November 1976, pp. 49–56, 61–68. Geng's article is deceptive because full of partial truths based on "inside" knowledge. It served the patriarchs of publishing well, being a sophisticated pronouncement by a woman that "the women's movement" is dead. When and if they choose to resurrect this "movement," Journeyers will be aware that such re-births have no more reality than such deaths.

## CHAPTER 14. THE METAPATRIARCHAL JOURNEY OF EXORCISM AND ECSTASY

1 See Morton W. Bloomfield, *The Seven Deadly Sins: An Introduction to the History of a Religious Concept, with Special Reference to Medieval English Literature* (East Lansing: Michigan State University Press, 1967), especially pp. 7–27. Bloomfield discusses the tradition of the Otherworld Journey in connection with the Deadly Sins. On p. 12 he writes: "The Sins are a by-product of an eschatological belief which has been called the Soul Drama or Soul Journey. . . . The seven cardinal sins are the remnant of some Gnostic Soul Journey which existed probably in Egypt or

Syria in the early Christian centuries. But the Soul Journey is itself part of a much vaster eschatological conception, the Otherworld Journey. . . ."

2 This listing became common in catholic doctrine. The number seven came to be favored for the cardinal sins, although there have been many different lists of the sins. See Bloomfield, *The Seven Deadly Sins.*

3 See Dolores Bargowski, "Moving Media: The Exorcist," *Quest: A Feminist Quarterly,* Vol. 1, No. 1 (Summer 1974), pp. 53–57.

4 Conversation, Boston, October 1976.

5 See Mary Daly, "The Qualitative Leap Beyond Patriarchal Religion," *Quest: A Feminist Quarterly,* Vol. 1, No. 4 (Spring 1975), pp. 20–40.

6 Françoise d'Eaubonne uses the term *phallocratisme* in her book, *La Féminisme ou la mort* (Paris: Pierre Horay, 1974), especially pp. 113–24.

7 We should not forget that countless women's lives have been consumed in the sweatshops of textile manufacturers and garment makers as well as in the everyday tedium of sewing, mending, laundering, and ironing. [Editors' note: Originally a footnote, p. 5.]

8 Conversation, Boston, September 1976.

9 Adrienne Rich, *Of Woman Born: Motherhood as Experience and Institution* (New York: W. W. Norton, 1976), p. 95.

10 See Daly, "The Qualitative Leap."

11 [Editors' note: Daly's evocation of Plato's cave is unexpected from this determined Thomistic Aristotelean!]

12 See Daly, *Beyond God the Father: Toward a Philosophy of Women's Liberation*, passim.

13 D'Eaubonne, *Le Féminisme*, pp. 213–52.

14 Rich, *Of Woman Born*, p. 153.

15 The technical term *iatrogenic*, used to describe the epidemic of doctor-made disease, is composed of the Greek words for physician (*iatros*) and for origins (*genesis*). [Editors' note: Originally a footnote, p. 10.]

16 Clearly, some women sometimes are helped through emergency situations by priests, ministers, gynecologists, therapists—but this is largely in spite of their institutions/professions within which they work. A great deal of the work of such exceptional professionals consists in repairing damages caused by their colleagues and by the methods of their professions. One serious liability associated with their ministrations is the conditioning of women to depend upon them rather than upon our own natural resources. It should not be necessary to repeat this distinction throughout this book, which criticizes patriarchal institutions and those who conform to them. [Editors' note: Originally a footnote, p. 10.]

17 By *biophilic* I mean life-loving. This term is not in the dictionary, although the term *necrophilic* is there, and is commonly used. [Editors' note: Originally a footnote, p. 10.]

18 See Monique Wittig, *Les Guérillères*, trans. David Le Vay (New York: Viking Press, 1971).

19 Conversation, Boston, December 1975.

20 See Adrienne Rich, "Women and Honor: Some Notes on Lying," *Heresies: A Feminist Publication on Art and Politics*, No. 1 (January 1977), pp. 23–26; reprinted by Motheroot Publications/Pittsburgh Women Writers.

21 Barbara Starrett, "I Dream in Female: The Metaphors of Evolution," *Amazon Quarterly*, Vol. 3, No. 1 (November 1974), pp. 13–27.

22 Emily Culpepper, "Female History/Myth Making," *The Second Wave*, Vol. 4, No. 1 (Spring 1975), pp. 14–17.

23 See Harold H. Titus and Morris Keaton, *Ethics for Today* (New York: D. Van Nostrand, 1973), p. 366.

24 See Robert Graves, *The Greek Myths* (Baltimore, Md.: Penguin Books, 1975). I, 9. *d, 9.1.* See also Jane Harrison, *Prolegomena to the Study of Greek Religion*, 3rd ed. (Cleveland and New York: World Publishing Company, 1966), pp. 302–3.

25 Catherine Nicholson, "How Rage Mothered My Third Birth," *Sinister Wisdom*, Vol. 1, No. 1 (July 1976), pp. 40–45.

26 Contemporary christian "theologians of hope," such as Jürgen Moltmann, have attempted to apply the idea of "call to an open future" to the judeo-christian god. The results are incongruous and unconvincing. See Moltmann, *Theology of Hope: On the Ground and Implications of Christian Eschatology.*

27 *Nightmare* is said to be derived from the Middle English terms *night* plus *mare*, meaning spirit. The first definition given in Merriam-Webster is "an evil spirit formerly thought to oppress people during sleep." Another definition is "a hag sometimes believed to be accompanied by nine attendant spirits." For Hags this should be a friendly gathering.

28 Crones can well be suspicious of dictionaries which, in listing possible etymologies for *crone*, suggest that it is derived from a term meaning carrion. The *Oxford English Dictionary* discusses this possibility, but also suggests that *crone* is probably from *carogne*, meaning "a cantankerous or mischievous woman." This meaning seems somewhat appropriate. It is noteworthy that Merriam-Webster gives as the etymology of *crony* the Greek *chronios*, meaning long-lasting, which in turn is from *chronos*, meaning time. It would seem eminently logical to think that *crone* is rooted in the word for "long-lasting," for this is what Crones are. [Editors' note: What follows was originally a footnote, p. 16.] The status of Crones is not determined merely by chronological age, but by Crone-logical considerations. A woman becomes a Crone as a result of Surviving early stages of the Otherworld Journey and therefore having dis-covered depths of courage, strength, and wisdom in her Self.

29 *The Burning Times* is a Crone-logical term which refers not only to the period of the European witchcraze (the fifteenth, sixteenth, and seventeenth centuries) but to the perpetual witchcraze which is the entire period of patriarchal rule. [Editors' note: Originally a footnote, p. 16.]

30 Conversation with Denise Connors, Watertown, Mass., November 1976.

31 Julia P. Stanley and Susan W. Robbins, "Going through the Changes: The Pronoun *She* in Middle English," *Papers in Linguistics*, Vol. 9, Nos. 3–4 (Fall 1977).

32 Monique Wittig, *The Lesbian Body*, trans. by David Le Vay (New York: William Morrow, 1975); author's note, pp. 10–11.

33 Rich, *Of Woman Born*, pp. 235–37.

34 [Editors' note: Daly's growing concern with word origins can be seen here in her pejorative use of the word "seminal"; Daly used the word as if it were benign in *The Church and the Second Sex*: "These seminal elements must be distinguished from the oppressive, life-destroying ideas with which they have been confused." See chapter 1 in this collection.]

35 [Editors' note: Daly's assessment that Carson had been overlooked and slighted was accurate when she wrote this passage. In the decades since, both because of the worsening environmental crisis and the entry of more women into the sciences, Carson has become better known, almost to the point of becoming iconic, for better or worse.]

36 See, for example, Barry Commoner, *The Closing Circles: Nature, Man, and Technology* (New York: Bantam, 1972), p. 200. Commoner makes only one brief reference to Rachel Carson, crediting her with unearthing the ecological facts about DDT and drawing them to public attention. The brevity and limitation of his acknowledgement of her work is a subtle kind of erasure, putting her in her unrightful place.

37 For an illuminating analysis of integrity, see Janice Raymond, "The Illusion of Androgyny," *Quest: A Feminist Quarterly*, Vol. 2, No. 1 (Summer 1975), pp. 57–66.

38 [Editors' note: This passage, recalling the earlier reference to the cave, suggests that those other beings—animals, plants, stars, and men—in whom biophilia lives will respond to the movement of women: "by breaking the imposed silence we help to spring other prisoners of patriarchy whose biophilic tendencies have not been completely blighted and blocked."]

39 This name, appropriately, is the title of a feminist journal—*Chrysalis: A Magazine of Women's Culture*.

40 Daly, *Beyond God the Father*, pp. 7–12. [Editors' note: See chapter 6 in this volume.]

41 Daly, *The Church and the Second Sex*, p. 49.

42 The term *chairperson* does not disclose the sexual identity of the "person." The solution to the problem presented by this word's inadequacy does not lie in the direction of regressing to the pseudo-generic *chairman*. Rather, Hags—if we are interested in "chairs" at all—will be specific. A Hag holding a chair is a *chairwoman*, or a *chaircrone*. Males can be *chairpersons* or *chairmen*—it doesn't matter.

43 I prefer the power of the term *Prehistory* to name the prior importance of the interconnected significant events of women's living and dying. *Her-story*, I think, shortcircuits the intent of radical feminism by implying a desire to parallel the record of men's achievements. It fails because it imitates male *history*. Inherently, it has an "odor" of mere reactive maneuvering, which is humiliating to women. It conveys an image of history's junior partner. The point is not simply that this term is "etymologically incorrect." It is enlightening to compare this term with such

woman-made constructs as *man-ipulated* or *the/rapist*, which are also "incorrect," but do succeed in targeting/humiliating the *right* objects. [Editors' note: Originally a footnote, p. 24.]

44 They appear also to want to break the silence of silent reading, demanding to be read out loud. Attentive journeyers of this book will notice that this is most likely to happen in the course of the First and Third Passages. [Editors' note: Originally a footnote, p. 25.]

45 I prefer to reserve the term *Lesbian* to describe women who are woman-identified, having rejected false loyalties to men on all levels. The terms *gay* or *female homosexual* more accurately describe women who, although they relate genitally to women, give their allegiance to men and male myths, ideologies, styles, practices, institutions, and professions. [Editors' note: Originally a footnote, p. 26.]

46 Gertrude Stein, "Poetry and Grammar," in *Gertrude Stein: Writings and Lectures 1909–1945*, ed. by Patricia Meyerowitz, with an introduction by Elizabeth Sprigge (Baltimore, Md.: Penguin Books, 1974), p. 133.

47 For a good analysis of these terms see Sarah Hoagland, "On the Status of the Concepts of Masculinity and Femininity," *Transactions of the Nebraska Academy of Sciences*, Vol. 5 (August 1977), pp. 169–72.

48 Edwin Newman, *Strictly Speaking: Will America Be the Death of English?* (Indianapolis: Bobbs-Merrill, 1974), p. ix.

49 Conversation, Wellesley, Mass., August 1976.

50 The following are some basic feminist sources not already cited: Phyllis Chesler, *Women and Madness* (Garden City, N.Y.: Doubleday, 1972); Davis, *The First Sex*; de Beauvoir, *The Second Sex*; Millett, *Sexual Politics*; Robin Morgan, ed., *Sisterhood Is Powerful: An Anthology of Writings from the Women's Liberation Movement* (New York: Random House, 1970).

51 In addition to the works cited above, see: Susan Brownmiller, *Against Our Will: Men, Women and Rape* (New York: Simon and Schuster, 1975); Gena Corea, *The Hidden Malpractice: How American Medicine Treats Women as Patients and Professionals* (New York: William Morrow, 1977); Barbara Ehrenreich and Deirdre English, *Complaints and Disorders: The Sexual Politics of Sickness* (Old Westbury, N.Y.: Feminist Press, 1973) and *Witches, Midwives and Nurses* (Old Westbury, N.Y.: Feminist Press, 1973); Ellen Frankfort, *Vaginal Politics* (New York: Quadrangle Books, 1972); Linda Gordon, *Woman's Body, Woman's Right: A Social History of Birth Control in America* (New York: Penguin Books, 1977); Barbara Seaman, *The Doctors' Case Against the Pill* (New York: Avon Books, 1970); Barbara Seaman and Gideon Seaman, M.D., *Women and the Crisis in Sex Hormones* (New York: Rawson Associates, 1977).

52 See notes to Chapters Three to Seven of this book. [Editors' note: Chapters 3–7 of *Gyn/Ecology*, which Daly termed "The Second Passage," detail each of these named atrocities against women.]

53 In addition to the sources cited above, see Diana E. H. Russell and Nicole Van de Ven, eds., *Crimes Against Women: Proceedings of the International Tribunal* (Millbrae, Calif.: Les Femmes, 1976).
54 Irene Peslikis, "Resistances to Consciousness," *Sisterhood Is Powerful*, p. 337.
55 Bloomfield, *The Seven Deadly Sins*, p. 13.
56 [Editors' note: And now, in the twenty-first century, we add, their man-splaining.]
57 Woolf, *Three Guineas*, p. 63.
58 *Ibid.*, p. 99.
59 *Ibid.*, p. 74.

## CHAPTER 15. SECULAR S AND M

1 *Time*, February 7, 1977.
2 Hannah Tillich, *From Time to Time* (New York: Stein and Day, 1973), p. 14.
3 See Elliott Wright, "Paul Tillich as Hero: An Interview with Rollo May," *The Christian Century* (May 15, 1974), pp. 530–33. The psychologist's arguments against Hannah Tillich's account of her life with Paul Tillich are fascinating. May complains: "The things that make Tillich significant are left out. What this does, unless the reader already knows him, is to give a warped portrait; another dirty old man." Indeed, and Hannah Tillich knew him well. May goes on with impeccable illogic, explaining that he had tried to persuade Hannah not to publish this book, which would be "most humiliating *to her* [emphasis mine]." May was asked if he thought his version was "more factual on the sensual side of Tillich." He responded: "I do. An admiring student may not be the most objective judge of a teacher, but a wife is considerably less reliable. No man is a hero to his valet." May goes on to explain some of Hannah Tillich's chores as "valet," such as always driving the car and making travel arrangements. With psychological acumen he continues: "At times I felt sorry for her. Yet she seemed to enjoy it; she liked to meet the important people she met because she was Mrs. Paul Tillich."
4 Hannah Tillich, *From Time to Time*, p. 241.
5 [Editors' note: For readers in the early twenty-first century, the explicit pictures of torture by American military prison guards at Abu Ghraib prison in Iraq sadly repeated the patterns Daly describes here.]
6 For analysis of the horror of modern medical techniques, see Ivan Illich, *Medical Nemesis: The Expropriation of Health* (New York: Pantheon, 1976). Illich discussed the use of "medicine," including life-prolonging equipment, in the torture of political prisoners, in a talk at Harvard University in 1976. For an unwitting self-exposé by psychiatric torturers, see Vernon Mark and Frank Ervin, *Violence and the Brain* (New York: Harper and Row, 1970). Even the title of Mark and Ervin's book is a reversal of the fact that *they* are the perpetrators of violence against their patients. The Nazi death camps will be discussed in The Second Passage of this book. [Editors' note: This refers to the conclusion to the Second Passage in *Gyn/Ecology*, pp. 293–312.]

7 See *Amnesty International Report on Torture* (London: Duckworth, in association with Amnesty International Publications, 1973), p. 61.

## CHAPTER 16. AFRICAN GENITAL MUTILATION

1 [Editors' note: Daly would be happy to learn that Nigeria, where female genital mutilation was most prevalent, has outlawed the practice (as of 2015), which is now prohibited in many countries. See "Nigeria Outlaws Female Genital Mutilation," NSNBC International, May 30, 2015, http://nsnbc.me for more information on the Nigerian ban.]

2 I have chosen to name these practices for what they are: barbaric rituals/atrocities. Critics from Western countries are constantly being intimidated by accusations of "racism," to the point of misnaming, non-naming, and not seeing these sado-rituals. The accusations of "racism" may come from ignorance, but they serve only the interests of males, not of women. This kind of accusation and intimidation constitutes an astounding and damaging reversal, for it is clearly in the interest of Black women that feminists of all races should speak out. Moreover, it is in the interests of women of all races to see African genital mutilation in the context of planetary patriarchy, of which it is but one manifestation. As I am demonstrating, it is of the same pattern as the other atrocities I discuss. [Editors' note: Originally a footnote, p. 154.]

3 Lest Westerners feel smugly distant from these rituals, it would be well to recall some facts of "our" culture. In a later chapter I will discuss the implications of the fact that clitoridectomies and other mutilations have been inflicted by American gynecologists. It should be noted also that slashing and mutilation of genitals are common features of contemporary gang rape, which is "as American as apple pie." Moreover, there has been a time-honored christian European tradition of infibulation and the chastity belt. According to some, this was done in the same way as the infibulation of mares practiced in the veterinary profession, consisting of fastening together the labia by means of a ring, a buckle, or a padlock. According to Davis, the upper classes resorted less frequently to infibulation, but used instead the chastity belt, which was supposedly less painful. When one considers that some women were locked up in these for months or even years while their lords were away, the torture of accumulated excrement and of infection is beyond imagination. Such items are of course still on display at European museums, objects of merriment for guides and visitors, including female visitors who often do not comprehend their implications. See Davis, *The First Sex*, pp. 163–67. [Editors' note: Originally a footnote, p. 155.]

4 Theologians such as Paul Tillich have noted that while there may in some sense be "sins," in a more original sense there is Sin, which is a state. However, Tillich and other theologians of patriarchy are not in a position to name this State accurately. This is demonstrated in Paul Tillich's *Systematic Theology*, v. II, pp. 44–47.

5 See *Women's International Network News*, ed. by Fran P. Hosken (187 Grant Street, Lexington, Mass. 02173), Vol. 1, No. 3 (June 1975), Vol. 1, No. 4 (October 1975), Vol. 2, No. 1 (January 1976), Vol. 2, No. 2 (Spring 1976), Vol. 2, No. 3 (Summer 1976).

In the last-mentioned issue, Hosken gives an extensive bibliography. The reader is advised to consult *WIN News* for up-to-date information.

6 See Hosken, *WIN News,* Vol. 2, No. 1 (January 1976), p. 30. See also J. A. Verzin, M.D., "Sequelae of Female Circumcision," *Tropical Doctor*, October 1975, p. 163. I have cited only the first three of the types of circumcision described by Verzin. He lists a fourth type, which he believes is practiced only among the Ditta Pitta tribes in Australia: "*Type IV: Itrocision.* This is the cutting into the vagina or splitting of the perineum, either digitally or by means of a sharp instrument, and is the severest form of female circumcision." Verzin maintains that Type III (Pharaonic circumcision) is practiced throughout the Sudan, Ethiopia and Somaliland.

7 Jacques Lantier, *La Cité magique et magie en afrique noire* (Paris: Librairie Arthème Fayard, 1972), p. 279.

8 *Ibid.*, pp. 279–80. Lantier describes marriage among the Somali. When the bride goes to her husband's house he takes off her clothes and beats her until the blood flows. Since he cannot "deflower" her (that is, break the scar) with his penis, he uses a knife. Before using the knife, he forces a piece of wood, "specially tailored," into the vaginal orifice—a precaution designed to protect the perineum, in order not to cause a fistula on the rectum. Then he plunges in the knife before having intercourse with her. There is more:

> "Selon la tradition, le mari doit avoir durant huit jours des rapports réiterés et prolongés. Ce 'travail' a pour objet de 'fabriquer' un vestibule en empèchant la cicatrice de se refermer. Pendant ces huits jours, la femme reste étendue et bouge le moins possible afin de tenir la plaie béante. Au lendemain de la nuit des noces, le mari fixe sur son épaule son poignard ensanglanté; il va faire des visites afin de recueillir l'admiration générale. Cette 'formalité' remplie, il rentre aussitôt chez lui reprendre son ouvrage."

Another source on infibulation and defibulation is Eugenio Lenzi, "Damage Caused by Infibulation and Infertility," *Acta Europaea Fertilitatis*, Vol. 2, No. 47 (1970), pp. 47–58. Asim Zaki Mustafa, in his article, "Female Circumcision and Infibulation in the Sudan," *Journal of Obstetrics and Gynaecology of the British Commonwealth*, Vol. 73, pp. 302–6, discusses infibulation in the Sudan, with an emphasis upon resultant complications. He imparts the interesting information that an individual named Tiggani, who was the only psychiatrist in the Sudan for several years, in a personal communication in 1965 conveyed his opinion that circumcision provides a "happy social occasion" for Sudanese women who normally enjoy little in the way of entertainment. This psychiatrist maintains that "had it been unpleasant or unacceptable it would have perished long ago." Mustafa also informs us: "Rectal intercourse not infrequently takes place in error because the vaginal introitus has been obliterated" (p. 305). See also M. F. Ashley Montagu, "Infibulation and Defibulation in the Old and New Worlds," *American Anthropologist,* n.s. 47 (1945), pp. 464–67; Allan Worsley, "Infibulaton and Female Circumcision: A Study of a Little-Known Custom," *Journal of Obstetrics and Gynaecology of the British Empire*, Vol. 45 (1938), pp. 686–91.

9 Linda Barufaldi observed that the circumcision of the male requires only the removal of the foreskin, which not only leaves his organ of sexual pleasure intact but also makes him *less* susceptible to infection (conversation, Boston, January 1978). [Editors' note: Originally a footnote, p. 157.]

See Hosken, *WIN News*, Vol. 2, No. 1 (January 1976), p. 36. See also Verzin, "Sequelae of Female Circumcision"; Mustafa, "Female Circumcision"; Lenzi, "Damage Caused by Infibulation." See also the article (unsigned), "Excision in Africa," *ISIS International Bulletin*, No. 2 (October 1976), pp. 12–15. ISIS is a collective of women providing an information and communication service for the women's movement internationally. The address in Switzerland is Case Postale 301, 1227, Carouge, Switzerland. Money orders can be sent to this address. Subscriptions for individual women and women's groups are $10.00; for libraries and other institutions, $20.00.

10 See Hosken, *WIN News*, Vol. 1, No. 3 (June 1975), p. 41.

11 As Hosken shows, a few doctors have spoken out in recent years. The evidence is to be found in a few medical journal articles, some of which are cited in this chapter. Particularly useful are the articles of J. A. Verzin, A. A. Shandall, and G. Pieters. [Editors' note: Originally a footnote, p. 158.] See Hosken, *WIN News*, Vol. 2, No. 1 (January 1976), p. 30.

12 Jomo Kenyatta, *Facing Mount Kenya: The Tribal Life of the Gikuyu*, with an introduction by B. Malinowski (New York: Vintage, 1965), p. 125 ff. In his introduction, the prestigious scholar Malinowski writes: "As a first-hand account of a representative African culture, as an invaluable document in the principles underlying culture-contact and change; last, not least, as a personal statement of the new outlook of a progressive African, this book will rank as a pioneering achievement of outstanding merit."

13 Benoîte Groult, *Ainsi soit-elle* (Paris: Bernard Grasset, 1975), p. 96. The entire fourth chapter of this book, entitled, "La Haine du C.," pp. 93–118, is worth reading. Since the author does not document her work, however, the Searcher will want to consult also more primary sources, such as those indicated in these notes.

14 "Excision in Africa," *ISIS*, p. 14. See Lenzi, "Damage Caused by Infibulation," p. 55; Worsley, "Infibulation and Female Circumcision," p. 688; Hosken in "Genital Mutilation of Females in Africa: Summary/Facts," a fact sheet available from *WIN News*, points out that in the Sudan, where most of the women, including city-dwellers, are infibulated, the ceremony is called *tahur*, which means "cleansing."

15 G. Pieters, "Gynécologie au pays des femmes cousues," *Acta Chururgica Belgica*, No. 3 (May 1972), p. 180. This article, on gynecology "in the country of the sewn women," is extremely valuable.

16 "Excision in Africa," *ISIS*, pp. 12–14.

17 When reading this passage, Emily Culpepper pointed out the possibility that these genitally reconstructed women are designed to offer their masters a kind of sexual experience comparable to that obtained by anal intercourse with other men. These "tight" women are never allowed to become too loose, for this would

decrease the strong stimulation of the penis which men experience in anal coitus. For the women's genital structure has been reduced and simplified to the dimension of a small hole. In a metaphorical sense, too, these women can never be "loose." This fact may give rise to the thought that in Western society both "tight" women ("dried-up old maids") and "loose" women ("dirty whores") are sexually *wrong* by male standards. For in fact female sexuality—as an expression of female be-ing—is essentially wrong by androcratic, heterosexist standards. [Editors' note: Originally a footnote, p. 160.]

**18** "Excision in Africa," *ISIS*, pp. 12.

**19** See Verzin, "Sequelae of Female Circumcision," in which he maintains that "circumcision" is done not only throughout Africa, but in Brazil, Eastern Mexico, Peru, several Asian countries, Australia, and, in Europe, among the Skopsi, a christian Russian sect, to ensure "perpetual virginity." Another strong argument for wide geographical distribution is given by Dr. Ahmed Abu-El-Futuh Shandall, in his article "Circumcision and Infibulation of Females," in *Sudan Medical Journal*, Vol. 5, No. 4 (1967), pp. 180–81. See also Ben R. Huelsman, "An Anthropological View of Clitoral and Other Female Genital Mutilations," in *The Clitoris*, ed. by Thomas P. Lowry, M.D., and Thea Snyder Lowry, M.A. (St. Louis, Mo.: Warren H. Green, 1976), p. 121.

**20** Hosken, *WIN News*, Vol. 2, No. 1 (January 1976), p. 30.

**21** *Ibid.*, p. 32.

**22** Montagu, "Infibulation and Defibulation," pp. 464–67.

**23** M. F. Ashley Montagu, "Ritual Mutilation among Primitive Peoples," *Ciba Symposia*, Vol. 8, No. 7 (October 1946), pp. 421–36.

**24** According to Hosken, female genital mutilation takes place in some tribes in the following countries: Kenya, Tanzania, Ethiopia, southern Egypt, Sudan, Uganda, northern Zaire, Chad, northern Cameroon, Nigeria, Dahomey, Togo, northern Ghana, Upper Volta, Mali, northern Ivory Coast, Liberia, Sierra Leone, Guinea, Guinea Bissau, the Gambia, Senegal, Mauritania. See Hosken, *WIN News*, Vol. II, No. 3 (Summer 1976), p. 22. Benoîte Groult states that excision in small girls still takes place in Yemen, Saudi Arabia, Iraq, Jordan, and Syria (*Ainsi soit-elle*, pp. 93–118). [Editors' note: originally a footnote, p. 161.]

**25** Huelsman, "An Anthropological View," p. 123.

**26** *Ibid.*, p. 124.

**27** Shandall, "Circumcision and Infibulation," pp. 178–79.

**28** Groult, *Ainsi soit-elle*, p. 94.

**29** Montagu, "Ritual Mutilation," p. 434.

**30** See Huelsman, "An Anthropological View," p. 121.

**31** Diana E. H. Russell and Nicole Van de Ven, eds., *The Proceedings of the International Tribunal on Crimes Against Women*, p. 151.

**32** In its origin, the term *castrate* is akin to the Sanskrit *śasati*, meaning, "he cuts to pieces." This describes precisely what is done to women's bodies/minds/spirits under patriarchy: they are divided and fragmented into disconnected pieces. [Editors' note: Originally a footnote, p. 164.]

33 Montagu, "Infibulation and Defibulation," pp. 465–66.

34 *Ibid.*, p. 466.

35 There are other details of the infibulated woman's life that support the evidence concerning who is behind the scenes controlling the gynocidal set-up. Thus Pieters points to the fact that in some parts of Arabia salt is stuffed into the vagina after childbirth in order to shrink the orifice so that intercourse will be more pleasurable for the husband. A common result of this is vaginal stenosis. See Pieters, "Gynécologie au pays," p. 189. Pieters refers to B. M. L. Underhill, "Salt Induced Vaginal Stenosis in Arabia," *Journal of Obstetrics and Gynaecology of the British Commonwealth*, 1963, Vol. 71, No. 293.

36 Lantier, *La Cité magique*, p. 278: "La mère achève son intervention en veillant à ménager un orifice très étroit, destiné a ne laisser passer que les urines et les mestrues. Il y va de son honneur que le trou soit le plus petit possible, car, chez les Somali, plus le passage artificial est étroit et plus la femme est considerée."

37 Henny Harald Hansen, "Clitoridectomy: Female Circumcision in Egypt," *Folk*, Vol. 14–15 (1972/73), p. 18.

38 Montagu, "Infibulation and Defibulation," p. 465.

39 Felix Bryk, *Dark Rapture: The Sex-Life of the African Negro*, English version by Dr. Arthur J. Norton (New York: Walden Publications, 1939), pp. 89–90.

40 Arnold van Gennep, *The Rites of Passage*, trans. by Monika B. Vizedom and Gabrielle L. Caffee (Chicago: University of Chicago Press, 1960), p. 71.

41 *Ibid.*, p. 86.

42 *Ibid.*, p. 87.

43 Kenyatta, *Facing Mount Kenya*, pp. 127–28. On page 130, Kenyatta expounds upon his thesis as follows: "For years there has been much criticism and agitation against *irua* [genital mutilation] of girls by certain misinformed missionary societies in East Africa, who see only the surgical side of the *irua*, and, without investigating the psychological importance attached to this custom by the Gikuyu, these missionaries draw their conclusion that the *irua* of girls is nothing but a barbarous practice and, as such, should be abolished by law.

"On the other hand, the Gikuyu look upon these religious fanatics with great suspicion. . . . The abolition of *irua* will destroy the tribal symbol which identifies age-groups, and prevent the Gikuyu from perpetuating that spirit of collectivism and national solidarity which they have been able to maintain from time immemorial."

44 It is interesting to compare these attempts to feminize women with the feminization of male-to-constructed-female transsexuals. The latter, who consider themselves to be "women" (referring to "other" women as "native women") undergo operations which remove the testicles and penis and give them artificial vaginas, but no clitoris. Both of these mutilating attempts at feminization receive a large amount of legitimation by phallocracy. See Janice Raymond, *The Transsexual Empire: The Making of the She-Male* (Boston: Beacon Press, 1979).

45 It may be helpful in this connection to recall Simone de Beauvoir's famous axiom: "One is not born, but rather becomes a woman." (*The Second Sex*, p. 301). In this

book of course, I use the term *woman* to refer to females generally and reserve the term *feminine* to connote the male-created construct/stereotype. However, *woman* is often used by others to refer to the androcractically constructed (destroyed) female, who is, of course, considered "natural." There is, for example, the "total woman" of Marabel Morgan, and the "true woman" of Pope Pius XII and Pope Paul VI.

46 Lantier, *La Cité magique*, pp. 271–72: "(Dieu) a donné le clitoris à la femme pour qu'elle puisse l'utiliser avant le mariage afin d'éprouver le plaisir de l'amour tout en restant pure. . . .

"On ne tranche pas le clitoris des toutes petites filles puisqu'il leur sert à se masturber. On tranche celui des jeunes filles que l'on juge disposées à la procreation et au mariage. Quand on leur a enlevé le clitoris, elles ne se masturbent plus. Cela les prive beaucoup. Alors tout le désir se porte vers l'intérieur, Elles cherchent donc à se marier promptement. Une fois mariées, au lieu d'éprouver des sensations disperses et faibles, elles concentrent tout au même endroit et les couples connaissent beaucoup de bonheur, ce qui est normal."

47 Pieters, "Gynécologie au pays," pp. 182–83.

48 Hosken, *WIN News*, Vol. 2, No. 1 (January 1976), p. 35.

49 Pieters, "Gynécologie au pays," pp. 180–81.

50 Bryk, *Dark Rapture*, pp. 87–88.

51 *Ibid.*, p. 100.

52 *Ibid.*, p. 90.

53 *Ibid.*, p. 27.

54 *Ibid.*, p. 28.

55 Van Gennep, *The Rites of Passage*, p. 72, note 2.

56 *Ibid.*, p. 73.

57 Marie Bonaparte, *Female Sexuality* (New York: International Universities Press, 1953), p. 191.

58 *Ibid.*, p. 204.

59 *Ibid.*, p. 207.

60 Mircea Eliade, *Rites and Symbols of Initiation: The Mysteries of Birth and Rebirth*, trans. by Willard R. Trask (New York: Harper Torchbooks, 1965), p. 42.

61 *Ibid.*, p. 43.

62 *Ibid.*, pp. 45–46.

63 *Ibid.*, p. 46.

64 In the summer of 1976 I saw a living confirmation of this "mythological memory of a permanent tension" at a folklore festival in Heraklion, Crete. The theme of one of the folk dances was the theft of spindles from a group of young girls by some invasive "playful" males after which the latter danced around with these stolen spindles/sticks held between their legs in the position of erect penises.

## CHAPTER 18. NEWSPEAK VERSUS NEW WORDS

1 Stefan Kanfer, "Sispeak: A Msguided Attempt to Change Herstory," *Time*, October 23, 1972, p. 79. Another article in the same vein and of the same vintage was L. E.

Sissman, "Innocent Bystander: Plastic English," in *Atlantic Monthly*, October 1972, pp. 32–37.

2 Kanfer, "Sispeak," p. 79.
3 George Orwell, *1984* (New York: New American Library, 1961), p. 247.
4 *Ibid.*, pp. 250–51.
5 *Ibid.*, p. 251.
6 *Ibid.*, p. 252.
7 *Ibid.*, p. 253.
8 *Ibid.*, p. 254. An interesting analysis of such words can be found in Casey Miller and Kate Swift, *Words and Women* (Garden City, N.Y.: Anchor Books, 1976). This entire work of Miller and Swift deserves careful study by the serious Searcher.
9 Sartre, *Being and Nothingness*, especially pp. 765–84.
10 Peggy Holland, "Jean-Paul Sartre as a NO to Women," *Sinister Wisdom* 6 (Summer 1978).
11 Orwell, *1984*, p. 231.

## CHAPTER 19. SPARKING

1 Jan Raymond, class lecture given at University of Massachusetts at Amherst, fall 1976.
2 De Beauvoir, *The Second Sex*, p. 468.
3 See Daly, *Beyond God the Father: Toward a Philosophy of Women's Liberation*. [Editors' note: Daly may well be referring to the illustration by Emily Culpepper that follows the end of the index in *Beyond God the Father*.]
4 [Editors' note: Daly had referenced the "wicked stepmother" in *The Church and the Second Sex:*

> The symbol, however, has seductive power. It is grasped without effort, and it generally conveys some recognizable truth. Distortion occurs when this truth is accepted as the whole truth. The "old man" serves well enough as a symbol for wisdom and the "step-mother" for wickedness, but old men are not always wise, nor are stepmothers always wicked. (p. 122)]

5 Jan Raymond, class lecture, fall 1976.

## CHAPTER 20. THE DISSEMBLY OF EXORCISM

1 The Voyager of this book is familiar with the demons' manifestations. However, she may wish to spin back to the Introduction [Editors' note: See the discussion of the Eight Deadly Sins of the Fathers in chapter 14 of this volume] for a brief refresher course in Haggard naming/listing/defining of the Sins of the Fathers, which the demons represent. [Editors' note: Originally a footnote, p. 418.]
2 Many movie-monitoring Hags note the resemblance of this attire to the apparel of the husbands who are the casual killers of *The Stepford Wives.*
3 [Editors' note: These animal names were evoked earlier in *Gyn/Ecology*; see chapter 14 of this volume.]
4 *Sinister Wisdom* is, of course, the name of a well-known Lesbian-Feminist journal.

5 Creative Anger and Bravery are rooted in a passion for Justice. As Dr. Elizabeth Farians has demonstrated, both in her writings and in her actions: "Justice is an active virtue. One must do something about justice." See her article, "Justice: The Hard Line," *Andover Newton Quarterly*, Vol. 12, No. 4 (March 1972), pp. 191–200.

## CHAPTER 21. DALY ON MATILDA JOSLYN GAGE

1 See the foundation's website at www.matildajoslyngage.org.

## CHAPTER 22. ON LUST AND THE LUSTY

1 *Webster*: "A weaver; a. as the designation of a woman." *Oxford English Dictionary.* [Editors' note: Originally a footnote, p. 1.]

2 *Wickedary*: "Archaic: a wicked/wiccen dictionary." *Websters' First New Intergalactic Wickedary of the English Language.* The adjective *wicked* can be traced to the same Indo-European root (*weik-*) as *wicce*, the Old English word meaning witch (*American Heritage Dictionary of the English Language*). The adjective *wiccen* is here constructed from the noun *wicce.* A *Wickedary* is a dictionary for Wicked/ Wiccen Women. [Editors' note: Originally a footnote, p. 1.]

3 Except when otherwise indicated, all definitions given in this work are from *Webster's Third New International Dictionary of the English Language.* [Editors' note: Originally a footnote, p. 2.]

4 I use *be-ing* in this hyphenated form to signify that this is intended not as a noun but as a verb, meaning participation in the Ultimate/Intimate Reality: *Be-ing*, the Verb. [Editors' note: Originally a footnote, p. 2.]

5 The *final cause*, according to an old scholastic philosophical axiom, is the "cause of causes, because it is the cause of the causality of all the other causes." According to Aristotelian and scholastic philosophy, it is one of the four causes. As I explained in *Beyond God the Father*, pp. 180–81: "When Aristotle wrote of the 'final cause,' he intended 'cause' to mean that which brings about an effect. Scholastic philosophers followed the Aristotelian theory of the 'four causes' to explain change. . . . The final cause is the purpose which starts the whole process in motion. . . . The final cause is the first cause, since it moves the agent to act upon the matter, bringing forth a new form." Thus the efficient cause (agent), the material cause (matter), and the formal cause (form) are all actualized by the final cause. Deep ontological purposefulness, or telic centering, is the target of phallic lust. Final causality, in this profound sense, is the object of attack within patriarchal society. [Editors' note: Originally a footnote, p. 2. See chapter 12 of this book.]

6 Conversation with Anne Dellenbaugh, Leverett, Mass., 1981.

7 The idea of *tribes* of women was suggested to me by Sue Bellamy. Conversation, Sydney, Australia, 1981.

8 One of these man-made racetracks, is, of course, racism. When I write of the Race of Women as participating in the Race of Elemental be-ing, I am Naming active struggle to overcome and transcend phallocracy, the social, political, ideological system that spawns racism and genocide as well as rapism and gynocide.

Confronting phallocracy includes opposing it in all of its forms/manifestations. I initially developed this thesis in *Beyond God the Father* (1973). Its implications were further expanded in *Gyn/Ecology* (1978), and it is further elaborated in this book. [Editors' note: Originally a footnote, p. 5.]

**9** Woolf, *Three Guineas*, p. 109.

**10** Matilda Joslyn Gage noted: "The famous works of Paracelsus were but compilations of the knowledge of these 'wise women' as he himself stated." *Woman, Church and State* (c. 1893; reprint edition, Watertown, Mass.: Persephone Press, 1980), p. 104. Moreover, in 1527, at Basel, Paracelsus reportedly "threw all his medical works, including those of Hippocrates and Galen, into the fire, saying that he knew nothing except what he had learned from the witches." *Ibid.*, p.104. See Michelet, *Satanism and Witchcraft*, p. 80.

Moreover, other students of Paracelsus, without explicitly recognizing the meaning of their comments, confirm this. Manley P. Hall, for example, writes: "He liked to visit hermits living in huts and caves, and to explore the myths and legends of the gypsies, alchemists, and herbalists, and even magicians and sorcerers." *The Mystical and Medical Philosophy of Paracelsus* (Los Angeles: The Philosophical Research Society, Inc., 1964), p. 45.

**11** Hall, *The Mystical and Medical Philosophy of Paracelsus*, p. 53.

**12** [Editors' note: Daly herSelf had experienced such moments of insight; these are in this book in chapters 32 and 33, describing her encounter with a clover blossom and the Dream of Green.]

**13** See Aristotle, *Metaphysics*: "For it is owing to their wonder that men [*sic*] both now begin and at first began to philosophize; they wondered originally at the obvious difficulties, then advanced little by little and stated difficulties about the greater matters, e.g. about the phenomena of the moon and those of the sun and of the stars, and about the genesis of the universe. And a man who is puzzled and wonders thinks himself ignorant (whence even the lover of myth is in a sense a lover of Wisdom, for the myth is composed of wonders)." I, 2.

**14** Brontë uses the term *heaven* here in the christian otherworldly sense. I would use this term in an Elemental Otherwordly sense and thereby reclaim it for feminists, as meaning something Other than both the patriarchal "this world" and the patriarchal "otherworld." That is, I would reclaim it to Name the "this world" of women and all Wild beings, who are Other than patriarchal. In any case, this passage expresses—in traditional terms—a love of earth shared by Elemental women. [Editors' note: Originally a footnote, p. 9.] Emily Brontë, *Wuthering Heights* (New York: The Modern Library, 1950), p. 84.

**15** Raymond T. Stamm, "Exegesis of the Epistle to the Galatians, 4:3," in *The Interpreter's Bible*, 12 vols. (New York: Abingdon-Cokesbury Press, 1952–57), X, 521.

**16** *Archaic* is derived from the Greek *arche*, meaning first principle, primal element. [Editors' note: Originally a footnote, p. 12.]

## CHAPTER 23. METAPHORS OF METABEING

1 Paul Tillich, *Dynamics of Faith* (New York: Harper and Row, 1957), p. 43.

2 Conversation with Nelle Morton, Claremont, Calif., 1981. See also Morton, "The Rising Woman Consciousness in a Male Language Structure"; "How Images Function," *Quest: A Feminist Quarterly*, vol. 3, no. 2 (Fall 1976), pp. 54–59; "Beloved Image" paper delivered at the National Conference of the American Academy of Religion, San Francisco, December 28, 1977, p. 4. These and other writings by Nelle Morton will be published in a forthcoming volume, *The Journey Is Home*, composed of her papers and articles from 1970 to 1979. This book reflects the development of her thought and of the women's movement during that period and contains writings from each year of that decade. [Editors' note: The book was published by Beacon Press, 1986.]

3 Julian Jaynes has written nicely about metaphors: "Let us speak of metaphor. The most fascinating property of language is its capacity to make metaphors. But what an understatement! For metaphor is not a mere extra trick of language, as it is so often slighted in the old schoolbooks on composition; it is the very constitutive ground of language." See *The Origin of Consciousness in the Breakdown of the Bicameral Mind* (Boston: Houghton Mifflin Company, 1976), p. 48. [Editors' note: Originally a footnote, p. 25.]

4 Classical metaphysics spurns metaphorical analogy in favor of what is technically called *the analogy of being*. Elemental philosophy, since it is concerned with participation in Be-ing *requires* metaphorical analogy. [Editors' note: Originally a footnote, p. 26.]

5 Adrienne Rich, *The Dream of a Common Language: Poems 1974–1977* (New York: W. W. Norton and Company, 1978).

6 In *Beyond God the Father: Toward a Philosophy of Women's Liberation*, I have analyzed at length my use of *Be-ing* as Verb—as intransitive Verb—to Name ultimate reality. At the time of writing that book I still used the term *God* to Name that reality. The symbol, God as Verb, was an essential step in my intellectual process to the Metaphor, Goddess as Verb. Often feminists try to eliminate this step, with the unfortunate result that "The Goddess" functions as a static symbol, simply replacing the noun *God*. In writing *Beyond God the Father*, I also used the expression *Power of Be-ing* to refer to ultimate/intimate reality. This emphasized the Verb, but I now think that it gives less than adequate emphasis to the multiple aspects of transcendence. I therefore now use the plural, *Powers of Be-ing*.

Behind this semantic struggle lies, of course, the problem of the one and the many. It is important to be explicitly aware of this problem. Some feminists, with good reason, prefer to use the singular Name, *The Goddess*. Others, also with good reasons, prefer to speak of *Goddesses*. Although the latter choice is motivated by an understanding of the necessity for, and fact of, multiplicity and diversity in symbols/metaphors of the Goddess, there is, it seems to me, an unresolved problem, if one ignores the principle of unity: the One. When

Be-ing is understood as Verb, the focus of the discussion changes. It would be foolish to speak of "Be-ings." But women can and do speak of different Powers and manifestations of Be-ing, which are sometimes imaged as Goddesses.

7 Langer, *Philosophy in a New Key*, p. 114.

8 *Ibid.*, p. 113.

9 "Snool" is a word that Daly reclaimed in the introduction to *Pure Lust* to describe the "normal inhabitants of sadosociety, characterized by sadism and masochism combined; stereotypic hero and/or saint of the sadostate" (*Wickedary*, p. 227). As she says, "Nags use words like *snool*, not to define the essence of any sentient being but to Name agents *as agents* of the atrocities of the sadostate" (*Pure Lust*, p. 21).

10 My allusion here is to Elizabeth Gould Davis, *The First Sex*—the work of a courageous Crone.

11 I have selected Tillich as an example precisely because of the vast scope and rigor of his thought, which sometimes inspires thinking beyond such limitations. In other words, I have chosen him because of his stature, because his work is worth studying and criticizing by those who would embark upon the adventure of discovering Elemental philosophy (provided, of course, that we employ his writings only as springboards for our own original analysis). [Editors' note: Originally a footnote, p. 29.]

12 Tillich, *Systematic Theology*, I, 163.

13 *Ibid.*, pp. 163–64.

## CHAPTER 24. BEYOND THE SADO-SUBLIME

1 See Mary Daly, *Gyn/Ecology: The Metaethics of Radical Feminism* (Boston: Beacon, 1978), pp. 223–92, footnotes. See G. J. Barker-Benfield, *The Horrors of the Half-Known Life* (New York: Harper and Row, 1976), especially pp. 61–132. See also Seale Harris, M.D., *Woman's Surgeon: The Life Story of J. Marion Sims*, with the collaboration of Frances Williams Browin (New York: The Macmillan Company, 1950). The pomposity and plethora of hypocritical excuses for Sims, the hero of Harris, can be appreciated only by reading the book, which actually glorifies the atrocities of Sims.

2 See Lillian Faderman, *Surpassing the Love of Men* (New York: William Morrow and Company, Inc., 1981), especially pp. 233–38.

3 Suzanne Arms, *Immaculate Deception: A New Look at Women and Childbirth in America* (New York: Bantam Books, 1975).

4 "Original sin" refers to a condition believed to be inherited by all descendents of the "first parents." According to catholic doctrine, no one can be saved except through the infusion of supernatural grace, which removes "original sin" as well as actual, personal sins. However, the "remains" of original sin stay in the soul, namely a darkening of the intellect, a weakening of the will, and an inclination to concupiscence. According to catholic doctrine, only Mary was spared this inheritance. In "poetic" language, she became "our tainted nature's solitary boast." [Editors' note: Originally a footnote, p. 103.]

5 See Daly, *Gyn/Ecology*, pp. 83–85.
6 Lecture given at Boston College during the Feminist Lecture Series, Winter 1980.
7 This more moderate view had been held by Thomas Aquinas, *Summa theologiae* III, q. 27.
8 Again, it may be necessary to emphasize that whether or not this intent was/is fully "conscious" and explicit is not the issue. My point is that there is an inherent program/message in this revision of Goddess myth, and that it functions to serve the interest of the dogma dealers. [Editors' note: Originally a footnote, p. 104.]
9 The idea that there are some women so oppressed that "they have never had a Self" is widespread among women concerned with the horrors of oppression. Some activists who totally repudiate christian myth on an overt, conscious level express this idea. In fact, on a subliminal level they are buying into the patriarchal/hierarchical belief system that is so blatantly illustrated in the doctrine of the "Immaculate Conception," and unwittingly propagating this belief system. Women who believe that they are totally beyond the influence of such christian doctrines and that discussion of such material is "irrelevant," could profit from a re-examination of this opinion, for the influence of such seemingly confined beliefs is vast and subterranean. To suggest that Third World women and others who are extremely oppressed "never have been allowed to have a Self" is a way of saying that such women were immaculately conceived. Such a view of severely oppressed women is grossly—indeed, ontologically—insulting. Moreover, the logical conclusion to be drawn from such a view of any woman would be that oppression is justified by the fact that she has no Self. This, of course, is exactly the "reasoning" of patriarchal oppressors, such as the executives of the multinational corporations that exploit female workers, to legitimate their exploitation. As Emily Culpepper points out: "To base self-definition on our oppressed state of affairs is the essence of perpetuating a derivative, secondary and oppressive definition. . . . Indeed, the oppressive conditions are a shock, a weight, a drain, precisely because they are a shock to something, a weight on something, a drain of something. That something is the sense of integrity of Self—a Self that may only or mostly exist as potential—but that potential is real." See Emily Culpepper, "Philosophia in a Feminist Key: Revolt of the Symbols" (unpublished ThD dissertation, Harvard University, 1983), pp. 107–08. [Editors' note: Originally a footnote, pp. 104–5.]
10 Conversation, Boston, January 1981.
11 [Editors' note: This analysis can help victims of rape to understand the entirely irrational feelings of guilt they may experience.]
12 Conversation, Boston, January 1981. [Editors' note: What follows was originally a footnote, p. 106.] The use of the word *virgin*, then, in this context, is a particularly horrifying example of a faded and broken metaphor.
13 [Editors' note: See chapter 3 in this collection, from *The Church and the Second Sex*, on the excesses of Marianism.]
14 I am not saying that women have to use this terminology, of course. Nor are any words for this process really adequate. The point is that metapatriarchal con-

sciousness needs somehow to be expressed. [Editors' note: Originally a footnote, p. 107.]

15 The reader who wants to see this maneuver in mythic-historical perspective should recall that the transsexing of the Goddess had been accomplished thousands of years before through the conversion of the Goddess (Iahu) into Jahweh—a phenomenon which I have discussed in *Gyn/Ecology* (chapter 2). In christianity the triplicity of the Goddess is re-covered in the all-male trinity, in which the "feminine" aspect is relegated to the holy ghost. "His" impregnation of Mary, who is also a remnant of the Goddess, can be seen as a parody of parthenogenesis, since the Goddess appears to be impregnating herself. The holy ghost in this scenario is a caricature of her will and Mary is her body, broken off from spirit/will. The union accomplished when "he" impregnates "her" is not at all a re-membering of original integrity. It is merely an integration/impregnation which further estranges the mythic Mary from her Source.

Seen in this context, the dogma of the "Immaculate Conception" might appear to be a sort of overkill. What more could be done to the symbol of female divinity? It may be helpful to see that theology resembles pornography, that a good deal of the time it functions as sublimed pornography. Like pornographers, theologians exercise "creativity" by inventing variations on the same theme and sometimes by manufacturing heightened horrors. Just as pornography overtly promotes unimaginable sadism against women's bodies, a great deal of theology covertly promotes mutilation and dismemberment of women's psyches. The latter is sublimed sadism. Its strategy of overkill is not essentially dissimilar to such propensities in pornography. [Editors' note: Originally a footnote, pp. 107–8.]

16 Modern tokenizing of women in the professions is a recent and refined adaptation of the very old patriarchal strategy of tokenism. In its cruder forms, it involves the use of women as token torturers of other women (and girls). A classic example is the footbinding (footmaiming) of daughters by their mothers in China—an atrocity that prevailed in Chinese society for almost a thousand years and that was terminated only a few decades ago. [Editors' note: Originally a footnote, pp. 108–9.]

17 Judith Long Laws, "The Psychology of Tokenism: An Analysis," *Sex Roles*, vol. 1, no. 1 (1975), p. 58.

18 Ralf Dahrendorf, *Class and Class Conflict in Industrial Society* (Stanford: Stanford University Press, 1959), p. 60.

19 Laws, "The Psychology of Tokenism," p. 55.

20 *Ibid.*, p. 64.

21 *Ibid.*, p. 63.

22 [Editors' note: A concept originally put forth by Paolo Freire in *Pedagogy of the Oppressed*, horizontal violence describes the taking out of one's anger against the oppressor by acting out against members of one's own group. Freire postulated that this behavior occurs because it is safer than challenging the oppressor directly.]

## CHAPTER 25. RESTORATION AND THE PROBLEM OF MEMORY

1 In criticizing de Beauvoir or any feminist it is important to keep in mind the extreme isolation and the harsh sanctions endured by such prophets. From the perspective of the 1980s it is possible to see some limitations that were impossible to perceive when de Beauvoir was writing in the 1940s. This point was emphasized in a conversation with Marisa Zavalloni and Nicole Brossard, Montréal, August 1983. [Editors' note: Originally a footnote, p. 137.]

2 De Beauvoir, *The Second Sex*, pp. xxi-xxii.

3 *Ibid.*, p. 69.

4 *Ibid.*, p. 87.

5 *Ibid.*, p. xxii. [Editors' note: What follows was originally a footnote, p. 137.] Emily Culpepper suggests that "it is a measure of how far we have come that within her own lifetime, de Beauvoir has lived to see feminists cast doubt on all of these assertions." She also suggests that de Beauvoir can be read as "accepting 'the worst possible case' and going on to claim that—even if thus it has always been—it need not remain so." Culpepper, "Philosophia in a Feminist Key: Revolt of the Symbols," pp. 111–13.

6 Restorationist "knowledge" is to Elemental knowing as a dysfunctional prosthesis is to a natural part of the body. [Editors' note: Originally a footnote, p. 138.]

7 See Gage, *Woman, Church and State*; Davis, *The First Sex*. Also see Merlin Stone, *When God Was a Woman* (New York: Harcourt Brace Jovanovich, Harvest Books, 1976).

8 Hall, *The Mystical and Medical Philosophy of Paracelsus*, p. 54.

9 As Emily Culpepper has remarked, it is ironically true that our first major institutional training in patriarchal roles is "elementary school." Conversation, Leverett, Mass., April 1983. [Editors' note: Originally a footnote, p. 139.]

10 Thomas Aquinas was explicit on this point: "First and chiefly, the image of the Trinity is to be found in the acts of the soul, that is, inasmuch as from the knowledge which we possess, by actual thought we form an internal word; and thence break forth into love." See *Summa theologiae* I, q. 93, a. 7c.

## CHAPTER 26. PHALLIC POWER OF ABSENCE

1 Daly, *Amazon Grace*, pp. 2, 16; see also *Wickedary*, pp. 86–87 on Original Sin.

2 Daly, *Beyond God the Father*, pp. 41–42. [See chapter 7 in this book.]

3 It can still be distressing even to an experienced Searcher, when a scholar such as Julian Jaynes sweeps over significant information as if it were barely worth noting, when such information relates to powers of women. He writes: "And a comment can be added here about sexual differences. It is now well known that women are biologically somewhat *less lateralized* in brain function than men. This means simply that psychological functions in women are not localized into one or the other hemisphere of the brain to the same degree as in men. Mental abilities in women are more spread over both hemispheres. . . . And it is common knowledge

that elderly men with a stroke or hemorrhage in the left hemisphere are *more speechless* than elderly women with a similar diagnosis. Accordingly we might expect more residual language function in the right hemisphere of women, *making it easier for women to learn to be oracles.* And indeed the majority of oracles and Sibyls, at least in European cultures, were women" [all emphasis mine]. See *The Origin of Consciousness in the Breakdown of the Bicameral Mind*, pp. 343–44. This fascinating point is mentioned in only one other place in the book, and there even more scantily (p. 350). Shrewd Shrews will notice that Jaynes' language is deceptive and patronizing to women. For by his syntax he manages to belittle the oracular gifts of women and the Elemental integrity of female mental faculties, while at the same time obscuring the negative implications of overly localized psychological functions in males. For example, in this passage "less lateralized" and "more speechless" illustrate this bias.

Male terror of such Elemental integrity in women is directly related to many of the phenomena discussed by Jaynes, although he fails to make this connection. For example, his split awareness is manifested in his discussion of the christian doctrine of the "hypostatic union"—the union of the divine and human natures in Christ. Referring to this doctrine as the "Bicameral Word Made Flesh," he fails to raise the question of why male theologians felt the need to insist dogmatically upon a miraculous union of two natures in a *god-man* (divine male). Jaynes does not suggest the possibility (so obvious to any Nag-Gnostic) that the reification of oracular powers as the "Bicameral Word Made [Male] Flesh" is a dogmatic cover-up designed to distract from his own admission that oracular powers have been more widespread among women than among males. [Editors' note: Originally a footnote, pp. 148–49.]

4 Orwell, *1984*, p. 63.

5 *Ibid.*, p. 26.

6 *Daughter* is the term chosen by scientists to mean "the immediate product of radioactive decay of an element such as uranium; also known as decay product or radioactive decay product." (*McGraw-Hill Dictionary of Scientific and Technical Terms* [New York: McGraw-Hill Publishing Co., 1974, 1981].) [Editors' note: Originally a footnote, p. 150.]

7 Rev. Walter W. Skeal, *A Concise Etymological Dictionary of the English Language* (Oxford: At the Clarendon Press, 1911).

8 Joseph Campbell, *The Masks of God: Oriental Mythology* (New York: Viking Press, 1962), p. 66.

## CHAPTER 27. REALIZING REASON

1 In modern philosophy, *realism* means that material objects exist externally to us and independently of our sense experience. Modern realism takes a number of conflicting forms, including the new realism, perspective realism, common-sense realism, representative realism, critical realism. See R. J. Hirst, "Realism," *The Encyclopedia of Philosophy*, ed. by Paul Edwards, Editor-in-Chief (New York: Mac-

millan Publishing Co. and the Free Press, 1967), VII, 77–83. Tillich is probably right in his assessment of the situation when he states: "The word 'realism' means today almost what 'nominalism' meant in the Middle Ages, while the 'realism' of the Middle Ages expresses almost exactly what we call 'idealism' today. It might be suggested that, whenever one speaks of classical realism, one should call it 'mystical realism.'" See Tillich, *Systematic Theology*, I, 178, note. I suggest that it be called *classical realism*, which is what it is. [Editors' note: Originally a footnote, p. 161; a strong critique of Tillich immediately precedes this excerpt in *Pure Lust*, pp. 155–60.]

2 James Hillman, *Re-Visioning Psychology* (New York: Harper and Row, 1975), p. 5.

3 Tillich, *Systematic Theology*, I, p. 177.

4 The expression "Realizing reason" is double-edged. It is even multiple-edged. On the one hand, it Names the *act* of Realizing (actualizing) reason. It also Names the *power* which Realizes, that is, reason itself. In the second case, "Realizing" functions adjectivally, to describe the power of reason. As a consequence of Realizing her *realizing reason*, a woman participates ever more fully in the source of this structure—Powers of Be-ing. [Editors' note: Originally a footnote, pp. 162–63.]

5 Conversation with Mary Schultz, Leverett, Mass., January 1981.

6 I am *not* saying that when/if the patriarchal sadosociety is exorcised from our existence the mystery of evil will disappear. I am developing the thesis that phallocracy is the most basic, radical, and universal societal manifestation of evil, underlying not only gynocide but also genocide, not only rapism but also racism, not only nuclear and chemical contamination but also spiritual pollution. I am further developing my thesis, first presented in *Beyond God the Father*, that "a declaration of identity beyond good and evil of patriarchy's world. . . . [is] a massive exorcism. Repudiation of the scapegoat role and the myth of the Fall by the primordial scapegoats may be the dawn of real confrontation with the mystery of evil" (p. 66). [Editors' note: Originally a footnote, p. 164.]

7 Daly, *Beyond God the Father*, pp. 34–35. [Editors' note: In chapter 7 of this volume.]

8 Andrea Dworkin, *Our Blood* (New York: Harper and Row, 1976), p. 24.

9 See Aristotle, *Metaphysics* IX, 1.

10 Clearly, I am not saying that no Women's Studies courses are successful. Some, indeed, are excellent, given the conditions under which they are conceived and taught. I am saying that in a society that castrates female reason in such a primal way, women are impeded from imagining freely what such courses of study could be. Frequently this blunting of imagination is achieved through reducing Women's Studies to courses obsessively fixated upon details of the past, in the name of Academic Credibility, thus serving the interests of bore-ocracy and making feminism seem irrelevant and boring. The challenge facing Wise Women/Prudes who are struggling to create Women's Studies "on the boundary" of androcratic academia is to trust our Selves and break the mindbindings that still impede us from Realizing freely our Elemental powers of intellect and imagination. [Editors' note: Originally a footnote, p. 168.]

11 Conversation with Louky Bersianik, Stanley House, New Richmond, New Brunswick, Canada, August 1980.

12 See Denise Donnell Connors, "Sickness unto Death: Medicine as Mythic, Necrophilic, and Iatrogenic," *Advances in Nursing Science*, vol. 2, no. 3 (April 1980), pp. 39–51.

13 Woolf, *Moments of Being*, p. 67.

14 Barbara Myerhoff, *Number Our Days* (New York: Simon and Schuster, 1978), p. 39. [Editors' note: Myerhoff's book was an important breakthrough in sociological/anthropological methodology, for taking the stories of elderly people, and Jewish women in particular, seriously.]

15 Conversation with Frances Theoret, Stanley House, New Richmond, New Brunswick, Canada, August 1980.

16 Muriel Rukeyser, "Käthe Kollwitz," III, St. 4, *The Speed of Darkness* (New York: Random House, 1968), p. 103.

17 Woolf, *Moments of Being*, p. 72.

18 [Editors' note: See chapter 32 in this volume for Daly's experience of a clover blossom.]

19 Woolf, *Moments of Being*, p. 73.

20 The expression "re-membering reason"—like "Realizing reason"—is double-edged, multiple-edged. [Editors' note: Originally a footnote, p. 173.]

21 Woolf, *Moments of Being*, p. 70.

22 *Ibid.*, p. 72.

23 *Ibid.*, p. 93.

24 *Ibid.*, p. 72.

25 Alice Walker, "In Search of Our Mothers' Gardens," *Ms.*, May 1974, pp. 66–67.

26 Gloria Anzaldúa, "Speaking in Tongues: A Letter to Third World Women Writers," in *This Bridge Called My Back: Writings by Radical Women of Color*, ed. by Cherríe Moraga and Gloria Anzaldúa (Watertown, Mass.: Persephone Press, 1981), p. 170.

27 See Tillie Olsen, *Silences* (New York: Delacorte Press/Seymour Lawrence, 1978).

28 Rachel Carson, *The Sea Around Us* (New York: New American Library, 1961), p. 144.

29 Janice Raymond, "A Genealogy of Female Friendship," *Trivia: A Journal of Ideas*, no. 1 (Fall 1982), p. 25.

30 Carson, *The Sea Around Us*, pp. 154–55.

## CHAPTER 28. THE RAGING RACE

1 [Editors' note: See chapter 22 in this volume for the full context of Daly's definition of "race."]

## CHAPTER 29. FROM "JUSTICE" TO NEMESIS

1 Aquinas, *Summa theologiae*, II-II, q. 58, a. 1c.

2 Paul Tillich, *Love, Power, and Justice* (New York: Oxford University Press, 1954), p. 86.

3 Elizabeth Oakes Smith, speech delivered at Woman's Rights Convention, 1852, in *History of Woman Suffrage*, ed. by Elizabeth Cady Stanton, Susan B. Anthony, and Matilda Joslyn Gage (New York: Fowler and Wells, 1881), I, 522–23.
4 Florynce Kennedy, "Institutionalized Oppression *vs.* the Female," in Morgan, *Sisterhood Is Powerful*, pp. 445–46.
5 Joyce Carol Oates, *Do with Me What You Will* (New York: The Vanguard Press, Inc., 1973), p. 284.
6 See Maxine Hong Kingston, *The Woman Warrior* (New York: Random House, Vintage Books, 1975, 1976).
7 Wittig, *Les Guérillères*.
8 The Australian novelist Gabrielle Lord conjures a powerful story that illustrates the powers of female warriorhood in *Fortress* (Sydney, Australia and London: Aurora Press, 1980).
9 J. C. Cooper, *An Illustrated Encyclopedia of Traditional Symbols* (London: Thames and Hudson, 1978), p. 82.
10 *Ibid.*
11 Elizabeth Cady Stanton, Letter to Woman's Suffrage Convention, 1851, in *History of Woman Suffrage*, I, 816.
12 Millicent Garrett Fawcett, *The Women's Victory—and After: Personal Reminiscences, 1911–1918* (London: Sidgwick and Jackson, Ltd., 1920), p. 66.
13 H. M. Tomlinson, *The Sea and the Jungle* (New York: The Modern Library, 1928), pp. 158–59.
14 *Ibid.*, pp. 213–14.
15 *Ibid.*, p. 158.

CHAPTER 30. THE "SOUL" AS METAPHOR FOR TELIC PRINCIPLE

1 Aquinas, *Summa theologiae* I, q. 75, 76. See Aristotle, *De Anima* II, ch. 1 and 2.
2 Aquinas, *Summa theologiae* I, q. 76, a. 1c. See Aristotle, *De Anima* II, 2.
3 Aquinas, *Summa theologiae* I, q. 76, a. 8c.
4 *Ibid.*, I, q. 76, a. 8c.
5 *Ibid.*, I, q. 76, a. 3c.
6 Larry Dossey, M.D., *Space, Time and Medicine* (Boulder and London: Shambhala Publications, 1982), p. 103.
7 Karl Pribram, interviewed by Daniel Goleman, "Holographic Memory," *Psychology Today*, February 1979, pp. 71–84.
8 Dossey, *Space, Time and Medicine*, p. 107. See David Bohm, *Wholeness and the Implicate Order* (London: Routledge and Kegan Paul, Ltd., 1980).
9 Robin Morgan uses the holographic analogy in a thought-provoking way to view feminism. See *The Anatomy of Freedom* (Garden City, N.Y.: Doubleday and Company, 1982). [Editors' note: Originally a footnote, p. 347.]
10 According to Leibniz (1646–1716), for example, the universe is composed of a hierarchy of "monads," each of which is a microcosm reflecting the world with differing degrees of clarity. See Gottfried Wilhelm von Leibniz, *The Monadology*

*and Other Philosophical Writings*, trans. by Robert Latta (London: Oxford University Press, 1925).

CHAPTER 31. BE-FRIENDING

1 Raymond, "A Genealogy of Female Friendship," p. 6.

2 Sarah M. Grimké, "A Seamstress Is Punished," in *Black Women in White America: A Documentary History*, ed. Gerda Lerner (New York: Random House, 1972), p. 18.

3 *Ibid.*, pp. 18–19.

4 Solomon Northup, "The Slaveholder's Mistress," in *Black Women in White America*, pp. 50–51. [Editors' note: This narrative of Patsey's torture is now better-known because of the film *Twelve Years a Slave*, which won the Oscar for best picture in 2013, directed by Steve McQueen; Patsey's life and agony were portrayed by Lupita Nyong'o, who won the Oscar for best female supporting actor.]

5 See, for example, "Racism Is the Issue," *Heresies*, vol. 4, no. 3, issue 15 (1982).

PART IV. SPIRALING ONWARD (1985–2010)

1 Jane Caputi's books include *The Age of Sex Crime* (1987); *Gossips, Gorgons and Crones* (1988); and *Goddesses and Monsters: Women, Myth, Power and Popular Culture* (2004).

2 Audre Lorde, *Zami: A New Spelling of My Name* (Trumansburg, NY: Crossing, 1982).

CHAPTER 32. EARLY MOMENTS

1 *Outercourse*, p. 342.

2 This was Sister Athanasia Gurry, C.S.J., who taught me English throughout my four years of high school at St. Joseph's Academy in Schenectady.

3 There was and still is a taboo against women studying philosophy seriously and becoming teachers and scholars in the "field" of philosophy. Even mere uncritical teaching and writing of scholarly articles about male philosophers was and to some extent still is taboo. But this is not what I am referring to in this passage. I am referring to breaking the *Terrible Taboo* against a woman's striving to become a philosopher in her own right. I already knew that my Quest was *to be* a philosopher, and—although I did not have the words for it—I knew that this was an Elemental Quest, implying Intimacy/Ultimacy. See Mary Daly, *Pure Lust: Elemental Feminist Philosophy* (1984; San Francisco: HarperSanFrancisco, 1992; London: The Women's Press Ltd., 1984), pp. 243–53.

4 See Chapter Four [of *Outercourse*]. My dissertation, subsequently published in Rome, entitled *Natural Knowledge of God in the Philosophy of Jacques Maritain*, was written for the doctorate in philosophy at the University of Fribourg, Switzerland, in the mid-sixties. Although it centers on the meaning and implications of the "intuition of being" in Maritain's philosophy, on a subliminal level I was really trying to understand the meaning and implications of my own intuition of be-ing

for my own philosophical Quest—for my own be-ing. I did not spell this word (*be-ing*) with a hyphen then but that was the sense of it. I later developed my own philosophy of be-ing as a verb (not a noun). See Daly, *Beyond God the Father: Toward a Philosophy of Women's Liberation*. See also my subsequent books.

### CHAPTER 33. THE DREAM OF GREEN

1 It was called a "dissertation" rather than merely a "thesis." There was a concerted effort at that institution at the time to upgrade the M.A. by imposing stringent course requirements and by making the dissertation a very challenging and serious scholarly project.

2 Despite the reality of male privilege, the fact is that La Drière was the first gifted male teacher whom I had ever encountered. Moreover, he was an exception among his colleagues at Catholic University. [Editors' note: originally a footnote, p. 49.]

### CHAPTER 34. THE ANTI-MODERNIST OATH

1 The word *modernism* has a number of meanings. *Webster's* succinctly defines the roman catholic usage as "a system of interpretation of Christian doctrine developed at the end of the 19th century and condemned by Pope Pius X in 1907 that denied the objective truth of revelation and the whole supernatural world and maintained that the only vital element in any religion and Catholicism in particular was its power to preserve and communicate to others the best religious experiences of the race."

### CHAPTER 35. MY DOCTORAL DISSERTATION IN PHILOSOPHY

1 As the disabling devices of phallic fragmentation and dis-memberment have worked to undermine the insights of Feminism—especially since the mid-1980s—the importance of Furious Focus becomes evident. For example, we can see the necessity for avoiding disintegration into anti-intellectuality and, at the seemingly opposite end, dryasdust elite/effete academic studies and discussions (sometimes under the aegis of "Women's Studies" or "Gender Studies") that turn back the clock and endlessly reiterate tired old "problems" that were intelligently discussed and moved beyond two decades before. [Editors' note: Originally a footnote, p. 75.]

2 See "Prelude to The Second Spiral Galaxy" for further discussion of Piracy. [Editors' note: This is an internal reference to *Outercourse*; originally a footnote, p. 75.]

3 Correspondence on "Women and the Church," *Commonweal* (February 14, 1964), p. 603.

4 Mary F. Daly, "Catholic Women and the Modern Era," in *Wir schweigen nicht länger!—We Won't Keep Silence Any Longer!* ed. by Gertrud Heinzelmann (Zurich: Interfeminas Verlag, 1965), pp. 106–110.

5 Mary Daly, "A Built-In Bias," *Commonweal* LXXXI (January 15, 1965), pp. 508–11.

6 Daly, "Autobiographical Preface to the 1975 Edition," *The Church and the Second Sex*, p. 11.

7 My philosophical dissertation was published the next year as a book: Mary F. Daly, *Natural Knowledge of God in the Philosophy of Jacques Maritain* (Rome: Catholic Book Agency, 1966). Even though I had completed all work for the doctorate in July 1965, I was granted only a "Certificat Provisoire" (Provisional Certificate) at that time. This document stated that "according to the regulations regarding the doctoral examination Mademoiselle Mary F. Daly will not have the right to use the title 'Doctor' until after remittance of the Diploma, which will be delivered to her upon reception of 150 printed copies of the Dissertation. This Provisional Certificate is valid for only two years." What this meant was that I was obliged to self-publish and donate 150 copies of my dissertation to the library in order to have evidence that I had earned the degree, and that if I didn't manage to accomplish this within two years, well, that was my loss! It seems that the library used these dissertations in an exchange system with other libraries in order to build up its collection. As for the "Catholic Book Agency," to which I paid several hundred dollars (a fortune to me at the time), I never recouped any of my investment, even though apparently my book was rather widely distributed/sold to libraries in Europe and America. [Editors' note: What follows was originally a footnote, p. 78.] I requested and received a further increase of my loan from the Medora A. Feehan Fund to cover the expense of publication. This brought my accumulated debt to $5,200, which was a lot then, but I knew that I could and would pay it all back.

8 Gary dashed off a quick outline of his process. Although I cannot Now remember all of the details, I recall the basic structural elements. He suggested that I write a letter to a friend describing what I wanted to do. He said that he generally began with a chapter whose function was "setting the scene." This presented the contemporary context. Then there would be a chapter analyzing the problems inherent in "the scene." This was followed by historical chapters presenting the background of these current problems. His final chapters offered new approaches to solving these problems. Although all of this may seem very general, it was just what I needed to Spin off from. My block about structuring a book was gone forever. This memory of the procedure was reconfirmed in a discussion with Gary while in the process of writing *Outercourse* (Conversation, Boston, June 1990). [Editors' note: Originally a footnote, p. 79.]

9 For further astonishing details, see my "Autobiographical Preface to the 1975 Edition," *The Church and the Second Sex*, pp. 5–14.

## CHAPTER 36. THE TIME OF THE TIGERS

1 The text of this sermon, together with introductory remarks by me and several letters from "The Exodus Community," were published in my article entitled "The Women's Movement: An Exodus Community," in *Religious Education* 67 (September–October 1972), pp. 327–35. The letters were written by Emily Culpepper, Linda Barufaldi, Elizabeth Rice, Mary Rodda, and myself.

2 Daly, "The Women's Movement," pp. 332–33.

3 *Ibid.*, p. 334.

## CHAPTER 37. RE-CALLING MY LESBIAN IDENTITY

1 See Anne Koedt, "Loving Another Woman—Interview," in *Radical Feminism*, edited by Anne Koedt, Ellen Levine, Anita Rapone (New York: Quadrangle Books, 1973), pp. 85–93. This anthology contains a number of articles from *Notes from the Second Year* and *Notes from the Third Year.*

2 *Ibid.*, p. 87.

3 *Ibid.*, p. 88.

4 These expressions are defined in Chapter Two [of *Outercourse*]. *Touching Powers* are "Pyrogenetic Powers of Communication, actualized by women who break the Terrible Taboo and thus break out of the touchable caste" (*Wickedary*). The expression *touchable caste* Names the "fixed status imposed upon women and all of nature; condition of those condemned by phallocrats to be touched—physically, emotionally, intellectually, spiritually—by those in possession of a penis; condition of those systematically subjected to phallic violation, e.g., by rape, battering, medical experimentation, and butchery" (*Wickedary*). See Daly, *Pure Lust*, Chapter Six. [Editors' note: Originally a footnote, p. 144.]

## CHAPTER 38. SOME BE-MUSING MOMENTS

1 *Be-Musing* means "be-ing a Muse for oneself and for Other Muses; refusing Musing to a-Musing scribblers; Spinning great dreams and reveries of Female creations of Lesbian nations" (*Wickedary*). [Editors' note: Originally a footnote, p. 152. The "Cove" to which Daly refers in this sentence was her apartment on Commonwealth Avenue in Brighton, Massachusetts.]

2 Transcontinental transtemporal telephone conversation with Linda Barufaldi, August 15, 1989.

3 [Editors' note: Elizabeth "Betty" Farians (1923–2013) was an outstanding pioneer feminist activist and thinker, with a passion for animal rights. A thoughtful memoir by Elizabeth Miller can be found on the Feminist Studies in Religion blog, "Elizabeth Farians: Catholic Feminist Pioneer," July 15, 2014, www.fsrinc.org.]

4 This insight occurred in a conversation with Nelle, probably in 1972, in her home in Madison, New Jersey. [Editors' note: Originally a footnote, p. 158.]

5 The word *Be-ing* refers to "the constantly Unfolding Verb of Verbs which is intransitive, having no object that limits its dynamism." It is "the Final Cause, the Good who is Self-communicating, who is the Verb from whom, in whom, and with whom all true movements move" (*Wickedary*). When *be-ing* is not capitalized, it refers to "actual participation in the Ultimate/Intimate Reality—Be-ing, the Verb" (*Wickedary*). In *Beyond God the Father* I did not yet consistently hyphenate Be-ing or be-ing in order to spell out, so to speak, my intention of Naming the Verb and participation in the Verb. [Editors' note: Originally a footnote, p. 158.]

## CHAPTER 39. THE FATHERS' FOLLIES

1 My whirlwind speaking tours of the winter and spring of 1975 brought me to the Aquinas Institute at Princeton University in Princeton, New Jersey; Denison University in Granville, Ohio; Rutgers University in New Brunswick, New Jersey; Carleton College in Northfield, Minnesota; Barat College in Lake Forest, Illinois; Florida State University in Tallahassee; University of Maine in Orono; Harvard Medical School in Cambridge, Massachusetts; Harvard University in Cambridge, Massachusetts; Keene State College in Keene, New Hampshire. I also spoke at the Cambridge Forum in Cambridge, Massachusetts and at the Woodstock Women's Center in Woodstock, New York.

2 See *Outercourse*, Chapter Nine.

3 I had published (in addition to dissertations) two major books—*The Church and the Second Sex* and *Beyond God the Father: Toward a Philosophy of Women's Liberation*. By the fall of 1974 the latter was used as a required text in universities and seminaries across the country and was excerpted in several publications. In addition I had made contributions to more than ten books and had published more than twenty articles in professional journals as well as in Feminist periodicals. I had done substantial committee work in a variety of areas, had given more than seventy public lectures, and had presented papers at learned [*sic*] societies. I was listed in a dozen or so *Who's Who* dictionaries and encyclopedias. I also had seven degrees, three of them doctorates. [Editors' note: Originally a footnote, p. 206.]

4 *The Heights*, February 10, 1975.

5 *Ibid*. See *Outercourse*, Chapter Nine.

6 See Janice G. Raymond, who cites the proceedings of that meeting in "Mary Daly: A Decade of Academic Harassment and Feminist Survival," in *Handbook for Women Scholars: Strategies for Success*, ed. by Mary L. Spencer, Monika Kehoe, and Karen Speece (San Francisco: America's Behavioral Research Corporation, 1982), p. 84. This was also reported in an article by Joan Quinlan in *The Heights*, March 3, 1975, p. 3.

7 See Raymond, "Mary Daly," p. 84, which cites the legal memorandum of that meeting. Quinlan's article in *The Heights* (March 3, 1975, p. 3) cites McBrien's pathetic claim that there were "not enough footnotes" in *Beyond God the Father* "in the areas of Christology, Ecclesiology, and the Old Testament." Although it is difficult to have the patience to respond to such charges, I did patiently explain that the book has more than adequate footnotes. It is noteworthy that the outside experts, whose favorable views of my work were dismissed, were: (1) John Bennett, former president of Union Theological Seminary; (2) John Cobb, renowned theologian on the faculty of The School of Theology at Claremont, California; (3) James Luther Adams, Professor Emeritus associated with Harvard Divinity School. The only persons whose judgments "counted" were members of the Boston College department of theology.

8 We used the term *Foremothers* at that time. Shortly thereafter, many of us began using *Foresisters* instead. This word has seemed more accurate. Not all women are mothers, whereas all can be sisters. *Foresisters* implies an egalitarian relationship, rather than a "maternal" role.
9 [Editors' note: Robin Morgan's recollections of this are in her preface to this volume.]
10 The article was published in *The Heights*, February 10, 1975.
11 [Editors' note: Also speaking was Joyce Marieb, who described herself as a motel desk clerk with a Ph.D. in religious and philosophical studies.]
12 The women educators who spoke, who were in various "fields" in diverse universities, related experiences of discrimination, denial of tenure, and firing at these institutions. In my speech I elaborated upon the nature of Feminist Studies and the ways in which it was thwarted in universities. I proclaimed that 1975 was the Year of the Backlash against women. Jan Raymond made an important point in her speech concerning her own case. "My final and greatest sin was female identification and bonding. I performed the unforgivable act of studying seriously—of identifying professionally—with a woman. In an educational sense, I was not the 'daughter of an educated man,' to use Virginia Woolf's phrase, but the daughter of an educated woman. Had I chosen to study under and seriously associate myself and my work with a renowned and internationally recognized male scholar, my status at BC would undoubtedly be most different today."
13 The Forum was not reported in major newspapers, although reporters had been called. This silence illustrated the fact that 1975 was indeed the year of the beginning of the backlash. It was, however, excellently recorded in *The Heights*, March 3, 1975, especially in an article by Maureen Dezell (pp. 1, 15). It was reported also in Feminist media. Most importantly, it was recorded deeply in the Memories of the hundreds of women who were Present.

## CHAPTER 40. CLASSROOM TEACHING OF WOMEN AND OF MEN

1 *Pure Lust*, p. 372. Sarah Hoagland has written eloquently about this.
2 As I have already explained, I have never refused to teach a registered, *bona fide*, qualified male student who expressed a desire to study with me.
3 At this point the reader will have noticed that in The Third Spiral Galaxy the resolution of each counterpoint breaks ground for the resolution of the next. [Editors' note: Originally a footnote, p. 328.]

## CHAPTER 41. ON HOW I JUMPED OVER THE MOON

1 See Nicholas D. Kristof, "Stark Data on Women: 100 Million Women Are Missing," *The New York Times*, November 5, 1991, pp. C1, C12. Kristof states: "A traditional preference for boys translates quickly—in China, India, and many other developing countries—into neglect and death for girls." Stating that the problem appears to be getting worse in Asia, he cites Harvard economist Amartya Sen: "Professor Sen estimates that considerably more than 100 million females are missing around the world, and he asserts that the reason the shortfall is getting worse in some

areas is that girls are not allowed to benefit as much as boys from improvements in health care and nutrition that are lowering death rates in developing countries." Numerous demographers seem to agree that millions of women die because they're women. As Kristof states: "It is only in the overall statistics that the shortfall becomes clear." In addition to infanticide and neglect of female children, there is another problem, arising from modern technology. Kristof comments: "These days technology has presented parents with a tidier option than infanticide: ultrasound tests that determine the sex of a fetus." Kristof writes of a United Nations report which "cited 8,000 abortions in Bombay after the parents learned of the sex of the fetus, *only one of which involved a male* [emphasis mine]." And *Science and Technology* quoted a Chinese peasant as saying: "Ultrasound is really worthwhile, even though my wife had to go through four abortions to get a son."

2 See *Outercourse*, Chapter Thirteen.

CHAPTER 42. MAGNETIC COURAGE

1 See Nevill Drury, *Dictionary of Mysticism and the Esoteric Traditions*, rev. ed. (Bridport, Dorset, England: Prism Press, 1992), p. 99.

2 *Ibid.*

3 "The Young Physicists," *The New York Times*, January 3, 1984, pp. C1, C5.

4 *Wickedary*, p. 256.

5 See Andrew Kimbrell, "Biocolonization: The Patenting of Life and the Global Market in Body Parts," in *The Case Against the Global Economy and for a Turn Toward the Local*, ed. by Jerry Mander and Edward Goldsmith (San Francisco: Sierra Club Books, 1996), pp. 131–32.

6 Andy Coghlan, "One Small Step for a Sheep . . . ," *New Scientist*, March 1, 1997, p. 4.

7 Gina Kolata, "On Cloning Humans, 'Never' Turns Swiftly into 'Why Not?'" *The New York Times*, December 2, 1997, pp. A1, A24.

8 *Ibid.*, p. A24.

9 *Ibid.*

10 I intend the expression *Metapatriarchal Metaphor* in the deepest sense. As first introduced in *Pure Lust* and later defined in the *Wickedary* (p. 82), it means: "words that function to Name Metapatriarchal transformation and therefore to elicit such change; the language/vehicles of transcendent Spiraling. . . ." [Editors' note: Originally a footnote, pp. 95–96.]

11 By *Fey Faith* I mean "the Faith of a woman who identifies with the Fates; Faith which implies the natural clairvoyance of those who reject master-minded mediation of sense experience; the source of the Hope that is characteristic of Hags." See *Pure Lust*, pp. 307–11, and *Wickedary*, pp. 75–76. [Editors note: Originally a footnote, p. 96.]

## CHAPTER 43. QUINTESSENCE

1 See Hildegarde, St., *New Catholic Encyclopedia*, 1967, VI, 1117. Word-Witches continue to wonder and speculate about this "lost" language and "lost" alphabet. Destroyed by the church, perhaps?

2 See *Illuminations of Hildegard of Bingen*, text by Hildegard of Bingen, with commentary by Matthew Fox (Santa Fe, N.M.: Bear and Company, 1985), p. 117.

3 Barbara G. Walker writes:

> Fathers of the Christian church strongly opposed the worship of Mary because they were well aware that she was only a composite of Mariamne, the Semitic God-Mother and Queen of Heaven, Aphrodite-Mari, the Syrian version of Ishtar; Juno the Blessed Virgin; Isis as Stella Maris, Star of the Sea; Maya the Oriental Virgin Mother of the Redeemer; the Moerae or trinity of Fates; and many other versions of the Great Goddess. Even Diana Lucifera the Morning-Star Goddess was assimilated to the Christian myth as Mary's "mother," Anna or Dinah. Churchmen knew the same titles were applied to Mary as to her pagan forerunners: "queen of heaven, empress of hell, lady of all the world."

The *Speculum beatae Mariae* said Mary was like the Juno-Artemis-Hecate trinity: "queen of heaven where she is enthroned in the midst of angels, queen of earth where she constantly manifests her power, and queen of hell where she has authority over the demons." According to the Office of the Virgin, she was the primordial being, "created from the beginning and before the centuries." Christian patriarchs therefore sought to humanize and belittle Mary, to prove her unworthy of adoration.

See Barbara G. Walker, *The Woman's Encyclopedia of Myths and Secrets* (San Francisco: Harper and Row, 1983), pp. 602–3. [Editors' note: Originally a footnote, p. 220.]

4 Lawrence M. Krauss, *The Fifth Essence: The Search for Dark Matter in the Universe* (New York: HarperCollins, Basic Books, 1989), pp. 11–13.

5 I have developed this idea in *Pure Lust*.

6 These realities are described vividly by Madeleine L'Engle in *A Wrinkle in Time* (New York: Dell Publishing Company, 1962). Equally enlightening is another book by Madeleine L'Engle, *A Wind in the Door* (New York: Dell Publishing Company, 1973).

## CHAPTER 44. A HEIGHTENED EXPERIENCE OF LOSING AND FINDING

1 [Editors' note: This request motivated the editors to include all of chapters 1 and 5 from *Gyn/Ecology*, chapters 14 and 16, respectively, in this collection.]

2 Mary Daly, *Outercourse: The Be-Dazzling Voyage* (New York: HarperSanFrancisco, 1992; London: The Women's Press, 1993; distributed in the US by Trafalgar Square Publishing), pp. 231–33.

3 *Ibid.*, p. 233, note.
4 Alexis De Veaux, *Warrior Poet: A Biography of Audre Lorde* (New York: W. W. Norton & Co., 2004).
5 Personal correspondence from Alexis De Veaux, September 30, 2003.

## CHAPTER 45. WHAT TERRIFIC SHOCK WILL BE SHOCKING ENOUGH?

1 Ida Husted Harper, *The Life and Work of Susan B. Anthony*, vol. III (Indianapolis: The Hollenbeck Press, c. 1898–1908), p. 366.
2 Thomas Oliphant, "Two Leaps Forward on Global Warming," *The Boston Globe* (June 4, 2002), p. A15.
3 See *Be-ing* in Mary Daly, *Websters' First New Intergalactic Wickedary of the English Language*, Conjured in Cahoots with Jane Caputi (Boston: Beacon Press, 1987; New York: HarperSanFrancisco, 1994), W-W 1.
4 [Editors' note: The clover blossom is discussed in chapter 32 of this collection.]
5 Daly, *Beyond God the Father: Toward a Philosophy of Women's Liberation*, pp. 203–04, note 28.
6 *Ibid.*, p. 204, note 28.
7 Harper, *Life and Work of Susan B. Anthony*, vol. III, p. 366.
8 See *patriarchy* in Daly, *Wickedary*, W-W 1. *Speciesism* will be added to the original definition of *patriarchy* in future editions. [Editors' note: The word "speciesism" in square brackets was inserted by Daly.]

# WORKS BY MARY DALY: A BIBLIOGRAPHY


BOOKS

*Amazon Grace: Re-Calling the Courage to Sin Big.* New York: Palgrave Macmillan, 2006.

*Beyond God the Father: Toward a Philosophy of Women's Liberation.* Boston: Beacon, 1973. Reprinted, with an "Original Reintroduction," Boston: Beacon, 1985. Published in the United Kingdom with "Original Reintroduction," London: Women's Press, 1986.

*The Church and the Second Sex.* New York: Harper and Row, 1968. Reprinted, with an "Autobiographical Preface to the Colophon Edition" and "Feminist Postchristian Introduction," New York: Harper Colophon, 1975. Reprinted, with a "New Archaic Afterwords," in *The Church and the Second Sex: With the Feminist Postchristian Introduction and New Archaic Afterwords by the Author*, Boston: Beacon, 1985.

*Gyn/Ecology: The Metaethics of Radical Feminism.* Boston: Beacon, 1978. Reprinted, with a "New Intergalactic Introduction by the Author," Boston: Beacon, 1990. Published in the United Kingdom, London: Women's Press, 1979.

*Outercourse: The Bedazzling Voyage, Containing Recollections from My Logbook of a Radical Feminist Philosopher.* San Francisco: HarperSanFrancisco, 1992.

*Pure Lust: Elemental Feminist Philosophy.* Boston: Beacon, 1984. Reprint, San Francisco: HarperSanFrancisco, 1992. Published in the United Kingdom, London: Women's Press, 1984.

*Quintessence . . . Realizing the Archaic Future: A Radical Elemental Feminist Manifesto.* Boston: Beacon, 1998.

*Websters' First New Intergalactic Wickedary of the English Language.* Conjured in Cahoots with Jane Caputi. Boston: Beacon, 1987. Published in the United Kingdom, London: Women's Press, 1988, and in Ireland, Dublin: Attic Press, 1988.

ARTICLES

"Abortion and Sexual Caste." *Commonweal* 95, no. 18 (February 4, 1972): 415–19.

"African Genital Mutilation: The Unspeakable Atrocities." In *The Gender Reader*, edited by Evelyn Ashton-Jones, Gary A. Olson, and Merry Perry, 462–85. 2nd ed. Boston: Allyn and Bacon, 2000.

"After the Death of God the Father: Women's Liberation and the Transformation of Christian Consciousness." *Commonweal* 94, no. 1 (March 12, 1971): 7–11. Reprinted in *Feminism in Our Time: The Essential Writings, World War II to the Present*, ed. Miriam Schneir, 260–71. New York: Vintage, 1994.

"Antifeminism in the Church." *Information Documentation on the Conciliar Church* No. 68–44 (1968).

"Be-Friending: The Lust to Share Happiness." In *For Lesbians Only: A Separatist Anthology*, edited by Sarah Lucia Hoagland and Julia Penelope, 200–211. London: Onlywomen Press, 1988.

"Be-Friending: Weaving Contexts, Creating Atmospheres." In *Weaving the Visions: New Patterns in Feminist Spirituality*, edited by Judith Plaskow and Carol P. Christ, 199–207. San Francisco: Harper and Row, 1989.

"Be-Laughing." *Woman of Power* 8 (Winter 1988): 76–80.

"A Built-in Bias: The Forgotten Sex." *Commonweal* 81, no. 16 (January 15, 1965): 508–11.

"A Call for the Castration of Sexist Religion." *Unitarian Universalist Christian* 27 (Autumn/Winter 1972): 23–27.

"Christian Mission after the Death of God." In *Demands for Christian Renewal*, edited by William J. Wilson, 1–18. New York: Maryknoll, 1968.

"The Courage to Leave: A Response to John Cobb's Theology." In *John Cobb's Theology in Process*, edited by D. R. Griffin and T. J. J. Altizer, 84–98. Philadelphia: Westminster, 1977.

"The Courage to See." *Christian Century* 88, no. 38 (September 22, 1971): 1108–11.

"Dispensing with Trivia." *Commonweal* 88, no. 11 (May 31, 1968): 322–25.

Foreword to *Woman, Church and State*, by Matilda Joslyn Gage, vii-x. Watertown, MA: Persephone, 1980.

"God Is a Verb." *Ms.*, December 1974, 58–62, 96–98.

"Gyn/Ecology: Spinning New Time/Space." In *The Politics of Women's Spirituality: Essays on the Rise of Spiritual Power within the Feminist Movement*, edited by Charlene Spretnak, 207–12. New York: Anchor Press/Doubleday, 1982.

"Hans Kung." In *The New Day: Catholic Theologians of the Renewal*, edited by William J. Boney and Lawrence E. Molumby, 129–42. Richmond: John Knox, 1968.

"I Thank Thee, Lord, That Thou Has Not Created Me a Woman." In *The Gender Reader*, edited by Evelyn Ashton-Jones, Gary A. Olson, and Merry Perry, 164–68. 2nd ed., Boston: Allyn and Bacon, 2000.

"The Looking Glass Society." In *Feminist Theology: A Reader*, edited by Ann Loades, 189–94. Louisville, KY: Westminster John Knox, 1990.

"A Manifestation of Goddess." *On the Issues 7, no.* 2 (Spring 1998): 14–15.

"Mary Daly on the Church: Questions and Answers and Questions and Answers." *Commonweal* 91, no. 7 (November 14, 1969): 215.

"Post-Christian Theology: Some Connections between Idolatry and Methodolatry, between Deicide and Methodicide." In *Women and Religion 1973*, edited by Joan Arnold Romero, 33–38. Tallahassee, FL: American Academy of Religion/Scholars' Press, 1973.

"Prelude to the First Passage." *Feminist Studies* 4, no. 3 (1978): 81–86.

"The Problem of Hope: Can We Judge the Theology of Hope an Unmixed Blessing?" *Commonweal* 92, no. 14 (June 26, 1970): 314–17.

"The Problem of Speculative Theology." *Thomist* 29 (1965): 177–216.

"The Qualitative Leap beyond Patriarchal Religion." *Quest* 1, no. 4 (Spring 1975): 20–40. Republished in *Women and Values: Readings in Recent Feminist Philosophy*, edited by Marilyn Pearsall, 198–210. Belmont, CA: Wadsworth, 1986.

"Return of the Protestant Principle: The Stakes: The Survival of Christianity." *Commonweal* 90, no. 12 (June 6, 1969): 338–41.

"Separation: Room of One's Own." In *For Lesbians Only: A Separatist Anthology*, edited by Sarah Lucia Hoagland and Julia Penelope, 367–71. London: Onlywomen Press, 1988.

"A Short Essay on Hearing and the Qualitative Leap of Radical Feminism." *Horizons* 2 (1975): 120–24.

"Sin Big." *New Yorker*, February 26–March 4, 1996, 76–84.

"Sisterhood as a Cosmic Covenant." In *The Politics of Women's Spirituality: Essays on the Rise of Spiritual Power Within the Feminist Movement*, edited by Charlene Spretnak, 351–61. New York: Anchor Press/Doubleday, 1982.

"Sparking: The Fire of Female Friendship." *Chrysalis* 6 (1978): 27–35.

"Spiraling into the Nineties." *Woman of Power* 17 (1990): 6–12.

"The Spiritual Dimension of Women's Liberation." In *Notes from the Third Year: Women's Liberation*, edited by Anne Koedt and Shulamith Firestone. New York: n.p., 1971. Reprinted in *Radical Feminism*, edited by Anne Koedt, Ellen Levine, and Anita Rapone, 259–67. New York: Quadrangle, 1973. Reprinted in *Feminist Knowledge: Critique and Construct*, edited by Sneja Gunew, 335–41. London: Routledge, 1991.

"The Spiritual Revolution: Women's Liberation as Theological Re-education." *Andover Newton Quarterly* 12 (1972): 163–72 and *Notre Dame Journal of Education* 2 (1972): 300–312. Reprinted in *Feminist Theological Ethics: A Reader*, edited by Lois K. Daly, 121–34. Louisville, KY: Westminster John Knox, 1994.

"Theology after the Demise of God the Father: A Call for the Castration of Sexist Religion." In *Women and Religion*, edited by Judith Plaskow and Joan Arnold, 3–19. Rev ed. Missoula, MT: American Academy of Religion/Scholars Press, 1974. Also in *Sexist Religion and Women in the Church: No More Silence!*, edited by Alice L. Ageman, 125–42. New York: Association Press, 1974.

"Toward Partnership in the Church." In *Voices of the New Feminism*, edited by Mary Lou Thompson, 136–51. Boston: Beacon, 1970.

"The Transformation of Silence into Language and Action." Panel presentation, Lesbians and Literature section of the Modern Language Association 1977 meeting. *Sinister Wisdom* 6 (1978): 5–11.

"Underground Theology: An Exchange of Views." *Commonweal* 88, no. 18 (August 9, 1968): 532–34, a response to Aquinas Ferrara.

"Vorwort zur deutschen Ausgabe von *Beyond God the Father*." In *Jenseits von Gottvater Sohn & Co.: Aufbruch zu einer Philosophie der Frauenbefreiung*, 5–10. Munich: Frauenoffensive, 1980.

"Why Speak about God?" In *Womanspirit Rising: A Feminist Reader in Religion*, edited by Carol Christ and Judith Plaskow, 210–18. San Francisco: Harper and Row, 1979.

"The Witches Return: Patriarchy on Trial." In *Radically Speaking: Feminism Reclaimed*, edited by Diana Bell and Renate Klein, 551–56. North Melbourne, Australia: Spinifex, 1996.

"Women and the Catholic Church." In *Sisterhood Is Powerful: An Anthology of Writings from the Women's Liberation Movement*, edited by Robin Morgan, 124–38. New York: Random House, 1970.

"Women and the Church." *Commonweal* 79, no. 20 (1964): 603.

"The Women's Movement: An Exodus Community." *Religious Education* 67, no. 5 (September–October 1972): 327–35. Republished in *Women and Religion: A Feminist Sourcebook of Christian Thought*, edited by Elizabeth Clark and Herbert Richardson, 265–71. New York: Harper and Row, 1977.

"Zeroing in on Freedom: Can the Charles Currans Be Freed?" *Commonweal* 86, no. 11 (June 2, 1967): 316–17.

### THESES/DISSERTATIONS

*Natural Knowledge of God in the Philosophy of Jacques Maritain: A Critical Study*. Rome: Officium Libri Catholici, Catholic Book Agency, 1966.

*The Problem of Speculative Theology*. Washington: Thomist Press, 1965.

### TRANSLATIONS

#### *Beyond God the Father*

DUTCH: *Voorbij God de Vader: Op weg naar een feministische bevrijdingsfilosofie*. Translated by Else Pars, Trudi Klijn, and Catharina J. M. Halkes. Amsterdam: De Horstink, 1983.

GERMAN: *Jenseits von Gottvater Sohn & Co.: Aufbruch zu einer Philosophie der Frauenbefreiung*. Translated by Marianne Reppekus and Barbara Henninges. Munich: Frauenoffensive, 1980.

ITALIAN: *Al di là di Dio Padre: Verso una filosofia della liberazione delle donne*. Rome: Editori Riuniti,1990.

KOREAN: *Hananim Abŏji rŭl nŏmŏsŏ: Yŏsŏngdŭl ŭi haebang ch'ŏrhak ŭl hyanghayŏ*. Translated by Hye-suk Hwang. Seoul: Ihwa Yŏja Taehakkyo Ch'ulp'anbu, 1996.

#### *The Church and the Second Sex*

FRENCH: *Le deuxième sexe conteste*. Translated by Suzanne Valles. Tours: Mame, 1969; Montréal: HMH, 1969.

GERMAN: *Kirche, Frau und Sexus*. Translated by Dietgard Erb. Olten: Walter-Verlag, 1970.

ITALIAN: *La Chiesa e il secondo sesso*. Translated by Liliana Lanzarini. Milan: Rizzoli, 1982.

KOREAN: *Kyohoe wa che-2 ŭi sŏng*. Translated by Hye-suk Hwang. Seoul: Yŏsŏng Sinmunsa, 1997.

*Gyn/Ecology*

GERMAN: *Gyn/Ökologie: Eine Meta-Ethik des radikalen Feminismus*. Translated by Erika Wisselinck. Munich: Frauenoffensive, 1980.

*Outercourse*

GERMAN: *Auswärts reisen: Die strahlkräftige Fahrt; darin Erinnerungen aus meinem Logbuch einer radikalen feministischen Philosophin*. Translated by Erika Wisselinck. Munich: Frauenoffensive, 1994.

*Pure Lust*

GERMAN: *Reine Lust: Elemental-feministische Philosophie*. Translated by Erika Wisselinck. Munich: Frauenoffensive, 1986.

*Quintessence*

ITALIAN: *Quintessenza: Realizzare il future arcaico: Un manifesto femminista elementare radicale*. Rome: Venexia, 2006.

TRANSLATIONS OF ARTICLES

"El Antifeminismo en la Iglesia." Rome: Información y documentación sobre la Iglesia Conciliar, 1969.

"El cristianismo: Una história de contradicciones." Translated by Elena Olivos. In *Del cielo a la tierra: Una antología de teología feminista*, edited by Mary Judith Ress, Ute Seibert-Cuadra, and Lene Sjørup, 61–96. Santiago: Sello Azul, Editorial de Mujeres, 1994. Chapter from The Church and the Second Sex. Also available at http://servicioskoinonia.org/.

"Después de la muerte de Dios Padre: La liberación de las mujeres y la transformación de la conciencia cristiana." Translated by Ondina Victoriano. In *Del cielo a la tierra: Una antología de teología feminista*, edited by Mary Judith Ress, Ute Seibert-Cuadra, and Lene Sjørup. Santiago: Sello Azul, Editorial de Mujeres, 1994, pp. 97–105.

*Notes pour une ontologie du féminisme radical*. Translated by Michèle Causse. Outremont, Québec: L'Intégrale, 1982. Published as a pamphlet.

"Der qualitative Sprung über die patriarchale Religion." Translated by Barbara Henninges. *Frauenoffensive Journal* (Munich) 9 (1978): 2–13; republished in *Frau und Religion: Gotteserfahrungen im Patriarchat; mit Texten von Gertrud Bäumer, Lily Braun, Mary Daly, Hedwig Dohm, Ricarda Huch, Louise Otto-Peters, Anna Paulsen, Luise Rinser, Dorothee Sölle*, edited by Elisabeth Moltmann-Wendel, 110–23. Frankfurt: Fischer Taschenbuch-Verlag, 1984.

"El salto caulitativo más allá de la religión patriarchal." Translated by Elena Olivos. In *Del cielo a la tierra: Una antología de teología feminista*, edited by Mary Judith

Ress, Ute Seibert-Cuadra, and Lene Sjørup, 106–25. Santiago: Sello Azul, Editorial de Mujeres, 1994. Translation of article from Quest entitled "The Qualitative Leap beyond Patriarchal Religion."

## INTERVIEWS

Bridle, Susan. "No Man's Land: An Interview with Mary Daly." *What Is Enlightenment* 16 (1999). Reprinted in the *Catholic New Times*, March 7, 2011, 4.

Madsen, Catherine. "The Thin Thread of Conversation: An Interview with Mary Daly." *CrossCurrents* 50, no. 3 (2000): 332–48.

# SECONDARY SOURCES ON MARY DALY


Adams, Carol J. "Ecofeminism and the Eating of Animals." *Hypatia* 6, no. 1 (1991): 125–45.

———. "Finding Necrophilia in Meat Eating: Mary Daly's Evolving FemVeg Perspective." *Journal of Feminist Studies in Religion* 28, no. 2 (2012): 93–98.

———. Review of *Outercourse: The Be-Dazzling Voyage*, by Mary Daly. *Women's Review of Books* 10, no. 6 (1993): 1.

———. *The Sexual Politics of Meat: A Feminist-Vegetarian Critical Theory*. New York: Continuum, 1989. Twentieth anniversary edition dedicated to Mary Daly, New York: Continuum, 2010.

Adams, Harriet Farwell. "Work in the Interstices: Woman in Academe." *Women's Studies International Forum* 6, no. 2 (1983): 135–41.

Ahranjani, Maryam. "Mary Daly v. Boston College: The Impermissibility of Single-Sex Classrooms within a Private University." *American University Journal of Gender, Social Policy and the Law* 9 (2001): 179–205.

Alcoff, Linda. "Cultural Feminism versus Post-Structuralism: The Identity Crisis in Feminist Theory." *Signs* 13, no. 3 (Spring 1988): 405–36.

Allen, Christine Garside. "Self-Creation and Loss of Self: Mary Daly and St. Teresa of Avila." *Studies in Religion/Sciences Religieuses* 6, no. 1 (1976): 67–72.

Alvizo, Xóchitl. "Celebrating and Con-Questioning Mary Daly." *Journal of Feminist Studies in Religion* 28, no. 2 (2012): 98–100.

Anderson, Carol, and Jennifer Rycenga. "Mary Daly: Grand Agitator and Revolting Hag." *Feminist Theology: The Journal of the Britain and Ireland School of Feminist Theology* 24 (May 2000): 9–12.

Anderson, Kristine. "The Encyclopedic Dictionary as Utopian Genre: Two Feminist Ventures." *Utopian Studies* 2 (1991): 124–30.

Andolsen, Barbara Hilkert. "Agape in Feminist Ethics." *Journal of Religious Ethics* 9, no. 1 (1981): 69–83.

Armour, Ellen T. "Questioning 'Woman' in Feminist/Womanist Theology: Irigaray, Ruether, and Daly." In *Transfigurations: Theology and the French Feminists*, edited by C. W. Maggie Kim, Susan St. Ville, and Susan Simonaitis. Minneapolis: Fortress, 1993.

———. "Writing/Reading Selves, Writing/Reading Race." *Philosophy Today* 41 (Winter 1997 supplement): 110–17.

Barr, Marleen S. "Goodnight, *Gynesis,* Goodnight *Gyn/Ecology.*" *Extrapolation* 36 (1995): 181–83.

Batz, Jeanette. "'Smuggle Back What's Lost,' Wild Mary Daly Tells Women." *National Catholic Reporter*, May 31, 1996, 18.

Berry, Wanda Warren. "Feminist Theology: The Verbing of Ultimate/Intimate Reality in Mary Daly in Women's Studies." *Ultimate Reality and Meaning* 11, no. 3 (1988): 212–32. Reprinted in *Feminist Interpretations of Mary Daly*, edited by Sarah Lucia Hoagland and Marilyn Frye, 27–54. State College: Pennsylvania State University Press, 2000.

———. "Images of Sin and Salvation in Feminist Theology." *Anglican Theological Review* 60 (1978): 25–54.

Biehl, Janet. *Rethinking Ecofeminist Politics*. Boston: South End, 1991.

Bircher-Bischof, Bettina. "Die Rede von Gott in der feministischen Theologie: Eine Darstellung der theologischen Ansätze von C. Halkes, M. Daly und R. Ruether." University of Freiburg, 1987.

Brewer, Kathleen. "The Self as Temporalizer: Time, Space, and Salvation for Women." *Radical Religion* 1, nos. 3–4 (Summer–Fall 1974): 52–60.

Brodbeck, Doris. *Siehe, ich schaffe Neues: Aufbrüche von Frauen in Protestantismus, Katholizismus, Christkatholizismus und Judentum*. Bern: eFeF-Verlag, 1998.

Bulkin, Elly. "Racism and Writing: Some Implications for White Lesbian Critics." *Sinister Wisdom* 13 (Spring 1980): 3–22. Reprinted in *Sinister Wisdom* 43–44 (1991): 114–34.

Busch, Irmgard Maria. "De kunst van het kaaien: Mythe en werkelijkheid in het boek Gyn-Ecology van Mary Daly." Thesis. Tilburg: Theologische Faculteit Tilburg, 1985.

Campbell, Debra. "Be-ing Is Be/Leaving." In *Feminist Interpretations of Mary Daly*, edited by Sarah Lucia Hoagland and Marilyn Frye, 164–93. State College: Pennsylvania State University Press, 2000.

Caputi, Jane. "Feeding Green Fire." *Journal for the Study of Religion, Nature & Culture* 5, no. 4 (2011): 410–36.

———. "Quintessentialism." *Feminist Theology: The Journal of the Britain and Ireland School of Feminist Theology* 24 (May 2000): 13–18.

Carr, Anne. "Is a Christian Feminist Theology Possible?" *Theological Studies* 43 (1982): 279–97.

Chittister, Joan. "For Mary Daly: In Memory of Courage Walking." *National Catholic Reporter* 46 (2010): 7–10.

Christ, Carol. "A Work of Female Erraticism." *New Women's Times*, December 1984.

Clack, Beverley. "'Just Dare and Care': Mary Daly 16 October 1928–3 January 2010." *Feminist Theology: The Journal of the Britain and Ireland School of Feminist Theology* 18, no. 3 (2010): 254–56.

Corbett, Sara. "Mary Daly: Gyno-Theologian." *New York Times Magazine*, December 26, 2010, 14–15.

Cortiel, Jeanne. *Passion für das Unmögliche: Befreiung als Narrativ in der amerikanischen feministischen Theologie*. Essen: Verlag Die Blaue Eule, 2001.

Culpepper, Emily. "In Memory of Mary Daly." *Journal of Feminist Studies in Religion* 28, no. 2 (2012): 89–90.

———. "Philosophia in a Feminist Key: Revolt of the Symbols." ThD dissertation, Harvard Divinity School, 1983.

———. "The Spiritual Movement of Radical Feminist Consciousness." In *Understanding the New Religions*, edited by George Baker and Jacob Needleman, 220–34. New York: Seabury, 1978.

D'Angelo, Mary Rose. "'Abba' and 'Father': Imperial Theology and the Jesus Traditions." *Journal of Biblical Literature*, 1992, 611–30.

———. "Remembering Her: Feminist Christian Readings of the Christian Tradition." *Toronto Journal of Theology* 2 (1986): 118–26.

D'Enbeau, Suzy. "Feminine and Feminist Transformation in Popular Culture: An Application of Mary Daly's Radical Philosophies to *Bust* Magazine." *Feminist Media Studies* 9, no. 1 (2009): 17–36.

De Haardt, Maaike. "Woedende woorden, woorden van hoop: De ontwikkeling in het denken van Mary Daly." Thesis. Tilburg: Stichting Theologische Faculteit Tilburg, 1985.

De Veaux, Alexis. *Warrior Poet: A Biography of Audre Lorde.* New York: Norton, 2004.

Dion, Michel. "L'aliénation ontologique et le processus de libération du soi des femmes chez Mary Daly." Dissertation, Université Laval, Montreal, 1983.

———. *Libération féministe et salut chrétien: Mary Daly et Paul Tillich.* Montreal: Bellarmin, 1995.

———. "Mary Daly, théologienne et philosophe féministe." *Études Théologiques et Religieuses* 62 (1987): 515–34.

———. "Pour une réinterprétation féministe de l'idée chrétienne de Dieu." *Laval Théologique et Philosophique* 47, no. 2 (1991): 169–84.

———. "La théologie/philosophie féministe de Mary Daly et le socialisme religieux de Paul Tillich." *Studies in Religion/Sciences Religieuses* 25 (1996): 379–96.

Donovan, Josephine. *Feminist Theory: The Intellectual Traditions of American Feminism.* New York: Continuum, 1992.

Douglas, Carol Anne. *Love and Politics: Radical Feminist and Lesbian Theories.* San Francisco: ism Press, 1990.

———. Review of *Outercourse: The Be-Dazzling Voyage*, by Mary Daly. *off our backs*, January 1993, 19.

———. Review of *Pure Lust: Elemental Feminist Philosophy*, by Mary Daly. *off our backs*, June 1984, 20–22.

———. Review of *Quintessence: Realizing the Archaic Future*, by Mary Daly. *off our backs*, December 1998, 14.

Dragiewicz, Molly. "Women's Voices, Women's Words: Reading Acquaintance Rape Discourse." In *Feminist Interpretations of Mary Daly*, edited by Sarah Lucia Hoagland and Marilyn Frye, 194–221. State College: Pennsylvania State University Press, 2000.

Driver, Anne Barstow. "Religion." *Signs* 2, no. 2 (1976): 434–42.

Dumais, Monique. "Pour que les noces aient lieu entre Dieu et les femmes." *Studies in Religion/Sciences Religieuses* 16 (1987): 53–64.

———. "Voyage vers les sources: Quelques discours féministes sur la nature." *Studies in Religion/Sciences Religieuses* 13, no. 3 (Summer 1984): 345–52.

Dunlap, Lauren Glen. Review of *Outercourse: The Be-Dazzling Voyage*, by Mary Daly. *Belles Lettres* 8 (1993): 42.

Durham, Paula Hope. "Patriarchy and Self-Hate: Mary Daly's Assessment of Patriarchal Religion Appraised and Evaluated in the Context of Karen Horney's Psychoanalytic Theory." *Journal of Feminist Studies in Religion* 13 (1997): 119–30.

Dworkin, Andrea. *Intercourse*. New York: Basic Books, 1987.

Echols, Alice. "The Taming of the Id: Feminist Sexual Politics, 1968–83." In *Pleasure and Danger: Exploring Female Sexuality,* edited by Carol Vance, 50–72. New York: Routledge, 1984.

Eisenstein, Hester. *Contemporary Feminist Thought.* Boston: G. K. Hall, 1983.

Elshtain, Jean Bethke. "Feminist Discourse and Its Discontents: Language, Power, and Meaning." *Signs* 7, no. 3 (1982): 603–21.

Ettorre, Elizabeth. "Exploring Lesbian Archetypes or Reviving 'Drooping Wings.'" *Journal of Lesbian Studies* 4, no. 1 (2000): 127–43.

Everson, Susan Corey. "Bodyself: Women's Bodily Experience in Recent Feminist Theology and Literature." PhD dissertation, University of Minnesota, 1984.

Felstiner, Mary Lowenthal. "Seeing *The Second Sex* through the Second Wave." *Feminist Studies* 6, no. 2 (1980): 247–76.

Ferguson, Ann. "A Feminist Aspect Theory of the Self." In *Women, Knowledge and Reality: Explorations in Feminist Philosophy*, edited by Ann Garry and Marilyn Pearsall, 93–107. Boston: Unwin and Hyman, 1989.

Field-Bibb, Jacqueline. "From *The Church* to *Wickedary*: The Theology and Philosophy of Mary Daly." *Modern Churchman*, n.s., 30 (1989): 35–41.

Fitts, Catherine Louise. "Reading Flannery O'Connor by the Light of Feminist Theology." PhD dissertation, Texas Christian University, 1990.

Flotow, Luise von. "Mutual Pun-ishment? Translating Radical Feminist Wordplay: Mary Daly's *Gyn/Ecology* in German." In *Traductio: Essays on Punning and Translation,* edited by Dirk Delabastita, 45–66. New York: Routledge, 1997.

Foss, Karen A., Sonja K. Foss, and Cindy L. Griffin. *Feminist Rhetorical Theories*. Long Grove, IL: Waveland, 1999.

Foss, Sonja. "Feminism Confronts Catholicism: A Study of the Use of Perspective by Incongruity." *Women's Studies in Communication* 3, no. 1 (1979): 7–15.

Fröse, Marlies. *Utopos—kein Ort: Mary Daly's Patriarchatskritik und feministische Politik, ein Lesebuch*. Bielefeld: AJZ-Druck, 1988.

Frye, Marilyn. "Famous Lust Words." Review of *Pure Lust: Elemental Feminist Philosophy*, by Mary Daly. *Women's Review of Books* 1, no. 11 (1984): 3–4.

———. *Willful Virgin: Essays in Feminism, 1976–1992*. Freedom, CA: Crossing, 1992.

Gelpi, Barbara Charlesworth. "The Politics of Androgyny." *Women's Studies: An Interdisciplinary Journal* 2, no. 2 (1974): 151–60.

Giles, Mary E. *The Feminist Mystic, and Other Essays on Women and Spirituality*. New York: Crossroad, 1982.

Goldenberg, Naomi R. "A Feminist Critique of Jung." *Signs* 2, no. 2 (1976): 443–49.

Gray, Frances. "Elemental Philosophy: Language and Ontology in Mary Daly's Texts." In *Feminist Interpretations of Mary Daly*, edited by Sarah Lucia Hoagland and Marilyn Frye, 222–45. State College: Pennsylvania State University Press, 2000.

Grey, Mary. "Feminist Theology: A Critical Theology of Liberation." In *The Cambridge Companion to Liberation Theology*, edited by Christopher Rowland, 2nd ed., 105–22. Cambridge: Cambridge University Press, 2007.

Griffin, Cindy L. "Women as Communicators: Mary Daly's Hagography as Rhetoric." *Communications Monographs* 60, no. 2 (1993): 158–77.

Griffin, Wendy. "The Embodied Goddess: Feminist Witchcraft and Female Divinity." *Sociology of Religion* 56, no. 1 (1995): 35–48.

Grigg, Richard. *When God Becomes Goddess: The Transformation of American Religion.* New York: Continuum, 1995.

Grimshaw, Jean. "Autonomy and Identity in Feminist Thinking." In *Feminist Perspectives in Philosophy*, edited by Morwenna Griffiths and Margaret Whitford, 90–108. Bloomington: Indiana University Press, 1988.

Gudorf, Christine E. Review of *Outercourse: The Be-Dazzling Voyage*, by Mary Daly. *National Catholic Reporter*, February 5, 1993, 37.

Halberstam, Judith. "Automating Gender: Postmodern Feminism in the Age of the Intelligent Machine." *Feminist Studies* 17, no. 3 (1991): 439–60.

Hampton, Daphne. *Theology and Feminism: Signposts in Theology.* Malden, MA: Blackwell, 1990.

Harrison, Beverly Wildung. "The Power of Anger in the Work of Love." *Union Seminary Quarterly Review* 36 (1981 Supplementary Issue): 41–57.

Hedley, Jane. "Surviving to Speak a New Language: Mary Daly and Adrienne Rich." *Hypatia* 7, no. 2 (1992): 40–62.

Hedrick, Elizabeth. "The Early Career of Mary Daly: A Retrospective." *Feminist Studies* 39, no. 2 (2013): 457–83.

Hendricks, Christina, and Kelly Oliver, eds. *Language and Liberation: Feminism, Philosophy, and Language.* Albany: State University of New York Press, 1999.

Henking, Susan E. "The Personal Is the Theological: Autobiographical Acts in Contemporary Feminist Theology." *Journal of the American Academy of Religion* 59 (1991): 511–25.

———. "Rejected, Reclaimed, Renamed: Mary Daly on Psychology and Religion." *Journal of Psychology and Theology* 21, no. 3 (1993): 199–207.

Henold, Mary J. *Catholic and Feminist: The Surprising History of the American Catholic Feminist Movement.* Chapel Hill: University of North Carolina Press, 2008.

Hewitt, Marsha. *Critical Theory of Religion: A Feminist Analysis.* Minneapolis: Augburg Fortress, 1995.

Heyward, Carter. "Rubyfruit Tangles: Response to Mary Daly." *Feminist Theology: The Journal of the Britain and Ireland School of Feminist Theology* 24 (May 2000): 19–22.

———. "Ruether and Daly: Theologians Speaking and Sparking, Building and Burning." *Christianity and Crisis* 39 (1979): 66–72.

Hill, Susan E. "(Dis)inheriting Augustine: Constructing the Alienated Self in the Autobiographical Works of Paul Monette and Mary Daly." *Literature and Theology* 13, no. 2 (1999): 149–65.

Hoagland, Sarah Lucia, and Marilyn Frye, eds. *Feminist Interpretations of Mary Daly*. State College: Pennsylvania State University Press, 2000.

Honkanen, Katriina. *Mary Daly: Feministi. Teoksessa Feministejä–Aikamme ajattelijoita*. Edited by Anneli Anttonen et al. Tampere: Vastapaino, 2000.

Howell, Nancy R. "Radical Relatedness and Feminist Separatism." *Process Studies* 18 (1989): 118–26.

Huber, Monika. "Die politische Relevanz der feministisch-theologischen Konzepte von Heide Göttner-Abendroth, Elisabeth Schüssler-Fiorenza und Mary Daly: Ein Beitrag zur ideologiekritischen Selbstreflexion feministischer Theologie." Thesis. University of Freiburg, 1987.

Hull, Fritz. *Earth and Spirit: The Spiritual Dimension of the Environmental Crisis*. New York: Burns and Oates, 1993.

Hunt, Mary E. "Celebrating and Cerebrating Mary Daly (1928–2010)." *Journal of Feminist Studies in Religion* 28, no. 2 (2012): 90–93.

———. "Future Visions: Response to Mary Daly." *Feminist Theology: The Journal of the Britain and Ireland School of Feminist Theology*, no. 24 (May 2000): 23–30.

———. "On Mary Daly." *Journal of Feminist Studies in Religion* 26, no. 2 (2010): 7–9.

———. "Pure Complexity: Mary Daly's Catholic Legacy." *Feminist Theology: The Journal of the Britain and Ireland School of Feminist Theology* 22, no. 3 (2014): 219–28.

———. "Religious Resources for Survival: Ecofeminism and Earth Community." In *Living Cosmology: Christian Responses to the Journey of the Universe*, edited by Mary Evelyn Tucker and John Grim. Maryknoll, NY: Orbis, 2016.

Jaggar, Alison. *Feminist Politics and Human Nature*. Totowa, NJ: Rowman and Allenheld, 1983.

Jantzen, Grace. *Becoming Divine: Towards a Feminist Philosophy of Religion*. Bloomington: Indiana University Press, 1999.

Johnson, Ella L. "Metaphors for Metamorphosis: Mary Daly Meets Gertrud the Great of Helfta." *Magistra* 15, no. 1 (2009): 3–31.

Johnson, Fern L. "Coming to Terms with Women's Language." *Quarterly Journal of Speech* 72 (1986): 318–30.

Juett, Joanne Crum. "Feminism in the Work of Mary Daly, Toni Morrison, Pauline Oliveros, and Laurie Anderson." PhD dissertation, University of Georgia, 1994.

Karagianis, Maria. "Mary, Mary, Quite Contrary." *Ms.* 9, no. 4 (1999): 56–59.

Kassam, Zayn. "Necrophilia and Voyaging: Some Curious Connections." *Journal of Feminist Studies in Religion* 28, no. 2 (2012): 104–9.

Katharine, Amber L. "'A Too Early Morning': Audre Lorde's 'An Open Letter to Mary Daly' and Daly's Decision Not to Respond in Kind." In *Feminist Interpretations of Mary Daly*, edited by Sarah Lucia Hoagland and Marilyn Frye, 266–97. State College: Pennsylvania State University Press, 2000.

———. "(Re)reading Mary Daly as a Sister Insider." In *Feminist Interpretations of Mary Daly*, edited by Sarah Lucia Hoagland and Marilyn Frye, 298–321. State College: Pennsylvania State University Press, 2000.

Keating, AnaLouise. "Back to the Mother? Feminist Mythmaking with a Difference." In *Feminist Interpretations of Mary Daly*, edited by Sarah Lucia Hoagland and Marilyn Frye, 349–88. State College: Pennsylvania State University Press, 2000.

Keller, Catherine. *From a Broken Web: Separation, Sexism, and Self.* Boston: Beacon, 1986.

Keshgegian, Flora Angel. "To Know by Heart: Toward a Theology of Remembering for Salvation." PhD dissertation, Boston College, 1992.

King, Ynestra. "Feminism and the Revolt of Nature." In *Thinking about the Environment: Readings on Politics, Property, and the Physical World*, edited by Matthew Alan Cahn and Rory O'Brien, 179–84. New York: M. E. Sharpe, 1997.

Knutsen, Mary M. "Beyond God the Father: Toward a Trinitarian Theology of the Cross." PhD dissertation, University of Chicago, 1994.

Korte, Anne-Marie. "Deliver Us from Evil: Bad versus Better Faith in Mary Daly's Feminist Writings." Translated by Mischa F. C. Hoyinck. In *Feminist Interpretations of Mary Daly*, edited by Sarah Lucia Hoagland and Marilyn Frye, 76–111. State College: Pennsylvania State University Press, 2000.

———. "Een gemeenschap waarin te geloven valt: Over de spirituele en de politieke betekenis van het geloof van vrouwen aan de hand van de 'ommekeer' van Anna Maria van Schurman en Mary Daly." Master's thesis, Catholic University of Nijmegen, Netherlands, 1985.

———. "Just/ice in Time: On Temporality in Mary Daly's Quintessence." In *Feminist Interpretations of Mary Daly*, edited by Sarah Lucia Hoagland and Marilyn Frye, 418–28. State College: Pennsylvania State University Press, 2000.

———. *Een passie voor transcendentie: Feminisme, theologie en moderniteit in het denken van Mary Daly.* Kampen, Overijssel, Netherlands: J. H. Kok Uitgeversmaatschappij, 1992.

Köstenberger, Margaret E. "A Critique of Feminist and Egalitarian Hermeneutics and Exegesis: With Special Focus on Jesus' Approach to Women." ThD dissertation, University of South Africa, Pretoria, Unisa, 2005.

Kraemer, Ross S. Review of *Gyn/Ecology: The Metaethics of Radical Feminism*, by Mary Daly. *Signs* 5 (1979): 354–56.

Lansbury, Coral. "What Snools These Mortals Be." Review of *Websters' First New Intergalactic Wickedary of the English Language*, by Mary Daly. *New York Times Book Review*, January 17, 1988, 9.

Lester, Neal A. "At the Heart of Shange's Feminism: An Interview." *Black American Literature Forum* 24, no. 4 (1990): 717–30.

Levitt, Laura S. "A Letter to Mary Daly." *Journal of Feminist Studies in Religion* 28, no. 2 (2012): 109–12.

Liddle, Joanna, and Shirin Rai. "Feminism, Imperialism and Orientalism: The Challenge of the 'Indian Woman.'" *Women's History Review* 7, no. 4 (1998): 495–520.

Lienert, Tania. "On Who Is Calling Radical Feminists 'Cultural Feminists' and Other Historical Sleights of Hand." In *Radically Speaking: Feminism Reclaimed*, edited by Diane Bell and Renate Klein, 155–68. North Melbourne, Australia: Spinifex, 1996.

Lorde, Audre. "An Open Letter to Mary Daly." In *Sister Outsider: Essays and Speeches*, 66–71. Trumansburg: Crossing Press, 1984. Also in *This Bridge Called My Back: Writings by Radical Women of Color*, edited by Cherrie Moraga and Gloria Anzaldúa, 94–97. Watertown, MA: Persephone Press, 1981. German translation "Offener Brief an Mary Daly." In *Lichtflut: Neue Texte*, 13–17. Berlin: Orlanda, 1988.

Love, Myra. "Christa Wolf and Feminism: Breaking the Patriarchal Connection." *New German Critique* 16 (Winter 1979): 31–53.

Lugones, María. "Wicked Caló: A Matter of the Authority of Improper Words." In *Feminist Interpretations of Mary Daly*, edited by Sarah Lucia Hoagland and Marilyn Frye, 246–65. State College: Pennsylvania State University Press, 2000.

MacKinnon, Catharine A. "Feminism, Marxism, Method, and the State: Toward Feminist Jurisprudence." *Signs* 8, no. 4 (1983): 635–58.

McManus, Jim. "BC Students Protest over Daly Bread." *National Catholic Reporter*, April 7, 1989, 5.

McNeil, Helen. "Hag-ography." Review of *Gyn/Ecology: The Metaethics of Radical Feminism*, by Mary Daly. *New Statesman*, April 4, 1980, 514–15.

Maher, Mary. Review of *Pure Lust: Elemental Feminist Philosophy*, by Mary Daly. *Women and Therapy* 4 (1985): 76–78.

Mellor, Mary. *Feminism and Ecology*. New York: New York University Press, 1998.

Meyer-Wilmes, Hedwig. "About the Schizophrenia in Women's Beings: A Re-reading of Mary Daly." *Feminist Theology*, May 1994, 67–81.

Moane, Geraldine. "Psychic Liberation: Feminist Practices for Transformation among Irish Women." In *Feminist Interpretations of Mary Daly*, edited by Sarah Lucia Hoagland and Marilyn Frye, 389–417. State College: Pennsylvania State University Press, 2000.

Mogford, Sheilagh A. "The Murder of the Goddess in Everywoman: Mary Daly's Sado-Ritual Syndrome and Margaret Atwood's *The Handmaid's Tale*." In *Feminist Interpretations of Mary Daly*, edited by Sarah Lucia Hoagland and Marilyn Frye, 132–63. State College: Pennsylvania State University Press, 2000.

Mohanty, Chandra Talpade. "Under Western Eyes: Feminist Scholarship and Colonial Discourses." *Feminist Review* 30 (Autumn 1988): 61–88.

Mombo, Esther. "Reflections on Peace in the Decade to Overcome Violence." *Ecumenical Review* 63, no. 1 (2011): 71–76.

Moody, Linda A. *Women Encounter God: Theology across the Boundaries of Difference*. Maryknoll, NY: Orbis, 1996.

Morgan, Robin. "Mary Daly." *Time*, January 25, 2010, 3.

Morgan, Sue. *The Feminist History Reader*. New York: Routledge, 2006.

Morris, Meaghan. *The Pirate's Fiancée: Feminism, Reading, Postmodernism*. London: Verso, 1988.

Morstad, Jill Suzanne. "Fuzzy Logic: Toward a Feminist Philosophy of Language and the Animals." PhD dissertation, University of Nebraska, 1994.

Narayan, Uma. *Dislocating Cultures: Identities, Traditions, and Third World Feminism.* New York: Routledge, 1997.

Neitz, Mary Jo. "Queering the Dragonfest: Changing Sexualities in a Post-Patriarchal Religion." *Sociology of Religion*, 2000, 369–91.

Nutt, Frederike Aurica. "Gott, Geschlecht und Leiden: Die feministische Theologie Elizabeth A. Johnsons im Vergleich mit den Theologien David Tracys und Mary Dalys." Thesis, Proefschrift Universiteit van Tilburg, 2008.

Olds, Linda E. "Metaphors of Hierarchy and Interrelatedness in Hildegard of Bingen and Mary Daly." *Listening* 24 (1989): 54–66.

Pangerl, Susan M. "Radical Feminism and Self-Psychology in Dialogue: A Critical Evaluation of the Models of Women's Experience in the Works of Mary Daly and Heinz Kohut." PhD dissertation, University of Chicago, 1992.

Papavoine, Marian, and Lieve Troch, eds. *Nelle Morton, Mary Daly, Rosemary Radford Ruether, Elisabeth Schüssler Fiorenza: Beeldenschokkend, ondersteboven, spanningsveld, transformatie: Een inleiding in haar denken.* Heerlen: UTP, 1990.

Pearce, Elizabeth Helen. "Mary Daly and Feminist Dis-Coveries." Master's thesis, University of St. Michael's College, Toronto, 1993.

Pears, Angie. "When Leaving Is Believing: The Feminist Ethical Imperative of Mary Daly's Rejection of Traditional Religion." *Feminist Theology* 10, no. 2 (2002): 9–18.

Percovich, Luciana, ed. *Il viaggio metapatriarcale di rabbia e speranza di Mary Daly.* Milan: Associazione per una Libera Università delle Donne, 2002.

Plaskow, Judith. "Lessons from Mary Daly." *Journal of Feminist Studies in Religion* 28, no. 2 (2012): 100–104.

Pollitt, Katha. "No Males Need Apply?" *Nation* 269, no. 6 (August 23, 1999): 10.

Poppe, Terre. Review of *Gyn/Ecology: The Metaethics of Radical Feminism*, by Mary Daly. *off our backs*, March 1979, 20.

Porper, Rebecca. Review of *Gyn/Ecology: The Metaethics of Radical Feminism*, by Mary Daly. *Union Seminary Quarterly Review* 35 (1980): 126–28.

Porterfield, Amanda. "Feminist Theology as a Revitalization Movement." *Sociological Analysis* 48 (1987): 234–44.

Pusch, Luise F. *Alle Menschen werden Schwestern: Feministische Sprachkritik*. Frankfurt: Suhrkamp, 1990.

Randour, Mary Lou, ed. *Exploring Sacred Landscapes: Religious and Spiritual Experiences in Psychotherapy*. New York: Columbia University Press, 1993.

Raphael, Melissa. "Thealogy, Redemption, and the Call of the Wild." *Feminist Theology*, May 1997, 55–72.

Raschke, Carl. "The Death of God the Father." *Iliff Review* 35 (1978): 55–64.

Ratcliffe, Krista. *Anglo-American Feminist Challenges to the Rhetorical Traditions: Virginia Woolf, Mary Daly, Adrienne Rich*. Carbondale: Southern Illinois University Press, 1996.

Ratzel, Eveline. *The Big Sin: Die Lust zum Sündigen: Mary Daly und ihr Werk*. Rüsselsheim: Göttert, 2011.

Raymond, Janice. "Mary Daly: A Decade of Academic Harassment and Feminist Survival." In *Handbook for Women Scholars: Strategies for Success*, edited by Mary Spencer, Monia Kehoe, and Karen Speece. San Francisco: American Behavioral Research Corporation, 1982.

Reininger-Shapiro, Meredith. "Traces of Misogyny in Women's Schooling." EdD dissertation, University of Rochester, 1982.

Ress, Mary Judith, Ute Seibert-Cuadra, and Lene Sjørup. *Del cielo a la tierra: Una antología de teología feminista*. Santiago: Sello Azul, Editorial de Mujeres, 1994.

Rich, Adrienne. "Compulsory Heterosexuality and Lesbian Existence." *Signs* 5, no. 4 (1980): 631–60.

———. "That Women Be Themselves." Review of *Gyn/Ecology: The Metaethics of Radical Feminism*, by Mary Daly. *New York Times Book Review*, February 4, 1979, 10.

Riswold, Caryn. "From a Babylonian Captivity to the Otherworld: Martin Luther and Mary Daly." *Currents in Theology and Mission* 24, no. 1 (1997): 50–58.

———. "Two Reformers: Martin Luther and Mary Daly as Political Theologians?" *Political Theology* 7, no. 4 (2010): 491–506.

Rodkey, Christopher Demuth. "Extraordinary Ecclesiology: Radical Theology in Practice." In *Resurrecting the Death of God: The Origins, Influence, and Return of Radical Theology*, edited by Daniel J. Peterson and G. Michael Zbaraschuk, 125–40. Albany: State University of New York Press, 2014.

———. "In the Horizon of the Infinite." PhD dissertation, Drew University, 2008.

———. "The Nemesis Hex: Mary Daly and the Pirated Proto-Patriarchal Paulus." In *Retrieving the Radical Tillich: His Legacy and Contemporary Importance*, edited by Russell Re Manning, 65–80. New York: Palgrave Macmillan, 2015.

Ross, Mary Ellen. "Feminism and the Problem of Moral Character." *Journal of Feminist Studies in Religion* 5, no. 2 (1989): 47–64.

Rosser, Sue V. "Are There Feminist Methodologies Appropriate for the Natural Sciences and Do They Make a Difference?" *Women's Studies International Forum* 15 (1992): 5.

Rowland, Robyn, and Renate D. Klein. "Radical Feminism: Critique and Construct." In *A Reader in Feminist Knowledge*, edited by Sneja Marina Gunew, 271–303. London: Routledge, 1991.

———. "Radical Feminism: History, Politics, Action." In *Radically Speaking: Feminism Reclaimed*, edited by Diana Bell and Renate D. Klein, 9–36. North Melbourne, Australia: Spinifex, 1996.

Ruether, Rosemary Radford. "Theology by Sex." *New Republic* 169, no. 19 (November 10, 1973): 24–26.

Russ, Joanna. Review of *Gyn/Ecology: The Metaethics of Radical Feminism*, by Mary Daly. *Frontiers* 4 (1979): 68–70.

Ryan, Zoe. "Stepping Up during the Days of Vatican II." *National Catholic Reporter* 49, no. 19 (July 5, 2013).

Rycenga, Jennifer. "Passionate Struggle Is Not an Intuition: An Argument and Appreciation of Mary Daly." *Feminist Theology: The Journal of the Britain and Ireland School of Feminist Theology* 24 (May 2000): 31–35.

Sands, Kathleen M. "Uses of the Thea(o)logian: Sex and Theodicy in Religious Feminism." *Journal of Feminist Studies in Religion* 8, no. 1 (1992): 7–33.

Santoni, Ronald E. "Paean to Women." Review of *Beyond God the Father*, by Mary Daly. *Progressive*, May 1974, 59–60.

Schmeiser, Peggy. "Visions of the Future." *Feminist Theology: The Journal of the Britain and Ireland School of Feminist Theology* 24 (May 2000): 36–39.

Schneider, Laurel. "The Courage to See and to Sin: Mary Daly's Elemental Transformation of Paul Tillich's Ontology." In *Feminist Interpretations of Mary Daly*, edited by Sarah Lucia Hoagland and Marilyn Frye, 55–75. State College: Pennsylvania State University Press, 2000.

Schultz, Debra. "An Antidote for Academentia." Review of *Websters' First New Intergalactic Wickedary of the English Language*, by Mary Daly. *Belle Lettres* 3 (1988): 4.

Seelhoff, Cheryl Lindsey. "A Feminist Hullabaloo: The Historic Reunion of the Wild Sisters." *off our backs* 37, nos. 2–3 (2007): 56–61.

Sharma, Renuka, and Purushottama Bilimoria. "Where Silence Burns: *Sati* (suttee) in India, Mary Daly's Gynocritique, and Resistant Spirituality." In *Feminist Interpretations of Mary Daly*, edited by Sarah Lucia Hoagland and Marilyn Frye, 322–48. State College: Pennsylvania State University Press, 2000.

Showalter, Elaine. "Feminist Criticism in the Wilderness." *Critical Inquiry* 8, no. 2 (Winter 1981): 179–205.

———. "Towards a Feminist Poetics." In *Women Writing and Writing about Women*, edited by Mary Jacobus. London: Croom Helm, 1979.

Simons, Margaret A. "Racism and Feminism: A Schism in the Sisterhood." *Feminist Studies* 5, no. 2 (Summer 1979): 384–401.

Spelman, Elizabeth V. *Inessential Woman: Problems of Exclusion in Feminist Thought.* Boston: Beacon, 1988.

Spender, Dale. *For the Record: The Making and Meaning of Feminist Knowledge.* London: Women's Press, 1985.

———. *Women of Ideas and What Men Have Done to Them.* London: Routledge and Kegan Paul, 1982.

Stacey, Jackie. "Untangling Feminist Theory." In *Introducing Women's Studies: Feminist Theory and Practice*, edited by Victoria Robinson and Diane Richardson, 49–73. New York: New York University Press, 1993.

Star, Susan Leigh. "To Dwell among Ourselves." Review of *Gyn/Ecology: The Metaethics of Radical Feminism*, by Mary Daly. *Sinister Wisdom* 8 (1979): 87–98.

Stenger, Mary Ann. "A Critical Analysis of the Influence of Paul Tillich on Mary Daly's Feminist Theology." *Encounter* 43 (1982): 219–38. Also in *Theonomy and Autonomy: Studies in Paul Tillich's Engagement with Modern Culture*, edited by John C. Carey. Macon: Mercer University Press, 1984.

Stimpson, Catharine R. "The Androgyne and the Homosexual." *Women's Studies: An Interdisciplinary Journal* 2, no. 2 (1974): 237–47.

Stofer, Judith Ann. "Von der Thomistin zur Häxe: Mary Dalys Weg der Radikalisierung: Die Verabschiedung der patriarchalen Religion und Gesellschaft bei Mary Daly." Thesis. University of Freiburg, 1987.

Sturgeon, Rebecca L. "Jeanette Winterson's Postmodernist Spirituality." Master's thesis, University of Louisville, 1995.

Sturgis, Susanna. "Mary Daly, Revolting Hag." *Women's Review of Books* 27, no. 3 (2010): 30–31.

———. "Priests Monitor Hag." *off our backs*, April 1979, 11.

———. Review of *Gyn/Ecology*, by Mary Daly. *off our backs*, March 1979, 18–19.

Suchocki, Marjorie. "The Challenge of Mary Daly." *Encounter* 41 (1980): 307–17.

———. "The Idea of God in Feminist Philosophy." *Hypatia* 9, no. 4 (1994): 57–68.

Suhonen, Marja. "Toward Biophilic Be-ing: Mary Daly's Feminist Metaethics and the Question of Essentialism." In *Feminist Interpretations of Mary Daly*, edited by Sarah Lucia Hoagland and Marilyn Frye, 112–31. State College: Pennsylvania State University Press, 2000.

Taylor, Verta, and Leila J. Rupp. "Women's Culture and Lesbian Feminist Activism: A Reconsideration of Cultural Feminism." *Signs* 19, no. 1 (Autumn 1993): 32–61.

Thompson, Denise. "What Does It Mean to Call Feminism 'White and Middle-Class?'" http://users.spin.net.au. Accessed October 20, 2014.

Tomaselli, Sylvana. "The Enlightenment Debate on Women." *History Workshop Journal* 20, no. 1 (1985): 101–24.

Tomassone, Letizia, ed. *Un vulcano nel vulcano: Mary Daly e gli spostamenti della teologia*. Conference proceedings. Cantalupa, Turin: Effatà, 2012.

Tong, Rosemarie. *Feminine and Feminist Ethics*. Belmont, CA: Wadsworth, 1993.

———. *Feminist Thought: A More Comprehensive Introduction*. Boulder: Harper-Westview, 1989.

Tupil, Marie. "Religion." In *Feminist Knowledge: Critique and Construct*, edited by Sneja Gunew, 229–68. London: Routledge, 1991.

Tyminski, Marie. "Divinity, Transcendence, and Female Subjectivity in the Works of Mary Daly." PhD dissertation, University of Toronto, 1996.

van der Vleuten, Harriët. "'De uitdrijving van het kwaad uit Eva': Beschrijving van de inhoud en een analyse van een kollege over feministische theologie." Thesis. Tilburg University, 1984.

Weaver, Mary Jo. "Daly, Daly, Sing to Mary." Review of *Pure Lust: Elemental Feminist Philosophy*, by Mary Daly. *CrossCurrents* 14 (1985): 111–15.

———. "Notes of a Nag-Gnostic." Review of *Outercourse: The Be-Dazzling Voyage*, by Mary Daly. *New York Times Book Review*, January 24, 1993, 15.

———. "Who Is the Goddess and Where Does She Get Us?" *Journal of Feminist Studies in Religion* 5, no. 1 (1989): 49–64.

Wehr, Demaris. "Fracturing the Language of Patriarchy." Review of *Pure Lust: Elemental Feminist Philosophy*, by Mary Daly. *New York Times Book Review*, July 22, 1984, 14.

Weil, Lise. Review of *Quintessence . . . Realizing the Archaic Future*, by Mary Daly. *Women's Review of Books* 16, no. 6 (1991): 21.

Williams, Brooke. "Toward a Semiotic beyond Feminism." In *Semiotics 1980*, edited by Michael Herzfeld and Margot D. Lenhart, 549–59. New York: Plenum, 1982.

Wilson, Richard Francis. "Human Liberation and Theology: An Examination of the Theology of Gustavo Gutierrez, James H. Cone, and Mary Daly." PhD dissertation, Southern Baptist Theological Seminary, 1982.

Young, Iris Marion. "Humanism, Gynocentrism and Feminist Politics." *Women's Studies International Forum* 8, no. 3 (1985): 173–83.

Zappone, Katherine. *The Hope for Wholeness: A Spirituality for Feminists.* Mystic, CT: Twenty-Third Publications, 1991.

# INDEX

## ABOUT THE AUTHOR

Mary Daly was a Positively Revolting Hag, Amazonian adventurer, and Radical Lesbian-Feminist Philosopher. She Spun Her Webs on This Planet from 1928 until 2010.

# ABOUT THE EDITORS

Jennifer Rycenga is Professor of Comparative Religious Studies at San José State University. She has co-edited two books: *Frontline Feminisms: Women, War, and Resistance*, with Marguerite Waller; and *Queering the Popular Pitch*, with Sheila Whiteley. She writes on Abolition history, women's religious history, feminism and music, Lesbian philosophy, and panentheism.

Linda Barufaldi is a lifelong radical feminist activist who has worked in the peace, civil rights, women's, LGBT, and environmental movements. She founded a holistic health center and practiced complementary medicine for nearly twenty years. She was a student of Mary Daly for four years in the early 1970s and was a reader/editor of *Beyond God the Father* and *Gyn/Ecology*. She and Daly maintained a forty-year friendship until Daly's death in 2010. She is retired and lives in La Mesa, California, with Joyce Marieb, her partner of forty-three years.